Jes Battis
Thinking Queerly

Premodern Transgressive Literatures

Edited by
Alicia Spencer-Hall

Editorial Board
Blake Gutt, University of Michigan, USA
Carissa Harris, Temple University, USA
Jonathan Hsy, George Washington University, USA
Roberta Magnani, Swansea University, UK
Elizabeth Robertson, University of Glasgow, UK

Volume 1

Jes Battis
Thinking Queerly

Medievalism, Wizardry, and Neurodiversity in Young Adult Texts

ISBN 978-1-5015-2320-5
e-ISBN (PDF) 978-1-5015-1533-0
e-ISBN (EPUB) 978-1-5015-1535-4
ISSN 2702-9824

Library of Congress Control Number: 2021932151

Bibliographic information published by the Deutsche Nationalbibliothek
The Deutsche Nationalbibliothek lists this publication in the Deutsche Nationalbibliografie;
detailed bibliographic data are available on the internet at http://dnb.dnb.de.

© 2024 Walter de Gruyter GmbH, Berlin/Boston
This volume is text- and page-identical with the hardback published in 2021.
Cover image: valentinrussanov/E+/Getty Images
Typesetting: Integra Software Services Pvt.

www.degruyter.com

Acknowledgments

In many ways, the acknowledgments for this book could be the entire book. So many people helped along the way, checked in, answered questions, kept me on track, and reminded me why I wanted to write this in the first place. I finished the draft manuscript at the start of a global pandemic, which meant that I had limited access to research materials. Luckily, I *did* still have access to a lovely a community of scholars on Twitter. So many people were willing to reach out, answer questions, help with thorny translations, and even send along PDF scans of texts. These colleagues include, but are not limited to: Carolyne Larrington, Shiloh Carroll, Jonah Coman, James Gifford, Katie DeCoste, Ellis Amity Light, Dainy Bernstein, Blake Gutt, Claudia Wittig, Kara Maloney, Steven Kruger, Matt McCall, Gabrielle M. W. Bychowski, Brooke Findley, Juliette de Bertole, Curtis Runstedler, Kara McShane, Anne Brannen, Taylor Driggers-McDowall, Steven Bruso, A. E. Whitacre, Kavita Mudan Finn, and Esther Liberman Cuenca. I'm also grateful for the ongoing anti-racist work of medievalists like Dorothy Kim, Jonathan Hsy, and Mary Rambaran-Olm. The medieval analysis in this book would not have been possible without all of you, and I love our community.

This is also a book about disability and neurodiversity across time, and I'm particularly indebted to work on medieval disability studies by Cameron Hunt McNabb, Joshua Eyler, and Will Rogers. My own analysis has also been enriched by the work of disabled and neurodivergent scholars: Alison Kafer, Eli Clare, Melanie Yergeau, Julia Miele Rodas, Margaret Price, and Petra Kuppers. Special thanks to Travis Chi Wing Lau for sending me his work on cripping academic time, and John Loeppky, for all his efforts to amplify creative work by disabled artists in Regina (and for always being the one to send a gentle text or DM asking me how I'm doing). Kathryn Nogue's keen editorial eye also helped to shape the book's introduction, and I'm grateful for her own scholarly and community work.

Many of the ideas for this book emerged from classroom conversations, where my students offered brilliant and critical readings of disability representation in pop culture. I'm especially thankful for the contributions of Hannah Grover, Kris Ferguson, Taylor Gilkes-Reed, Joshua Kopriva, Yasmin Woolridge, Quinn Hosking, Amy Langen, Hannah Eiserman, Eric Piapot, and Carrie Fehr. I've been inspired by the fantasy literature of my creative writing students, including Courtney Stroh, Laetitia Adams, Farron Ager, and Matt MacDonald, as well as scholarship on gender and heroism by Apolline Lucyk. I'm grateful for Cody Jackson's work on queer disability studies, and Rosemary McAllister's work on fandom and neurodiversity.

There were multiple podcasts that helped shape this book's discussion. *Hazel & Katniss & Harry & Starr* was invaluable for its treatment of YA literature (and the precious banter between Joe Lipsett and Brenna Clarke Gray was a balm when I was recovering from surgery). Clarke Gray's educational technology podcast, *You Got This*, also helped me to innovate my online teaching. *Witch Please*, hosted by Hannah McGregor and Marcelle Kosman (produced by Ariana Martinez) offered fascinating discussions of the Potterverse and its impact on YA genres. Matt Baume's *Sewers of Paris* podcast was a source of fascinating interviews, including a perfect discussion with Anthony Oliveira about medievalism in *He-Man*. Andrew Gurza's *Disability after Dark* also influenced my discussion of disability representation, and *Queer As Fact* provided some great historical and literary examples.

My friends and colleagues at the University of Regina have inspired and sustained me throughout this project. Medrie Purdham, there aren't enough words for how much I love you and your family. Mark Lajoie, thanks for always being a voice of reason (I'm devastated I missed out on your mulled wine this year). Rowan Lajoie, you once told me that I should lift everyone I love to see the moon, and I've tried to keep doing that—I'm continually inspired by the person you're growing into. Victor Lajoie, your energy is boundless, and you can do anything. Alexis McQuigge, your friendship is invaluable to me, and I love that you can crack me up with a look. Thanks for renewing my interest in Lady Mary Wortley Montagu, and for introducing me to other fascinating eighteenth-century authors. Jon Wight, thanks for always being available to talk about spaceships, and for the time you drove me to the hospital late at night (Alexis drove me twice that same year—it was a banner year for emergency visits).

Susan Johnston, thanks for your excellent work on Tolkien and *Game of Thrones*, and for the many conversations we've had about fantasy literature over the years. Marcel DeCoste, thanks for your kindness as department head when I was having a particularly rough time, and for your sense of hospitality. Jason Demers, thanks for your vital public scholarship on incarceration, and for the many quick but sweet conversations by the photocopier (in the before times). Melanie Schnell, thanks for your writing, and for always letting me melt into a puddle of anxiety. Troni Grande, thanks for your poetry, and for all the support you've given me over the years. Michelle Coupal, thanks for your work on the legacy of residential schools, and for all that you bring to our department and community. Jean Hillabold, thanks for your generosity as a writer and reviewer, and for all your community work.

West Coast thanks go to June Scudeler, for all the conversations we've had over the years about academia and beyond. And to Shelley Boyd, for our chats over dinner, and for including my oddball essay on queer food studies in your excellent volume, *Canadian Culinary Imaginations*. To Bea, for all the reasons. To my parents, for instilling in me a love of reading, research, and medieval history. To Guinevere, whose medievalist name only fueled her tenacity as a cat (she once dispelled an actual dragon from my bedroom).

I wrote this book as a settler scholar living on multiple territories. Treaty 4: traditional homelands of the Nêhiyawak, Anihšināpēk, Dakota, Lakota, and Nakoda peoples, as well as the Métis Nation. And Unceded Coast Salish territory: traditional homelands of the Musqueam, Squamish, Stó:lō, and Tsleil-Waututh nations. I acknowledge that I am a guest on these territories, and that I am invested in working towards efforts of decolonization, both in the classroom and beyond.

Finally, this book is a love letter to queer, trans, nonbinary, and neurodivergent scholars, students, readers, and viewers. I hope you keep seeing yourself in the diverse Middle Ages.

Contents

Acknowledgments —— V

Introduction: Wizardry, Medievalism, and Queer Thinking —— 1
    Origins —— 1
    Medieval Adolescence: Or, Waxing up Sideways —— 4
    Medieval and Medievalist Neurodiversity —— 10
    Medievalist YA —— 20

Chapter 1
My So-Called Merlin: Wizardry and Neurodiversity —— 27
    Medieval Magic and the Wizard —— 31
    Merlin in the Arthurian Tradition —— 32
    De Boron: Merlin's Childhood and Adolescence —— 33
    Monmouth's *Vita Merlini*: Merlin Looking Backwards —— 39
    The Middle English Merlin —— 43
    The Sword in the Stone —— 48
    Once and Future —— 51
    Red Scrolls of Magic —— 53

Chapter 2
The Futures of Morgan le Fay: Solidarity and Knowledge in *Sabrina* and *Tiffany Aching* —— 59
    Medieval Morgans —— 61
    Sabrina Spellman —— 74
    Tiffany Aching —— 82

Chapter 3
Wizards in School: Queering the Magical Academy —— 93
    Medieval Magic Schools and the Spell-Casting Tradition —— 94
    Medieval Roots of the Wizard School —— 95
    Earthsea and the Roke School of Wizardry —— 99
    The Magicians: Magic and Disappointment —— 102
    Carrying on with Queer Wizards —— 113

Chapter 4
Bad Magic: Wizardry and Queer Failures of Communication —— 127
    Failing in the Middle Ages —— 128
    The Last Unicorn —— 135
    Elliot Schafer in Sarah Reese Brennan's *In Other Lands* —— 142
    Oscar and Autistic Medievalism in *The Real Boy* —— 146

Chapter 5
Do You Really Want to Snyrt Me? Queer Adolescence in *Sir Gawain and the Green Knight* —— 157
    The Rise of Gawain —— 159
    Gawain's Offshoots —— 162
    Queer Youth in *Sir Gawain and the Green Knight* —— 165
    Just a Kiss? —— 167
    Green, G, or PG-13? —— 175

Epilogue: Gandalf's Charm —— 189

Appendix: Texts and Media —— 203

Bibliography —— 219

Index —— 235

Introduction: Wizardry, Medievalism, and Queer Thinking

> Therefore I cannot wonder across this world
> why my mind does not muster in the murk
> when I ponder pervading all the lives of men,
> how they suddenly abandoned their halls,
> the proud young thanes. So this entire middle-earth
> tumbles and falls every day. ("The Wanderer," tr. Aaron Hostetter)[1]

> We're too young to know any better, to know we won't triumph and be heroes, that we won't be returned to the other world as if no time had passed, that the lies in the stories aren't about mermaids or harpies—the lies are about us. (Sara Brennan, *In Other Lands*, 219)

Origins

The idea for this book emerged from a chaotic semester when I was teaching classes on both medieval literature and young adult (YA) texts. During one long day, I taught Chaucer in the morning and a class on *Buffy the Vampire Slayer* at night, where issues of youth and medievalism were productively blurred. I seemed to be living through Carolyn Dinshaw's argument, in *How Soon Is Now?*, about medievalism's "asynchrony: different time frames or temporal systems colliding in a single moment of *now*" (5). In the queer middle between pardoners and vampires, I was also teaching a third class explicitly on teen fiction. Rainbow Rowell's *Carry On*, about a queer teen wizard and his vampire boyfriend, was the YA text that unexpectedly linked all of these classes together. *Carry On* takes place in a medievalist wizard school, and as an open adaptation of *Harry Potter*, it asks tough questions about magic and medievalism. At the same time, it's a strikingly contemporary story about a neurodivergent teen dealing with trauma in a world that forces him to be a hero. With this text as a lens, my students were able to trace medievalist concepts across the field of YA: witches and wizards, magic schools, and monsters. Those conversations encouraged me to think of *medieval YA* as a

---

[1] Forþon ic geþencan ne mæg geond þas woruld
for hwan modsefa min ne gesweorce,
þonne ic eorla lif eal geondþence,
hu hi færlice flet ofgeafon,
modge maguþegnas. Swa þes middangeard
ealra dogra gehwam dreoseð ond fealleþ (L58–63, Delanty and Matto 2011).

sub-genre of teen fiction that was hidden in plain sight among dystopian futures and more realist novels.

The quotations above—one medieval, the other medievalist—echo this book's discussion of being caught between eras, worlds, and desires. Hostetter's translation of the early medieval poem "The Wanderer" manages to preserve the evocative phrase "middangeard," as well as the "modge maguþegnas" who burn in the speaker's memory. The adjective *modge* suggests an impetuous young retainer, so the speaker cites a medieval adolescence already in ruins. *In Other Lands* is a YA novel about youth and magic's failure. Elliot, the book's transcendently snarky protagonist, tells a room full of children that all of their dreams are actually false. Of course, he's also talking about his own dreams, as he tries to reconcile the flawed fantasy world around him with the magic he once desired. Separated across time, both narrators mention an impossible youth, a longed-for past that was never quite real, as they wander through some kind of middle territory. As I'll argue throughout this book, medievalist YA transports the middleness of adolescence to what scholars like Jeffrey J. Cohen and Eileen Joy have termed "the medieval middle" (as the title of their medieval blog). The figures who most often traverse that dangerous middle territory are wizards and enchantresses. From Merlin and Morgan le Fay to Simon Snow and Sabrina, the wizard figure has endured as a key to medievalism. Kevin and Brent Moberly suggest that "the relationship between play and medievalism is more fraught and traumatic then it first appears" (Emery 175). I'll argue that the medieval wizard is the character who occupies that fraught space, linking the power of magic with the trauma of a supernatural and queer adolescence. Throughout the book, I'll also unpack terms like "wizard," "warlock," and "witch" to think about the gendered differences between these terms.

At the same time, we also need to discuss how these figures are read as part of falsely homogenous and white medieval culture, propagated in part by scholars like J. R. R. Tolkien. In her essay "The Question of Race in *Beowulf*," Dorothy Kim points out that "Black scholars have been systematically shut out of Old English literature"—in part due to the de-politicized medieval readings of scholars like Tolkien—and this has disrupted the formation of "[a] critical mass of black intellectuals, writers, and poets who can talk back to the early English literary corpus and the large-looming white supremacist gatekeepers." As I'll discuss throughout this book, scholars such as Ebony Elizabeth Thomas and Maria Sachiko Cecire have argued that the children's and YA fantasy traditions, based on Tolkien's model of medieval studies, did not welcome them as young racialized readers. Since wizards are bound up in a scholarly medieval tradition that has also been hostile to Black, Indigenous, and POC (person of color) scholars, it becomes all the more important to interrogate what me mean when we say "wizard."

Who does this character resemble? Which communities do they cross, and how can we prise "wizard" from white supremacist notions of what it means to be "medieval" in the first place? How do we ensure that wizards can create space for readers beyond privileged white, straight, and abled communities?

There are a number of reasons that I wanted to write this book. My dissertation focused on wizardry and sexuality in medievalist texts, so I've been heated about wizards and their role in pop culture since grad school. I've had numerous conversations with students in fantasy-themed courses about the wizard as a complex figure, yet there's surprisingly little published scholarship on the history of the literary wizard. Most scholarly treatments of magic-users focus almost exclusively on children's literature, while this book examines how the wizard evolves in teen and middle-grade works: that is, how is the wizard a potentially useful figure for discussing adolescence? How do wizards grow up with us? Aside from all that, one of the questions that drives this work is personal. *What kind of wizards do we need?*

Years ago, I attempted to publish an article about drag culture and wizardry. More specifically, I was arguing that Gandalf, the wizard hero of Tolkien's *The Hobbit* and *Lord of the Rings* series, shared a kinship with drag queens. After all, so much of wizardry is performance. A reviewer took offense to this reading and offered what has perhaps become one of my favorite reviews: "Gandalf is a member of an angelic order, and deserves more respect." The reviewer, in essence, was telling me that I didn't respect wizards. This points to a continual divide between "respectable" wizards, like Gandalf, and "other" wizards who proliferate along the margins of the YA genre. It's that tension that I'm interested in—the space where wizards can be messy, wild, relatable. How is a wizard supposed to act? Who made those rules? And how does the teen genre challenge them by giving us queer wizards, disabled wizards, anxious wizards, failed wizards?

As a queer kid on the spectrum, I grew up desiring medieval wizards in the same way that Tolkien desired dragons—with a mixture of longing and fear. I struggled to communicate with neurotypical kids my age. The world was a bizarre set of rules, and I lacked the spell-book to decode them. But wizards gave me a model of survival. In *The Boy's King Arthur*, the picture that stood out most to me was Merlin, solitary, complete. The wizard seemed to offer a vital middle ground for a queer, socially awkward kid who didn't want to be a knight. Years later, the medievalist fiction writer Chaz Brenchley would tell me, in a whispered aside, that queer people "were the real wizards." We survived in spite of all the knights. This book, in many ways, is an attempt to transmit the wizardry of queer youth while exploring the impact of medieval literature on diverse futures. What do medieval texts teach us about growing up, and how do their many fantastic adaptations contribute to the field of medievalism studies? As someone who works "in the middle" of various conversations on sexuality, history, and disability, I also want to explore the place of medieval/medievalist literature within disability studies. How do characters with disabilities negotiate these medievalist worlds, and how might they play with medieval ways of thinking about disability and neurodiversity?

Medieval Adolescence: Or, Waxing up Sideways

The title of this section borrows from Katherine Bond Stockton's *The Queer Child*, where she discusses the "ghostly gay child—the publicly impossible child" whose experience is "an act of growing sideways" (11). The child, already queer by mixing so many ideas, is always "sideways" rather than straight. Medieval literature in the English and Latin traditions tend to discuss adolescence in highly uncertain terms, since the long medieval era (if we track it from roughly 500 to 1500 CE) utilized several different "ages" to explore the development of children into adults. It can be hard to pin down what *adolescentia* really meant to medieval audiences, just as it can be hard to pin down any clear transition between the medieval and early modern eras. But various medieval romances, and texts on childhood development, seem to agree that the ages of fourteen and fifteen were transitional, which we'll discuss below. This was the time when a young person might enroll in university or undertake an apprenticeship.

Medieval literature also uses the metaphor of the growing tree as a symbol of adolescence. The thirteenth-century Middle English romance *King Horn* focuses on a young monarch-to-be. Horn is told that he must "waxe more / Bi fulle seve yere"[2] (L99–100) before he sets off on his own adventures. The twelfth-century romance *Havelok the Dane* focuses on two young heirs who must reclaim their rightful kingdoms. The titular character is portrayed as a hungry teen who might eat his hermit foster parents out of house and home. When called a child, he responds sharply: "Ich am now no grom! / Ich am wel waxen and wel may eten" (L791–92).[3] The University of Michigan's *Middle English Dictionary* defines the charming word *grom* as "an infant boy," but also as "a young man." A diminutive version of the word *gomen*—both man and game—that playfully slides throughout *Sir Gawain and the Green Knight*. Havelok is a hungry middle, refusing to be satisfied with any category. Youth are supposed to grow like trees, but what happens when they grow sideways, like the fairy tree of the thirteenth-century romance *Orfeo*, which seems to have represented a collapse of boundaries? I want

---

2 "Grow for seven more years."
3 "Now I am full grown, and may eat as a man!"

this section to riff on Eve Sedgwick's essay "How to Bring Your Kids up Gay," by imagining how to bring your medieval kids up queer. What were the "wrong" ways to grow up medieval, and how did failing that test often produce the most interesting lives?

Medieval conduct literature arguably begins with the tenth-century *Colloquy* of the abbot and grammarian Aelfric of Eynsham, which was directed at young students. This genre reached its height with chivalry manuals and fifteenth-century texts like *How the Good Wife Taught Her Daughter*, written as an anonymous text between mother and daughter. One thing all of these texts agree on is an essential straightness in every sense of the word. Growing youth must avoid *slyness*, which is exemplified by trickery or artifice. In his fourteenth-century *Book of Chivalry*, Geoffroi de Charny cautions against becoming "those who are too ingenious or over subtle" (149).[4] A knight should never engage in "cunning schemes"[5] or "fail to act according to natural good sense"[6] (149; 51). You have to be straight, hard, and plain (though, as we'll discuss later, the Middle English (ME) word for "hard" was actually "sad," with many connotations). The fifteenth-century *ABC of Aristotle*, designed as conduct literature for children, also advises against being "to queynte, ne / to qurelose"[7] (Kline 73). Children should be neither too crafty, nor too quarrelsome. Of course, *queynte* has a number of other meanings that Chaucer will exploit, but we might think of it as the dark side of "hendy."[8] Too sly for one's own good. When Aelfric's students say "we want to be wise" (Kline 125), they seem to be turning away from slyness. But when the teacher-narrator asks them to identify bad students, one of the pupils asks: "Why do you ask me about them? I don't dare give up our secrets" (ibid.). So a bit of slyness remains.

Various medieval scholars identify *adolescentia* as a time of great turmoil, fiery emotions, willfulness, and temptation. In *From Boys to Men*, Ruth Mazo Karras notes that "the question of what constituted childhood, adolescence, and adulthood in the Middle Ages is easily as complicated as the question of what constituted masculinity and femininity" (12). A youth might enter university as early as twelve, or as late as twenty, depending upon what program and outcome they were seeking. Karras observes that there was also "great variation in the age at which apprenticeship began" (116), though twelve to fifteen was the general range. Many scholars based their definitions of childhood on Aristotle,

---

4 "Se en y a d'autres que li aucuns tiennent a saiges" (148).
5 "Subtilz engin" (148).
6 "Et pour ce n'est ce mie tout le bien de sens" (150).
7 "Too quaint (clever), nor too querulous."
8 The ME "hendy" has a number of definitions, but is often glossed as "handy" or "tricky."

who saw the beard as a threshold moment for boys becoming teens (he wasn't nearly as concerned with discussing the adolescence of girls). The seventh-century polymath Isidore of Seville, whose work would be faithfully adapted by later writers, identified "six stages in a lifetime: infancy, childhood, adolescence, youth, maturity, and old age" (242). Youth, or *adolescentia*, represented those who were "mature enough for procreating and lasts until the twenty-eighth year" (ibid.). We often discuss the "attenuated" teen period of the twenty-first century, with generic categories like *new adult,* as something new. Complaints about young adults often suggest that a particular new generation has somehow demanded a longer adolescent period, and are refusing to "be adults." But medieval audiences were also prepared to view adolescence as a much longer stretch of time. For Isidore, as with other scholars, the age of fourteen represented a watershed moment. But it was still just one stop along an adolescent journey.

The thirteenth-century scholar Bartholomaeus goes into further detail. Childhood lasts "to the ende of fourteene yeare . . . [and] after that commeth the age that is called *Adolescentia*, the age of a young striplyng" (Batman 70). We have the image of the tree in the word "striplyng," as well as the impression that the tree should wax up straight. Bartholomaeus goes on to say that in "this age the members are softe and tender, and able to stretch: and therefore they grow by vertue of heate that hath masterye in them" (ibid.). This explains the young, hotheaded Arthur in *Sir Gawain and the Green Knight.* Youth is a time of pliability and unmanageable fire. It's also signaled by the peculiar sound of a changing voice, as Bartholomaeus suggests: "In children the voyce chaungeth not, untill the desiring of *Venus* come: For when childrens voyce chaungeth it is a token of *Puberte*" (72). Medieval thinkers, like contemporary ones, were divided on exactly what youth was. But they agreed that it was a time, of variable duration, when humans burned and stretched in-between one thing and another. I'll discuss the medieval adolescent phenomenon throughout this book, and how it gets adapted by writers of medievalist YA, from teen wizards and university students to life in the cloisters.

Queerness was a paradoxical issue for this time of life—often suggested or hinted at, but rarely codified in conduct literature. At the same time, there was a tradition of medieval homoerotic verse going back to early writers like the fourth-century Ausonius. In one of his poems, he writes about a "handsome boy" who is "paene puella," or "nearly a girl" (Stehling 3). The twelfth-century French poet Marbod of Rennes describes an androgynous boy who is "rough and thankless / like a tiger cub" (Stehling 33),[9] too proud to yield to a lover's pleas. There's an

---

9 "Asper et ingratus, tanquam de tigride natus" (Stehling 32).

echo in several poems of what I've come to think of as the *proud femme boy*, arrogant in his beauty, somehow wasting what these poets feel entitled to. Baudri of Bourgeuil, a contemporary of Marbod's, writes in a similar vein. He chastises those with "rude manners . . . / Certainly a boy is bad who has such arrogant ways" (Stehling 39).[10] This bad boy doesn't smile at older men, like he's supposed to. He's doubly vexing for insisting upon his own queer personhood. Bourgeuil hates "pompous young men, hard as flint" (Stehling 41).[11] But sometimes this flint-boy gets center-stage. The popular character Ganymede—Jove's young cup-bearer, famously abducted by the god—shows up as a presence in multiple Latin poems between the twelfth and thirteenth centuries, which suggests that he was an enduring queer symbol. Often called *semivir*, or "half-man," we might also think of him as a *middle man*: a flexible middle that non-traditional youth could occupy. In the remarkable thirteenth-century "Debate between Ganymede and Helen," young Ganymede is pictured as a "morning star"[12] who "seems to disdain everything with his eyes" (Stehling 109). When Helen challenges Ganymede for engaging in sex that isn't procreative, he responds: "I don't want my face duplicated / I'd rather have it attract men with its uniqueness" (Stehling 113).[13] He describes two male bodies fitting together as *"eleganti copula,"* an elegant conjunction: something a boy might actually strive for.

As Terry Castle has observed, premodern same-sex encounters between women have an "apparitional" quality, seldom as recorded as male encounters were. There may have been a certain freedom in this lack of codification. In a recent Twitter conversation, Rosemary McAllister (@DubiousCA) summed this up: "I love the idea of medieval girls just being *super gay* because nobody technically told them that they weren't allowed to" (April 14, 2020). Monastic guides like the early thirteenth-century *Ancrene Wisse*, or Guide for Anchoresses—designed specifically for women living outside of conventional spaces—warned against sins that were *unspeakable*, and Victoria Blud has connected the earlier, *unasecgendlic* (unspeakable) and *fullic* (impure) desires mentioned cryptically by Saint Mary of Egypt with same-sex attraction (Blud 36). In a remarkable passage of his didactic twelfth-century *Livre des manières*, written to advise the Countess of Hereford, Étienne De Fougères includes a warning against same-sex relationships between young women. He uses a fishing metaphor to describe women who fish "without a rod" (ne vont pas chercher de gaule), in search of the *turbot* or "flat fish" (91).

---

10 "Quippe supercilio puer improbus utere tanto" (Stehling 38).
11 "Odi pomposos, odi juvenes silicinos" (Stehling 40).
12 "Qualis solet lucifer diem prevenire" (Stehling 108).
13 "Non hanc meam faciem volo reparari / sed placere singulis forma singulari" (Stehling 112).

These women, he says, "have invented a game / of two holes [or hills] that form a knot," rubbing until they "strike sparks" (89).[14] I'll return to this knotty image when we discuss Geraldine Heng's reading of the feminine knot in *Sir Gawain and the Green Knight*. Fougères specifies that this "game" is common among chambermaids, but worries that it will spread to aristocratic ladies.

The thirteenth-century Occitan *Trobairitz* poet Bieris de Romans, in her poem "Na Maria" ("Lady Maria"), echoes the ancient Greek poet Sappho in her expression of anxious queer desire:

> [Give] me, lovely woman, if it's pleasing to you,
> the gift in which I have most joy and hope.
> For in you I have fixed my heart and desire,
> and from you I have derived all my happiness,
> and from you—so many times—my painful yearning. (Thiébaux 257)[15]

The poem's desire wavers between propriety and pain, both mirroring a system of patronage while exceeding that frame with its passion. In an evocative twelfth-century poem by Hamda bin Ziyad (from Islamic Iberia), the speaker is swimming near her friends when she notices "a joydoe who's palmed my heart and unsleeped my eyes" (Al-Udhari 236). Al-Udhari's translation of "unsleeped" echoes Sappho's anxiety of being intensely aware of desire, while having no language to express it. Ziyad's speaker goes on to say: "When she unpins her hair you see the moon in a dark horizon, as though the dawn has lost a brother," fluid as water.

As I'll discuss further in my chapter on Merlin's adolescence, there were also young trans and nonbinary characters within the medieval romance tradition. The titular character of the thirteenth-century *Roman de silence* is AFAB (assigned female at birth), but lives as a boy in order to satisfy their parents' anxieties of inheritance. There's a lengthy and remarkable passage detailing how Nature forms Silence through her "million molds," and M. W. Gabrielle

---

14 "Ces dames ont inventé un jeu:
de deux trous elles font un nœud,
heurtent cercueil contre cercueil,
allument leur feu sans fusil" (89).

15 "Per çò vos prèc, si'us platz, que Fin' Amors
E gauziment e dous umilitatz
Me puòsca far ab vos tant de secours
Que mi donetz, bèla Dòmna, si'us platz,
Çò dont plus ai d'aver jòi esperança;
Car en vois ai mon còr e mon talan
E per vois ai tot çò qu'ai d'alegrança,
E por vos vauc mantas vetz sospiran" (Bec 73).

Bychowski has written brilliantly on the role of *Silence* within a corpus of medieval trans writing. I'll discuss later the figure of Grisandolus, a young transmasculine knight who features within the late Middle English *Prose Merlin*. Trans women also appear in the story of Grisandolus, and Monmouth's earlier *Vita Merlini* features a young page disguised as a girl. Though both Grisandolus and Silence are "exposed" by Merlin (who cannot endure anything that doesn't fit within his own prophecy), both characters present enduring narratives of trans adolescence. Blake Gutt notes that medieval narratives of transformation and transition, in spite of their subtle or visible violences against trans bodies, can also "present the journey (or transition) of 'trans' as a personal trajectory whose start and end points need not be rigidly defined" (133). The story of Grisandolus has perhaps a more flexible ending for its transmasculine protagonist, which we'll discuss in that chapter.

Finally, here are two examples of "right" and "wrong" medieval adolescence, drawn from two linked Arthurian texts: *The Vulgate* and Robert de Boron's *Merlin*. What medievalists call *The Vulgate* is a series of interwoven Arthurian stories written in Old French, and composed in the early thirteenth century—the basis for Thomas Malory's later *Morte Darthur*. Robert de Boron's *Merlin*, on the other hand, is part of his late twelfth-century series of three linked tales about Joseph of Arimethea as the guardian of the grail. De Boron wanted to Christianize the Merlin figure, though his work still contains supernatural elements. Both sources include Merlin, though the anti-hero of the *Vulgate* is clearly Lancelot. If Lancelot is the upright child, Merlin is the cuckoo, the sly, queer child who grew sideways. First, an image of teen Lancelot, from the thirteenth-century French *Vulgate*:

> He was, says the story, the handsomest lad in the world, with the most beautifully formed torso and limbs. Nor may the details of his face be overlooked; they need to be described for all people who like to hear about the great beauty in a youth. He had a perfect complexion, neither too fair nor too dark . . . [His] eyes were bright and smiling and full of delight as long as he was in a good mood, but when he was angry they looked just like glowing coals. (Lacy 95)[16]

Lancelot is the perfect mercurial youth—beautiful and dangerous—and the writer understands that their audience has a hunger for just this type of stripling. "There is no point in wondering about his neck," the writer goes on (somewhat creepily, as my Arthurian Lit students observed). "Even as the neck of a beautiful woman,

---

16 "Et che fu que dist li contes li plus biax enfes del monde. & li mieux taillies de cors & de tous menbres. Ne sa fachons ne fait pas a oubier en cont . . . [les] iex vairs & rians & plains de ioie tant com il estoir lies. Mais quant il fu iries a chertes che sambloit carbon esprit" (Sommer, VIII, 34).

it would have been very becoming" (ibid.).[17] Lancelot's androgyny makes him an object of desire to both men and women, though his martial skills ensure that nobody could see him as anything but the perfect knight. This is not to say that Lancelot *is* actually straight. In the sprawling thirteenth-century *Vulgate*, he shares a passionate relationship with the princely knight Galehaut, who dies of grief when he realizes Lancelot has chosen Guinevere over him. Thomas Malory's *Morte*, designed to edit these sprawling stories for a fifteenth-century audience, also flattens the love square—Lancelot + Galehaut + Guinevere + Arthur—into the more traditional triangle.

Now, let's contrast this with Robert de Boron's description of young Merlin:

> One day [King Vortigern's men] were passing through a field outside of town where a group of children were playing a game with a stick and ball. Merlin, who knew everything that had been happening, was one of the players. When he saw Vortigern's messengers, he went up to one of the wealthiest children of the town and struck him across the leg with the stick, knowing he would react angrily. The child began to cry and hurl insults at Merlin, accusing him of being born without a father. (Bryant 68)

Both Merlin and Lancelot have uncertain parentage, but while Lancelot is fostered by one of the benign Ladies of the Lake, Merlin's father is understood to be a demon. He is, in many ways, the antithesis to Lancelot's straight boyhood. An awkward kid who's terrible at stick-ball, he decides to hit one of the other kids, instead of playing fair. Merlin understands that there *is* no fair play, no real chivalry—only prophecy. In de Boron's version, he begins life as a hairy toddler who speaks in full sentences, challenging the judge who tries to condemn his mother. Everyone's spooked by him. As a neurodivergent child, Merlin grows sideways. When we place his youthful description alongside that of Lancelot, awkwardness clashes with mastery, slyness with fair play. Merlin's wizardry queers his adolescence, and we'll see this replicated in medievalist YA adaptations like Capetta and McCarthy's *Once and Future*: a 2019 text that reimagines Arthurian legend through a queer and more diverse lens. What I'll argue is that these adaptations aren't entirely revisionist—Merlin was always a sideways child.

Medieval and Medievalist Neurodiversity

One of the arguments of this book is that medieval wizards—and their counterparts in contemporary medievalist fiction—think differently, *queerly*. I want to connect the wizard with the term "neuro-queer," popularized by Nick Walker, Melanie

---

[17] "De son col ne fait il mie a demander. Car sil fust en une tres bele dame" (ibid.).

Yergeau, and Julia Miele Rodas, along with the broader idea of neurodiversity. In her book *Autistic Disturbances*, Rodas notes that the term *neuro-queer* "gestures toward a cultural history shared by neurodivergent and queer peoples," and "reclaims identity from clinical and popular arenas" (xvi–vii). It encompasses the unique rhetorical and cognitive practices of people on a broad spectrum of neuro-atypicality. Yergeau argues in *Authoring Autism* that people on the spectrum are often denied the sense of being "rhetorical" when their non-traditional communication styles are seen as marginal, even non-existent. Certainly, as someone on the spectrum, I have struggled with neurotypical communication. I can recall countless instances of being told to "speak up," or "get to the point," or "make proper eye contact." My silences, pauses, and inarticulate moments have placed me in opposition to the ableist model of academia, which demands specific performance of rigor and collegiality (more on those later, informed by the work of Margaret Price).

So where does the medieval wizard fit into this discussion that crosses both disability studies and cultures of neurodiversity? In the autistic-authored *Loud Hands* collection, Nick Walker succinctly defines neurodiversity: "There is no 'normal' style of human brain or human mind" (228). This is often presented as the "operating system" model of human cognition, arguing that we all run slightly different operating systems, but our minds are equal. John Loeppky reiterates this in his work on accessibility: "[Able-bodied] people are wary of those who think we get everything for free just because our legs don't work or our brain has a different operating system" ("Disabilities Are Not Curses"). In a world sponsored by Mac, neurodivergent people are working on platforms and systems that, although vital and varied, are rendered incompatible by the dominant paradigms of social software. Also, our spell-books have different codes. Neuro-queer rhetorics (and runes) provide ways of being sly and crafty in the face of overwhelmingly ableist narratives about how we should exist in public space.

Characters with physical impairments are still somewhat uncommon in the YA fantasy genre, though their presence is growing. Distinctions between impairment and disability are often contested, but Eli Clare offers the following contrast between models of disability:

> The medical model of disability defines disability as a medical problem located in individual bodies and frames those problems as curable, or at least treatable, by the medical-industrial complex; in essence giving doctors complete authority over the embodied experiences of disabled people. In resistance to the medical model, the disability rights movement has created a social model that separates impairment—a physical, emotional, cognitive, and/or developmental limitation, difference and/or variation—and ableism—the material and social conditions that restrict people with impairments. This model declares that ableism is far more disabling than impairment. (Interview, *Upping the Anti*)

Clare's division between medical and community-based models of disability creates a living space for all kinds of bodies, and presents impairment as a form of difference, rather than strictly a type of limitation. My own use of terms like "impairment" is guided by the work of Clare and other disability rights activists. These discussions take on complicated dimensions when we link them to neurodiversity. For instance—I know that my brain has some uncommon wiring, and this produces physical issues: environmental sensitivity, problems with light/sound and texture, a heightened fight/flight response, problems with verbal communication, and meltdowns that are physically exhausting. That's my experience—I can't speak for others. Would I define these bodily phenomena as impairments? They certainly interfere with my attempts to adapt to a world that values only one type of physicality and sociability. But on good days, I can see these as strengths, rather than barriers—intensities of experience that remind me of being vitally different, and which might signal to others that being different is queer and good.

YA texts deal with these varieties of physical difference in ways that range from inventive to reductive. J. K. Rowling's Mad-Eye Moody, for instance, has one eye, though he compensates for this with his magic eye as a type of assistive device. In *Otherbound*, Corinne Duyvis includes a protagonist, Nolan, who has been physically disabled as a result of magic. The book's other protagonist, Amara, communicates through sign within a medievalist world. Claire Bartlett's *We Rule the Night* has a magic-user protagonist, Revna, who's a double-amputee, and Mackenzi Lee's *Gentleman's Guide to Vice and Virtue* features a queer character who's epileptic (though the novel also veers into a fraught storyline where a character becomes disabled as a form of sacrifice). Hogwarts is notoriously inaccessible as a school, though the mobile game *Harry Potter: Hogwarts Mystery* (2019) has added a young wizard who's also a wheelchair-user named Murphy McNully. The character states: "[I] will always be 'that wizard in a wheelchair.' Which I am, of course . . . [But] I'm all of those other things too. So I'm always trying to show everyone all that I am, all at once, and all at the moment I meet them" (Machemer).

McNully is both white and blonde, which recalls a recent conversation between disability activists Carson Tueller and Andrew Gurza on the notion of palatability privilege in disability politics. Tueller notes that his acquired disability (a spinal cord injury), as well as his white attractiveness as an Instagram star, gives him a palatability while also conferring the responsibility "to advocate for disabled people in a way that is congruent with the way that people listen to me . . . [I'm] very safe" (*Disability after Dark*, E186, April 19, 2020). Gurza and Tueller both go on to discuss how queer disabled people challenge notions of queer normativity by presenting non-traditional sex lives that are equally valid. A character like McNully is, perhaps, the safest version possible of a disabled wizard in Rowling's world. His affable desire to please, "to show everyone all that I am," is the sort of thing that exhausts activists like Gurza. His inclusion doesn't rewrite the ableism of Rowling's medievalist world, but it does offer players the chance to see themselves represented as a wizard who's also a wheelchair-user. Fanfiction.net has a section of disability-centered fanfic stories, called *Potter Impaired*, where authors have attempted to challenge the ableism of Hogwarts. The user Teddylonglong's story, "To Whom It May Concern," imagines Harry dealing with a heart defect, for instance (2009), while the story "Thicker Than Blood" (by user The Lilac Elf of Lothlorien) imagines Harry living with a spinal cord injury (2008). Fanfiction is clearly willing to envision disability in the series as a realistic variation of human experience, rather than a kind of metaphor, as Rowling does in the case of her werewolf characters.

Rowling's social media presence in 2020 has unleashed a storm of transphobia. The author has been soundly criticized for many flaws within the *HP* series, including the whiteness of the main characters, Dumbledore's after-the-fact queerness, the exoticization of characters like Nagini, and the anti-Semitic connotations of her goblin bankers. The author's recent and strident defense of gender essentialism signals a catastrophic betrayal of her queer, trans, and nonbinary readers—particularly young readers who are vulnerable and searching for some form of positive representation in fantasy literature. In their *Vox* article, "Harry Potter and the Author Who Failed Us," Aja Romano cites the character Tonks as someone who could be read as nonbinary, in spite of Rowling's later efforts to "tame" the character and make them more clearly feminine. Romano states that "we can no longer talk about *Harry Potter* without foregrounding the prejudice lurking beneath the surface-level morality of Rowling's stories." This places some critical limits on the transformative potential of Rowling's wizards—though, as Romano suggests, it's still possible to connect with a character like Tonks for their nonbinary potential, and to ignore the prejudices of the author who keeps trying to erase that potential. Rowling's work belongs to us, and not to her. It can still resonate for queer, trans, and nonbinary readers, though we have to keep challenging its author, and make way for more inclusive stories that also deserve the same amount of global attention.

I want to use the wizard as a particularly flexible and enduring symbol for looking at different modes of cognition, both in medieval literature and its medievalist adaptations. As I'll discuss in the chapter on Merlin (and throughout the book), wizards can also be deeply anxious, in ways that produce kinship between these medieval figures and young neurodivergent readers. Magic is anxious, magic is queer, and these medieval ideas both structure and reflect YA's contemporary concerns with power, cognitive development, and sexuality. Wizards also have a peculiarly epic way of thinking, informed by power and prophecy, but also shaped by their social marginality as figures who exist on the edge of various communities. This aligns them with the developmental narratives of the YA genre, where teen passions often feel just as epic, just as "life-or-death" as the decisions that a wizard might make.

In my class on teen fiction, we discussed a number of magic-centric YA texts (Rainbow Rowell's *Carry On*, Haisla/Heiltsuk writer Eden Robinson's *Son of a Trickster*, *The Philosopher's Stone*). My students observed that the cost of being a witch or wizard seemed to always involve some kind of trauma. Several of these young wizards were neurodivergent: Simon Snow, from *Carry On*, has anxiety and issues with verbal communication; Harry Potter was traumatized by his abusive foster family; the witch Sarah, from Robinson's *Son of a Trickster*, lives with depression (while identifying as nonbinary). In class, we talked about how saving the world demanded an impossible psychic toll, while at the same time, characters who were already anxious seemed drawn to magic. I had the students design a strategic plan for Hogwarts School of Witchcraft and Wizardry, and what they demanded most clearly was more counseling support for these characters. It became impossible to talk about wizards without talking about mental health, and that connection made me think more clearly about the role of the wizard in discussions of disability and neurodiversity.

Our classroom conversations also addressed the role of gender in these magical texts. The terms *wizard* and *witch* have different roots: *wizard* comes from the Old English "wīs" (wise), and signals a learned man. But *witch* seems to have two Old English sources: "wicca" (originally gender-neutral, eventually becoming the feminine "wicce"), and "hægtesse," from which we derive the word *hag*. In popular fantasy culture, witches are virtually always women—though Terry Pratchett's *Discworld* series has some exceptions, which we'll discuss. Ambiguous terms like *warlock* (Old English "wærloga," meaning traitor) have narrowed to mean a type of evil wizard. But characters like Ambrose in *Chilling Adventures of Sabrina* also identifies as a warlock, though he's more on the neutral-good side.

Early medieval anti-magical texts would often decry witches, wizards, and Valkyries, all in the same sentence, but the most organized pogrom against so-called magic-users was directed at women in the late Middle Ages, as the witch trials sought to combat a perceived "organizing" among supernatural practitioners. In class, we discussed how women were historically punished for being witches, though men could take on the role of wizard and simply be mysterious. Witches like Willow Rosenberg in *Buffy the Vampire Slayer* took on emotional labor as well—serving as Buffy's main confidante—while characters like Warren used magic for selfish ends. *Buffy* seemed interested in valorizing the witch as a figure, even as it fussed over magic being aligned with drug use. Throughout this book, we'll return to the ways in which magic and gender are related, and how the responsibilities—and barriers—experienced by witches are often different than the experiences of their wizardly counterparts.

Our conversations moved between gender, sexuality, and disability when thinking about magic-users, and this book expands upon the role of wizards and witches in both disability literature and LGBTQ+ literature. In his 2019 volume on disability in YA, Jacob Stratman notes that "there is still a dearth of scholarship that explores the intersections of young adult literature and disability" (1). He also argues, in a way relevant to my own discussion, that "both queer and disability studies thrive in making the normal strange, odd, and unfamiliar" (6). YA fantasy texts also queer the normal in this regard, using magic to explore the unfamiliar, while making the ordinary seem strange. In his chapter on queer and Deaf narratives in YA, Angel Daniel Matos goes on to describe how disability narratives in YA "[assist] readers in considering the strangeness of normativity" (222). This speaks to the larger project of #OwnVoices YA—texts for communities, written by people within those communities—and the inclusion of central characters who aren't just able-bodied, white, straight, and cisgender.

Neurodiversity isn't a new concept, even if it's only been more recently included within the umbrella of disability studies (and there's no agreed-upon consensus for the term, especially when we visualize it as a spectrum that might include many perspectives and realities). This term can signal the deceptively simple fact that everyone's brain works differently, or that all brains have slightly different operating systems. A spectrum of neurodiversity includes all sorts of cognitive models, and defies the "high/low-functioning" terminology often used to draw ableist distinctions between these models. Neurodiversity has also become a space for marketing—I just ordered a mask with a rainbow brain stamped on it, including the slogan *embrace neurodiversity*—and rainbow symbolism has emerged as a link between neurodivergent and queer experiences. We'll explore the idea of neuro-queerness in a bit. Melanie Yergeau notes that "terms like *neurodiversity* are welcomed with broader social currency" (4), though this doesn't necessarily signal better lives for neurodivergent people. Like diversity, neurodiversity as a term has the advantage of being palatable and broad. For that very reason, we need to continually tease out its vital specificities and communities.

There was also no "correct" mind within medieval discussions of cognition; or, perhaps we can point to all the untidy minds and unwieldy perspectives that come out in medieval literature. Mystics like Hildegard of Bingen recorded sensory experiences that were difficult to classify. Late medieval writers represent experiences of anxiety, trauma, and what we might think of as deep introversion, like Thomas Hoccleve in his fifteenth-century poem *My Compleinte*. In the 2020 *Medieval Disability Sourcebook*, Will Rogers states that "Hoccleve's poem gestures to a complex view of impairment and disability in the fifteenth century" (313). Hoccleve writes:

> Noon abood, noon areest, but al brainseke.
> Another spake and of me seide also,
> My feet weren ay wauynge to and fro,
> Whanne þat I stonde shulde and wiþ men talke,
> And þat myn yen souȝten euery halke. (Rogers 317)

> [Never still, never steady, always feverish,
> Another [friend] spoke this of me as well,
> My feet were always wending to and fro,
> When they should be planted firm to talk with friends,
> Instead, my eyes bounced off the very walls.]

The description is remarkably like an anxiety attack. I've certainly felt this way in crowded spaces, my feet restless, my already sketchy eye contact dissolving into quick glances while I fall into sensory overload. Hoccleve's speaker knows what they should be doing in this social situation, but they can't manage it: a feeling many of us can relate to. There's also a moment when the speaker goes "streit unto my myrrowr and my glas / to loke how that me of my chere thowght" (straight to my mirror / to see if my face seemed cheerful). As a kid who used to practice "appropriate" facial expressions in the mirror, I can relate to this.

Joshua Eyler notes that "there were many lenses through which medieval societies viewed disability" (3). Though Thomas Aquinas and other medieval theologians sought to study cognition and even brain structure, there was no unifying perspective on how minds worked. One of the Old English words for mind is *mod*, and the *mod* is unhinged: in Leslie Lockett's words, it "whistl[es] . . . like a boiling tea kettle" (70). Medieval visualizations of the mind actually come close to approximating more recent terms, like "bodymind," since they visualize a holistic connection between mind and heart. By seeing the mind as something open, snarly, a bit unmanageable, these thinkers were creating medieval models for neurodiversity. Across the long medieval era, there is no single definition of impairment. Adapting work by disability scholars like Rosemary Garland Thomson, Tory Pearman has argued that medieval women exist on a continuum of disability, since "the use of the [medieval] gendered model makes evident the connections between discursive productions of the female body and the disabled body" (7). By exploring contexts of feminist disability in medieval literature, Pearman expands Thomson's argument that "disability is a culturally fabricated narrative of the body, similar to what we understand as the fictions of race and gender" (5). Pearman goes on to explore these connections in her reading of the medieval conduct text *Book of the Knight,* and its paradoxical treatment of women: the author honors his daughters, on whom he wishes to bestow these lessons, while simultaneously vilifying wives and daughters in the *Book*. Cameron Hunt McNabb links "medieval" with "disability" as similarly contested terms: "The term 'disability' presents complexities similar to 'the Middle Ages,' including under its umbrella disabilities marked as physical, emotional, and mental; chronic and acute; visible and invisible" (13). Reading connections between disability and neurodiversity in medieval literature can help us to avoid the nostalgic (and inevitably racist) views of the Middle Ages as a "simpler" time. Beyond being nostalgic, these views are historically inaccurate—as we'll discuss throughout this monograph, the medieval world demonstrates racial diversity, gender complexity, and cognitive difference. Their conversations about mentality and embodiment were every bit as complex as the ones currently circulating within YA literature, and ideas shifted across a long arc of time.

There's a tradition of both established and emerging conversations around medieval disability studies, which attempts to link our current models of disability with varied medieval experiences. Throughout this book, I'll come back to work by Cameron Hunt McNabb, Joshua Eyler, and Tory Pearman, who all discuss how medieval understandings of the body might have created a form of early disability studies. Edward Wheatley bridges the medieval and the modern, arguing that "the church's control over discourse related to disability [is] in a manner analogous to the way modern medicine attempts to maintain control over it now" (9). In his work on medieval disability studies and digital cultures, Rick Godden notes that both disabled people and queer people "occupy a varied, highly individualized, and at times troubled temporality similar to a queer temporality" ("Getting Medieval in Real Time" 268). He links this to work on queer time by Carolyn Dinshaw—which I'll also come back to—and he cites lack of accessibility at events designed to connect medieval scholars (like the International Congress on Medieval Studies at Kalamazoo). I'll return to Godden's work on both accessibility and temporality, and connect it with similar work by Alison Kafer. Both scholars think about the queerness of time—something relevant to studying a remote era—and how disabled and neurodivergent people might experience time differently.

Medieval literature also presents a number of individuals who struggled to deal with a fast-paced world, and seemed to value a quiet, bookish life over the buzz of court or the violent energy of the battlefield. In effect, they were attempting to create their own sensitive temporalities. In his dream vision, *The Parliament of Fowls*, Chaucer's narrator has his nose in a book, nestled in a comfortably cluttered space and musing about how other people go about their lives—the wild dreams of hunters, or the wheels that occupy the mind of the carter. Chaucer's contemporary, John Gower, dedicates his *Confessio Amantis* ("Lover's Confession") to a young Richard II. The text is ostensibly about love, but includes a number of didactic stories and fables. Gower presents the unlikely figure of Diogenes, the ancient Greek philosopher who preferred the retiring life. In volume 2, he presents the tale of Diogenes and Alexander the Great, which is supposed to be a cautionary tale about homicide. Diogenes has the wisdom to stay at home, which seems like a sure-fire way to avoid fatalities, in spite of Alexander's desire to pay him a visit. He also has a home constructed out of a barrel, which is then anchored to a tree. It's a space that blurs public and private, and it signals a defiance to traditional sociability: *We can interact, but on my terms.* When Alexander the Great offers him a favor, Diogenes is thought to have replied simply: *Step out of my light* ("Quod he, 'Thanne hove out of mi sonne, / And let it schyne into mi tonne'"). A sentiment that anyone caught up in a book can probably agree with.

What Diogenes feels is presented less as a mood towards staying in, and more as a kind of secular asceticism:

> For he therinne sitte scholde
> And torne himself so as he wolde,
> To take th'eir and se the hevene
> And deme of the planetes sevene,
> As he which cowthe mochel what.
> And thus fulofte there he sat
> To muse in his philosophie
> Solein withoute compaignie. (1206–1220)

> [For he should sit therein
> and turn himself as he liked
> to take the air and watch the heavens
> and study the seven planets
> since he knew so much about them.
> And thus he often sat there
> to muse on his philosophy
> Solo, without company.]

The image is a singular one: a man reading in an over-sized barrel, able "to take th'eir and se the hevene" while still maintaining his own forcefield of privacy. It's remarkably similar to the image of someone on public transit with their headphones on, reading something on a screen, both part of the world and at a remove from it. Diogenes would have loved earbuds. What he demands: "To muse in his philosophie / Solein withoute compaignie." As someone on the spectrum, this speaks to me on a visceral level: the need to be left alone, to recharge, to read as therapy and have the freedom to choose my social interactions. Neurodivergent readers might also see a kindred spirit in Diogenes and say: *Step out of our light.*

Finally, what Mary Carruthers has described as "the medieval craft of memory" tends to privilege a form of knowing that, I'd argue, has a lot in common with neurodivergent perspectives. She argues that medieval society had a "privileged cultural role of memory" (12) which seems to run counter to our modern celebration of creativity. While we cite innovation as a pillar of genius, "ancient and medieval people reserved *their* awe for memory" (1). I think about this when my friend's kid demonstrates their encyclopedic knowledge of Pokémon. They experience a deep excitement and artistry within that archive of Pokémon data, a wild pleasure in relating to me all the alliances, tricks, contradictions, and patterns within this multi-media universe. I'll never know as much as they do, but there are still ways into the conversation.

Carruthers notes the "chain" or *catena* memory technique, used by Aquinas and other scholars, to link biblical texts together by particular phrases (6). Manuscripts could be framed visually in a way that aided in memory, and the trick "lies in the imposition of a rigid order to which clearly prepared pieces of textual content are attached" (9). I'd argue that this chainmail mode of memoria *feels* rigid, but can actually allow for great variation. The evolutions of Pokémon seem formulaic, with one shape leading to another, but there are also playful varieties—and of course the whole system is based on *evolution*. This brilliant kid—who used to fight sleep with bleary eyes while I read *Doctor Seuss* to them—now slides up to me with their screen, grinning with pleasure to share a new pattern, a new chain in the universe.

By tracing how these medieval ideas on cognition and embodiment are adapted in medievalist YA literature, we can also enter into broader conversations about neurodiversity and disability studies. My own work is informed particularly by Margaret Price (*Mad at School*) and Jay Dolmage (*Academic Ableism*), who both discuss the experiences of disabled academics and how we negotiate the classroom, as well as the ableist structures of academia. Alison Kafer (*Feminist, Queer, Crip*) animates my thinking on what it means to link queerness with disability, and the ways in which "crip time" acts as a necessary, more flexible alternative to the capitalist temporal rhythms of the university. We'll return to discussions of this temporal term, but Kafer describes it as "a challenge to normative and normalizing expectations of pace and scheduling" (27). All three of these scholars address the practice of teaching, and since this book emerges from classroom discussions and interactions with disabled students, I'll focus on how medieval/medievalist texts link up with these dialogues. YA is often didactic, and it's important to track not only the (often ableist) lessons the genre wants to impart, but also how we treat those lessons within a diverse classroom setting. Eli Clare's work on disability and transness in *Brilliant Imperfection* has also shaped how this book discusses trans and nonbinary characters across a variety of texts.

The broader lens for these conversations will most often be the social model of disability—discussed by activists like Eli Clare—as opposed to the medical model. I'm also influenced by Tom Shakespeare's critical realist model of disability, which includes "the independent existence of bodies which sometimes hurt, regardless of what we may think or say about those bodies" (73). As a person with a complex diagnostic history, I'm invested in the capacity of disabled and neurodivergent people to define themselves, and how that capacity translates into literature.

Medievalist YA

This final section outlines the unique subgenre of medievalist YA, which differs from medievalist children's literature in several important ways. The field of YA studies is still growing and has less of a firm critical tradition than children's literature studies. In fact, YA is still often considered a subset of children's literature, and while there's overlap between the readerships, YA tends to deal with more distinct concerns: gender and sexuality, class issues, the high school experience, and sometimes college (in the New Adult category). Scholars like Beverly Lyon Clark, Perry Nodelman, Mavis Reimer, and Colin Manlove have worked to establish a critical tradition that surveys the origins of children's literature in North America, and the UK. But surveys of the YA genre are less common, perhaps because YA feels "newer" and harder to locate. In *Young Adult Literature: From Romance to Realism* (reprinted in 2017), Michael Cart identifies the origins of YA in the work of S. E. Hinton (*The Outsiders*). He quotes a 1967 newspaper column in which Hinton observes: "Teenagers today want to read about teenagers today" (quoted in Cart 21). This focus on the present has often been a shifting target in YA, since novels that depend upon "current" teen discourses quickly become obsolete, while children's literature can address more timeless concepts. As early as 1965, however, Nancy Larrick published her article "The All-White World of Children's Books" for the *Saturday Review*, suggesting that these "timeless" stories weren't inclusive. As linked genres, both children's literature and YA deal with a lack of diversity, made all the more difficult by white authors calling out BIPOC (Black, Indigenous, and other people of color) authors for writing "issue-driven" books.

In *The Dark Fantastic*, Ebony Elizabeth Thomas locates what she calls "the imagination gap" when it comes to diversity in children's and YA literature: "When people of color seek passageways into the fantastic, we have often discovered that the doors are barred" (Introduction). An important aspect of historical YA literature, then, and medievalist YA in particular, is reflecting the diversity of the actual Middle Ages. It's vital for young readers to see themselves echoed in these stories about growing up in the past. In the chapter specifically on Arthurian material, I'll discuss the pushback that a medieval fantasy program like the BBC's *Merlin* experienced when casting a Black actress (Angel Coulby) in the role of young Guinevere; it's all the more important to discuss how diverse characters move through these medievalist realms. I'll discuss throughout this book how a tradition of medievalist YA has existed since Tolkien's publication of *The Hobbit* (which arguably sits somewhere between children's literature and YA), but it's important to track how this genre is distinct from children's fantasy literature. Authors like Ursula Le Guin and Lloyd Alexander were some of the first writers to imagine a particularly adolescent version of medievalist fiction, and their characters come of age in ways that link the diverse Middle Ages with YA's more current concerns of adolescent identity. When considering the pervasive white Englishness of YA fantasy in her book *Re-Enchanted*, Maria Sachiko Cecire asks: "What are the cultural implications of locating youthful heroics in environments steeped in long-standing raced, gendered, and classed hierarchies?" (Introduction). Coming of age in a castle necessarily changes the teen experience, but teens are still voraciously reading about medieval fantasy, and learning lessons that are influenced by our adaptation of that time period.

In addition to this anti-racist work in YA studies, a great deal of significant work on genre analysis and adaptation is happening on digital platforms. I'll draw upon podcasts like Oh Witch Please and *Hazel & Katniss & Harry & Starr* (*HKHS*), which both discuss how YA texts are transformed through the adaptation process. In Season 1, Episode 25 of *HKHS*, Brenna Clarke Gray provides a broad and useful analysis of YA fiction: "YA is focalized through a teen. It's not YA when it's an adult remembering . . . [that's] really important because that's part of what makes YA feel so immediate and vivid, and why the emotions are so raw in YA." I'll return to this affective definition of YA throughout the book, in order to examine how that "focalizing" aspect is significant when discussing something as contested as *adolescentia*. Often, it isn't just the classification of a book that makes it YA, but rather the protagonist's voice, and that "vivid" feeling applies to both medieval and contemporary teens. Clarke Gray also describes *The Hobbit* as a YA text, since the lessons of that novel—and Bilbo's emotional narrative—are closely in line with the experiences of teen readers. My own definition of medievalist YA is a flexible one: the genre features an adolescent focalizing narrative, and the protagonist comes of age within some type of medieval space, or in proximity to medieval cultures. This includes YA novels that are visible adaptations of medieval literature, like Amy Rose Capetta and Cori McCarthy's *Once and Future* (which I'll discuss further in the chapter on Merlin). But it also includes YA titles that "feel medieval" in an important way.

An example of this flexibility is David Rees's obscure 1979 novel *In the Tent*, about a Catholic gay teen growing up in Exeter, UK. Much of the novel's action takes place in the titular tent, where Tim, the protagonist, must deal with his growing attraction to his friend Aaron. The space of the tent recalls a biblical landscape, and Tim interprets his own sexuality through the weight of a Catholic tradition that he can't easily part with. The first page of the novel imagines medieval Exeter: "He was standing on the battlements of a city . . . [A] teeming, densely populated city in medieval times" (7). We're told that "history was Tim's delight" (12), and his passion for the English Civil War is always pulling him out of the present, in order to imagine his place in a longer arc of history. His description of the countryside around Exeter would fit in with a medieval bucolic poem, or one of Virgil's Georgic images:

> Light was failing. The huge wide world falling away from the summit of the Great Gable was a marvel beyond imagining . . . [The] turning world: he knew it was spinning, infinitely little, infinitely enormous. At the edges, the sea . . . [Cloud], soft cotton wool wraps of it slowly rolling over the steeple and haycock . . . [The] slopes! The depths! The heights! The sky!. (Rees 17)

Tim's attention to clouds reminds us of the Gawain poet's description of "misty hats" on mountains. In the medieval poem, Gawain is supposed to be fending off monsters, but the landscape itself becomes a fascinating character. Tim is also in love with the medieval landscape, just as he's in love with the evocatively named Aaron. He tries not to reveal himself, but his thoughts are a song of songs: "Aaron, stretch out a hand and touch me, put your hand where mine is!" (20). Tim's meditations on mortal sin are the same anxieties that Baudry of Borgeuil and Marbod of Rennes have set down in their poetry, which wavers between shame and desire.

In the Tent recalls Carolyn Dinshaw's discussion of amateur medievalism as a queer passion, where "love and knowledge are as inextricable as the links in chain mail" (xv). Dinshaw notes that she feels "a kinship with the amateur that I can only call queer" (32). And there is something elegantly amateur—in Dinshaw's sense of *amator*/lover—about Rees's book. It sold poorly, and while it wasn't as criticized as his later teen novels, it contained just enough queer content to make readers uncomfortable. More queer content, in fact, than John Donovan's 1976 YA novel *I'll Get There, It Better Be Worth the Trip*, which Michael Cart and Derritt Mason have analyzed as one of the earliest queer-inclusive YA titles. Rees died of AIDS in the early 1990s, and all of his books are out of print. His work has both a medieval feeling, and a sense of being lost that recalls fragile manuscripts and vanished texts. Yet *In the Tent* speaks to queer communities just as directly as more recent properties, like Becky Albertalli's *Simon vs. the Homo Sapiens Agenda* (adapted as the film *Love, Simon*). Tim and his friend Ray sleep together in no uncertain terms (the tent wins!), and afterwards, Ray discusses early gay spaces in Exeter: "There's places at home where people like us meet . . . [A] pub. And some group that meets in somebody's house . . . [They're] people like anybody else" (Rees 105). Here, Tim's medieval framework collides with Ray's modern sense of queerness, anticipating (in 1979) what Michael Cart describes as "queer consciousness/community" (*Representing the Rainbow* 142) in YA literature. Tim's sense of the very old makes *In the Tent* medievalist, while Ray's embrace of the fragile new makes it relatably queer YA that plays with asynchronous time.

This book surveys the evolution of medievalist YA literature, from Tolkien's *The Hobbit* to current texts like *Once and Future*, *Carry On*, and *Chilling Adventures of Sabrina*. By placing literary texts in conversation with films and TV shows, I aim to present a wider field of medievalist adaptation, while engaging with the media texts that young readers are most likely to stream. This broad range of analysis takes medieval material beyond university syllabi, and imagines how the medieval actually structures our lives across the trans-media landscape that we currently inhabit. All of these texts draw upon Kevin and Brent Moberly's playful definition of medievalism: "Although the imagined worlds of popular medievalism are not, as many scholars have pointed out, the 'real Middle Ages,' they are nevertheless also 'not *not*' the real Middle Ages" (174). Medievalist magic schools like Watford (from *Carry On*) and Brakebills (from Grossman's *The Magicians*), along with fantasy realms like Middle-Earth, Prydain, and Valdemar, compel us to think about what makes the "real" Middle Ages. The protagonists in these novels challenge our medieval definitions of heroism, and the wizard figures in particular show us queer old/new ways of thinking and surviving. The Merlin of *Once and Future* falls in love with the knight Percival; Simon Snow wields a medieval sword that he can barely control; Sabrina Spellman draws upon the slyness of Morgan to challenge the medieval trappings of her contemporary witch community. As we follow these young wizards and witches on trials that will change them (and us), I want us to consider the reciprocal relationship between medieval and medievalist texts. Not simply how medieval literature has influenced these adaptations, but what these adaptations can teach us about medieval literature. In order to understand how Capetta and McCarthy are adapting Malory's *Morte Darthur*, we also need to examine Malory's source text as an equally subversive web of stories (and a YA text in its own right, given how William Caxton would market these stories as educational for youth).

I draw upon medieval criticism by scholars whose work demonstrates what Jonathan Hsy calls "co-disciplinarity" in its productive blurring of communities. Touchstones will include: work by Carolyn Dinshaw and Tison Pugh on queer medievalism; work by Mary Rambaran-Olm, Dorothy Kim, and Geraldine Heng on intersections between race and gender in medieval studies; and work on medieval disability studies by Cameron Hunt McNabb, Joshua Eyler, and Tory Pearman. As I explore both medieval and medievalist characters who are trans and nonbinary, I engage with work by Gabrielle M.W. Bychowski, Blake Gutt, and Ellis Amity Light. With Merlin and Morgan le Fay as touchstone characters, I'll focus two chapters on Arthurian literature. But, like medievalism itself, this book's treatment of the long medieval era will be capacious. As I explore how medieval magic is adapted by YA texts, I'll examine early medieval riddles and spells, twelfth-century romances, and late medieval accounts of university students, in order to identify a body of medieval magical texts. Ruth Mazo Karras will be an important source of information on medieval adolescence, along with other scholars of medieval childhood: Nicholas Orme, J. Allan Mitchell, and Eve Salisbury. Clare Bradford's work on medievalist children's literature has been immensely valuable to the formulation of my own discussion, particularly her observation that "imaginings of the Middle Ages propose and advocate values, offer models (negative and positive) of human behaviour and sociality, and speculate about future worlds" (10). Finally, Sara Ahmed's work on the "willful child," and Jack Halberstam's discussions of "queer failure," will animate various sections of this book.

Chapter 1, "My So-Called Merlin," focuses on Merlin as an originary wizard figure in medieval literature. I draw on scholarship by Steven Knight and Peter Goodrich to explore Merlin as a teenager in the medieval work of Geoffrey of Monmouth, Robert de Boron, and the anonymous Middle English *Prose Merlin*. This chapter argues that one of Merlin's defining attributes is a sense of fragmentation and unknowability. I'll compare him with the famous Merlyn of T. H White's *Sword in the Stone*, as well as the intergalactic teen wizard from Amy Capetta and Cori McCarthy's *Once and Future*. I argue that Merlin represents a queer and neurodivergent medieval teen—halfway between a demon and a human boy—whose very in-betweenness places him within a position that marginalized teens can understand.

Chapter 2, "The Futures of Morgan le Fay," will take up medievalist adaptations of the famous enchantress Morgan le Fay. Work by Barbara Lupack has examined Morgan's place in Victorian literature, but this chapter breaks new ground by examining her continuous adaptation in the teen genre. Carolyne Larrington's work in *King Arthur's Enchantresses* will inform my discussion of Morgan as she appears in early texts like Monmouth's *Vita Merlini*, the *Vulgate*, and later texts like *Sir Gawain and the Green Knight* and the *Prophésies de Merlin* (where she's part of an enchantress community). I'll use Geraldine Heng's work on the "knot" of Morgan's presence in *Gawain* to link her with two other enchantresses in YA texts: Tiffany Aching in the work of Terry Pratchett, and Sabrina Spellman in *Chilling Adventures of Sabrina*. Drawing upon Amy Kaufman's discussion of feminine agency in the *Morte*, I'll consider how Morgan reflects Merlin's thinking, but reframes it to include the complexity of Arthurian women.

Chapter 3, "Wizards in School," considers the explicit links between medievalism, wizardry, and education. This chapter begins by considering the medieval university experience, which was already surprisingly linked with issues of magic. I'll engage with work on the medieval university by Ruth Mazo Karras and Juanita Ruys, as well as accounts of medieval student life in *The Canterbury Tales*, *Carmina Burana*, and fifteenth-century schoolbooks. I'll then examine how the YA wizard school tradition adapts these medieval sources, through YA texts like Le Guin's *The Wizard of Earthsea*, Rowell's *Carry On*, and Lev Grossman's *The Magicians*. Since characters in both Rowell's and Grossman's novels are neurodivergent, this discussion continues with the book's exploration of how medieval modes of thinking might inform contemporary neurodiversity.

Chapter 4, "Bad Magic," deals with minor and "failed" wizards in medievalist literature. Specifically, I'll look at failures of communication in these medievalist texts, and how these characters use what Julia Rodas calls "language hacking" to disrupt neurotypical ideals of speech and learning. We'll examine the character of Schmendrick "the Magnificent" in Peter S. Beagle's *The Last Unicorn*, as well as Anne Ursu's autistic protagonist Oscar in *The Real Boy*. This chapter also takes up the medieval apothecary as a site for "practical magic," which Ursu adapts. These characters draw upon the medieval wizarding tradition, while failing to fulfill the promise of their own power. In this way, I argue, these minor wizards offer *in medias* positions for readers who may not fully align with the wizard's historical role. As a final example, I consider Elliot Schafer, the bisexual protagonist of Sarah Brennan's *In Other Lands*, whose critical snark and trauma end up defining his heroism within a medievalist world.

Chapter 5, "Do You Really Want to Snyrt Me," addresses the young figure of Gawain in a variety of medieval texts, from *Sir Gawain and the Green Knight* (*SGGK*) to the Latin *Rise of Gawain* and Middle Dutch *Walewein*. In particular, I examine Gawain's contested sexuality in *SGGK* by analyzing how his infamous kisses with Lord Bertilak are represented in children's and middle-grade adaptations of the medieval poem. These include Michael Morpurgo's 2001 *Sir Gawain and the Green Knight*, and the 2002 BAFTA-award-winning animated film of the same name by Tim Fernee. I'll discuss how these adaptations either avoid or celebrate the kissing game, in order to modernize the medieval material for young audiences. This chapter also considers the role of chivalry manuals in shaping medieval boyhood, as well as the process of "saddening" (literally, hardening), which Gawain can't quite accept—instead, he chooses a queer middle ground throughout the poem, transforming it into an ambiguous conduct manual for teens.

The epilogue, "Gandalf's Charm," focuses on Gandalf in *The Hobbit* as a classic figure who also contains a multitude of queer surprises. In particular, I read Gandalf as a nonbinary wizard—since the Maiar are technically angelic beings who only take on physical form to live in the world. We'll return to the image of an older, more fragile Merlin in Monmouth's *Vita Merlini*, and think about the "charm" as a form of indefinable magic in Gandalf's toolkit. I'll discuss Tolkien's wizard as a neuro-queer icon and think about where *The Hobbit* sits within a YA canon, while returning to the book's central ideas.

This book ends where it began, with an acknowledgment of how the inherent queerness in medievalism—its category disruption and refusal to settle upon a binary—has shaped it into a force for empowerment within contemporary teen fiction. This refers not only to the oddness of the Middle Ages as a period that readers might not immediately connect with, but also the queering potential of medievalist adaptation—taking something remote and making it accessible, even campy. Most often, I'll argue, that queer force is embodied by the wizard, both inside/outside of community. But just as medieval literature could not decide precisely upon one definition of *wizard*, so has the YA genre diversified and reimagined that character as powerful, inclusive, wyrd.

Chapter 1
My So-Called Merlin: Wizardry and Neurodiversity

I was nine when I first met Merlin. I encountered him in the pages of *King Arthur and His Knights*, a Victorian adaptation of Malory's *Morte Darthur*, by James Knowles. My copy was from 1986, and I wonder if Knowles—crafting prose stories alongside his more famous poet friend, Alfred Lord Tennyson—dreamed that a queer 1980s kid would someday be reading his work. My mother found me that copy at The Book Nook, a used bookstore in Chilliwack that was practically a second home. The illustrations were by Louis Rhead, and one in particular caught my eye: Merlin, in black and white, communing with a crow. The knights were always in action poses, or sidling up to damsels, but Merlin seemed still and self-contained. I knew, even at nine, that I was reading this book the wrong way. Like a medieval chivalry manual, the stories of King Arthur were designed to teach straight boys how to be knights; the same way that my piles of forgotten hockey cards were supposed to teach me how to be an NHL star. What I wanted to be was that solitary wizard, chilling with his bird.

The title of this chapter plays on a mid-1990s teen drama, *My So-Called Life*, which was canceled after one season. Like Merlin, it was an acquired taste, though it launched the career of a young Claire Danes and Jared Leto. The show was notable for its voiceovers, where the main character, Angela Chase, described high school as a battlefield. Merlin was also traumatized on a medieval battlefield, though his later versions in Malory seem to have forgotten. Both Merlin and Angela struggle to negotiate complex societies while boiling in their own feelings. I think of him as "so-called Merlin" because he's had other names—Myrddin and Lailoken in the Welsh traditions—and because there are so many versions of the sly, fragile enchanter. We can never quite pin him down, just as no one can ever truly fix teen Angela within a particular identity. This chapter examines younger versions of Merlin in medieval and medievalist literature, as well as older incarnations. We'll look at Merlin's early appearances in *The Black Book of Carmarthen*, his awkward childhood in Robert de Boron's *Merlin and the Grail*, and Malory's more pragmatic enchanter. I'll place these medieval source texts in conversation with YA adaptations: T. H. White's *Sword in the Stone*; *Once and Future*, by Amy Rose Capetta and Cori McCarthy; and *The Red Scrolls of Magic*, by Cassandra Clare and Wesley Chu.

This first chapter comprises discussion of medieval magic in general, with Merlin as a character who crosses a number of supernatural genres. I'll discuss some of the ways in which the medieval supernatural productively blurred distinctions between "dark" magic (*maleficia*), helpful charms, and the type of ascetic concentration that would become a staple of wizardry narratives. This provides a foundation to discuss how Morgan le Fay challenges aspects of male-centered magic (in Chapter 2), and how ritual magic influences medievalist YA fiction that engages with the wizard school tradition. We can track the evolution of these magic systems through Merlin, because his various iterations draw upon early medieval magic, as well as more established narratives of sorcery in the romance tradition. He allows us to explore the medieval tension between casting spells, weaving prophecies, and manipulating political events, as Malory's savvy (somewhat chilling) Merlin often does.

At the same time, Merlin is a paradoxical figure in medieval literature—both everywhere and nowhere. Like Arthur, he makes early appearances in the Old Welsh *Gododdin* (difficult to date, but likely composed between 600 and 800 CE), as well as *The Black Book of Carmarthen* (written down in 1250 but with content going back to the sixth century). Merlin is often several different people: a recluse and wild man named Lailoken; a prophet named Myrddin who's been traumatized by war; and a counselor named Merlinus who facilitates the birth of Arthur through questionable magic. Even within the earliest Welsh tradition, Meirion Pennar notes that Merlin shifts between "a virile warrior" and "a raving insomniac" (25). In "Myrddin Converses with Taliesin," he conveys inexpressible sadness after witnessing the sixth-century battle between Elgan and Maelgwn Gwynned, rulers of South and North Wales: "So sad am I / so sad . . . / [The] noise of the battle was shrill" (Pennar 40). We move from this battlefield consciousness to the *Oianau* ("The Ohs of Merlin"), where the prophet speaks to a beloved pig—likely the inspiration for the oracular pig Henwen in Lloyd Alexander's *The Black Cauldron*. In this poem, Merlin shifts from playfully addressing the pig as "happy porker" and "restless grunter," to the image of a figure "deprived and threadbare, wintering in the forest with icicles in his hair" (Pennar 25). He sleeps little, sings to his pig, and will provide a template for the reclusive forest-dweller of Monmouth's twelfth-century *Vita Merlini*. By the time we get to Malory's fifteenth-century *Morte*, the character has become terse and marginal, a collection of myths and fragments that are difficult to piece together.

Merlin and Taliesin were both prophet-figures who emerged from an early Welsh tradition, rooted in differentiating medieval Welsh culture from Germanic colonizers (and later, Norman colonizers). In examples as late as the fifteenth century—like the Middle English *Prose Merlin*—both figures are seen in relation to each other. In Geoffrey of Monmouth's twelfth-century *Life of Merlin*, Taliesin and Merlin weave prophecies together. Taliesin is often considered the younger character, and more of a bard than an actual wizard. His discussions in *The Life of Merlin* could be classified as medieval natural science, though the boundaries of this discipline often collapse into magic, as well. J. Gwenogvrn Evans calls Taliesin "a well-authenticated historical character" who "was a subject of the Earl of Chester [in the sixth century]" (xiii). *The Book of Taliesin* was copied in the fourteenth century, though much of its content is as early as the tenth century, and adapts even earlier oral material. Taliesin the poet asks questions like "whose idea was the wind?" (3).[1] "The earth, what is its extent, / or how great its thickness?" (19).[2] His questions form a balanced counterpoint to Merlin's more chaotic mysticism, and we might see them as two philosophers—one a poet, the other a recovering soldier and royal administrator. Though Taliesin has no explicit powers, his curiosity about the world makes him the ideal pupil for Merlin (though we have to assume, given his misanthropy, that Merlin would not be a student-centered instructor).

We find echoes of Taliesin and Merlin in Diane Duane's YA *Young Wizards* series. Her magic system is scientific in its close focus on language, but also has much of the supernatural flavor of Merlin's wizardry. A central character in Diane Duane's YA book *A Wizard Alone*, Darryl McAllister, is explicitly written as autistic. I'll link Merlin's varied experiences to the autism spectrum throughout this chapter, though it's not my intention to diagnose a wizard across time—simply to show how a character like Merlin can resonate for neurodivergent readers. Duane initially wrote *A Wizard Alone* in 2003, but revised it in 2014 to be more sensitive to current discussions of autism. Darryl is, as far as I know, the only explicitly defined autistic teen wizard in the YA fantasy canon. He's also African-American, though Duane doesn't delve into the specifically racialized ableism that he would likely be subject to. In Duane's universe, young wizards embark on a magical test called "errantry," and Darryl seems to be mentally trapped within this process. Such a storyline could easily play to autistic stereotypes, but the book carefully veers from this. Kit Rodriguez, the young wizard sent after Darryl, is also racialized as a Latinx character, and he's forced to confront his own lack of knowledge about autism. Kit's mentor, the older, gay wizard Tom, reminds Kit that "if [Darryl] has been offered wizardry, that means that there's some problem to which *he* is the solution" (Ch 2). It later turns out that Darryl's hyper-focus has allowed him to capture the main antagonist of the series—the Lone Power—in a complex psychic landscape. The Lone Power, who resembles a more intergalactic version of the fallen Lucifer, tempts Darryl with even further magical prowess. "Don't imagine," the Lone Power says, "that you have any further power to confine me." Darryl responds: "Yeah, I *do* imagine that," (Ch 9) challenging any clinical idea that he might experience some failure of imagination.

---

1 "Dychymig pwy yw?" (2).
2 "Y ðaear, pwy i lled, / neu vaint i thewhed?" (18).

Darryl does end up trapping a small part of the Lone Power through his own hyper-focus: "I've got news for you. I am really, *really* good at concentrating on things." Luckily, he also has the ability of "co-location," which allows him to exist in multiple spaces at once. This connects him even more closely with Merlin, who also seems able to pop in and out of various spaces and narratives. The novel ends with Darryl announcing that he wants to leave the school for high-needs kids (which hasn't actually helped him) and begin an entirely different and more independent life. When Kit observes that he's "different" rather than broken, as some might think, Darryl's response cites physical and mental sovereignty in a way that reminds me of Chaucer's Wife of Bath, whose prologue in *The Canterbury Tales* also insists upon women's bodily autonomy. Darryl says: "The brain and nerves and mind I've got . . . [they're] mine. They're *me*. I've got the right to them." Like Merlin, as well, he asserts his right to live outside of social norms that don't define him.

Duane's earlier series—*The Middle Kingdoms*—also featured a queer wizard. The first novel, *A Door into Fire*, came out in 1979,[3] so it's quite remarkable that it dealt with multiple queer characters. In this medievalist world, the wizard Herewiss uses a rare and dangerous form of magic to protect his lover, the exiled (and roguish) Prince Freelorn. The cover copy describes Freelorn as a "dear friend," but in the Middle Kingdoms, pansexuality is the norm, and the two are in a committed partnership. I was around thirteen when I read this book, and I vividly remember a scene where Freelorn and Herewiss recall getting caught in bed together while they were still teenagers. Herewiss asks:

> "Lorn, remember the first time we shared[4] at your place?"
> "That was a long time ago."
> "It seems that way."
> "—and my father yelled up the stairs, 'what are you dooooooooing?'"
> "—and you yelled back, 'we're *fuck*innnnnnnnnnnng!'"
> "—and it was quiet for so long—"
> "—and then he started laughing—." (270)

Though I preferred the teen characters in her *Young Wizards* series, who were closer to my age at the time, this scene from *Door into Fire* still took me apart on a cellular level. Not only were these two characters queer—and having sex as teenagers—but their *medieval* parents didn't mind? I was still figuring my sexuality

---

3 Duane has re-released e-editions of the *Middle Kingdoms* books, and continued stories in this universe suggest that the series has always had a certain fandom, though it's largely gone under the radar.
4 "Share" is the book's slang for sex with an emotional component.

out, and the book probably would have hit harder if I'd read it in my later teens. But even then, it was a surprising flash of queer love, without the tragedy, in a fantasy novel. And it showed how wizards have been queer from the very beginning, in their thinking, and their desires.

Medieval Magic and the Wizard

Merlin is the most famous wizard in medieval literature, but there were plenty of other examples, including biblical figures who used magic of various shades. I'll mention several of these figures in Chapter 3 ("Wizards in School"), as well as Chapter 4 ("Bad Magic"). In his wonderfully titled book *Wizards: A History*, P. G. Maxwell-Stuart notes that the odd title *wizard* is "a word formed from the Middle English *wys*—wise—and the suffix *ard* which . . . has the sense of 'someone who does something to excess'" (11). Wizardry always carries this sense of potential decadence and addiction, just as queer desire was seen as a too-powerful pleasure in the Middle Ages. As the poems by Rennes and Bourgeuil demonstrate in the introduction, same-sex desire between men was a kind of intense pleasure— something that you could lose yourself in. Magic could also top you, and destroy your spirituality in the process, even though it was paradoxically spiritual itself.

Maxwell-Stuart points to biblical figures like the Witch of Endor, whose magic controls the dead, and Simon Magus, described in Acts 8:9 as "seducens gente Samariae" (seducing the citizens of Samaria) with his sorcery (*Biblia Vulgata*, 1073). Simon is called *magus*, while the Witch of Endor is called *pythonem* (soothsayer) in 1 Samuel 28:8 (*Biblia Vulgata*, 245), with the word's slithery connotations referring to the serpent at Delphi. We'll return to her in Chapter 2, on Morgan and Sabrina. In the second-century *Acts of St. Peter*, Simon challenges Peter to a magic contest: "Next day, he said, he would leave the earth and fly up to God in front of everyone" (Maxwell-Stuart 55). Simon *does* fly, but when Peter speaks a word, the arrogant magus falls and breaks his leg. These early stories establish a context of punishment for magic: it's available, but too much could get you killed.

There's no single magical form within the long Middle Ages. Early Medieval charms like "Against a Sudden Stitch" provide a fascinating, Valkyrian context for thinking about magic. This charm is designed to repel "elf-shot," or the tiny arrows that might cause a wound to fester. The charm had a practical purpose, while a spell could be broader—creating a state of love, for instance, rather than simply healing a wound. But the poem itself begins with a speaker who witnesses giant women dancing around a tree, somewhat like Valkyries incanting battle magic. The poem's speaker hears the battle-cries of *mihtigan wif* (giant spear-maidens) who will lend power to a charm against "elf-shot" (Delanty and Matto 482). There are also more specific spells against miscarriage, and spells to soothe the pain of losing a child. By the time we get to the later romance tradition, wizards and witches are often marginal characters who either help or frustrate the hero. Geraldine Heng argues that romance's blending of magic and science is both fantastic and forward-looking: "In medieval romance, science will still feel like magic, even if it also feels like a magic of the future," ushering in "the creation of more marvels than even medieval romance might dream of or desire" (*Empire of Magic* 303). This idea of the *marvel* circulates alongside magic in medieval literature, from the marvel demanded by young Arthur in *Sir Gawain and the Green Knight* (which he insists upon before eating: enter the Green Knight), to the technological magic in *Once and Future*. And medieval magic-users provide useful adaptations, since their powers are often mysterious. The necromancer Clinschor—a minor but memorable character in Wolfram von Eschenbach's thirteenth-century *Parzival*—is a ghostly presence who wreaks havoc from a tower. The perfect antecedent to Tolkien's spectral antagonist, Sauron.

As Juanita Ruys discusses in *Demons in the Middle Ages*, these shadowy forces were also part of medieval university curricula: both angels and demons, the fuel of magic, "offered themselves so amenably to thought experiments" (65). We'll return to this in Chapter 3, but it serves as initial context for thinking about how capacious (and institutionalized) magic really was. Merlin is part of this tradition nearly from its inception, and his afterlives in YA fantasy have allowed that tradition to evolve with young readers. Different authors and eras approach Merlin's magic in distinct ways, but it's always connected with the politics of the time, making the wizard an always-current figure. And we should remember that, throughout the Middle Ages, definitions like "wizard," "angel," and "demon" were assigned by men. Women mystics often sought to challenge the patriarchal church by describing their own mystical experiences, but these still needed to be authorized by male scribes and teachers. Medievalist YA challenges this dynamic with its witch characters, like Sabrina and Tiffany, who make their own definitions.

Merlin in the Arthurian Tradition

Peter Goodrich notes of the Arthurian Merlin figure: "It is as if he can step outside the conventional reality of the narrative world and re-enter it anywhere he desires" (12). This act of teleportation explains how Merlin cruises through medieval texts by Geoffrey of Monmouth (*Vita Merlini*), Robert de Boron (*Merlin and the Grail*), and the Middle English *Prose Merlin*, never quite coming to rest in a particular space. Malory's Merlin is perhaps the least present, and Stephen

Knight describes him as "a fifteenth-century senior bureaucrat" (*Merlin* 94) who's mostly stripped of his powers—yet his magic engenders Arthur. He flashes to life in the first chapter of the *Morte*, then flickers out for the rest of it. The epic thirteenth-century *Vulgate* dispenses with him early, preferring to focus on Lancelot as the story's fallible hero. Gawain hears Merlin's ghost, asking: "Don't you recognize me?" (Lacy 90), and he's quickly told by the invisible wizard: "You'll never see me . . . [and] after you leave here, I'll never speak to you or to anyone else" (91). The writer (or writers) of the *Vulgate*, like Malory, run into the same problem: how do you solve a problem like Merlin? I'll return to this in the final chapter on Gandalf, Dumbledore, and ghostly queer wizards.

Arthurian literature is vast—it stretches across at least nine languages, from Latin to Occitan, and continues in current adaptations. Roberta Krueger notes that Arthurian romances in English, beginning with the thirteenth-century poet Wace, created a "popular and vernacular history" (2) that explored both England's link to the ancient world, and the contested Englishness of Arthur as a cultural hero. But these myths emerged from a cultural fusion, to the point that Marie de France's Anglo-French *lais*—already an adaptation of Breton stories—were translated into the Old Norse *Strengleikar* (stringed instruments). Writing in the twelfth century alongside Chrétien de Troyes, Marie de France interpreted Arthurian myths in a way that centered women. While de Troyes's poetry always focused on male knights, de France's *lais* had more significant roles for women, and were often more concerned with the interiority of their characters. These myths are musical, motile, difficult to track but glorious in their intersections. And Merlin crosses many of them. Historical work on the evolution of Merlin has been done by Peter Goodrich (*Merlin: A Casebook*), Stephen Knight (*Merlin: Knowledge and Power*), and Tim Clarkson (*Scotland's Merlin*). These studies trace Merlin from his Welsh origins to more current adaptations. This chapter is interested in Merlin's journey from young to old, which we see in Robert de Boron's *Merlin and the Grail*, and Geoffrey of Monmouth's *Vita Merlini*. With those as the central medieval texts (plus the amiable *Prose Merlin*), I'll move onto YA adaptations: T. H. White's *Sword in the Stone*, Capetta and McCarthy's *Once and Future*, and Clare and Chu's *Red Scrolls*.

De Boron: Merlin's Childhood and Adolescence

Robert de Boron's *Merlin* is part of a trilogy that includes *Joseph of Arimathea* and *Perceval*, though it's likely that he didn't write the entire collection (sections of *Merlin* mention de Boron in the third person, suggesting that a second part was added later). In this more explicitly Christian adaptation of the earlier Merlin and

Arthur stories, Joseph of Arimethea was regarded as the guardian of the grail. Merlin appears throughout the cycle, eventually passing on the narrative to the young knight Percival (famous for seeking the grail). Little is known of de Boron's life, though he refers to himself as both "clerk" and "knight" at various points in the trilogy. The early thirteenth-century French prose may pale in comparison to the sparkling verse of Chrétien de Troyes, but in his study of the complete Modena manuscript, Nigel Bryant clarifies that "the sparseness with which it is written" is actually due to "a highly developed sense of what would work startlingly and movingly when performed" (12). Since de Boron represents a kind of middle for Merlin—twelfth century shading into thirteenth—I've decided to start *in medias res*, with his interpretation of Merlin's childhood and adolescence.

De Boron adapts Monmouth's slightly earlier version of Merlin, delving more into his supernatural parentage. In this account, Merlin is the child of a demon and a mortal woman. As a toddler, he's already talking about destiny and defending his mother in court. His dual lineage gives him knowledge of both the past and the future: "The child inherited knowledge of the past from the Enemy, and, in addition, knowledge of things to come was bequeathed to him by God. It was up to him which way he inclined" (55). De Boron's Merlin calls himself "a figure of secrecy" (62), and goes on to explain his lack of sociability: "You must understand," he says to Pendragon, "that I sometimes need to be away from people . . . [however] much you may desire my company, don't be upset when I leave you" (84). Gandalf insists upon similar departures in *The Hobbit*, and though these are for the purpose of the greater mission, we can also see them as instances of multi-tasking and wizard's time. Wizards perceive time differently, after all, than other characters in these stories. The Merlyn character in T. H. White's *Sword in the Stone* is both out of time, and looking at time "backwards," as we'll soon get to. In many ways, this connects with definitions of "crip time" by Alison Kafer, Eli Clare, and Rick Godden, who all argue for a more flexible alternative to the ableist deadlines of late capitalism.

What fascinates me most about this Merlin is his pervasive need to be alone. Merlin often goes mad in earlier traditions, but de Boron's Merlin seems to express more of a delicacy when it comes to worldly interaction. We might just as easily read his retiring nature as the strategy of someone who is easily overwhelmed—someone who flees to the woods in order to escape the sensory overload of court. Wizards think differently, after all. As we'll discuss later, T. H. White's Merlyn tells Wart that he "was born at the wrong end of time, and I have to live *backwards* from in front, while surrounded by a lot of people living forwards from behind" (53). This backsight makes him wary of all human interactions, and perhaps this is true of all wizards. Certainly, the metaphor of being on the "wrong planet," or at the "wrong end of time," is something keenly understood by neurodivergent readers who also get sensorily overwhelmed.

The tween Merlin of de Boron's cycle is particularly interesting because we get to see him as a kid, which is relatively rare. Goodrich, in the *Merlin Casebook*, notes how the YA genre skips over Merlin's adolescence:

> Most children's literature has bypassed the medieval tradition of Merlin's own birth and childhood . . . [literature] before the twentieth century always portrays the young Merlin as a miniature adult who is born in the body of an infant but is fully developed both mentally and verbally, and whose physical maturation is essentially passed over. (55)

In contrast, de Boron gives us an awkward child Merlin—half demon, half human—who scares everyone around him. When a creepy toddler can see into your past and future, you tend to avoid them.

Alexandre Micha notes of this Merlin: "[It's] his precocious skill in speaking and reasoning that makes him a prodigy—and a disturbing child, who frightens anyone who speaks to him" (297). I'd argue that a lot of hyper-verbal kids on the spectrum will get this portrayal of a kid who tends to unnerve adults with nontraditional language. Non-verbal kids on the spectrum run into similar problems as a result of their silence, which is never actually silence, but rather non-verbal interaction. Autistic kids who struggle with traditional communication are often subjected to applied behavioral analysis—a form of "therapy" that punishes them for any verbal or physical behaviors that aren't strictly in line with neurotypical communication. This could even include punishments that feel like torture, such as having your hands tied to keep you from stimming or flapping. In *Autistic Disturbances*, Julia Miele Rodas describes neurodivergent language as "language hacking, the joyful breaking down and retooling of conventional language in ways that defamiliarize and implicitly critique seemingly seamless and intuitive communicative practice" (8). I'd argue that Merlin does something similar here by slicing through courtly language to deliver a core of anxious truth.

My favorite moment from de Boron's text is that throwaway scene of young Merlin playing stick-ball, which I mentioned in the introduction. Let's return to it. Hard to say how old he is here—twelve or younger. The scene is designed to move us from Merlin's youth to his adulthood as an enchanter who allows Pendragon to seize power. But in the interim, we get this weird little image of a kid who can't quite play ball with the other kids:

> One day they were passing through a field outside of town where a group of children were playing a game with a stick and a ball. Merlin, who knew everything that had been happening, was one of the players . . . [he] went up to one of the wealthiest children of the town and struck him across the leg with the stick, knowing he would react angrily. The child began to cry and hurl insults at Merlin, accusing him of being born without a father. (68)

So much is happening here. Merlin can see both the past and the future, like an anxiety buffet laid out before him, but he's stuck playing ball. He knows, in this instance, that he has to draw attention to himself by hurting one of the other kids. It's the only way that passing knights will notice him. So he does the most un-wizardly thing possible: he hits this boy with the stick. This boy is rich, privileged, and Merlin knows that he'll wail. The rich kid retaliates by calling Merlin a fatherless child, which is not precisely true. Merlin's father is a shape-shifting demon, "one of a kind of demons called Hequibedes, who inhabit the air" (60). His ancestry is air, shadow, impossible choices between raw truth and the fiction of courtly sociability. To prophesize, or not? Merlin opens up this wound in his past because the insult is the only thing that can fulfill this particular prophecy. It reminds me of what Didier Eribon, in his book *Insult and the Making of the Gay Self*, calls the "horizon" of insult that renders queer kids as vulnerable subjects. I also imagine Merlin, for a moment, as the kid from *Young Sheldon*, both a constellation of stereotypes and an authentically neuro-queer kid, trying and wanting and failing to play ball with the others. Inviting the insult that will make him real in the eyes of the knights, the wizard's position.

Young Sheldon is a spinoff developed by the creators of *Big Bang Theory*, in order to explore the childhood of acerbic physicist Sheldon Cooper. I should clarify that the show isn't about a child on the autism spectrum—the creators have always avoided labeling Sheldon, though much of his behavior seems based on stereotypical portrayals of autism. At nine years old, Sheldon displays traits that might resonate not only with viewers on the spectrum, but also with viewers who are anxious, living with ADD/ADHD, or OCD. He's scared of loud noises, bright lights, and crowds. He's touch-averse to the point of wearing mittens to hold hands (though he makes an exception in one episode, holding his father's hand when he thinks it might comfort him). Much of the show's humor is based on Sheldon's neuro-atypical reactions to common situations, which mark him as a different type of child. But, whereas adult Sheldon is often met with exasperation, child Sheldon receives more tenderness and understanding from his family and peers.

Young Sheldon mentions to his grandmother that he identifies with the character Spock, who is always logical. In the pilot episode, Sheldon describes performing solitary experiments as the height of pleasure: "I felt like Neil Armstrong on the moon—alone and happy." In the same episode, while negotiating the anxieties of public school, Sheldon hears some strains of music coming from behind a closed door. It lures him in, siren-like, and the look on his face while listening to the cello is a mixture of curiosity and peace. In the loud jungle of the school, this classical music is a welcome release. Like Merlin, he finds a space where he can escape the crowds and uncertainty. The show can be frustrating—it often places a vulnerable, neurodivergent character in situations designed to make him uncomfortable—but it also signals that some kids think differently, queerly.

The term "neuro-queer" emerged more or less simultaneously from three different scholars on the spectrum: Nick Walker, Melanie Yergeau, and Athena Dillon. Walker defines this in a number of ways, including "being neurodivergent and approaching one's neurodivergence as a form of queerness" and "engaging in practices intended to 'undo' one's cultural conditioning toward conformity and compliance with dominant norms" (*Neurocosmopolitanism*, n.p.). You can queer your brain; your brain can be queer; and your way of thinking can be an act of queerness, just as powerful as any erotic or relational act. In *Authoring Autism*, Melanie Yergeau defines neuro-queerness as a type of non-traditional rhetoric often shared by people on the spectrum. In her passionate manifesto for the rights of autistic people, she states: "I want a rhetoric that tics, a rhetoric that stims, . . . [a] rhetoric that averts eye contact" (31). Her central argument is that autistic people are not seen as possessing rhetoric, which means that we aren't seen as possessing humanity. Neuro-queerness insists upon alternative mental rhetorics, brain scripts, and runes like the ones scratched on Bilbo's door by a sly and curious Gandalf.

I mentioned earlier the odd, anti-social moment where de Boron's Merlin explains to Pendragon that he needs to be alone sometimes: "[However] much you may desire my company, don't be upset when I leave you" (84). The Middle French original has a slightly more complex sentiment, as Micha points out in his chapter on de Boron: "Il me convient, dit Merlin, par fine force de nature estre parfois eschis de la gent" (P39, L46–47; quoted in Micha 300). I translate this as follows: "It suits me, sometimes, by fine force of [my] nature, to avoid others." *Eschire* is a double-voiced verb that can mean "avoid" or "escape," but which also alludes to inherent shyness. Losing people, losing sociability, losing the world—Merlin has mastered these arts, insisting upon their relevance to his survival. His bodymind is a "fine force" that gets overloaded by the court and its obnoxious noise. Merlin himself has a "fine" nature, an environmental sensitivity, which makes him flee to the forest in search of peace and quiet. Unlike Lailoken or Monmouth's wizard, he isn't mad—just sensitive. Micha calls him a "sylvan creature" (296), and this fits. Not someone meant for the court. Neurodivergent kids might see, in Merlin's claim to silence, an empowering strategy. He demands time away. He insists upon, but does not apologize for, his fine nature.

In an episode of *Big Bang Theory* ("The 48 Peculiarity," S6E8), Sheldon Cooper says something similar to his friends Leonard and Raj: "You may not realize it, but I have difficulty navigating certain aspects of daily life. You know, understanding sarcasm, feigning interest in others, not talking about trains as much as I want. It's exhausting!" I've written previously about Sheldon as an autistic stereotype, but he also coheres, for many viewers on the spectrum, as a potential future: an autistic scientist with (mostly) supportive friends and family. In a scene in S7E24, Sheldon crystallizes this need for alone time in a description that, to me, is resonant of anxiety on the spectrum: "Leonard, I am overwhelmed. Everything is changing, and it's simply too much. I need to get away to think." His call-out to Leonard serves to humanize his statement: a plea from one friend to another. I was once a kid who felt terrorized by the intensity of the world (still do; still am), and I was lucky to have a Leonard. Sheldon and Leonard may not be the greatest autistic and allistic characters—so much about *Big Bang Theory* makes me cringe. But when I presented a paper on the show at the annual meeting of the Pop Culture Association, a mother introduced me to her autistic daughter, who saw in Sheldon an odd sibling, a kinship. It was enough.

There's a peculiar image of young Merlin in the British Library's fourteenth-century copy of de Boron's *Merlin* (MS Additional 38177, f. 161v), where the wizard is offering a tablet to Arthur and Guinevere. What's odd is that the Merlin in the miniature is also a *miniature Merlin*—a boy of indeterminate age—when the Merlin in de Boron's text would be an adult at this moment. He's smaller than the adult royalty, but not as childlike as the Merlin in Wace's *Brut* (MS Egerton 3028, fol. 24). Wace's Merlin is holding his mother's hand while standing before King Vortigern, the king to whom Merlin first offers a prophecy about two dragons—the Britons vs. the Saxons—when he's still a child. He wears a simple yellow robe, and almost appears to be hiding behind her. The Merlin in the Additional manuscript is larger, and dressed in striking blue. I magnify my digital copy to puzzle out his expression (wishing I could do the same in the real world). Is he annoyed? Slightly defiant? It's a curious set of the mouth for a child—certainly not deferential. *Look, I'm telling you.* Perhaps an anxious twelve-year-old with the weight of prophecy on his shoulders. A young Sheldon frozen at that awkward stage, before he crafted Stonehenge. Queerly out of time, just like his future selves.

Sheldon is a kind of Merlin—an overwhelmed enchanter, on the lookout for a companionable grove. Like Sheldon, Merlin is a character who can be both positive and negative for readers and viewers. His powers place him at a remove from sociability, just as Sheldon's absorption with science makes him an uneasy conversationalist. I've been frustrated by how Sheldon's character co-opts certain complex and rich neurodivergent phenomena in the service of comedy. But I've also heard from young autistic viewers who saw themselves reflected for the first time in Sheldon. Unlike Merlin—he has a community of friends, and that can make all the difference.

And some later texts (like the Middle English *Prose Merlin*) do present the magic-user within a loving court and community. He isn't always alone. The wizard's mind runs hot, like a kid on the spectrum. A wizard, like Merlin, offers possibilities for readers who don't see a place for themselves at the Round Table. There is, in fact, a place, next to Merlin, who's just as distracted as we are, probably dreaming of stillness, or birdsong, or a room full of books, or texture like fur. Stimming can be a spell, after all—a spell to ward off anxiety. The "sudden stitch" of being overwhelmed that you can't talk yourself out of. Instead, run your fingers down the soft tail-feathers of Archimedes, Merlyn's owl familiar. Get lost in the mirrors of the enchanter's gown, reflecting an infinity of queer futures, halfway between earth and air.

Monmouth's *Vita Merlini*: Merlin Looking Backwards

Geoffrey of Monmouth is most famous for writing *History of the Kings of Britain*—an accessible twelfth-century prose text that includes foundational Arthurian material. Monmouth lived during a time of political instability, when Stephen was fighting his cousin Matilda for control of a transitional England. Christopher Snyder notes that Monmouth is "a Latinized Norman name, but he describes himself as *pudibundus Brito*, 'a modest Briton'" (80). His *History* sides with the Bretons and the Cornish, though his immensely popular text has become a part of current British nationalism and its white supremacist idea of a "unified" medieval Britain (his England was actually in the midst of a civil war—far from unified). This section focuses not on the oft-taught prose *History*, but on the far less popular verse *Vita Merlini* (*Life of Merlin*). In his edition, Basil Clarke describes this enigmatic, often playful text as literally thorny: "One needs some image like that of long chains of many-hooked burrs to make the case" (15). Full of weird magic, natural science, Welsh antecedents, and twelfth-century English politics, the *Vita* gives us an electric version of Merlin in decadent Latin hexameter. Several of the students in my Arthurian Literature class described this Merlin as "unhinged," but also reported that it was one of their favorite texts on the syllabus. The epic poem has an uncanny, moving quality as it follows Merlin into a sunset of his own making. This text also marks the first appearance of Morgan le Fay, though we'll delve into that in Chapter 2.

Michael Faletra notes that the *Vita Merlini* "narrates the madness of Merlin at the end of his lifetime, having lived many years past the days of Vortigern and Arthur" (Monmouth, *History* 242). Monmouth frees himself from the tight and efficient style of the *History* and goes full-bore into Merlin's decay. Rather than a dangerous wizard, he appears to be an exhausted introvert, fleeing his beloved Celidon forest, where he can co-exist with birds and trees. In several Merlin stories, the wizard spends time in this space—the Caledonian forest of ancient Scotland—where he can gently unravel and mourn his battlefield losses. At one point, he attacks the bridegroom of Gwendolena, a love interest who appears in Monmouth's *Vita*, as well as in some of the earlier Welsh material. Merlin uses a pair of giant antlers to murder the groom. This is a Merlin who stalks, who startles, who unnerves everyone. His emotions are wild. He spins through the text like an uncontrollable firebrand, with no legible purpose. It's a Merlin, I think, that we can all relate to: finally having reached the end of his patience with society.

This older Merlin seems to dwell within a lifelong anxiety attack. But this makes him no less powerful or dangerous. In fact, having burned through his sociability, he's all the more unpredictable. Will he pull a leaf from your hair? Will he throw a baby dragon at you? Will he predict your violent death or ride through your wedding on a giant stag? I always feel, when reading this late work of Monmouth's, that he's having fun playing with Merlin's scattered myths. He's wondering: *what if this magical titan just stopped caring?* The result is a compelling and unpredictable character who tears through medieval society and the mythic record, enacting some of our weirdest and most anti-social fantasies.

After the battle of Cumbria, Merlin has a breakdown. He wails for his lost friends in the middle of the battlefield.[5] "Then he cast himself upon the earth and rolled back and forth" (244).[6] He flees to the forest to live with an old, white-haired wolf. They starve together, while Merlin screams about his lost apple tree: a symbol of his former prosperity in earlier Welsh poems, which will return—in a sinister fashion—in Monmouth's adaptation. Later in the text, he'll recall the unexpected gift of an apple. A man named Maeldin—one of his traveling companions, years ago—offers him the gift: "The man who first glimpsed [the apples] picked them up and gave them to me, laughing about this unusual gift" (273).[7] But the apple turns out to be cursed, and Merlin will need to use a magic spring to cure Maeldin, when they meet again years later. The Maeldin that Merlin knew was "a handsome and powerful knight," part of Merlin's retinue when "our youth was in full bloom" (ibid.).[8] We have so few glimpses of Merlin the youth. Awkward but cocky, full of prophecies and foresight which must make any relationship

---

[5] The translated material comes from Michael Faletra's edition of the *Vita Merlini*, in his edition of Monmouth's *History of the Kings of Britain*. The original Latin comes from Basil Clarke's verse edition of the *Vita Merlini*.

[6] "Pulveribus crines spargit vestesque rescindit
   et prostratus humi nunc hac illacque volutat" (L67–68, Clarke 54).

[7] "Mox ea collegit qui primus adiverat iste
   porrexitque michi subito pro munere ridens.
   Ergo distribui data poma sodalibus et me" (L1410–14, Clarke 128).

[8] "Non hec fuit ejus ymago / olim, dum nobis juvenilis floruit etas" (L1395–96, Clarke 128).

impossible. Taliesin is the only one who understands him, though Merlin is already old by the time he meets the bard. He tries, and fails, to explain his prophetic experience:

> I was outside of myself, and I knew of the deeds of people past and I predicted the future as if I were a spirit. I understood the secrets of nature and the flights of birds and the wanderings of the stars and the gliding of fish, but the unswerving laws of these things also haunted me, denying me the peace that is natural to a human mind. (268)[9]

He speaks of a past event—the feeling of being inspirited with this knowledge—but he's also out of time *all the time*, out of himself. The Latin word that begins this passage is *raptus* (Clarke L1160, 114). Merlin is kidnapped from himself, and becomes *quasi spiritus*, neither demon nor man. The older Merlin tries to express this, while remembering his younger self. To paraphrase Dinshaw, he is, himself, an amateur temporality, a wizard growing into his devastating potential. This is his first moment in wizard time, beyond the constraints of court and the frenzy of the battlefield. In an epic register, he sees things (*rerum*) as they are—he sees his place in the universe, as well. But in that moment by the clear spring, with the handsome knight, he's also just a boy palming a sweet apple—made all the sweeter by Maeldin's sheepish laughter, the unusual intimacy of the gift. These apples turn out to be enchanted weapons that will drive the men insane, including Maeldin. But amateur Merlin doesn't know that yet. He gives them away, like a backward country lord with no gold rings to offer his thanes, just wild fruit.

We're meant to see this text as Merlin's dramatic descent into madness. But even this deteriorating Merlin retains his sly power. When a boy messenger dressed as a girl is sent to confuse his prophecy, he replies: "Maiden or no maiden . . . [she] shall die in a river" (250).[10] When we encounter the wizard again in the later *Prose Merlin*, he'll be far more judgmental of the trans masculine knight Grisandolus, whose male presentation disrupts what Merlin sees as the natural order. Bychowski notes that Merlin needs to proclaim here "the reassuring fixedness of being" ("Quantum Objects" 13). That said, Merlin still has a grudging respect for Grisandolus, and while his textual reactions often err on the side of recrimination, his sly asides of laughter have a winking intimacy to them—both Merlin and Grisandolus are companions in their difference. This earlier Merlin finds everything

---

9 "Raptus eram michimet quasi spiritus acta sciebam
preteriti populi predicebamque futura.
Tunc rerum secreta sciens volucrumque volatus
stellarumque vagos motus lapsusque natantum
id me vexabat naturalemque negabat" (L1161–65, Clarke 114).
10 "'Hec virgo nec ne,' dixit, 'morietur in ampne'" (L338, Clarke 68).

funny. He laughs to see a poor man who's standing above a hidden cache of gold. He laughs again to see a man in the market, trying to repair his shoes, because Merlin knows that the man will die the same day. Those loved shoes will be of no use.

After laughing, Merlin "refused to go any further through the market because the people he was watching were staring at him" (253).[11] Merlin's anxious gaze disrupts the orderly market. He's content to study the people around him, but shies away from their own confused looks. To be fair, this sounds completely like me at a mall. What's consistent about Merlin from childhood to adulthood is a discomfort with bustling social settings. He'll gladly pass out apples among a group of close friends, but the market undoes him. The laughter, perhaps, re-orients him. Alexandre Micha calls Merlin's laughter "the irrepressible jubilation of a privileged being," but also says that it "has a darker origin and resonance" (301). The laughter of someone on the margins, someone who sees people as chess pieces. This is also an ableist vision that's often used against neurodivergent folk—that we lack empathy. But Merlin's laughter is the one thing that he has power over—a reaction, I'd argue, to nearly unbearable empathy. The wizard who mourns for his old wolf, who watched a tree grow from seed to sapling, who laughs at a dead man's forgotten shoes, is not someone who *lacks* feeling. He's bursting with it. Monmouth has a kind of love for this character. He elevates him from the typical wild man legends, re-weaves him as an eco-mage who runs with animals and would likely prefer to live inside a tree.

Though he longs for Celidon, Merlin does, at one point in the *Vita*, make a request for something more like a house. A house as he pictures it. After enduring a stint of gloomy captivity (which tends to happen when you violently disrupt a wedding), Merlin asks his sister the queen for a less sylvan, more permanent dwelling:

> Before other buildings, build me a house in a remote locale with seventy doors and seventy windows through which I may watch flaming Phoebus and Venus and behold the stars gliding through the heavens all night long: these things will inform me what will happen to the people of the realm . . . [You], my dear sister, should come there often, as well (255).[12]

---

[11] "Tunc iterum risit renuitque diutius ire / per fora spectandus populus quos inspicebat" (L497–99, Clarke 78).
[12] "Ante domos alias unam compone remotam
cui sex dena decum dabis hostia totque fenestras,
per quas ignivomum videam cum Venere Phebum
inspiciamque polo labentia sydera noctu
que me de populo regni ventura docebunt. . .
[Tu] quoque veni, soror o dilecta, meamque" (L555–62, Clarke 80).

Queen Ganieda fulfills his request. When your magical brother asks for a house with seventy doors and windows ("cui sex dena decem dabis hostia totque fenestras" [Clarke, L555]), what else can you do but comply? At first glance, it seems that Merlin is constructing a fortress of solitude. A barracks where he can retire from the world. But it's actually a more enchanting space than that. He calls it a "domos . . . in silvis" (Clarke, L550): a kind of cottage. He can see night sky (*sydera noctu*) from every window. He can marvel at full-length sunsets from any point. Prophecy can't sneak up on him, because he'll always see it coming: he demands an army of scribes to translate it from *carmen* (song) to *tabellis* (tablet), which mirrors the very structure of his *Vita*. The house is a window on the world, and Merlin gets to control the intensity of the gaze. He's simultaneously vulnerable and sheltered, keeping his eye on events, while indulging in the unexpected pleasures of being a witness. And he's not alone. The awkward kid who failed medieval gym class also has his sister, the queen, at his side. I imagine them chatting late into the night, punctuated by bursts of Merlin's laughter. Not dark in its source, but rather lit by the glow of so many stars flaring out their inscrutable lives before him.

The Middle English Merlin

As a figure who evolves through adaptation, Merlin offers us different versions of magical childhood in various Middle English texts. The most sustained of these is the *Prose Merlin*, sections of which are adapted from de Boron. John Conlee notes that "because it pre-dates Malory's work, the Middle English Prose Merlin is considered the earliest piece of Arthurian literature written in English prose" ("Introduction"). It details the birth of Merlin and guides us through the rise of Arthur, while still managing to pre-date Malory's *Morte*. There's something rollicking about this adaptation, which has Merlin wielding a baby dragon in battle. He's still slightly unhinged as a character, but not nearly as alone as he appears in earlier texts. When he's born, all covered in hair (a monstrous showing), he's lowered out of a high tower to be baptized. Nobody quite wants to get near him. But the women who raise Merlin call him a "merveyle" (marvel [Conlee 29]), and also seem in awe of him. They're eager to hear what this precocious, hyperlexic baby has to say: "We shull heire hym sey othir thynges" (We shall hear him say other things [28]).

Malory's *Morte* was published on William Caxton's printing press in 1485, though the Winchester manuscript places its composition somewhat earlier. Malory wanted to tie all the disparate threads of the Latin and Old French traditions into a palatable volume of stories that would center England. He writes these stories in a late form of Middle English, already shading into the more recognizable language of early modern writers like Lady Mary Wroth and Shakespeare. The anonymous *Prose Merlin* comes out in the middle of the fifteenth century, likely a few decades earlier than Malory had started working on the *Morte*. While Malory's intention is to condense the Merlin material, the author of the *Prose Merlin* offers what editor John Conlee calls "a straightforward and fairly accurate translation . . . [of] the Merlin section of the Old French Vulgate Cycle" (1)—that is, French stories composed in the thirteenth century. Digging into the Arthurian tradition always involves countless threads and contradictory narratives, and reveals that—like us—medieval audiences loved the process of adaptation. While Merlin is closely edited in the *Morte*, so Lancelot can really shine, the *Prose Merlin* retains much of the wild ambivalence of its French original.

The *Prose Merlin* also aims for solid entertainment. Like other contemporary ballads (such as the Middle English *Arthour and Merlin*), it feels like we're listening to a ballad in a rickety cart, on our way to some mysterious town where the secrets of Merlin will unfold. We see more extended hunting scenes, more conversation about daily matters and exchange of knowledge. This Merlin is more sociable about his supernatural side. He explains that his powers lie between angels and demons, which forces him to always choose the right side: "I have not loste the knowynge of here [demons'] engynes, but I holde of hem that I ought to conne" (Conlee 33).[13] The sense of *ought to conne* is a hard-scrabble, DIY kind of magic. Merlin takes what he needs from the pool of demonic knowledge.

In the scene where he attacks the rich boy—forcing the insult that will reveal him to the knights—we're told that young Merlin "wiste hym [the boy] moste fell and hasty [thought him rude and hot-headed]" (35). In other versions, the boy is simply described as rich or haughty, but calling him "fell" (same root as "foul") suggests that he's a bad apple. We can imagine anyone reading this silently cheering for Merlin, who takes on the late medieval equivalent of Draco Malfoy. As Merlin grows up and becomes an advisor to various kings, he retains a critical ambivalence. He offers up advice, but qualifies it with statements like: "Yef ye acorde to myn awarde, I shall telle yow; and yef I sey not wele, acordeth not therto" (72).[14] *Listen to me if you feel like it*, while flexible as advice, isn't necessarily what one wants to hear from a financial advisor or diplomat.

But there's something doggedly good-natured about this Merlin, in spite of his eccentricities. Aside from his mentor Blaise, his only friend is the younger bard Taliesin. I'd argue that wizardly mentorship can also mirror neurodivergent mentorship, as folks on the spectrum teach each other about how they experience

---

13 "I have not lost the crafty knowledge of those demons, though I take from it what I need."
14 "If you listen to my words, I'll explain [it] to you; and if you don't like what I have to say, then don't follow my advice."

the world—not just masking or passing, but *living*. Merlin seems to genuinely delight in their conversations about the stars, the weather, and the hidden fabric of the universe. These talks mostly occur behind closed doors, but the narrator assures us that Merlin teaches Taliesin a number of "feire pleyes" (100).

This notion of magic as playful, *aventure*, isn't something we find in the darker Welsh stories. These older stories communicate what Knight calls "a long-lasting position of exile" (*Merlin* 9). Merlin, scarred by battle trauma, is as dissociated as the character in the Old English elegy "The Wife's Lament." In this enigmatic poem, a woman tries to recall the events of her life—including how she ended up in what might be a cave—but some trauma has disrupted her narrative. This prosaic Merlin clearly has a past, but also appears to have a wild but essentially comforting life at court. He takes on various forms, including a "cherll"[15] whose country dress is described in detail and would have been familiar to fifteenth-century readers. As a churlish archer, he plays with the court and its expectations. He's described as "grete and longe and blakke and rowe rympled [shaggy bearded]" (Conlee 109).[16] Conlee glosses "blakke" as "sun-burnt," to distinguish it from an adjective like "swarthy" that would normally be applied to a person of color. But given Merlin's complete transformation here, a reader could easily view him as a wizard of color, like Le Guin's Ged or Ogion. This opens up space for medievalists who are also people of color, and readers searching for themselves in a wizard like Merlin. He thrives on adaptation, and Knight reminds us that all this shape-shifting "should not be called disguise . . . [what] Merlin does is transform" (*Merlin* 53).

The *Prose Merlin* also gives us Grisandolus, the trans masculine knight, with whom Merlin shares a secret laugh. They're both different in a world that wants them to be the same. He upbraids Grisandolus for what he's concealing, but recognizes a kinship between them, queer wizard and trans knight. Grisandolus and the titular character in the Anglo-Norman romance *Silence* are both medieval trans men, and in her *Public Medievalist* article, Bychowski argues that "the 'how' of medieval transgender life is as vast and diverse as its modern counterpart" (n.p.). In this section of *Prose Merlin* Grisandolus is the child of Duke Matan, and we first meet him playing with a group of young knights as they attack a quintain—a jousting target: some of the knights are successful, "but noon so well as dide Grisandoll" (but none so well as Grisandolus [Conlee 1]). Grisandolus enters the service of an emperor, who encounters Merlin in the form of a great

---

15 We still use the archaic "churl" to mean someone rude, though in the medieval sense, it could refer to someone living on the margins of society.
16 "Big and tall and dark, with a shaggy beard."

stag: "He caste his enchauntement that alle the dores and yates of the paleise opened so rudely that thei fly alle in peces" (2).[17] The image of the wizard in stag-form, blowing up his castle, makes a firm impression on the emperor. He sends Grisandolus to bring Merlin back to his court.

Along the way, Merlin initiates a cat-and-mouse game with Grisandolus. He speaks to the knight in stag-form, dead-naming him first, then chiding him: "Thow chacest folye, for thow maist not spede of thy queste in no maner" (2).[18] When Grisandolus finally catches him, Merlin calls the knight a "repaired image"[19]—conveying his displeasure with the knight's transition, while also pointing to its very possibility. This repair suggests that the original image was broken or incomplete, while the new one is whole. Merlin wants Grisandolus to revert to the old "image," not because the wizard denies his knightly prowess, but because he sees Grisandolus's transition as a kind of subterfuge—a piece of the prophecy that doesn't quite fit. Or perhaps the knight simply surprises him. Merlin doesn't quite resent his captor—in fact, when he sees both "images," he laughs in recognition. They're both marvels. The story is overwhelmed by Merlin's monologues—when Grisandolus does speak, he's usually just asking questions. Merlin finally exposes him before the emperor, in a move designed to restore courtly order. Grisandolus is then offered to the emperor in marriage. But Merlin places a caveat on the marriage: the emperor cannot deny *any* request of Grisandolus. As far as we know, he reverts back to knighthood the moment after the ceremony.

Bychowski notes that the tale dramatizes a battle of masculine and feminine "essences," with Merlin asserting a narrative of gender essentialism in spite of Grisandolus's transformation. In this sense he becomes bound by the specifics of his own prophecy, and though animal transformations are allowed, Merlin refuses to support the more radical transition of Grisandolus. Merlin is the only being allowed to have this power within the narrative (and we see this in the thirteenth-century Anglo-Norman romance *Silence*, as well). Merlin's transphobia places limits on the transformative potential of his own character, and reminds us that wizards can also be used in literature to violently enforce gender norms. His laughter is what makes Grisandolus—and the trans women who serve the emperor's wife—most unsafe, even as his power is what helps to create what might be a more empowering life for Grisandolus. Bychowski also observes that very little scholarly attention has been paid to the trans women in the story, whose ingenious "use of a hormone mimicking oil to prevent the growth

---

[17] "He cast his enchantment so that all the doors and the gates of the palace opened so suddenly that they flew to pieces."
[18] "'You do wrong [foul], for you cannot pursue your quest in this way.'"
[19] "Ymage repaired and disnatured fro Kynde" (L158, Conlee 3).

of facial hair" (12) resembles a kind of medieval hormone replacement therapy (HRT). The death of these women at the hands of Merlin only confirms what Bychowski calls his "startling . . . [violence] against trans bodies" (11). The wizard's analytical search for "truth," like any scientific claim to understanding gender "objectively," is what decimates trans lives. When I teach this tale, I emphasize its productive gaps, as well as its undeniable harm. Merlin as a wizard has many iterations, and this one in particular is used to normalize the transphobia of the Middle English narrative. *Only I get to change shape.* But not all Merlins take this hard line (Monmouth's Merlin is bemused when his sister dresses a boy in drag, and seems relatively untroubled by the switch between masculine/feminine presentation). The Merlin of YA texts like *Once and Future* will be explicitly queer and share space with trans and nonbinary allies—we need more of these Merlins. And Grisandolus, we hope, experiences sovereignty in his unwritten life after the wedding. And in the largely unobserved middle of the tale, as Bychowski observes, the trans maidens "pass" and "remain invisibly present . . . [influencing] events without giving away their definite location" (12).

This offers a sly zone of survival for medieval trans women in the lacunae of the story, and what Blake Gutt points to as "productive resonances between medieval texts and modern trans theory" (131). In no way do I want to assume, as Judith Butler did with the life of Venus Xtravaganza, that the trans maidens are "interesting" subjects of analysis. They are victims of fatal transphobic violence, and trans readers are deprived of hearing more about the nuance and ingenuity of their lives. But their existence is important, as well as the fissure the tale exposes between transmasculine and transfeminine presentations—the former being forgiven, the latter punished. This is in contrast with the fifteenth-century case of Eleanor Rykener, a trans woman and sex-worker, whose primary crime seems to have been solicitation—though we don't know the outcome, there's no mention of punishment for feminine presentation. Trans women must have remained "invisibly present" throughout the Middle Ages, in spite of the tale's suggestion that medieval transmisogyny had only one grim outcome.

Merlin shifts shape throughout the text, from child to stag to "churl" and back to wizard again. In one scene, after he's changed back to his former self, the whole court piles atop him like a teen football player in a movie: "Than thei ronne to hym and embraced hym and made hym grete joye, as thei that hym loved with gode herte. Than thei satte and japed and pleyde with hym alle togedyr" (Conlee 112).[20] One would love to know what it means to "pley" with Merlin.

---

[20] "Then they ran to [Merlin] and embraced him and made great joy, since they loved him with good hearts. And they sat and joked and played with him, all together."

Is it the same "pley" that he shares with Taliesin, intimate and magical? Or is it like Gandalf carting out fireworks for the hobbits? What games does he show them? I think of young Merlin, unable to join the stick-ball team, marked instead as a pawn of prophecy. Maybe they all play ball together. Merlin hikes up his gown and launches the ball into the sky, legitimate at last, no longer a fatherless child. This is the Merlin that we're presented with: dragon-wrangler, game-player, queen of transformation. But he remains a bit frayed around the edges, a bit exhausted by his role in these cosmic events. At various points, when people inquire about Merlin, they're told that he's resting. We imagine him curled on a king's bed, tangled in fine furs, like Marie de France's werewolf Bisclavret (who also advises and befriends a king). Legs twitching as he dreams about demons of the air, dragon eggs, and how to survive this sublunary world.

The Sword in the Stone

We'll conclude by discussing three YA adaptations, starting with T. H. White's 1938 *Sword in the Stone*. Published a year after Tolkien's *The Hobbit*, White's first Arthurian novel is a foundational text within the medievalist YA genre. It's medievalist in the clearest sense of adapting medieval material for a newer audience, while infusing that adaptation with historical knowledge. White's lavish descriptions of tournaments, castles, and falconry are all informed by deep research, and every time I re-read this text, I learn something new. But there's also a cheek that we'll see in the later work of Terry Pratchett, as White mixes 1930s slang with the complexities of courtly language. A perfect example of this occurs in the duel between Sir Pellinore and Sir Grummore, who argue over which one said *pax* first, or was it *pax non*? Their hems and haws and pauses reveal that neither really knows the rules of chivalric battle, like calling "pax" (peace) in order to yield. When Grummore offers Pellinore his feather bed—a break from hunting the Questing Beast—White is able to sneak in a queer romance behind the scenes of his playfully educational novel.

Just as Capetta and McCarthy's *Once and Future* will adapt White's novel, so does White adapt Malory's *Morte* with tongue firmly in cheek. One of the most remarkable scenes is the magic duel between Merlyn and the happily solitary witch Madame Mim—though we'll leave that for Chapter 2. The scene I'd like to dwell on, for now, is Merlyn's workshop. Searching for a lost hawk, Wart (young Arthur) comes across Merlyn's cottage. One of my Arthurian Literature students remarked that the coziness of Merlyn's dwelling may have been White's attempt to divorce Merlin's historical "madness" from the bucolic forest, thereby making the woods feel safe for young readers. When Wart first spies Merlin, what he sees is a paradox:

> The old gentleman that the Wart saw was a singular spectacle. He was dressed in a flowing gown with fur tippets which had the signs of the zodiac embroidered all over it . . . [with] queer crosses, leaves of trees, bones and birds and animals and a planetarium whose stars shone like bits of looking glass with the sun on them. (43)

Are we supposed to be scared of this enchanter with "bits of looking glass" sewed onto his gown and "fur tippets?" A tippet is both a narrow strip of cloth and a woman's scarf, so there's something queer about Merlyn from the beginning. The fifteenth-century author and mystic Margery Kempe—who also made people uncomfortable as a result of her impassioned experience of the mystical realm—wore fashionable tippets. Merlyn's study is a nerd's dream, though his house is a shambles. His owl familiar, Archimedes, has the habit of shitting on everything. We're even told that "the old gentleman was streaked with droppings over his shoulders, among the stars and triangles of his gown, and a large spider was slowly lowering itself from the tip of his hat" (44). This is one of my favorite sentences in any novel. The image of a wizard, shit mixed with stars, ignorant to the spider who's taken up residence on his hat. This is my Merlin. A shit-spattered introvert, unable to explain anything to Wart's satisfaction, whose life companion is a fussy owl. Surrounded by books and weird tools and trash and owl pellets and medieval impossibilities, draped in anachronism, forever backward.

This is the same Merlyn who darkly tells Wart that nothing was worth it—not the shape-shifting, not being taken prisoner by a perverse giant, not even drawing the sword from the stone (which signals the end of Merlyn's useful magic). What he does impart to Wart is a wizardly lesson. He commands the boy to find things out:

> You may grow old and trembling in your anatomies, you may lie awake at night listening to the disorder of your veins, you may miss your only love and lose your moneys to a monster, you may see the world about you devastated by evil lunatics, or know your honor trampled in the sewers of baser minds. There is only one thing for it then—to learn. Learn why the world wags and what wags it. (319)

Wizards want to know what wags the world. But, perhaps more subtly, Merlyn imparts to Wart a lesson about non-linear time: "There must have been something queer about Time [Wart thought], as well as its preciousness" (308). Time is a precious thing, a queer and present future that we can't judge from a knight's perspective, or even a king's. Only a shitty wizard's.

Merlyn's shittiness, perhaps, recalls Melanie Yergeau's discussion of the "shitty narratives" (3) that persist in popular discussions of autism, as well as the shittiness of having a body in the first place. I'd argue that Merlyn's sense of looking backward—of always being in the wrong time—mirrors Yergeau's idea of *neuro-queer rhetoric*. Merlyn tells Wart: "Ordinary people are born *forwards* in Time, if you understand what I mean, and nearly everything in the world goes forward too. This makes it quite easy for the ordinary people to live . . . [I], unfortunately, was born at the wrong end of time, and I have to live *backwards*" (White 53). Certainly, neurodivergent readers understand the idea of moving through a world not made for them, living back to front, or being on the "wrong planet," to quote the slogan of an autistic youth community. But Merlyn also calls this backwardness a gift, because it gives him "second sight." In defining a neuro-queer rhetoric, Melanie Yergeau cites "autistic people's cunning expertise in rhetorical landscapes that would otherwise render us inhuman" (5). This is a reclaiming of queer and backward rhetoricity. Neuro-queer rhetoric "comes into being through movement and the residues of movement, through creeping, sidling, ticcing, twitching, stimming, and stuttering" (Yergeau 76). All things I've done in the course of conversation. This unorthodox way of thinking and speaking "unsettles power structures at work in normative spaces" (Yergeau 84). We see it when Merlyn schools Wart in the sadness of snakes, when he cries at the thought of young Arthur forgetting him, and when he says, as they're about to die at the hands of a giant: "I don't think it was worth it at all" (White 304).

In his article on male pregnancy in medieval romances, Blake Gutt asks us to think about the "backward glance" as a form of anamorphosis: ways in which texts, like images, can yield different interpretations from different angles. Building upon the work of Katherine Stockton Bond on queer children "growing up sideways," Gutt defines "the queer look back [as] . . . recognizing and acknowledging characters who can be read as trans in medieval texts" (188). We can connect this productive form of reading with Merlyn's experience of looking back from some queer temporality: a feeling that can sometimes be isolating, but which also affords a unique perspective beyond the normative. Within the terms of academic analysis, Gutt calls this practice "looking back . . . [by] means of the crooked path of anamorphosis" (205), where we often find surprisingly affirming narratives of gender diversity. Merlyn is also teaching a young King Arthur to look queerly, beyond the structures of chivalry, in order to acknowledge his nonhuman relations and the durable love they offer him. We can telegraph some of this thinking to our own academic analyses and look back queerly at texts which often contain what Julian B. Carter calls "trancestors" (691): historical ancestors that we can connect with across time. Searching with Merlyn, we can approach old texts in new ways, and trace these communities in order to reveal vital queer and trans temporalities that have always existed.

Merlyn and the falconer Hob are both a little odd, both natural introverts: "When they could be alone together they could talk and talk, although each was naturally a silent man" (White 58). Yet Merlyn is also a teacher—and White's transformation is to move the enchanter from a king's counselor to a boy's companion. He is *wys* in the Middle English sense, and he must pass his own peculiar patterns of thought onto Wart. We might see this as a form of queer inheritance: passing down both wizardly and neurodivergent ways of being that challenge medieval forms of lineage. Merlyn is preparing Arthur to think a particular way—and to honor that mode of being—rather than preparing him to make a family. This includes his sense of what Jane Bennett would call "vibrant matter," or the idea that Arthur's realm includes important nonhuman life. When Wart talks to the snake, she doesn't recognize him as a king, but says simply: "You must forget about us . . . [there] is no History in me or you. We are individuals too small for our great sea to care for" (White 217). When he communicates with the stone, he hears its solitary, eternal thought: *cohere*. Everything in his realm, every snake and stone and star, is simply a mind with a different operating system. Medieval lapidaries teach us that stones have a life of their own, just as bestiaries reveal a slippage between human and animal. Though medieval authorities like Isidore were clear about human souls being the only rational ones, nonhuman life was still seen as charged with a kind of life. This kind of philosophy—existing as it did alongside sacred definitions of the human soul—is what allows Wart to address the sword as he pulls it from the stone: "Come sword . . . I must cry your mercy, and take you for a better cause" (349). And what allows him to see all his nonhuman subjects, giving him encouragement: "The lovers and helpers of Wart . . . [they] had come to help on account of love" (350). With Merlyn's mind as key, White reframes the Arthurian legend as a lesson in kinship and radical difference.

Once and Future

In Capetta and McCarthy's *Once and Future*, teen Merlin has already lived through dozens of Arthurs, as a result of his backward evolution: "I keep coming back and back and back, and I can't seem to make things better" (98). Now he's in a futuristic space dystopia, where Ari (Arthur) and her brother pilot a starship in search of their parents, who've been imprisoned by an evil corporation. The result is a delightful mash-up of *Firefly* (Joss Whedon's space opera western) and *Morte Darthur*, with asexual, aromantic, and nonbinary characters and a queer romance between Ari and Queen Gwen. Merlin discovers, upon waking up as a teenager in this fraught future, that adolescence comes with its own challenges—not the least of them being a subtle but powerful attraction to the space knight Val (Percival). Percival is known as a virgin in medieval texts, but Capetta and McCarthy overturn this with the character of Val, who is kind and patient, but also confident in his sexuality. None of the queer romances in this book turn to ruin—all of them flourish in some way, including the storyline of an ace knight, Jordan, who's more than happy to not have a physical relationship.

Merlin is born as a senior citizen of Camelot, "old and magical, with a tiny wooden falcon clutched in his hand" (Capetta 98). This paradox—old Merlin clutching the child's toy that bears his namesake—shows us the novel's vision of queer time. This Merlin is decidedly ambivalent about his immortality, enmeshed as it is in a web of queer failures and mythical mishaps. He lists a long line of Arthurs who die as a result of his choices, including an Arthur who killed him in a jealous rage. This Arthurian autopsy tells us that Merlin's many lives share that old Welsh tone of pain and trauma. He tries and fails to properly train Ari, the first woman (that he knows of) who takes on the Arthurian mantle. Like the Arthur of the Gawain Poet—described as being a bit childish—Ari is hot-headed and doesn't always think before she acts. But both king and mentor are united in their essential imposter syndrome. At one point, Merlin reveals to Ari that he fell in love with one of the many Arthurs: "He wasn't the best of the Arthurs. He wasn't the bravest or the most heroic. He was clever, though. And he said the most bluntly ridiculous things" (99). Merlin is drawn not to "the best of the Arthurs," but to the blunt one, the clever one, who tells him the truth. Merlin and Arthur share a moment in a grove, which we could easily imagine as the enchanter's beloved Celidon:

> They had kissed in the forest, under trees that seemed to hide them from an unfriendly sky. They had loved each other in a time when people pretended such things weren't happening . . . [the] rush of Art's kiss, the welcoming darkness. And then Merlin was pushing Art away, saying, "We can't do this forever," meaning those words quite literally. (99–100; 142)

We can't do this forever. But forever is all Merlin has. What else can he do? This clever Arthur, not the best of them, stops his spinning with a kiss. Capetta and McCarthy nod to medieval history by saying "they had loved each other in a time when people pretended such things weren't happening." The Arthurian myths don't necessarily pretend that queerness isn't happening, though they often cloak it. In the Winchester manuscript of Malory's *Morte Darthur*, there's a humorous throwaway scene where Lancelot accidentally gets into bed with Sir Pelleus. He leaps out of bed when he feels the knight's prickly beard, and both are full of deflections and apologies for the event. But it remains canonical—Lancelot in bed with another knight—and we have to wonder what kind of laughter (or ire) Malory wanted to invoke by retaining this scene from his "French book."

The Merlin of *Once and Future* is far from what Knight calls the medieval tradition's "sacrificeable seven-year-old" (*Merlin* 51). He may have a bird toy and a weirdly inflected view of human relations, but he's very much an anxious and embodied teen. And perhaps adolescence, after all, is something like a struggle to remember who we'll be, to sift through dreams and past versions of ourselves in search of the honest-to-shit truth. He calls this dystopian future "a new kind of Dark Age" (Capetta 136), which I'd argue is less of a misinterpretation, and more of an acknowledgment of the early medieval past and its many contradictions. Those "dark ages" also had myths, and technology, and light pouring through stained glass, and queers kissing and in groves, as well as greedy corporations and governments. An honest look at the arc of time.

Merlin's rival in the book is Morgana, who turns out to be a ghost with problems of her own. I'll discuss her further in Chapter 2. At one point, she tells Ari that "Merlin's purpose is calamity" (211). He's havoc and failure and disappointment all wrapped up in the body of an awkward teen. He continually fails Arthur, just as we fail our way through life, since we really can't do much else. Like Merlin's sense of time, we're strapped to "a roller coaster designed by a drunkard" (Capetta 136). This echoes Chaucer's image, in *The Parliament of Fowls*, of a drunkard making their shaky way home as the medieval streets tremble and spin around them. In that poem, the carter dreams of his carts, the knight of battles lost and won. Merlin dreams about finally saving Arthur, which he manages to do in *Once and Future*. He also manages to sleep with Val, in a scene of queer interstellar desire that links the mythic past with José Esteban's Muñoz's vision of queer futurity, which I'll discuss later: "[Val's] touch had a confidence that pinned Merlin into place after so much wandering through places and times that didn't belong to him . . . [After] lifetimes of saying no, Merlin found himself saying yes, and yes, and yes" (330–31). Unlike the wanderer, Merlin is no longer *anhaga*, mapless. Val's kiss makes them *uncer*, the Old English (OE) dual pronoun for *we two*. What do you call a knight and a wizard in love? A marvel.

Red Scrolls of Magic

In her YA *Mortal Instruments* series—which focuses on demon hunters and magic-users—Cassandra Clare introduces a witty warlock named Magnus Bane. He eventually falls for a demon-hunter named Alec, and the two get a spinoff series, which begins with *The Red Scrolls of Magic* (co-authored with Wesley Chu). In this book, we learn that Magnus was born in seventeenth-century Jakarta, to a mother who was half-Indonesian and half-Dutch. In the TV adaptation (*Shadowhunters*), Magnus is portrayed by Chinese-American actor Harry Shum Jr. In her teaching essay "Race in the European Middle Ages," Geraldine Heng discusses how the European Middle Ages are "*still* seen as outside the history of race," yet both medievalists and consumers of medievalism must acknowledge "that racial thinking, racial practices, and racial phenomena can occur before there is a vocabulary to name them for what they are" (n.p.). A character like Magnus can intervene in the white-washing of the Middle Ages, by showing that a wizard can be a person of color who wears a brooch inspired by Chaucer (who also wrote about people of color in multiple tales). His presence challenges what Dorothy Kim calls the "white, male hero story" presented as a model by Tolkien, whose "aesthetic, non-politicized, close reading" ("The Question of Race in *Beowulf*" n.p.) of medieval texts like *Beowulf* has covered over the diversity of the actual Middle Ages.

Clare's popular series began as fanfiction, with a focus on the relationship between Harry Potter and Draco Malfoy. In the classroom, I talk with students about the concept of medieval fanfiction—how medieval writers were often focused on adaptations of biblical texts, and we can see the medieval romance tradition as a form of sophisticated fanfiction. In her work on fanfiction and early modern literature, Kavita Mudan Finn notes that most canonical literature "is clearly written in response to or adapting a specific source text" ("Exit" 27). In light of this, it's important to affirm the value of fanfiction as a place where writers can experiment with existing worlds (some ideas for my first novel began as a *CSI* slash fanfiction cycle). Finn also argues that "fandom prizes qualities more often derided and refused in traditional academic circles: emotion, self-insertion, and subjectivity" ("Exit" 28). When we study texts that might have a resonance with particular communities, it's imperative to think about how these stories actually make us feel—not simply what scholarly utility they might have. Fanfiction was really the first genre where I found queer characters my age as a younger writer, before the YA genre became more inclusive of LGBTQ+ stories.[21] The principles of fanfiction also align with this book, since the genre is interested in both seeing queer content in existing texts, and making it visible.

Like Ambrose on *Sabrina the Teenage Witch*, Magnus is a demi-immortal warlock, cheerfully and openly queer in both his aesthetic and his desires. He wears fabulous nonbinary outfits, including a "shimmering white suit rumpled like bedsheets in the morning, his white cloak swaying after him like a moonbeam" (Clare and Chu 150). Next to Alec's well-worn leather jacket and quiet

---

[21] Britta Lundin's YA novel *Ship It* engages with issues of LGBTQ+ representation. It focuses on a show much like *Supernatural*, where the two male leads—demon and demon hunter—are often shipped together. Lundin makes the interesting decision to tell the story from two perspectives: Claire, a queer teen who ships the characters, and Forrest, the straight actor who doesn't understand why Claire needs his character to be queer so badly. The novel received mixed reviews from my students, with many observing that Claire's "obsessive" fandom was a negative fan stereotype, while others noted that Lundin was trying to generate a vital conversation about fandom and queer-baiting.

but very masc presentation, Magnus is every bit a firework as Merlin and Gandalf before him. The long years have given him an incorrigible sense of humor, and he tells Alec: "I would joke about anything" (28). When you've seen all of your friends die, you have to laugh.

This echoes the powerful and critical humor of the AIDS years, when irony could be both a sharp weapon and a swan-song against death. We're told that "chaos swirled and orbited around Magnus like a cloud of glitter" (35–36). *Red Scrolls* is unsubtle about Magnus being queer, but that's part of what's so endearing and surprising about the book. The hardcover depicts an image of Magnus and Alec, hand in hand, as clear silhouettes over a Paris skyline. The fantasy genre has a history of queer-friendly or simply thirst-worthy gay covers, from soft boy Vanyel in *Magic's Pawn* to bare-chested farm twink Garion in *The Castle of Sorcery*. As a young reader, I recall being extra aware of the painted cover to Raymond E. Feist's *Magician: Apprentice*, where sturdy orphan babe Pug comes in out of the rain, dripping all over the wizard's workshop. But the *Red Scrolls* marks the first instance of a primary queer couple on a popular YA fantasy novel cover, depicted *as* a couple in no uncertain terms (the cover to Rowell's *Carry On* comes close, but it's still slightly ambiguous, depicting either two profiles or Simon and Baz about to fight a fabulous purple dragon together).

Red Scrolls focuses on solving a mystery that Magnus himself created, though he doesn't quite remember how it happened. The final battle, like so many battle scenes in the genre, turns out to be metaphorical as well as literal. Magnus is fighting against his own imposter syndrome, and struggling to find a place among his shaky community of warlocks, hunters, and monsters. He's also struggling to form a "normal" relationship with Alec, which of course proves impossible, since their world doesn't really skew towards the traditional. Early on in the first season of *Shadowhunters*, Magnus makes a throwaway joke about the painter/poet Michelangelo being "excellent in bed, I might add" (S1E4). We get a sense here of the warlock's trans-historical sense of humor, which draws upon the fundamental queerness of immortality. I grew up with the *Highlander* films—about immortal warriors, often from a medieval timeline, struggling to survive in the contemporary world. It always struck me as odd that they weren't all queer, given how desires must broaden over time. There were a few queer-coded characters in the early-1990s *Highlander* TV series, but they were always villains or minor characters—more a testament to the homophobia of that televisual era than a comment on immortal gender.

Magnus casually mentions his attraction to Alec, who's quite nervous at the prospect. "It's nothing to be ashamed of," Magnus tells him (S1E4). In the following episode, he asks Alec out for a drink. It's a funny collision of the historical and the modern—a warlock, centuries old, proposing a cocktail. A bit weird when we recall that Alec is sixteen, and Magnus is around four hundred (Buffy and Angel have the same issue in *Buffy the Vampire Slayer*). But the fantasy framework allows Magus to inhabit a young person's body, and in many ways, he remains a queer teenager, unsure if his affections will be returned. Perhaps all that dating starts to feel like an eternal adolescence, after a while. Asking out Alec is just as brave as asking out the captain of the football team. Their relationship grows over the course of the *Mortal Instruments* series, until they appear as a firm couple in *Red Scrolls*.

The novel is quite funny in the way that it presents contemporary romance as a magical disaster. Magnus creates over-the-top romantic scenarios using magic, only to have them deflate or turn fatal or simply fail. Alec turns out to be more than a tall drink of water in a leather coat. At first, he feels alienated by all the years that Magnus has on him. But rather than holding that against the warlock, he turns it back on himself: "He wasn't just an open book, [Alec] thought. He was a short one. A slim volume compared to the chronicles of Magnus's long life" (201). Alec sees himself as nothing but a novella, compared to his mythic boyfriend. How can Alec's slim pages compare to the many chapters of Magnus, who "was somehow still a blazing riot of life and color, a source of joy for everyone around him" (204). We see that Magnus, like Merlin, has lived through innumerable traumas. He doesn't just laugh in the face of pain—he laughs in defiance of a world that wants to break him down. His magic, like the magic of T. H. White's Merlyn, is often campy—he floats all the books that he's reading simultaneously, exactly like Merlyn floating books in Disney's *Sword in the Stone*. But he's still capable of taking down a demon, all while wearing a Latin amulet that says *amor verus numquam moritur*. True love never dies. He's both a warlock and a hopeless romantic. The amulet reminds us of Chaucer's prioress, the religious figure who doesn't quite believe in celibacy, since her brooch declares: *love conquers all*. But the message of Magnus is slightly different—not that love conquers, but that love *survives*, even in the face of centuries of trauma.

There's a masquerade party in the middle of the book, which turns into a disaster. But before everything goes literally to hell, Alec spies Magnus dancing: "His mirrorlike mask was askew, his black hair wild, his slim body arching with the dance, and wrapped around his fingers like ten shimmering rings was the light of his magic" (150). The phrase that comes to my mind, as a 1980s kid, is *magic dance*, from the film *Labyrinth*. In this 1980s Jim Henson film, the Goblin King—played by David Bowie in high camp fashion—sings to his goblins about how magic should feel like dancing. You don't fear magic—you dance with it. As a queer kid with the tendency to hyper-focus, I watched that movie endless times, and wore out my tape of the soundtrack. I now realize this was a productive form of stimming—immersing myself in that fantasy soundscape, where a gorgeously queer king sang to me about dancing my way into existence and community. Like Magnus, Bowie's character wears a feathered cloak and seduces the viewer with a promise of queer magic.[22] In one memorable scene, he walks up M. C. Escher-style stairs at impossible angles, letting the space of the fairy tale fracture. Gutt's practice of "looking back queerly" serves me now, as I look back on that version of myself dancing queerly in that space where anything could happen.

Alec falls in love with Magnus for his imperfections, and we see in him a queer profusion of Merlins, all sly, all survivors, all born backwards but looking ever-forward. Like the Merlin of Capetta and McCarthy's *Once and Future*, Magnus "had always had a wanderer's heart" (344). As an actual immigrant wizard, his geographic perspective is broad. Merlin also has a variety of origin stories, ranging from Britain to Wales to Scotland. He begins as a figure in conflict with colonization—prophesying the survival of Welsh culture in the face of Saxon, and later Norman, invasion. His legend crossed Europe and appears as far as Iceland, revealing him to be a traveler, like Magnus. Alec seems to signal an end to Magnus's wandering: "Everywhere they kissed and everywhere they touched felt like alchemy, the transformation of the commonplace to gold" (343). Through medieval alchemy, they kiss their way to the philosopher's stone. Magnus, always out of time and unable to understand how mortals feel, mends into gold with Alec. Both Merlin and Magnus begin these separate series as wanderers, but end, a bit like Doctor Who, as fixed points in time and space.

The next chapter will turn to Merlin's co-ancestor in this story of magical thinking: Morgan le Fay. Morgan appears as early as the twelfth century in Monmouth's *Vita Merlini*, though she has antecedents in earlier enchantresses: Circe, Medea, and even the biblical Witch of Endor. I'll discuss how Morgan, as an enchantress, occupies a unique position somewhere between wizard and witch. She's a royal figure with a great deal of cultural power, even as later writers like Malory attempt to edit and control her. We'll talk more about how gender influences the role of the magic-user, and how Morgan can simultaneously appear as a kind of anti-hero in Arthurian myth, as well as a marginalized character. She sidles her way through these male-centered narratives, disrupting them, teasing them, and offering challenges to chivalry. Morgan also serves as a vital counterpart to Merlin, whose focus is often on epic events, rather than human particularities. Morgan, on the other hand, invests in educating a young Gawain, offering

---

[22] The first explicitly queer character I can remember seeing in a fantasy film was Otho, Catherine O'Hara's acerbic interior designer in *Beetlejuice* (1988). One of the characters makes a clear connection between queerness and the supernatural when she quips: "Paranormal—is that what they're calling your kind these days?" Otho manages to cast a spell in order to summon ghosts, and while he isn't precisely positive, there's the sense that he's appreciated by the Deetz family.

him a number of queer possibilities. The authors of the *Vulgate* try to paint her into particular roles, but she always exceeds these frames, surprising us. Like Merlin, Morgan encourages us to think differently, queerly, about things we might take for granted. We'll think about her origins, her challenges to medieval magical literature, and her many queer futures.

Chapter 2
The Futures of Morgan le Fay: Solidarity and Knowledge in *Sabrina* and *Tiffany Aching*

Morgan le Fay remains a contested character in the vast Arthurian tradition. Is she a villain, or some kind of anti-hero? Medieval writers interpret her variously: a scholar and physician; a grasping politician; a witch in league with the devil; even a playful aunt to young Sir Gawain. But who is Morgan really, and what's the effect of trying to capture her in a single frame or text? In popular medievalist films like *Excalibur*, Morgan is portrayed as the over-ambitious apprentice of Merlin—though this role is more often filled in medieval literature by the shadowy character of Vivian, who eventually traps Merlin in his own spell. Often, Merlin and Morgan seem to work independently of one another, like free agents. While Merlin focuses on the structures of prophecy, Morgan is the instigator who challenges the rules of Camelot. As we'll discuss, she's both a royal enchantress—Arthur's half-sister in many sources—and a character who seems to haunt the margins of Arthurian literature. She sets the stage for many powerful and queerly thinking witches, from Sabrina Spellman to Tiffany Aching.

I'll quote another ambiguous villain: Pizzazz, the snarky leader of the Misfits, who form the rival band in the 1980s cartoon *Jem and the Holograms*. This show captivated me as a kid, because it featured not only a shape-shifting character (Jerrica becoming Jem), but also a cyber-magical hologram named Synergy. Morgan is also a hologram in many ways, ghosting through her medieval texts; and Synergy held vital knowledge about the hero's mission. Pizzazz was not supposed to be the center of this narrative, but her glam hair and new wave guitar riffs tended to steal every scene. Like Morgan, Pizzazz is tired of playing second fiddle to the heroic Jem, and in a second season episode she sings about it. "Who is she, anyway?"

In my recent class on Arthurian Literature, Morgan was the character we discussed the most. My students were far more interested in the inscrutable enchantress than they were in, say, Lancelot (the fallible hero), or Arthur (the mythic source). She seemed to cut across every text, even when she wasn't quite present. They debated her motivations in *Sir Gawain and the Green Knight*, and connected with Geoffrey of Monmouth's early description of her, in the *Vita Merlini*, as a scholar and older sister (living on a magical island with her other siblings). They raged against her treatment in the *Vulgate*—all the ways she was shamed or silenced—while also discussing her curious forms of agency. As Carolyne Larrington and Amy S. Kaufman have discussed in their work, Morgan is a powerful actor within the Arthurian tradition, even if many writers don't quite know what to do with her. Kaufman describes feminine agency in Malory's *Morte* as complex: "Several of the female characters he adapts have amplified roles," and supernatural figures like Morgan "[provide] models that could disrupt our notions of Medieval Arthurian gender and power" (165; 170). These characters are never wholly victims or goddesses, but rather enact what Kaufman describes as a "witnessing" role as they critique chivalry's inequalities. Morgan occupies a productive middle space that makes her open to both interpretation and adaptation. Jill Hebert notes that "her ability to cross and/or blur boundaries . . . [literally] represents the concept of the potential for representation" (5), and this chapter will focus on how both medieval and medievalist authors have dealt with those various crossings. It's impossible to isolate Morgan across nearly four hundred years of medieval literature, but that's partially the point: she resists all attempts at classification. That defiance is what makes her the ancestor of contemporary witches like Sabrina and Tiffany Aching.

This chapter will read Morgan le Fay as an ancestor to the diverse and queer witches that have emerged in recent YA literature. Particularly, we'll see how a character like Morgan influences Sabrina Spellman (from *Chilling Adventures of Sabrina*) and Tiffany Aching (from Terry Pratchett's expansive *Discworld* series). We'll also look at how Morgan appears in children's adaptations of Arthuriana—in those defiant and playful images, we can see a character who is breaking the rules. In fact, she's breaking the very genre of Arthurian myth. In *Sir Gawain and the Green Knight*, for example, the character of Morgan seems to have cryptic motivation—if any at all—for engineering Gawain's test of manners. Geraldine Heng argues that the poem is really about the relationship between Morgan and Guinevere, but Morgan herself is a difficult knot, visible only as a kind of lacework throughout the poem's action. Heng describes this as the "imperfect knot . . . [that] situates identity as more tenuous and incomplete—a fragile, uncertain prospect that is always on the verge of unraveling" ("Feminine Knots" 504). The knot links Morgan with Guinevere, but it also comes to symbolize Morgan's own irreducible motivation in the text—her mental complexity as a character.

I'm interested in how this medieval focus on mental complexity might resonate for contemporary teens—especially those identifying as neurodivergent. I want us to think about the neuro-queerness of wizards and enchantresses. The context of being epic, of understanding prophecy and seeing beyond the text or the manuscript, brings with it a perspective that's both intriguing and unstable. How do you go about your life when all you can think about is death, in the case of Merlin, or revenge, in the case of Morgan? What's it like to realize that prophecy is using you? The YA genre explores these questions through a number of teen witches who need to balance medieval traditions with contemporary concerns. They live in both the past and the future, and embody what Carolyn Dinshaw has called the "asynchronous time" within medievalism—not quite now or then, not quite "authentic" or "amateur," but productively queer in its own way.

Medieval Morgans

There's no clear answer to the question: where does Morgan come from? Her earliest appearance by name is in Geoffrey of Monmouth's twelfth-century *Vita Merlini*, which Larrington describes as "[a] much less popular poem" (7) than his well-known *History of the Kings of Britain*. As we discussed in the previous chapter, the *Vita* is in many ways the opposite of the *History*. While its predecessor is crisp and accessible, the *Vita* opts for big emotions and complex poetry. Monmouth obviously wanted to make a creative statement—though, since only one manuscript copy survived, it wasn't a successful one. Morgan isn't officially part of the action in the *Vita*. She comes up as a kind of historical trivia in Merlin's prophetic exchange with the bard Taliesin. We're told about the Fortunate Isle, where everything is self-sufficient. The island is governed by nine sisters, "administering a very pleasant law code" (Clarke 263).[1] "Morgen" is the most accomplished: "[She is] most learned in the art of healing . . . [and] she has learned the helpful properties of all the various herbs" (ibid.).[2] This seems fairly straightforward, but the text goes on to say: "She also possesses the great skill of being able to transform her appearance."[3] In the Latin original, Monmouth uses *vult* to echo the power with which the enchantress can fly and take on various shapes:

> *Cum vult, est Bristi Carnoti sive Papie,*
> *cum vult, in vestris ex aere labitur horis*
> (L925–26, Clarke 100).
>
> [At will, she's in Brest, then Chartres, even Pavia,
> at will, she slips from the sky, down to your shores.]

The word *vult* (will) seems to glide through both lines, and Monmouth playfully separates *vestris* (plural your) from *horis* (shores), as if Morgen is plummeting through the gap. The phrase "your shores" is also a tad ominous, with its suggestion that the enchantress could appear in any of *your* spaces—an alien on

---

1 "Illic jura novum geniali lege sorores" (L916, Clarke 100).
2 "Quarum que prior est fit doctior arte medendi / exceditque suas forma prestante sorores" (L917–19, Clarke 100).
3 "Ars quoque nota sibi qua scit mutare figuram" (L922, Clarke 100).

human shores. But this version of Morgan is a benign scholar. She takes Arthur to the Fortunate Isle, and nurses him back to health on a golden bed. We imagine her solving devilish math problems while the king reposes on this matriarchal island. Did Monmouth have any idea how popular, and truly changeable, this character would become? That she would appear in Victorian art, in Edwardian children's stories, in twenty-first-century science-fiction novels? Like Marie de France's fairy queen in "Lanval," this version of the enchantress seems to exist in a parallel world, only checking in when prophecy demands it. But she has the potential to meddle in human affairs whenever she likes. Both Larrington and Maureen Fries have suggested that the sorceress Medea—known first for killing her children, but also skilled in the arts of magical apothecary—served as a template for Morgan. In the twelfth-century *Roman de Troie*, by Benoit de Saint-Maure, Medea is possessed of *grant saveir* (great knowledge), having learned magic through both *engin* (a combination of trickery and ingenuity) and *maistrie* (mastery) (L1204–5). Like Morgan, she has mastered the *arz* (arts) of both astronomy and sorcery. But Medea is also profoundly negative—frozen in the act of killing her children—while Morgan is a far more benevolent figure in Monmouth's story. All of the power and none of the baggage.

She appears a bit later in Hartmann von Aue's *Erec* (an adaptation of Chrétien de Troyes's *Erec et Enide*). This retelling of the knight Erec's story also introduces a fairy enchantress named Feimorgan (Fay-Morgan). Her minor but memorable role in *Erec* has an ominous flavor. Instead of the enchantress who might pop into your neighborhood, like a friendly Professor McGonagall, this version of Morgan "has kin deep in hell" (quoted in Larrington 12). She's surrounded by demons, and her magic is clearly the darker kind of necromancy, rather than the more ambiguous "sorcery." She's not entirely *evil* in von Aue's poem—she can be helpful—but certainly not a celestial math-wizard and healer. Maureen Fries argues that Morgan's later role as "sorceress" is far reduced from Monmouth's vision of her as "seer." By the time she appears in the thirteenth-century *Vulgate* stories, we see a "decline in her moral nature . . . [which] coincides with the virulent growth of women-hatred in both religious and lay society" (4). "Morgan Shape-Shifter," as Jill Hebert calls her, ends up shifting against her will—from prophet and healer to an ambivalent character who reveals "the inability of male Arthurian authors to cope with the image of a woman in power" (2). But Morgan does have one, unexpected thing in some of these ambivalent thirteenth-century representations: a community of enchantresses.

The fifth book of the *Vulgate* introduces us to Morgan's co-witches, Sebile and the Queen of North Gaul. These are both minor characters who, nonetheless, make several fascinating appearances in Arthurian texts of the thirteenth and early fourteenth century. By the time we get to Malory, they've been largely compressed. In Malory's "A Noble Tale of Sir Launcelot du Lake," the famous knight is taken prisoner by "four queens of great estate" (Okun 47). Morgan is the only queen that Malory names, though he mentions the Queen of North Gaul, the Queen of Eastland, and the Queen of the Out Isles (who is perhaps Malory's substitution for Sebile). Carolyne Larrington describes Sebile as "a crony of Morgan's" (43), which makes me think of the character Evil-Lyn in the medievalist 1980s cartoon *He-Man*.

He-Man and the Masters of the Universe was one of my earliest obsessions as a kid. The show focuses on a hybrid medievalist/science-fiction world, Eternia, where the warrior He-Man grapples with an undead sorcerer named Skeletor. I had the figurines, the sticker books, both castles (Grayskull and Snake Mountain, respectively), and even the disgusting toy that dumps green slime on unsuspecting characters. I can still remember what the villain Moss-Man smelled like when I dropped him in the bath (wet dog). Somewhat like the *Morte Darthur*, *He-Man* was supposed to focus on a band of heroes with a charismatic leader. But the show actually dealt in themes of queerness and secrecy, as the not-especially-competent Prince Adam concealed his true identity as a buff warrior. His nemesis, Skeletor, was campy and full of rage, stealing every scene. The show was full of magical characters whose power served to destabilize the narrative, including a winged sorceress, a floating comedic wizard, and the aptly named Evil-Lyn.

The 2017 documentary *Power of Grayskull* revealed that the creative team for *He-Man* included several pioneering women writers and directors, including Erika Scheimer and Barbara Hambly. We tend to think of *He-Man* as a franchise for boys—just as the *Morte* was a kind of late medieval version of the same thing—but the women of Eternia were just as significant as the male characters. Like Sebile, Evil-Lyn is a henchwoman, caught in the wake of a more powerful magic-user (Skeletor). She was often railing against the injustice of being a supporting character—much how Morgan seemed to possess a barely concealed rage at being marginalized by medieval narratives.

I still have an Evil-Lyn action figure in my office. So unapologetically *evil* that she announced it in her very name: could this also be a queer model? A character who knows exactly who they are? Noelle Stevenson's reboot of *She-Ra*[4] (the *He-Man* spinoff) includes an autistic character named Entrapta, who's more comfortable interacting with machines than humans. *She-Ra* takes place on Etheria, a mixed medievalist/tech-centered planet, where a community of rebels is fighting against interstellar colonists known as the Horde. Stevenson noted on Twitter that

---

4 It's worth noting that *She-Ra* includes three queer POC characters, including Bow, who viewers have long suspected is a trans boy. Stevenson has tentatively approved of this reading, though stated in interview that they would have hired a trans voice actor if Bow had explicitly been written as trans.

one of *She-Ra*'s board artists, Sam Szymanski, is also on the spectrum, and "had a huge part in shaping [Entrapta's] story and character" (Chappell n.p.). At first it seems like Entrapta might be an antagonist, but she ends up joining She-Ra's community of rebels and princesses (she's a princess herself). In S5E2, Entrapta gets so focused on tracking a signal—which will help the group save Princess Glimmer—that she unwittingly puts everyone in danger. After the other princesses accuse her of being reckless, she responds:

> I'm not good at people. But I am good at tech. I thought maybe, if I could use tech to help you, you'd like me. But I messed that up too. . . . I'm sorry I'm bad at listening. I'm sorry I mess everything up. But you need this signal and I'm gonna get it for you!

Entrapta is the only princess who doesn't seem to have elemental-related powers that resemble magic. Her power lies in understanding nonhuman beings, like robots, as well as computer networks. In this sense, she reads rhetorics that are beyond the understanding of the other princesses. Melanie Yergeau challenges the ableist notion that "one must be human in order to be rhetorical" (11), which places autistic people beyond the structures of conventional rhetoric, therefore denying humanity to anyone whose rhetoric is different. Entrapta is fluent in nonhuman rhetorics—not just coding, but how machines *feel*—and as the group comes to understand that, they also see what Entrapta adds to their cause. She possesses empathy for the machines that the Horde uses in their warfare, and that empathy is what allows her to disrupt the machine network that keeps Etheria under the Horde's control. Like Morgan, Entrapta thinks across different networks, and sees connections between human and nonhuman beings—connections that her companions can't quite apprehend. Her different ways of thinking are at first viewed with suspicion, but ultimately prized by the group.

On the other hand, feedback from autistic fans of the show has not been wholly positive.[5] @DubiousCA finds the character to be important "[because] she's autistic rep but she also carries a lot of problematic tropes" (August 24, 2020). @BitterBleue notes that Entrapta has "zero moral compass and did not care about the fact that the people she was creating these machines and doing research for were going to murder her friends" (August 23, 2020). It should be noted that Entrapta sides with the Horde because she's drawn to their technology, and this pursuit of a special interest—something often associated with people on the spectrum—places the other characters in danger. Back in 2018, Ana Mardoll criticized the fact that "the one ND [neurodivergent] team mate is

---

[5] In the episode mentioned above, Entrapta is literally put on a leash by another character to "keep her safe," an image that remains deeply jarring in its dehumanizing ableism.

basically turned evil because she's too much of a reckless fool to realize that evil is bad" (n.p.). There's also the fact that community consultation needs to be broad, rather than focused on a single positive endorsement, and @DubiousCA adds that "because 1 single autistic person consulted on her, she's considered above reproach" (August 24, 2020). I've had the same argument about a show like *Atypical* when people say: *but they consulted!* I recognized elements of myself in Entrapta, but also found it problematic that she identified primarily with robots and technology. This can be a really fascinating way of de-centering the human, as I've discussed above, but it can also perpetuate stereotypes about neurodivergent people and issues with communication.

Perhaps we can agree that there's a bit of Entrapta in Morgan, and vice versa, in the way that both think differently and look beyond the surface. Morgan changes shape at will, transforming to living stone (more on this in Chapter 5), and focuses a great deal of her attention on an artifact (Excalibur's magical scabbard). Like Entrapta, her precise motivations are often veiled, or difficult to read. But this doesn't necessarily make her a villain. Both Morgan and Entrapta challenge the narratives in which they've been placed, by asking different questions, and assuming non-traditional perspectives on the story. In the scene involving Lancelot's capture, Malory doesn't quite know what to do with Morgan and all her shadows. The thirteenth-century *Vulgate*, however, gives us an expanded version of this capture scene, where Morgan's fellow enchantresses vie for the spotlight. Obviously, it was important enough for Malory to reinterpret it, even though it's all about Lancelot's failure to be the ideal knight (he's literally caught sleeping).

Reading the *Vulgate* is a bit like binge-watching Arthurian stories. It's sprawling, overwhelming, sometimes disconnected, but you can still make connections and see how multiple writers attempted to frame these living legends. In class, we talked about how inaccessible the *Vulgate* is—unless you're an Arthurian scholar, you've probably never heard of it, and assume that Malory was working from scratch. Even Arthurian scholars find it unwieldy. At ten volumes, published by Boydell & Brewer, it's not exactly a coffee-table book. Few scholars actually own it, and few libraries can afford it. Reading it makes you appreciate Malory's editorial skill, and how Caxton's press made these stories widely available in the format we're now familiar with.

We can't underestimate the significance of making these stories accessible, over a variety of media. There's always been something secretive—even hermetic—about medieval studies. A difficult constellation of texts and languages, controlled primarily by male scholars at Ivy League schools. Part of the reason Tolkien was able to influence medieval studies to such an extent lay in his access to physical manuscripts. Most universities do not have access to a single medieval manuscript *leaf*, let alone an entire manuscript. My own institution can't compete with larger schools that have programs in rare book history and paleography (the study of manuscript production). The digital era has leveled this playing field in many ways, offering access to databases full of illuminated manuscripts. But that's only part of the experience of reading medieval literature: students also deserve the privilege of touching, even smelling, these fragile documents, made by animals, ink, and the crabbed hands of scribes. They can't be kept under lock and key at elite archives which only 10 percent of scholars have the funds to visit. If medieval studies is going to survive as an accessible field, we need to develop new strategies for bringing the physical reality of manuscripts and early medieval books into the classroom.

The *Vulgate* is also an ocean of mysteries, subtleties, contradictions, queer desires, and moments—like this one—where enchantresses are allowed to tread the stage. Morgan, Sebile, and the Queen of North Gaul come upon Lancelot sleeping. Knights are always unwisely falling asleep in these stories. They appreciate him for the snack that he is, admiring his body, which the *Vulgate* has already described as perfect. While Morgan is given her proper title of *la fee*, Sebile is described as *lenchanteresce* (the enchantress)—she is one of the "femmes del monde qui plus savoient denchantemens sans la dame del lac" (other than the Lady of the Lake, she was one of the women who knew the most spells in the world [Sommer 91]). In the *Vulgate*, there are multiple Ladies of the Lake: one of them raises Lancelot, while another offers up a replacement Excalibur when Arthur breaks the sword. If the Lady of the Lake is actually one person, she seems to be a benign enchantress, well-versed in the politics of Camelot, who appears in various guises to help Arthur and his knights. This gives us the sense of a global enchantress community that will vanish in later texts, where Morgan nearly always operates alone. Though we may think of these wizard and enchantress figures as marginal and solitary, the earlier Arthurian tradition presents them as part of an uneasy but like-minded group. You may think on an epic scale—may not get along with the heroes—but you can still belong. This offers an unexpectedly durable model of kinship for queer and neurodivergent readers, who may also feel as if a community is beyond their grasp.

Malory's more judicious version cuts off any dialogue between the queens. But in the *Vulgate*, they fall into a debate, with the Queen of North Gaul launching the first salvo. She argues that Lancelot should be hers, since she is a "plus riche dame" (most elegant lady) who possesses "tote la terre del monde en ma baillie" (everyone in my jurisdiction [Sommer 92]). Her literal use of what we'd now call *bailiwick* conveys both the social and geographic scope of her power. Morgan responds with a transgressive laugh—a literally rendered *Ha!* within the text. There's something delicious about the interjection. In many ways, the text that we'll end this section with—*Sir Gawain and the Green Knight*—is entirely

Morgan's *Ha!* But her own laughter in the poem is far more subtle, and only suggested in one scene. In the *Vulgate*, we have an audible act of resistance. It recalls Hélène Cixous's discussion of transgressive interruptions in "The Laugh of the Medusa," where she urges: "Write! Writing is for you, you are for you; your body is yours, take it" (876). Morgan takes it, and her laugh here is preserved as an act of sly and furious writing. She cuts off the queen, arguing that she is of higher birth. This is a relatively recent innovation within thirteenth-century Arthurian literature, since previous Morgans didn't share Arthur's bloodline. There's something new and transitional about the *Vulgate* Morgan, even as she strikes against the misogynistic confines of the text.

Sebile, the youngest enchantress, finds the loophole in the arguments of her peers: "encore le deuroie ie avoir mieuz que vous, quar ie sui plus bele & plus ione & plus enuoi" (the duty must be more mine than yours, for I am younger and prettier and have the better claim [Sommer ibid.]). She deftly reverses Morgan's claim to experience, and the Queen of North Gaul's claim to jurisdiction, by getting to the root of the matter: *We all know what we're going to do with him, and in this realm, I'm a double threat—young and gorgeous*. We can only imagine the look of annoyance that crosses their faces, as this upstart stakes a claim to Lancelot. Everyone has lost track of the sleeping knight, at this point. He drives the action of this scene, but he isn't the heart of it. In many ways, this scene reverses the lover/beloved equation of courtly love poetry—instead of a man pursuing a woman, Lancelot is pursued by multiple women. Like a damsel who's been sidelined, he waits in the background, while the real energy flashes between the group of enchantresses. There's also a bit of Tiffany Aching, in Sebile's refusal to respect authority—since Tiffany also resists the male hierarchy of wizards in her world. Morgan wins in the end, but Sebile remains a contender throughout the scene, and she'll return in a more obscure text: the early fourteenth-century *Prophésies de Merlin*.

There are a number of loosely connected medieval texts called "The Prophecies of Merlin" that circulated in the thirteenth and fourteenth centuries, in various languages. The oldest is a French prose text, likely composed in the second half of the thirteenth century, held in Venice (Str. App. 29). There are also different versions held in London, Rennes, and Cologny, ranging from 1303 to 1330 in composition. All are collections of Merlin's prophecies with vignettes of adventure sprinkled throughout. The version that I'll address—the above-mentioned *Prophésies de Merlin*—is from Cologny (Bodmer 116), and it was written in the first decade of the fourteenth century. It includes a rarely discussed magic duel, between Morgan, Sebile, and a figure called Dame d'Avalon, which Carolyne Larrington summarizes in *King Arthur's Enchantresses*. Larrington notes that "the moves in the competition make demonic involvement in enchantment clearly visible" (23–24). I was surprised that few critics had analyzed this remarkable scene—but the text itself is difficult to find. Anne Berthelot's modern French translation is out of print, and I'm unaware of any Arthurian volume that includes the story. Marvelously, the Bodmer manuscript is available online, through the library at the Fondation Bodmer. So, through a combination of the digitized manuscript, and commentary by Larrington and Fries, I was able to examine this remarkable text. A post-pandemic miracle. Whenever I use a digital manuscript in the classroom—where I can magnify the individual animal hairs on the parchment, to reveal both its complexity and its mammalian kinship with us—it's always a bit of a marvel. Like the Green Knight appearing out of time, ready to play.

Unfortunately, there are no illustrations depicting the magic battle, so we don't get to see Morgan—"Morgue" in this text—in all her glory. But this blank space also allows readers to fill in the outlines of the enchantress with whatever they need her to be. On fol. 168r, we're told that the mysterious Dame d'Avalon sends for the group of enchantresses: "Et lors monta la damoisiele avoec celes qui mout furent ioians et lies de cou que la dame d'Avalon avoit envoyet pour eles" (And then [Dame d'Avalon] sent for them, and they were joyful and lighthearted to receive her summons). Even though this is a competition, there's a sense of fellowship. The rival enchantresses are happy for the chance to meet and match their wills against one another. They're hoping to learn more powerful magic from this figure, in stark contrast to the ways in which they were disappointed by Merlin's knowledge. In this version, he trades sex for magic in quite a skeevy manner, and the enchantresses discuss him as a predator. This de-thrones Merlin as the archmage, giving Morgue and her community the space to have their own adventures. The *Prophésies* features a magic battle where Morgue is stripped naked by the Dame d'Avalon, and Maureen Fries reads this moment as a clear echo of misogyny. Larrington reads the magic battle as one of demonic excess, though also grounded in academia—since the character "Morgue"[6] casts spells from a book. What interests me most about this strange duel is how it plays with notions of community and rivalry. It's reminiscent of magic duels in White's *Sword in the Stone* and the 1980s fantasy film *Willow*—even if the deep obscurity of the manuscript precludes it from being an influence on either of these modern adaptations.

Sebile is dispensed with fairly early. Young and cocky, she uses her magic to envelope the Dame d'Avalon's castle in flames. But the Dame d'Avalon uses her magic ring (*anelet*) to counter the spell. Here, Sebile is only able to craft an

---

[6] By the fifteenth century at least, the phrase "pleine de morgue" signaled "full of arrogance." Though this manuscript is earlier, the author may still be playing on the sense of "morgue" as "haughty."

illusion, while Dame d'Avalon is more direct—she magics the clothes off their bodies. This understandably halts the competition, and two damsels have to bring in spare sets of clothing. It's both a low blow and a mercy—Dame d'Avalon does precisely what will shame the women most, then apologizes by bringing them replacement outfits. At this point, Larrington notes, "hearing of the other enchantresses' failure, Morgue is confident she can do better" (24). It's significant that Morgue is brought in as a pinch hitter, only after the other women have failed. There's a nod to her power and experience here, as well as, perhaps, her patience (since she waits to survey the first few rounds, before jumping into the final one). She doesn't hold back. On fol. 169v, Morgue summons up "les enchantemens y les arz" (spells and arts) in order to raise a "legion" of demonic spirits. This calls back to Medea in the *Roman de Troie*, whose mastery of magic's "art" gives her power over the realm of life and death. When the Dame d'Avalon dispenses with this, Morgue calls forth a dragon to burn her castle to cinders. Everyone is "en angouisce de morte" (scared to death) at the sight of the dragon, but the Dame d'Avalon looks past the monster. She locks her gaze, instead, on Morgue herself: "Ele voit venir maintenant Morghain entre sa maisnie lissant son livre" (And then she was able to see Morgan, among her household, reading her book). *Maisnie* could mean Dame d'Avalon's household staff, or retinue, which makes Morgan's placement doubly strange—is she hiding among the castle staff?

Dame d'Avalon sees Morgue mouthing the spell, and this sudden visibility of the enchantress—Morgan with her book, rather than Morgan, Queen of Dragons—is perhaps the most significant undressing within the competition. After "smashing" the dragon with her magic, the Dame d'Avalon brings the house down, in fol. 170r, with a signature spell: "Maintenant ist d'entre les iambes une flanbe" (then there issued forth a fiery arc from between her legs). She admits that she had to offer Merlin her virginity (*mon pucelage*) to learn this spell, which incinerates Morgan's clothes. This is after the Dame d'Avalon exposes Morgan's soft, human body, whose curves and wrinkles are put on display.

A similar moment will occur in the HBO series *Game of Thrones*, when Cersei Lannister is forced to walk naked through the streets of King's Landing. In both cases, the narrative attempts to render their bodies grotesque. But they are also realistic bodies, which bear the marks of living. While Cersei is transformed into a public spectacle in order to reinforce medievalist patriarchy, Morgue's de-robing is a curious mixture of pointed and playful—Dame d'Avalon punishes her, but immediately returns to their fellowship by offering her a new set of clothes. Kavita Mudan Finn and Jessica McCall note that Cersei's persona as a responsible queen is a "facade soon demolished" ("High and Mighty Queens of Westeros" 23), and she's eventually punished for her political maneuvering by this scene of "public penance in King's Landing . . . [a] conflation and exaggeration of actual medieval punishments" (27). Cersei's royal status links her with Morgue, whose punishment in the *Prophésies* may also be an adaptation of penance inflicted on medieval women. But Morgue's exposure here is different than it might be in the *Vulgate*, among mixed company. She is still within her community—these "dames plaines d'encantement" (women full of enchantment)—whose judgment is fundamentally different in spite of the narrator's misogynistic tone. This is similar to the magic duel between the evil Queen Bavmorda and the enchantress Fin Raziel in *Willow*. This fantasy film from the 1980s centered on an unlikely hero—a little person, Willow, played by actor Warwick Davis (who has spondyloepiphyseal dysplasia congenita). Whether the film meant this or not, it presented a fascinating subversion of the "dwarf" character in medieval romances—often a minor antagonist and othered due to appearing physically different. The show also focused on two older enchantresses, Bavmorda and Raziel, who are scene-stealing villains and cranky heroes, respectively. Raziel is likely in her seventies, and there's the suggestion that she was Bavmorda's teacher, long ago. In one, gleeful moment, like Dame d'Avalon, Raziel uses her wand to whip Bavmorda in the air, crying "na na na!" Both scenes revolve around competition, but also around supernatural community.

Morgan makes a famously cryptic cameo in *Sir Gawain and the Green Knight* (*SGGK*). I'll return to this text in Chapter 5, when we discuss Gawain as an adolescent knight. For now, I want to conclude this section by thinking about Morgan's *vult*, her intention, in *SGGK*. This anonymous fourteenth-century poem, written in a western dialect of Middle English, is often included on medieval studies syllabi. It focuses on the trial of a young Gawain, who must keep a grisly appointment with the unearthly Green Knight (who has promised to behead him). Both Fries and Heng discuss Morgan's strange presence in this poem: she's both central and marginal, the engine of conflict and the shadow that's never fully resolved. Like a double exposure, she's everywhere and nowhere in the poem, which is one of the reasons that students are often fascinated by her character. Larrington notes that a text like *SGGK* "deliberately gives us too little information to decide about Morgan" (68). She remains a wildcard. Her search for knowledge and power lays the foundations for future witches, like arch-nerd Willow Rosenberg from *Buffy the Vampire Slayer*, Sabrina Spellman, and Tiffany Aching. But who *is* Morgan in the *Gawain* poem? She doesn't appear until after Gawain has accepted the Green Knight's bargain (a blow for a blow), and he arrives at the conveniently placed Castle Hautdesert. Soon, he'll make a deceptively simple bargain with the host: both will give anything they "win" to the other. But before that fateful agreement, just as Mass is letting out, Gawain spies a beautiful lady "wener then Wenore" (more lovely than Guinevere [L945]). Beside her, and seeming to serve purely as contrast, is an older woman. The poem dwells on her aging body, just as *Prophésies de Merlin* dwells upon Morgan's curves and wrinkles:

> Rugh ronkled chekez that other on rolled . . .
> The tweyne yghen and the nase, the naked lyppez,
> And those were soure to se and sellyly blered;
> A mensk lady on molde mon may hire calle,
>   for Gode! (L953–65).

> [That other [lady] sagged with rough, wrinkled cheeks . . .
> Her eyes, her nose, her naked lips,
> So sour to see and strangely bleared;
> A truly noble lady, we might call her
>   by God!]

The poet is practically saying *pay no attention to this non-beautiful lady*, even as the description makes it impossible to turn away. Maureen Fries notes that the double-portrait "pairs Morgan as she has become with a beauty similar to what she once was" (6), rendering both women, effectively, as Morgan. As I mentioned earlier, Larrington has also argued that we're supposed to underestimate Morgan, to judge and misrecognize her, as Gawain does. This is one of the greatest spells that the poet casts on us. The sneering tone: *you could call her a lady*. But the poem never lies. You *could* call her a lady, and people do, because she's the king's sister. There's nothing wrong with her *ronkled chekez*, because she dresses modestly. In fact, she does everything to appear as invisible as possible—it's Gawain who leers at her. His youthful disdain is what paints each and every one of her unoffending wrinkles, her black eyebrows, the gaps where wimple meets soft skin. Her mouth is somehow *too much* even when she's saying nothing. The Morgue of the earlier *Prophésies de Merlin* has no trouble speaking—she uses magic words, reads aloud from books, and challenges Dame d'Avalon. This later Morgan is confined to a non-speaking part. Yet, she ultimately speaks through the host and the Green Knight himself, in the poem's conclusion. And in one evocative line, a bit later in Gawain's stay, we're told that he was entertained "by such a worthy pair / one old, the other young; / Much pleasure did they share" (L1316–17, Winny 75). The alliterative Middle English line places Gawain "bitwene two so dygne dame" (between two such dignified ladies). That sense of *bitwene* or middleness is Morgan's calling-card throughout the poem, and we'd dearly love to know more about the "pleasure" Gawain shares in the company of both women. Perhaps Morgan tells him everything, but he simply can't comprehend it.

Whenever I teach this poem, students want to un-knot (to borrow Heng's term) Morgan's motivation. That word, *motivation*, always comes up in connection with her shadowy presence. As early as 1960, Albert Friedman argued that the poet "fails to convince us that Morgan is organic to the poem" (158). One of my Arthurian students even made a meme about Morgan's motivation: it shows Felonius Gru from the *Despicable Me* franchise going through Morgan's plan on a notepad. After the Green Knight issues the challenge, the second step is "scares Guinevere to death," but the conclusion is "Guinevere lives." In the popular meme frame, Gru stares at the notepad in confusion, realizing his mistake. Several students pointed out that Morgan's motivation is flimsy for this very reason—the "plan" immediately fails, but she still goes on with Gawain's trial. We had fascinating debates about this. Does Morgan carry on with the *gomen* (game) as a challenge to chivalry? An educational exercise for Gawain? As an extended prank? An elaborate invitation for her nephew to come live with her? Larrington argues that Morgan, in *SGGK*, "offers the most complex challenge to chivalric ideals" (60). We didn't dispute this idea, but we did question what, exactly, that challenge was. Heng notes the "slippery reversals of hierarchy" ("Feminine Knots" 508) in the poem, and her conclusion about Morgan's motivation is equally slippery, open-ended: she is "the spectre of a knot" whose presence forces us to "constantly repeat the gestures of unraveling and reconstitution that are conditioned—indeed demanded—by the character of the knot itself" (509). In other words, Morgan fashions a knot that we must unravel, even though we can't—and at times, she *is* the knot. She stands in for the whole idea of close reading and criticism.

In the beginning of this chapter, I suggested that Morgan, like Merlin, could have a kind of neuro-queer rhetoric. Melanie Yergeau has described this previously as a way of communicating—and existing—that "comes into being through movement and the residues of movement, through creeping, sidling, ticcing, twitching, stimming, and stuttering" (76). Morgan certainly creeps and sidles through *SGGK*, always slightly out of frame, always avoiding our interpretation. Her knot holds things together—it isn't meant to be undone.

That clinical/academic desire to "solve" Morgan, in some ways, echoes the desire to "solve" neurodivergent people and bring them more in line with normative thinking and behavior. When we struggle to find the character's motivation—and ultimately conclude that she doesn't have any—we steal her rhetoric. We transform her into a concept, or an author's ploy, instead of admitting that her motivation could be woven into the poem itself. That Morgan might *be* the poem, enchanting us, teaching us to think divergently. Her slyness, her singularity, all connect her with the neuro-queer versions of Merlin that we've already discussed. But her approach, as an enchantress, is fundamentally different. She doesn't beat you with a stag's horns. She invites you to her castle, makes you comfortable, and then challenges everything you thought you knew about chivalry, masculinity, and magic. Morgan isn't a knot for untying—she's a *punctum*, or gathered point of fabric, signaling her own complexity. As Heng argues, this pointedness allows her to embody the very spirit of critical analysis—not solving a text, but listening in dialectic to its many embroidered voices.

The search for Morgan's motivation also reminds me of Margaret Price's anti-ableist work on "passing" in academia as a neurodivergent person. In *Mad at School*, she states that "some of the most important common topoi of academe intersect problematically with mental disability," including concepts such as "rationality . . . participation . . . [and] collegiality" (5). I certainly feel this in long department meetings, where I need to keep close control of my facial expressions, vocalizations, and movements in order to appear "collegial" at all times. Though lately, I've begun to play with a medieval fidget spinner: a coil of chainmail links that have a deeply satisfying feeling in my hand. My motivations are self-affirming. Movement helps me think, and makes a certain kind of thinking possible. My body isn't collegial in the strictest sense, because the blunt force of collegiality has already left my body bruised, and I no longer have any interest in conforming to it. Academia defines how disabled and neurodivergent people should take up space, but we can fidget out of that model.

Robert McRuer defines the oft-used term "compulsory able-bodiedness" as an actual desire of able-bodied people: "[It] repeatedly demands that people with disabilities embody for others an affirmative answer to the unspoken question, Yes, but in the end, wouldn't you rather be more like me?" (93). I'm particularly aware of this while running professional seminars for students, where we discuss topics like how to present at a conference, how to project your voice, how to occupy space. Academia's models for these activities are fundamentally ableist, and I try to short circuit the need for conformity by stressing difference instead. *Do whatever you need to do in order to be in that space.* There's no single vocal method or strategy of physical comportment. Morgan also moves through space in a curious manner, often leaping into a frame, guffawing, stealing scenes, shape-shifting, refusing Malory's implicit desire for her to "be more like me," as McRuer describes it. As a conference presenter, she'd be chaotic good under the best of circumstances, and that makes her presence all the more compelling.

When we ascribe normative motivations to Morgan, we lose the queer contours of her mind and shifting form. Price says that by labeling herself publicly as neuro-atypical, "I am trying to reassign meaning . . . [naming] myself pragmatically according to what context requires" (20). I often do the same thing by self-labeling as "weird" (or perhaps *wyrd*), so when folks protest that I'm not, I can say: *I like being weird. There's nothing wrong with it.* In the *Vulgate*, Morgan captures Lancelot and imprisons him in a dungeon, where he's forced to narrate his transgressions as paintings on the wall. Morgan's handmaiden asks her why she's done this, and Morgan replies: "I'll be glad to tell you . . . [if] by chance [his companions] come here I will take my vengeance on them gladly" (Lacy 261). She has a motive—the testing of Camelot. This is fuzzy in *SGGK*, but whatever Morgan actually desires, it doesn't need to slot perfectly into romance conventions because it's meant to productively denature those conventions. Her motivations are her own "privitee" (privacy). Similarly, young readers shouldn't need to have a single motivation for approaching these texts; rather, they should consume them for all sorts of reasons, even (perhaps especially) if they contravene ways in which academia has decided these texts ought to be read. Make Morgan your hero—she's already mine.

What emerges from these varied medieval texts is someone incredibly complex—not quite a witch, or a wizard, or a fairy queen—who survives beyond Merlin or Arthur. This unique combination of sly joy and thirst for knowledge is what creates other iconoclast witches, like Willow and Sabrina. She has an influence on witches like Willow Rosenberg from *Buffy*, and Kristina Pérez actually calls Morgan "the final girl" (1) of Arthurian literature—the one who survives—not unscathed—to tell the story. Pérez goes on to describe her as "[something] at the edge of the narrative that holds the entire Arthurian tradition together" (208). Let's look at how, in her way, Morgan holds these future witches together.

Sabrina Spellman

Chilling Adventures of Sabrina is a show that revels in its own queer excess. From her origins in the 1960s *Archie* comics, Sabrina was always an unsettling character. Her magic could be playful, or dangerous, depending on the circumstances, and it made her a non-conformist like Morgan. In her first appearance, in the 1962 issue of *Archie's Madhouse*, Sabrina says: "We *modern* witches believe life should be a ball," then smiles as she proclaims: "[Witches] can't cry." The comic adapts late medieval stereotypes about witches, and repurposes the material to create a character that's both ironic and powerful. Like Morgan, Sabrina doesn't apologize for power. The self-titled *Sabrina* comic arrived only a few years after anti-war protests in 1968, and the first few issues deal with counterculture and social norms vs. cultural autonomy. The 1990s saw a popular but safe remake—*Sabrina the Teenage Witch*—focusing on Sabrina's hijinks with her two supernatural aunts. The most enduring part of this version was the talking cat, Salem, whose sloppy puppetry imbued the show with a campiness that might have made it slightly more interesting for teens at the time. In many ways, this version felt like a gently conservative backlash against edgier teen dramas, and its lack of sexuality also served to make the magic more palatable for parents.

This background—both medieval and modern—sets the stage for the most recent TV adaptation by Roberto Aguirre-Sacasa, who makes Sabrina both individual—she's half witch, half human—and simultaneously a member of a queer family. Her fierce aunts, Hilda and Zelda, along with her pansexual cousin Ambrose, form an unconventional group—an echo of Morgan's community. But this queer kinship also plays with late medieval fears of witches organizing along the lines of a heretical family, or an unholy sabbath. In his work on the history of witchcraft, Ronald Hutton notes that by the late fourteenth century, the image of the lone witch had been refashioned into "an heretical sect in which Satan empowered its members with the ability to work harm against their neighbours on a grand scale" (177). This perceived organization was what made witches so dangerous, and it's precisely this image that *Sabrina* holds onto and subverts, by celebrating the main character's loving, odd, and often dangerous family. She has Morgan's power, along with the support and love that Morgan was denied.

The first episode asks us to envision "the town of Greendale, where it always feels like Halloween." Not only is Greendale a bit like a Renaissance fair, it also echoes the earlier point made by Carolyn Dinshaw about medievalism and its queer temporalities. Much of the show is focused on ensuring safe spaces for characters who don't fit in, with the most pressing case being that of Theo, a trans boy who insists upon being acknowledged with dignity. Theo also has a gender-nonconforming relative, Dorothea, who appears to him as a ghost. This recalls Bychowski's argument about trans individuals persisting under the radar in medieval literature, only in Theo's case, his ancestor is able to communicate with him. The show doesn't always handle this character well, but through Dorothea, it does manage to create a trans lineage for Theo, so he can feel as though he belongs to a community.

Sabrina is in a unique position as an insider-outsider, since the witch community doesn't accept her, while her human friends don't quite understand her. Aunt Zelda wants her to be more of a proper witch, and she channels Morgan's wicked joy as she celebrates Satan and "the extraordinary delicious gifts he bestows upon us." Hilda is more subtly supportive of Sabrina's attempts to mainstream, though in a particularly searing moment in the second episode, she reveals her daily anger as both a witch and a feminist. She had no choice but to sign the Dark Lord's book, and while tucking Sabrina in, she says, with a faraway look: "[Sometimes] I dream I'm walking through the forest at the peak of dry season with a torch in each hand, and I watch the whole forest burn like so much dry kindling" (S1E2). In a later episode, Hilda kills a rival with cyanide-laced cookies, fully embodying a kind of dark, *Hansel and Gretel* realness while stating: "If you hurt my family, there will be Heaven to pay." One of the strengths of the show is that, like a medieval romance, it's immersive. *Chilling Adventures* is what Farah Mendlesohn describes as "immersive fantasy," which "presents the fantastic without comment as the norm both for the protagonist and the reader" (xx). With a character like Willow in *Buffy*, the audience is eased into the supernatural world—discovering, alongside the teen witch, that it can be glamorous but also deadly. Sabrina already lives and breathes this world, and it's a world of blasphemy and blood magic that *should* be unsettling . . . and yet? The show's tone bounces between irony and melodrama, offering up medievalist symbols of witchcraft as something deeply camp and unexpectedly moving. There are so many scenes of the Spellmans eating glorious food at an inviting kitchen table, joking, sharing stories, having lives—it suggests a horizon of happiness for anyone who is different or outcast. This aligns with José Esteban Muñoz's argument about how queerness is always on the horizon: "We are not quite queer yet—that queerness, what we will really know as queerness, does not yet exist" (22). If we look forward to queerness—whether at the dinner table, or in a classroom—then we get to have a future and we need to stay alive for that ever-transforming moment.

In Season 2, Episode 7 ("Miracles"), Sabrina invites her mortal friends and her witch colleagues to the same party, in an effort to integrate her two worlds. There's a throwaway scene of two male extras sharing a kiss—a surprisingly rare moment on any show, let alone a show aimed at teens. It's a bit of asynchronous queerness. Not serving a storyline—just delightful background. Sabrina observes to Nick: "Witches and mortals together tapping the same beer keg . . . why can't this be the future?" Like Morgan, Sabrina is challenging the rules of her magical society, and questioning why mortals and witches can't live in community. The show adapts a medievalist framework here that's forward-looking. Elements like prophecy, even eschatology, combine to create a queer timeframe where binaries like mortal/witch break down. As Patrick Cheng observes in *Radical Love*, his work on queer theology: "Numerous boundaries . . . [are] dissolved and erased by radical love as we approach the eschatological horizon" (18). *Sabrina* participates in this queering of time, by challenging notions of immortality and riffing as well on Carolyn Dinshaw's analysis of medievalism as something queerly out of time. The show's setting contributes to this temporal ambivalence, since the town of Greendale—eternally performing Halloween—mingles the 1960s-feel of the *Sabrina* comics with the more noirish tone of a monster-hunting show like *Supernatural*. All of this works with Dinshaw's definition of medievalism as something that, magpie-like, borrows from different worlds, different times, in order to stitch together something both old and new.

At the same time, Sabrina belongs to an actual medieval university—the Unseen Academy—where she receives instruction in what the head of the school calls "[the] Corpus Arcanum—a shared body of infernal knowledge." This includes late medieval magic systems, like the Ars Notoria—a supernatural notary process of using diagrams and invocations to access divine knowledge. Magic was a niche but popular area of medieval academic study, though it was generally seen as a dangerous upper-class vice. Catherine Rider notes that "magical texts . . . [seem] to have been common among scholars and students at medieval universities. In 1277 they were among the books banned from the University of Paris by the city's bishop, Etienne Tempier, and the university issued another prohibition in 1398" (111). I'll talk a bit more about this in Chapter 3, on the wizard school experience. Since *Sabrina* focuses more on the title character's dissatisfaction with her school, the show often approaches magic in a sly way—a field of medieval study that can also be queer, camp, and, to quote Zelda, "delicious."

Sabrina's cousin Ambrose is a significant part of this witching tradition that empowers outsiders in the show. He's both a pansexual warlock and a person of color who gets nearly as much screen time as Sabrina herself. Perhaps more importantly, he isn't the *sole* person of color on the show—the cast is diverse, and the main storylines don't simply revolve around white performers. Later, the show introduces Marie LaFleur, a witch of color who will become Zelda's love interest—reminding us that Sabrina's own rebellious streak is modeled not only on ancestral witches, but on the sly styles of both Zelda and Hilda. There's a casually pan vibe to Season 1 of *Chilling Adventures*—witches and warlocks all seem to be into each other—though this fades in successive seasons as the show comes to focus more on straight romance. One wonders if this was an attempt to snag queer viewers in the beginning, only to ditch these more transgressive storylines in favor of a love triangle that subtly resembles the *Morte*: Sabrina, Nick (bad boy Lancelot), and Harvey (hapless Arthur). What's left out is the queerness of the original *Vulgate*, which also included Sir Galehaut and his love for Lancelot.

Ambrose is very out, and no one seems to mind this. He wears velvet bathrobes and picks up a male warlock at a funeral by chatting about iguanas. He's weird and unapologetically so. On Sabrina's first day of magic school, he reminds her: "You will meet interesting witches and warlocks from around the world. Some of them—a great deal many of them—will be hot" (S1E4). Magic on the show is a global queer affair. We can see how *Sabrina* is trying to improve upon the racial politics of shows like *Buffy*, which was groundbreaking but also wildly inaccurate in its depiction of California in the 1990s. *Buffy* introduced a Black slayer in Season 2 (Kendra), then summarily killed her. It also identified the first slayer, Sineya, as a Black woman, mostly deprived of a voice and seen as a kind of ancestral antagonist to the show's white hero. This points to the ways in which the fantasy genre often appropriates different cultural particularities—such as voodoo, or Indigenous traditions ripped from proper context—without actually including those cultures in a meaningful way.

The show's constant negotiation of past/future and rebellion/tradition provides a unique framework for talking about medievalism, which is fundamentally about using the past to interpret the present—and seeing how the present appropriates the past. Both Sabrina and Ambrose are interested in tapping into "a different kind of magic—one that isn't based on cause and effect." They escape the confines of their own prophetic narratives, just like Morgan, whose disruptive magic, Larrington argues, can be "successful in renegotiating [Romance's] priorities" (3). At the same time, this show offers a great deal of queer potential that it can't quite deliver on. A bit like the *Morte*, it weaves in characters that queer its world, but then doesn't quite know what to do with them. Ambrose has a playful queer relationship in Season 1, but by Season 3, he's locked into a doomed romance with Prudence. Her character—a powerful Black witch who creates her own found family among the Weird Sisters—is also critically under-served when she might be a far more dynamic anti-hero within the show. While Ambrose fades into the background, Nick Scratch does remain a bit stubbornly queer throughout. He begins as a challenge to the excruciatingly dull Sabrina/Harvey romance, flirting with Sabrina while hooking up with Ambrose. By Season 3, he's locked in a physical battle with the devil that feels like a sexy/macabre illustration by William Blake, or the lost soft-core canto of Dante's *Inferno* where the hero gets an education from the devil. This campiness is darker than the 1990s *Sabrina*, but still manages to lighten the drama of the show.

Sabrina also shows us witches and warlocks of various ages—a reminder that you don't need a particular type of body to be part of this community. Audiences are meant to underestimate Aunt Hilda, who seems neither young nor powerful and lives with her more vibrant sister, Zelda. But Hilda's knowledge is razor sharp. She calls out a high school bully for his abusive tactics, and says to him: "I know why you're a bully. What those boys did to you at summer camp" (S1E9). She seduces a werewolf, single-handedly protects Sabrina's high school from an evil coven, and helps Ambrose to astral-project on a date with a warlock. But we're meant to underestimate her, as we underestimate Morgan le Fay. The presence of Zelda and Hilda creates a continuum of magical role models for Sabrina. The show subverts stereotypes of witches as either old crones or hyper-sexual women, just as Morgan herself often hovers between appearances. Zelda's constantly burning cigarillo and shades, her powerful snark, creates a dynamic model for Sabrina to emulate. But Zelda is also a contradiction: someone who deeply honors the traditions of witchcraft, while simultaneously being a no-fucks-giving witch capable of upsetting the whole coven. Late in Season 3, when she enters into a relationship with Marie, Zelda reminds the audience—and Sabrina—that witches are fundamentally queer. Not just their desires, but their methods, and their minds. Zelda can listen to her ancestors, while still blazing a new path in the celestial sky.

Morgan can also be read as a supernatural auntie—someone we're meant to underestimate until it's too late. When she appears in the *Prose Merlin*, she's described as "a young lady, very cheerful and merry, but her face was very somber; she had a rounded build, not too thin" (Conlee 25). The narrator could just as well be describing Aunt Hildie, who's quick with a joke and a wink, but will also poison you with shortbread if you defy her. As Morgan shifts in the late medieval period from a healer to a mistress of demons, she, like Sabrina, gains a devilish family that aligns her with the witches in *Sabrina*. In his German adaptation of *Erec and Enide*, Hartmann von Aue describes Morgan as always changing, "indifferent as to whether she lived in the fire or . . . [in] the dew . . . [She] had kin deep in Hell: the Devil was her companion" (cited in Larrington 11). As a medievalist show, *Sabrina* explores similar witches with "kin deep in Hell," trying to live somewhere between the fire and the dew. Like Morgan, Sabrina depends upon her kin, and learns to appreciate the support she gets from her loving, infernal family.

Sabrina also has to balance high school with the lessons of the Unseen Academy. In the optimistic opening to Season 2, she tells Zelda that "the academy's curriculum is just more rigorous and rewarding than Baxter High" (S2E1). The school is a demonic inversion of high school, where students casually gather around a statue of Baphomet, the devil in goat form, to discuss homework and who's dating whom. The show plays with a concept like Hogwarts by reimagining it as a devilish school where *all* of the classes are the dark arts. But it's also a community of witches and warlocks who have fashioned this culture to escape oppression. When witch hunters invade the school near the end of the season, it's presented as an assault on their community. There are also several plot lines involving Sabrina using her hybrid knowledge to subvert the school's own curriculum. She demands to be named "head boy," and engages in potion-making and a trivia contest that she eventually wins through the help of her sympathetic classmates. She uses magic to get Theo on the boys' basketball team at Baxter High, and—more seriously—lends Theo a charm to seriously injure one of his bullies. Theo says: "I was just so angry . . . [angrier] than I've ever been before" (S2E2). Theo's anger is shaded by vulnerability, since the entire basketball team has been bullying him. What's interesting is that the student who instigates the bullying later apologizes to Theo. A bit like Malory's *Morte*, the show remains interested in recuperation for its characters. In spite of high school structures that often make empathy impossible, the characters still find ways to connect with each other.

There's an unexpected sweetness to *Chilling Adventures* that, perhaps, borrows from its 1990s incarnation. Near the end of Season 1, Theo has begun presenting exclusively as male, and needs help with his tie. Harvey—who never has a trace of judgment about Theo's transition—helps him with the knot while offering him advice about the prom. They stand in front of the mirror for a moment, two guys on a spectrum of masculinity, easily sharing space. Their reflections offer a living space for trans and nonbinary viewers who may be grappling with their own looking glasses. This recalls Gutt's discussion of mirroring angles and looking queerly. Theo eventually gets a love interest—Robin Goodfellow—who seems to be the embodiment of Shakespeare's fairy, Puck. Though their physical relationship is more tame than the show's straight partnerships, they share a sweet outsider intimacy with each other. Robin rejects his community to be with Theo, and their relationship is something in Theo's life that doesn't revolve around Sabrina. Robin is Theo's alone.

In S2E2 ("Lupercalia"), Theo comes out to his dad as trans, and explains that he's going to present as masculine from now on: "I feel more myself in boy's clothes . . . [I'm] a boy. I feel good when people call me 'he.'" His connection to Dorothea strengthens his self-presentation, and he even attempts a spell of metamorphosis in S2E4. The spell fails—revealing that magical transformation has its limits—and Theo continues to live as himself, without magic. Given his lack of powers, Theo is actually the most ordinary of Sabrina's friends. A bit like Xander from *Buffy*, he's seen as the default boy of the group, which is quietly radical in its own way. His explanation to his father, about why he needs to present as a boy, echoes the words of another historical trans man: Lou Sullivan, who kept diaries from 1961–1991. At the age of thirteen, he describes who he wants to be, and we can read this as a kind of spell—Sullivan casting himself into being:

> I wish I was a boy! God, do I want so bad to roam . . . [I] wanna look like what I am but I don't know what someone like me looks like. I mean, when people look at me I want them to think—there's one of those people that reasons, that is a philosopher, that has their own interpretation of happiness. (38; 40)

I imagine Grisandolus thinking the same thing—and he does get to roam, fighting in tournaments and seeking out Merlin.

Morgan also roams throughout the *Vulgate*, impossible to confine for long. In Book 8, she steals the magical scabbard of Excalibur and replaces it with a counterfeit, so that Arthur will fail in battle against the knight Accolon. When this plot fails, she steals the scabbard and throws it into the lake. But she's worried about being detected by Arthur's knights, so she turns herself and her allies to stone:

> Then she cast her spell and turned them all to stone—ladies, knights, and horses—so that if you had seen them, you would truly have thought they were made of the natural stone . . . [and] Morgan was also turned to stone, but not so that she could not undo her spell any time she wanted. Anybody who saw them at that moment would have said that truly they were people of stone. (*Lancelot-Grail* 8:204)

We see here that Morgan's transformative magic can create a seeming impossibility: living stone. What does that feel like? We might think of stone as cold and unyielding, but in his work on stone in medieval studies, Jeffrey Jerome Cohen says the opposite. Stones are "ancient allies in knowledge making . . . [neither] dead matter nor pliant utensil" (*Stone* 4). He cites Stonehenge as a structure that impresses itself on human consciousness, arguing that "stone brings story into being" (ibid.). Morgan's shape here is more liquid than it first seems. She spells herself into a new form, just as Theo re-weaves himself to "look like what I am" (Sullivan 40). Magic may sometimes fail, but enchantresses like Morgan teach us that bodies are meant to transform. This reminds me of a recent Tweet by] @HamletHologram: "If every single person transitioned that would still be fine" (July 12, 2020). These characters are always transforming and challenging the structures that attempt to confine them. Sabrina also challenges the very concepts of high school and witch school by transforming their curricula to suit her needs. She turns, instead, to the magical knowledge passed down by her aunts, as well as the messages she receives through dreams—a literal ghostly education. The result is a bit like medievalism itself: Sabrina borrows from multiple areas, while rejecting the sexism of the traditional academic space, in order to forge something new. This places her alongside other witch characters in YA literature who learn through matrilineal knowledge rather than university, including Tiffany Aching in Terry Pratchett's *Discworld* novels (more on her in a moment), and Roddy in Diana Wynne Jones's *Merlin Conspiracy*, who learns magic through the consciousness of an Iron Age witch—all of her spells are encrypted as flowers. In this way, the show presents us with a medieval liberal arts tradition, but ultimately rejects it in favor of family wisdom, passed down by those "kin deep in Hell."

Morgan le Fay is invoked on *Sabrina* as part of a long line of witches, from the ancient Greek figure Hecate (a patron of witches) to the biblical Witch of Endor. Even Anne Boleyn is included in the list, subverting the Tudor charge of witchcraft against her by suggesting that she really did have power. There's a staggering amount of horror intertext in the show, as documented in a 2018 article by Hanh Nguyen for *Indiewire*—including numerous references to witches and other horror divas. Because the idea of the witch transforms so drastically between the medieval and early modern eras, *Sabrina* draws upon many variations—not just Morgan and her sisters, but many Morgans, all the various and wild adaptations of her that make the character so enduring. The witch lives in adaptation, and Morgan's indeterminacy as a character, her many knotted afterlives, produce a medievalist myth that allows Sabrina to carve her own path in the world of witchcraft. The show's camp sensibility, and its attention to queer, trans, and nonbinary characters, also works in tandem with the diversity of the Middle Ages. The end result is a diverse show about magic, horror, and adolescence that can also work as an unexpected teaching tool for showing the figure of the witch through time. When we trace Sabrina's rule-breaking and quest for knowledge back to figures like Morgan, we can make medieval magic come alive for students, and point to a diversity of enchantresses who should not be underestimated. This lineage of ancestral witches also reveals that magic-using women have always existed, and Sabrina has access to their power and knowledge.

Tiffany Aching

The final part of this chapter will consider Tiffany Aching, from Terry Pratchett's enormously popular *Discworld* series, who grows from a ten-year-old witch in training to a formidable practitioner in her own right over the course of the series. Like Sabrina, Tiffany rejects a more structured tradition of magic, choosing instead the lessons passed down by her grandmother, Granny Aching. In a forthcoming chapter in Noone and Leverett's volume *Terry Pratchett's Ethical Worlds*, Kathleen Burt notes Tiffany's identity-based quest in *Wee Free Men*: "In order to beat a creature who uses illusions and doubt as weapons, Tiffany is forced to become aware of the difficulties and realities of identifying as a witch" (80). Tiffany serves as a counterpart to male wizards in the *Discworld* series, like the male wizard Rincewind, and her distance from the wizard's classroom serves to illustrate how magic is segregated by gender in Pratchett's world. In her article on women's relationships in the Aching books, Mary Jeanette Moran notes that witchcraft diverges from wizardry—rather than a structured education, it becomes "a mission of caregiving carried out primarily by women" (269).

Much of Pratchett's tongue-in-cheek narration throughout the novels confirms this by showing how male wizards have the privilege of dealing with spellbooks, while witches deal with reality. Moran's analysis reveals the importance of kinship among these witches, and this connects back to Morgan's place among other enchantresses in the *Vulgate*. Malory's late medieval sexism—driven as it is by growing polemical tracts designed to punish women—attempts to remove Morgan from this earlier community. But he can't quite manage it, since she still remains a queen among queens. In *The Shepherd's Crown*, Nanny Ogg tells Tiffany: "[Witchcraft's] not about shiny charms. Not about books. It's about bein' a witch to the bone in the darkness, an' dealing with the lamentation an' the tears. It's about bein' *real*" (78). Tiffany and Sabrina are very different practitioners of magic, though they both share the burden of saving the world at a young age. Sabrina inherits a world of witchcraft that she doesn't fully understand—a world she must reconcile with her desire to be an unremarkable teenager. Tiffany doesn't have two magical aunties to raise her with magical traditions, but she does have Granny

Aching, who runs the agricultural community known as the Chalk[7] with a firm but quiet rule. By the end of the series, Granny Aching is recognized as one of the "queens of wisdom" (*The Shepherd's Crown* 290), passing down both mystical and practical knowledge to her daughters and granddaughters. But in *The Wee Free Men*, the first novel in the Aching series, she's described merely as a silent, steady presence in Tiffany's life:

> [Grandma Aching] was the silence of the hills. Perhaps that's why she liked Tiffany, in her awkward, hesitant way . . . [Granny] Aching wrapped this silence around herself and made room inside it for Tiffany. (31)

Tiffany is also an awkward, serious child who asks too many questions, and so Granny Aching becomes what we might think of as a communication role model. She teaches Tiffany the value of silence and observation, the care with which words can be chosen, and the variety of magic as a force beyond books and academia.

Part of Pratchett's subversive project with the Aching books is to uproot magic from its high fantasy (and male-dominated) roots, and allow it to dwell within the space of the uncanny. Some of Tiffany's magic is epic, but some of it is a series of everyday choices that add up to living ethically. As she remarks in *Wintersmith*—a novel detailing her journey from apprentice to practitioner—"Witching was turning out to be mostly hard work . . . [There] was no school and nothing that was exactly like a lesson" (19). Witches visit each other, maintain relationships, and tend to vulnerable people who need help with daily tasks. They cut toenails, deliver babies, and stand vigil over the dead. They also bury each other, and maintain community by ensuring the dignity of witches everywhere. In their chapter on the Aching novels, Haberkorn and Reinhardt argue that this type of magical/mundane practice encourages "inquiry and critical thinking" beyond the space of the classroom, because "a witch must be nosy, inquisitive and direct . . . [and] should not be afraid of dealing with unpleasant responsibilities she never asked for" (Battis, *Supernatural Youth* 50). Magic in this series is about what Moran describes as "feminist relationality" (259), which becomes an integral part of being a witch and saving the world.

We can see this type of care in contemporary neurodivergent communities as well. When Sarah Kurchak recently reviewed the Netflix reality show *Love on the Spectrum*—designed to showcase the pitfalls of dating while autistic—she offered

---

[7] The Chalk has some similarities with medieval Scotland, and incorporates feudal structures, though in many ways it appears to be out of time—which brings it even further in line with Dinshaw's queer atemporality.

a thoughtful criticism of the program and its motivations. In her *TIME* article, she describes the show as "seemingly well-meaning and intermittently charming," but qualifies this by saying that the show "doesn't accurately reflect the autistic community in terms of race, gender, or sexuality" ("The Promise" n.p.). The couples are almost entirely straight, which ignores the common connections between autistic, queer, and trans communities. Kurchak ultimately wonders if neurotypical audiences will sympathize with the autistic individuals, or simply see them as entertainment. Within days of her article being published, it was quoted out-of-context by Australian Netflix, who edited her comments to make it appear as though an autistic cultural critic was endorsing the program.

I bring this up as an example of fellowship because of the support that Kurchak received on Twitter from people on the spectrum. Netflix's attempt to normalize the program actually created a nuanced online discussion among neurodivergent people, who could weigh in on their own dating experiences, and the ways in which they felt popular culture often made neurodiversity a spectacle. If we see Netflix as the "official," academic side of things, then Autistic Twitter created the practical magic: a response as varied and hybrid as the strategies that Tiffany and Sabrina were taught by their crafty relatives and ancestors.

While Sabrina's medievalist world is a dark adaptation of the medieval classroom, Tiffany lives in a medievalist world far from crowded cityscapes or unseen academies. We're reminded many times that the Chalk is in her bones, while also being told that the unstable surface of the Chalk doesn't normally produce witches. In this sense, both Tiffany and her grandmother are little miracles, sprung from a matrix of fossils, loose earth, silent rock. They are shepherds and farmers above all else, and Pratchett is able to subvert the traditional "farm boy turned hero" narrative of high fantasy by making his hero a shepherdess and a midwife. The blurry feudal structure of Discworld is always an object of criticism for Tiffany and Granny Aching, who mistrust these power structures because they have to deal with the consequences of their inequality. We learn at the beginning of *The Wee Free Men* that the Chalk is technically under a baron's jurisdiction, but really, it's Granny Aching who runs the community. In a formative moment, Tiffany remembers when Granny Aching witnesses a man beating his donkey in the village. Rather than appealing to the baron,

> Suddenly, so fast that her hand was a blur, Granny Aching sliced [the whip] across the man's face twice, leaving two long red marks . . . "[Hurts], don't it," said Granny pleasantly . . . "[If] I put out the word you'll have no business in my hills. Be told. Better to feed your beast than whip it . . . [Someone] has to speak up for them as has no voices."
> (187–88)

This lesson becomes a pillar of Tiffany's own witch practice. On the Chalk, a witch's word is her bond, and a witch's trust is more powerful than a medieval court. Though this trust in the word borrows from feudal conventions, it also remakes them, valuing women's words instead of the authorizing seals of barons.

Tiffany's first adventure, in *The Wee Free Men*, is focused on getting her little brother back from an evil fairy. It's also about her education as a new witch, and how she brings Granny Aching's own teachings to bear, in order to create something new. Her primary educator in the book is Miss Tick, who teaches her the rudiments of witchcraft (as it turns out, wearing a pointy hat is part of the overall performance). But Granny Aching also serves as a ghostly educator, whose past lessons inform the type of witch that Tiffany wants to become. Pratchett draws clear lines between Tiffany and Granny Aching—both are observant and logical, both prefer the silence of the Chalk, and both are extraordinarily focused on their duties. Tiffany notes that Granny Aching *practiced* silence in a way that was inclusive: "[She] wrapped this silence around herself and made room inside it for Tiffany" (31). After Granny Aching dies, Tiffany longs for that shared silence: "I want her back so much, because she didn't know how to talk to me and I was too scared to talk to her, and so we never talked and we turned silence into something to share" (121). In a way, the two fail to communicate, but that failure becomes a best practice—a gift. They dwell within each other's awkwardness and forge a language as spare and durable as the Chalk itself. In *Autistic Disturbances*, Julia Miele Rodas describes "the enduring cultural association between autism and silence" (36), which leads to exploitative organizations like Autism Speaks which claim to speak for us. Regardless of whether we view Granny Aching as neurodivergent or not, her silences are valued, and become a form of teaching and what Tiffany calls "holding."

We can model this type of holding space in the medieval studies classroom, as well. I've started including a section on my syllabus that describes my own experience of neurodiversity, my various anxieties and environmental issues, while pointing students to resources. By unmasking myself a bit, I can make space for students who might be otherwise hesitant about asking questions or talking about their own identities. Holding space in neurodivergent terms also means ensuring that this community doesn't simply refer to one specific type of individual: that is, a straight, cis white male with talents that are culturally valuable, such as physicist Sheldon Cooper from *Big Bang Theory*. Neurodiversity includes many queer minds, all types of cognitive difference, and instructors can't assume that their neurodivergent students will follow some kind of template. We need to create pathways between experiences: autism, ADHD, OCD, anxiety, depression, and other mentalities which the academic system tends to ignore. Women and nonbinary people on the spectrum are going to have different needs than cis men, and students are often afraid to vocalize what they need for fear that these accommodations won't be honored (or worse, that instructors might retaliate against them). Holding space in a classroom for these conversations can look a lot like a supportive witch's coven. Just as Tiffany learns that there's no one way to be a witch, academics need to learn that there's no one way to be neurodivergent in class. We all wear very different hats, and some are invisible.

Granny Aching tries to model both care and efficiency for her granddaughter, even when she struggles to communicate or find common ground. She's slightly baffled by conversation, but understands kinship. When she does finally utter more than a sentence, it turns out to be a description of something curiously mundane: her tobacco. This is one of many anachronistic flourishes in Pratchett's medievalist world, which allows him to poke fun at the high fantasy tradition. As she describes the image of the sailor on her tobacco wrapper, Granny Aching manages to describe the lure of adventure, side by side with the pull of home:

> "That's 'cos the bo-ut is just where you can't see it . . . [He's] got a bo-ut for chasin' the great white whale fish on the salt sea . . . [He wants] to catch it . . . [But] he never will, the reason being, the world is round like a big plate and so is the sea and so they're chasing one another, so it is almost like he is chasing hisself. Ye never want to go to sea, jiggit. That's where worse things happen. Everyone says that. You stop along here, wheres the hills is in yer bones." (*Wee Free Men* 142)

Like Merlin, Granny Aching delivers a prophecy here. Over the course of the series, Tiffany will travel to fairy realms, dreamscapes, castles, frozen landscapes, and disreputable magic shops. But *The Shepherd's Crown*, the final book in the series, sees her firmly rooted in the sketchy soil of the Chalk, precisely where she began her journey as a witch. She eventually finds a companionate and romantic relationship at the end of *The Shepherd's Crown*, with a shy medical student who respects her job as much as she respects his. But ultimately, she heeds Granny Aching's advice to "stop along here, wheres the hills is in yer bones." Tiffany chooses her job as a witch over having a more traditional relationship, and builds a permanent home on the Chalk to follow in Granny Aching's footsteps. She maintains the relationship long-distance, but it's just one part of her life. Janet Croft notes that much of the series is about "the training of a young person in how to use his or her budding talents wisely" (129). Male wizards in Discworld practice their craft in giant cities like Ankh-Morpork, while witches like Tiffany apply their talents to community-building and the practical business of running a village. She does manage to save the world several times, but her mission becomes passing down knowledge, "Aching to Aching, down the generations" (*The Shepherd's Crown* 290). Like an ache, a witch's magic stays with her, deep in the body. People with chronic pain (myself included) can sympathize with this ache, which is also a part of us. Sometimes magic is inseparable from pain, and we need to hold space for that as well, as part of our existence. Tiffany weaves Granny Aching's silences, her competencies, and her ethics into a position where knowledge is more important than magic. By attending to births and deaths, she confirms the witch's understanding that "the start and finish of things was always dangerous, lives most of all" (*Wintersmith* 141).

As a character, Tiffany might resonate with a variety of neurodivergent readers. The traits and knowledges shared by Tiffany and her grandmother—social awkwardness, blunt honesty, attention to detail, analysis and rejection of norms—tend to be the very things that make a successful witch. They're also social "problems" that can be turned into strengths, as discovered by many adult geeks who still remember childhoods that were awkward, alienating, and sometimes even traumatic. Certainly, kids who are neurodivergent—including kids on the spectrum, with ADHD, or other forms of neurological complexity—might sympathize with Tiffany's singularity. She's constantly thinking about her place in the world, and about her own thoughts, in a way that places her at meta-cognitive distance from other characters in the series. *The Wee Free Men* begins, in fact, with Tiffany's self-conscious observation that "[she] sometimes feels she is nothing more than a way of moving her boots around" (6). We also learn that she's read the entire dictionary—one of the only books in Granny Aching's collection—from beginning to end because "no one told her you weren't supposed to" (4). When reading in a fairy tale that a monster's eyes are the size of dinner plates, Tiffany demands to know the exact diameter of these metaphorical plates.

Tiffany's mentors—Miss Tick, Granny Weatherwax, Nanny Ogg—explain to her that this meta-cognitive way of thinking is particular to a witch's rhetorical toolkit. She learns that Second Thoughts are a form of philosophical analysis (thinking about thinking), while Third Thoughts are "thinking about how I think about what I'm thinking" (*The Wee Free Men* 194). The "wee free men" of the book's title—known as Feegles, who are a bit like Brownies—also have a wise woman of their own called a kelda. She says to Tiffany: "Ye've got that little bitty bit inside o' you that holds on, right? The bitty bit that watches the rest o' ye" (131). This part that "holds on" is a neuro-queer rhetoric that observes, analyzes, and collapses boundaries between self/other. The bitty bit of yourself that floats free from conversation and imagines what it *means* to have a conversation at all. In *A Hat Full of Sky*, we discover that Tiffany thinks in pictures rather than words: "She'd *always* found it easy to see herself, at least in her head. All her memories were like little pictures of herself doing things or watching things . . . [There] was a part of her that was always watching her" (10). She can't help but observe herself, a body/mind trying to find a place in the world. In his essay on composition and disability studies, Cody Jackson argues that "disabled bodyminds—disabled rhetoricians and compositionists—are oftentimes bodied forms of round pegs attempting to enter the square hole of disciplinarity" ("How Disability Labor Justice" n.p.). Granny Aching's particular style of composition, with its valued silences and queer edges, shows that you can be a round peg and still compose yourself, entirely, humanly.

Part of this acceptance of the non-traditional, I'd argue, comes from the epic temporal context of witches and wizards. Sabrina constantly has to think about the world ending, and how eschatology will collapse all the boundaries that make physical and social interaction meaningful. In medieval texts like *Sir Gawain and the Green Knight*, Morgan le Fay's mind is a complex knot that has to consider past, present, and future as these various horizons loop and thread into one another. Merlin thinks in prophecies, which doesn't exactly make you sociable (since no one wants to hear about how they'll die three times before sundown). Granny Aching, as well, is visibly uncomfortable in social settings, and we could explain this by citing the fact that she sees beyond the veil of reality. But both Tiffany and Granny Aching are also, at their core, nervous, hyperaware, and sensitive individuals who don't follow the neurotypical rhythms of conversation. They remain themselves in every interaction.

In *Wintersmith*, Tiffany notes: "[Witches] looked up above the everyday chores and wondered, What's all this about? How does it work? What should I do? What am I for?" (139). These are common questions for kids, who are always interrogating the fabric of the universe and the maze of social relations that they'll one day be expected to participate in. They're also common questions for folks on the spectrum—myself included—who ask "what should I do?" on a regular basis when confronted with the accepted rhythms of conversation, pedagogy, and active listening. It's a relief, to me, that witches ask the same kinds of critical questions! Tiffany often defies the world's head games—what Pratchett calls "headology"—by stubbornly insisting on being herself. This happens when an evil fairy plays actual head games—in effect, she traps Tiffany in her own mind. As Tiffany attempts to rescue her baby brother, the elf queen taunts her: "You never loved him. You have a heart like a little snowball. I can see it . . . [All] a witch cares about is what's hers" (223–24). She tries to frame Tiffany's self-knowledge as selfishness, her critical distance and inquisitive nature as a lack of human connection. This ties deeply into discussions of empathy, which are often weaponized against people on the spectrum. But in the end, Tiffany responds by being defiantly herself:

> The anger rose up joyfully. "Yes! I'm me! I am careful and logical and I look things up I don't understand! When I hear people use the wrong words I get edgy! I am good with cheese. I read books fast! I think! And I always have a piece of string! That's the kind of person I am!" (256)

I think of this as a witch's neuro-queer manifesto. Tiffany doesn't apologize for reading too much, thinking too deeply, feeling upset when someone uses the wrong definition. She wants, always, to be understood on her own terms. The anger in her response is also a scream of joy, a claim to individuality and human dignity. Sabrina Spellman also wants something similar—to exist as both a witch and a human, ordinary and extraordinary. Being a witch means thinking differently, even feeling differently, from those around you. It means always having a piece of string, always choosing reality over metaphors, always needing to measure twice so you can cut once. In her comedy special *Douglas*, Hannah Gadsby says that being diagnosed with autism was liberatory: "It felt like I'd been handed the keys to the city of me." Like a key turning in a medieval gate, this self-knowledge re-alters the world. Gadsby also describes the people on the spectrum who recognized her, even before she knew herself. They were saying: "I have a piece of information you seem to be missing. You may or may not be ready to hear this information, but I'll tell you anyway, because knowledge is power." A moment of wizards recognizing one another. And for Tiffany, that knowledge—the certainty of who she is—becomes bound up in her own magic as a witch. She is a witch precisely because she understands herself.

There's a queerness in the perspective that Tiffany describes. She inhabits a mind and body that don't necessarily line up with her society's expectations. And plenty of neurodivergent people identify as queer, trans, and nonbinary. The whole point of a concept like neuro-queerness is that it creates connections between how we think, how we desire, and how we feel embodied as humans. In her 2020 memoir, Sarah Kurchak draws a firm link between autism and queerness: "I firmly believe that heteronormativity is a curse for everyone. It's a particularly harmful lens through which to discuss autism and love, though, because we are significantly queerer than non-autistic people" (*I Overcame My Autism* Ch 6). I mention this not to speculate on Tiffany's sexuality, but to connect open desires with neuro-queer thinking. Witches are certainly queered in the sense of being "othered" in the series, but Pratchett also argues for their radical humanity. As Granny Weatherwax observes in *A Hat Full of Sky*: "If you don't know when to be a human being, you don't know when to be a witch" (324). Being a human, then, in Pratchett's world, is about being rhetorically different and critically thoughtful. It's an idea passed down by generations of witches, always changing and unbound by kings or the rules of fairy tales.

Your witch's hat doesn't need to look like anyone else's. As Tiffany learns: "The only hat worth wearing was the one you made for yourself" (332). Radical individuality is power in this series, and that is a gift to marginalized readers who may be exhausted from passing or trying to blend in. In a move that frustrates normative expectations, Tiffany settles for a non-traditional, long-distance relationship, in order to continue with the demands of her job. She even takes on a nonbinary apprentice, Geoffrey, who tells her: "I've never thought of myself as a man, Mistress Tiffany. I don't think I'm anything. I'm just me" (*Shepherd's Crown* 150). Tiffany proves that witches and wizards don't have to be defined by tradition, and that being different can be a supernatural act. This paves the way for readers with many different minds, and many different bodies, to see possibilities for empowerment in Discworld.

Since both Tiffany and Sabrina ultimately reject a traditional curriculum, what do these texts ultimately have to say about the wizard school tradition? Isabel Capdevila makes the point that Pratchett is actually proposing a more diverse and age-inclusive model of participatory education among witches: "[Pratchett] subverts the prejudices against the elderly, especially elderly women, that are prevalent in the present moment and validates the right of the old crone to be the protagonist" (59). Through a mixture of humor and sly criticism, he valorizes characters like Granny Weatherwax and Nanny Ogg, without romanticizing them. We see them as a both ordinary and mystical continuum, of which Tiffany is already a part. One day, Tiffany will have the same complaints as Granny Weatherwax, and will field an even greater understanding of "the algebra of mourning" (*The Shepherd's Crown* 86). In the same way, Sabrina will eventually occupy a role similar to Aunt Hilda and Aunt Zelda, instructing younger witches and dealing with ageism herself. Both series apply equal value to women of all ages, while arguing that more traditional classrooms might not reflect the diversity of knowledge practices that a witch actually needs to be successful and supported within their community. The Unseen Academy doesn't fulfill Sabrina's desires for inclusive education, and so she learns from her families, both biological and chosen. Tiffany buries her mentor—Granny Weatherwax—and then carves out a space as both a midwife and a community educator.

Like Sabrina, Morgan has both an academic and a more organic side. Monmouth's version of Morgan is educated in the liberal arts tradition—more on that medieval structure in the next chapter—while Malory imagines that Morgan has learned necromancy in an evil nunnery. What we lose, over the passage of centuries, is that sense of kinship that Morgan has with her sisters, benevolently ruling their sacred island. But even in late medieval texts that try to reduce her, Morgan unites these two elements of her story. She has education to negotiate complex structures of chivalry, but she also has Sebile and other enchantresses, who remind us that a magical community exists beneath the surface of Arthurian literature. She's sly in the way that medieval girls weren't supposed to be—and that slyness ends up being a means of survival within a hostile world of knights and warfare. Her character balances this sense of being different, with a need to communicate and participate in courtly society, which allows her to move forward while also staying exactly who she is.

Haberkorn and Reinhardt note that Tiffany "does what a witch is supposed to do: she is watching the edges" (Battis, *Supernatural Youth* 55). Sabrina focuses on the margins as well, by supporting Theo, and arguing more broadly for an updated and inclusive curriculum for the Unseen Academy. Near the end of Season 1, Miss Wardwell urges her to sign her name in the Book of the Beast, which would essentially be signing her soul over to her devilish father. "It isn't just power," Miss Wardwell says. "It's rage. It's the desire to change the world and the will to do it" (S1E10). But ultimately, Sabrina signs her name to save her friends, and to advocate for a better world: the kind of future where everyone taps the same queer keg. Like Tiffany, Sabrina searches for a model that isn't purely based on tradition. She tells Ambrose: "I've tapped into a different kind of magic—one that isn't based on cause and effect" (S2E7).

Both series reframe what it means to be a magical practitioner, by showing that magic is just as much about forming relationships as it is about casting spells. When the character Roz is blinded by her second sight, Sabrina and her friends unite to support her. While the show's portrayal of disability as a "price" is troubling, it still manages to craft a Black character with significant powers. Magic can alter the body in unexpected ways, and witches live with this. The relationships they form thrive in a space that celebrates radical difference, and in the case of Tiffany, a neuro-queer way of thinking that collapses boundaries and "[watches] the edges." As Pratchett argues, to be a witch is, ultimately, to look up and ask: *what's this all about?* Tiffany and Sabrina both ask this question, again and again, to upset the status quo of the wizarding tradition in medievalist YA texts. Following in Morgan's iconoclast footsteps, they produce their own strategic plans for inclusive education, and re-world the classroom by showing how power can hold us, like the Chalk, producing unlikely miracles.

As we've seen, witches have responsibilities that are different from their masculine, wizardly counterparts. They're expected to maintain relationships, and to manage the physical realities of death and injury. While Merlin tends to act with impunity, Sabrina and Tiffany use their powers to maintain a delicate balance between magic and mortality. Sabrina also has to combat a sexist academy based on medieval principles of exclusion, and Tiffany finds herself doing—and appreciating—the kind of unpaid work that academic mothers are intimately familiar with. A witch's work is care work, and this upends our view of magic as something entirely radical and transformative. It can also be relational, and indeed, *must* be so, if the practitioner intends to form a community that will allow them to survive. This is similar to the care work in both queer and disabled communities, where lines of kinship often form to replace (or enhance) the support of family. In her book *Care Work*, Leah Lakshmi Piepzna-Samarasinha describes these communities as "care webs," which allow disabled people with varied identities to "get what we need to love and live, interdependently, in the world and in our homes, without primarily relying on the state or, often, our biological families" (33). Tiffany and her witch colleagues are doing something similar—bringing this community to the edges of the Chalk, in order to ensure that everyone has access to basic care.

When I take a pandemic walk around the block with another queer person—that care web is as powerful as one of Morgan's spells. When another neurodivergent person texts me a gif about sensory overload, that's part of the web, too. Not just the care web, or the internet, but the web of fate that we call *wyrd* in Old English. Wizards are known for their powerful words, but Geraldine Heng's knotted metaphor applies here in ways that pertain to the formation of multiple communities. Morgan's work, like Tiffany's, has more to do with weaving and combining living threads. Like the actual Fates in ancient Greek mythology, witches seem to hold both threads of life and death in their hands, attending humans from the dangerous beginning to the very end. Morgan's slantwise thinking—her refusal to follow the "rules" of being a woman in Arthurian literature—weaves a web of defiance and survival that all manner of readers might identify with. She didn't learn this in school. She learned it from her sisters, her fellow enchantresses, and herself. Like Morgan, we can choose to be a singularity, a knot that's vital rather than difficult. The place where many threads meet, and the story itself offers an infinity of queer reflections where we can see ourselves.

The next chapter turns to the opposite: how we "academize" magic. How male students had access to actual magic texts in medieval universities, and what these texts can tell us about how magic intersected with the experience of being a student. We'll look at two narratives in particular where medievalist YA characters challenge the structure of the magic school: Rainbow Rowell's *Carry On*, and Lev Grossman's *The Magicians*. Both of these novels blur the outlines of the heroic young male wizard by queering the story, and both feature magical academies that ultimately fail their students. By connecting these contemporary stories with medieval material on academic magic, we can query the enduring popularity of tales about the wizardly classroom: the dangers of learning magic as part of your curriculum, and the ways in which young wizards can weave an entirely new syllabus. We'll see how the ghosts of Merlin and Morgan—with their queer thinking—manifest within these contemporary adaptations of a very medieval idea: the wizard's education.

Chapter 3
Wizards in School: Queering the Magical Academy

The idea of the wizard school is a curious piece of medievalism that also has roots in medieval literature and culture. But searching for a medieval or classical origin to this tradition is a bit like searching for the philosopher's stone. There's the infamous devil's school mentioned in Bram Stoker's *Dracula* (pulled from Transylvanian myth, where the devil teaches classes on magic); or Dom-Daniel academy, an invention of the romantic era, where wizards learned spells under the waves. T. H. White's Madame Mim earns her magical degree at Dom-Daniel, though it doesn't quite help her in the end. Most of these institutions were nineteenth-century dreams, emerging from the rise in popularity of the fantasy genre during this time. But there was, in fact, a long medieval tradition where wizardry met academia, sometimes in an actual classroom. Medieval parents were worried that their children might be learning magic at school, just as parents in the 1980s were worried that their children might be playing medievalist games like *Dungeons & Dragons*. Across time, the fear is still the same—who wants a teenager wielding the dark arts? This chapter examines both the possibilities and the limits of the wizard school tradition in medievalist YA. We'll look at Rainbow Rowell's *Carry On*, and Lev Grossman's *The Magicians*, along with Ursula Le Guin's *Wizard of Earthsea* as one of the earliest YA novels to embrace this idea. I'll draw connections to medieval traditions like the magic school founded by Hercules, academic wizards in the work of Chaucer, and magic in the university classroom. We'll also get practical by looking at two late medieval necromancy manuals: *The Sworn Book of Honorius*, and the Munich manuscript discovered by Richard Kieckhefer. To survive adolescence, it seems—whether medieval or contemporary—you need to cast some spells along the way.

J. K. Rowling's Hogwarts, Lev Grossman's Brakebills Academy, the Roke School of Magic in Ursula Le Guin's *Earthsea* series, and Rowell's Watford Academy—all are part of a medievalist wizarding school tradition in YA literature. All hidden schools with magical curricula designed to mold unpredictable teens into responsible magic-users. This chapter is interested in how these YA texts borrow medieval ideas to create classrooms where characters can literally shape-shift and alter their identities. Do these medievalist classrooms succeed, fail, or find a queer space in-between? In her work on Hogwarts, Pat Pinsent notes that these schools are often focused on imparting "the right kind of knowledge of the universe," and they pivot around a lesson: "If children meddle with knowledge beyond their years, they may regret it" (29). This echoes parental concerns around teens accessing knowledge too early, including vital knowledge about their own bodily autonomy, sexuality, and gender identity.

It also reminds the reader that teen heroes are often woefully unprepared to tackle adulthood, let alone to save the world. Emily Greensleeves, a minor (but important) character in Lev Grossman's *The Magicians*, sums this up while talking to the protagonist Quentin Coldwater about the impossibility of a magic school like Brakebills: "They're just kids, Quentin! With all that power! . . . [Somebody] needs to get control of that place" (397). We romanticize the idea of kids learning magic in a hidden school—we joke about never having received our invitations to Hogwarts—but what do these schools actually represent? What lessons about power do these students actually learn, and why are we so interested in linking magic with the language of education? I want to talk about wizards in training, and what that training actually entails in a classroom. I'll also focus on wizards who disrupt or otherwise queer the classroom.

Medieval Magic Schools and the Spell-Casting Tradition

As early as the first century CE, the Syrian writer Lucian discussed teaching magic in a satirical dialogue, and ritual magic appears in some of the earliest recorded texts, like the *Epic of Gilgamesh*, written around 1800 BCE. As we've discussed in earlier chapters, there was also an early medieval tradition of spells and charms that overlapped with clerical ritual. There were clerical spells attributed to Gildas and St. Patrick, called *loricae* (from the Latin word for "breastplate"), designed to invoke God as both spiritual and material armor. The tenth-century *Lacnunga*, or "Leech-Book," mentioned in Chapter 2 for its "Charm against a Sudden Stitch," mixes practical remedies with prayers and spells. Even the riddling tradition blurs the line between puzzle and invocation. The lorica enigma of the eighth-century writer Aldhelm, for instance, describes a coat of armor that "[does] not fear arrows drawn from long quivers" (spicula non uereor longis exempta faretris). Some of these twilight spells emerge from a tradition of medieval academia, while others are clearly passed down by word of mouth. But discussion of actual magic schools will coincide with what Juanita Ruys describes as "[the] epistemological revolution sweeping Western Europe in the twelfth and thirteenth centuries" (61). The rise of magic, and the rise of the medieval university, are intertwined.

The twelfth century saw a veritable explosion of information, comparable to the dawning of the "Internet age" in the late twentieth century. There was a proliferation of classical texts—both literary and scientific—circulating as never before thanks to "a Latin translation movement that would rewrite the western curriculum" (Ruys 61). Schools shifted in both method and location, moving from cathedral-centered places of spiritual learning, to centers of medicine and law. The University of Bologna, one of the oldest schools in the world, adopted a system where students "choose their material and their teacher, and oversee their own system of learning" (Toswell 48). Scholars like Peter Abelard introduced a dialectical way of teaching—based on debate—which we still see in universities today. It was inevitable that students would also discuss angels and demons in the classroom, since, as Ruys has mentioned, these supernatural beings provided the best "thought experiments." But this also opened a troubling gateway into the realm of the supernatural. If this gateway is similar to the hell-mouth in *Buffy the Vampire Slayer*, then it seems as though we've left it wide open. Both adult fantasy literature and the YA genre are filled with stories about magical education and its dangers. And the linked fantasy/horror genres have always offered a space to address contemporary issues within a fantastic setting. Medieval texts do the same thing: the fourteenth-century *Sir Gawain and the Green Knight* comments on the problems of chivalry, and even the dangers of rural spaces, while also reassuring the reader by setting these conversations within the atemporal space of romance.

Medieval Roots of the Wizard School

One of the longest-running medieval myths—one that spread across Europe—was the idea of the magic "school" of the ancient Greek figure of Hercules. This requires some global untangling, as it represents a fusion of culture, history, and national identity. When Christian-Visigoth Spain was absorbed by the Umayyad caliphate in the eighth century, a myth emerged about the last Visigoth king, Roderic. The earliest mention of this is in the ninth-century chronicle of Ahmad ibn Muhammad al-Razi, which survives in a twelfth-century copy. In the story, Roderic—desperate to defend the city of Toledo—breaks into a mysterious structure known as *la cueva de Ércoles* (Cave of Hercules). In the earliest versions, it's called *el edificio de los Cerrojos* ("the sealed building" or "structure of many locks"). Vasilis Tsiolis notes that this magical site was located "in the basement of the church of San Ginés" in Toledo, still a tourist spot, and that the original structure was actually "a giant, open-air cistern, connected with the Roman aqueduct" (740; 736). Once inside, Roderic discovers a cave full of marvels, including a statue with an inscription that foretells his ultimate defeat by the Umayyad caliphate.

By the time King Alfonso X adapts this story to his thirteenth-century *Crónica General*, Roderic becomes Rocas, a descendent of Hercules, who discovers "todos los saberes e las naturas de las cosas e cuemo savien dobrar" (all the world's knowledge, the nature of all things, and how they should be achieved [Pidal, quoted in Tsiolis 742]). In the medieval Spanish tradition, Hercules becomes a colonizer who invaded Hispania, leaving behind his mystical treasures. Pedro de Corral's fourteenth-century *Crónica del rey don Rodrigo* (pivoting back to Roderic) describes Hercules as a magic-user whose *encantamentos* were well-known. The sixteenth-century reprinted version stages the cave as a site of wonder, a TARDIS-sized interior, presided over by a menacing statue:

> La una parte del palacio era tan blanco como la nieve. E la otra que era en dereco era mas negra que la pez, e la otra era verde como la fina esmeralda. Y en dereco della la otra parte era mas bermeja que la sangre muy clara, e todo el palacio era muy claro e mas luziéte que el cristal. (de Corral 21)

> [One part of the palace was as white as the snow. The right-hand side was blacker than pitch, while another [side] was green like a subtle emerald. And the final side was vermilion, [flowing] like clear blood, and the entire palace blazed like fired glass.]

Rodrigo breaks open a sealed chest, only to be confronted with a flaming eagle that portends his military defeat. The myth is eventually reprinted in Caxton's fifteenth-century *Recuyell of the Historyes of Troye*, spreading to England, where Hercules becomes a benign necromancer "[who] louyd bookes aboue all the Rychesse of the world." In the city of "Salamanque . . . [he made] there in the erthe a grete rounde holl in manner of an estudye. And he set there the 7 scyences lyberall with many other bookes" (Sommer 426).[1] This odd transformation from Hercules the warrior, to Hercules the marvel-worker, shifts to dark magic as both Toledo and Salamanca develop an infamous reputation for necromancy. Ruiz de la Puerta notes that, by the sixteenth century, most authors "speak of the cave as a school of sorcery" (quoted in Castillo 148), where the "downfall" of Christian Spain was initially decreed. From the early chronicle of Al-Rais, to later texts like Miguel de Luna's "true history" of Roderic, this space both endures and transforms into the first medieval magic academy. Who knew that Hercules would take the place of a medieval Godric Gryffindor?

As we've already seen with the Arthurian tradition, wizards and enchantresses have to learn their craft from somewhere—but this is often vaguely defined. Texts like the *Prophésies de Merlin* suggest an intriguing community of enchantresses who teach each other (and compete in duels of magic). But late medieval writers like Malory are cagey about the subject: he says tersely of Morgan le Fay that she "was put to school in a nunnery, and there she learned so much that she was a great clerk of necromancy" (Okun 35). Necromancy, or

---

[1] "[He] loved books above all the riches of the world . . . [in] the city of Salamanca, he made there in the earth a great round hole in the manner of a study. And he set there the seven liberal sciences, with many books" (Sommer 426).

nigromancy, shifted in meaning over time, from magic focused on raising spirits to "black" magic that concerned itself with demons—from the Witch of Endor to Morgan, essentially. There are all kinds of minor magicians and marginal witches who surface within later medieval literature: fairy queens, hags, quack-alchemists, and scholars dabbling in demonic magic. The magician of Chaucer's "Franklin's Tale" is of particular interest since his magic is linked with academia. Eve Salisbury notes that several of the Canterbury Tales present "a playful yet serious competition between youth and age, earnest and game" (148). "Handy" clerks like Nicholas, with his pile of astrological texts, are often studying love as well as the trivium. Salisbury also identifies Chaucer's squire as someone vying not for love or war, but rather "for a win in Harry Bailly's storytelling contest" (160). Chaucer gives us a spectrum of medieval adolescents, and while critics mostly pay attention to Nicholas, Alisoun, or the squire, I want to consider the young magician in "The Franklin's Tale" as an analog to college-age wizards in YA.

The uppity Franklin tells the story of Dorigen, whose husband-to-be, Arveragus, leaves her alone in Brittany. During this interval, she's aggressively courted by Aurelius, and she eventually promises him—with the slyness of Penelope—that they might marry if he can manage to get rid of all the rocks on the coast. Aurelius hires a magician to do this, and what's of most interest is the magician's scholarly background and genteel home. The brother of Aurelius recalls a student at the University of Orléans, who, like his fellow "yonge clerkes," was "lykerous / to reden artes that been curious / Seken in every halk and every herne" (L410–12).[2] *Lykerous*—lusty—draws a direct link between magic and desire. Here we have not a wise old man, or a marginal witch, but a group of privileged boys looking for "magyk natureel" (natural magic). The would-be magician is also studying law, though magic is his true passion. His forbidden spell-book contains "operaciouns" (operations) of ritual magic, just like existing medieval spell-books, though the brother condemns them as "nat worth a flye" (not worth a fly). Aurelius is more enthusiastic as he recalls "tregetoures" (tricksters/illusionists) who could conjure up boats, lions, and spring flowers. Many of these examples are echoed in real spell-books, which we'll address a bit later. Aurelius goes to Orléans and finds the young clerk, who greets him civilly in Latin. Now he's described in no uncertain terms as a "magicien" (magician)—but he lives in neither a cave nor a palace. His well-appointed home, filled with books, "lakked no vitaille that myghte hem please"

---

2 Like his fellow "young clerks," the brother of Aurelius is "lustful / to read about the arts / sought out in every nook and cranny" (all quotes taken from *The Riverside Chaucer*, edited by Larry Benson).

(L478).³ Perhaps the real spell is this magician's middle-class lifestyle, which so impresses Aurelius.

The magician conjures a variety of things for Aurelius: deer and falcons, "knyghtes justyng in a playn" (knights jousting in a plain), and even Dorigen herself, to dance with him. Then, he abruptly ends the spell by clapping his hands, saying "And farewell! al oure revel was ago" (L495–96).⁴ Richard Hillman has noted the similarity between this and the "revels" of Shakespeare's Prospero, citing "his debt to Chaucer" (426) when constructing his own popular magus figure. The "subtil clerke" (subtle clerk) uses a variety of astrological calculations to perform his illusion, which is somewhere between a "jape" and "wrecchednesse." Arveragus eventually returns, and when Dorigen tells him what's happened, he praises her honesty. Aurelius relinquishes his claim—but he still has to pay the magician 500 pounds for his service. Cursing himself and the "philosopher," Aurelius delivers the payment. But the magician, surprisingly, declines it: "I releesse thee thy thousand pound . . . / Thou hast ypayed wel for my vitaille" (L905; 910).⁵ In spite of all the suspicions of Aurelius—and the useless curses he lays upon his supernatural employer—the magician turns out to be curiously honorable. His illusions may be "japes," but much of the terrestrial world in *The Canterbury Tales* is described in similar terms—like the wobbly perspective of a drunk man, sidling home at night.

We might remember, as well, that Chaucer's own narrator is an awkward and semi-magical figure. In the prologue to "Sir Thopas," Harry Bailly remarks that the narrator "semeth elvyssh by his contenaunce, / For unto no wight dooth he daliaunce" (L13–12).⁶ This characterization of the narrator as both "elvyssh" and a "popet" (puppet) is possibly what leads him to tell the story of toy-like Sir Thopas, which Seth Lerer and J. Alan Mitchell have both described as a piece of medieval children's literature. Sir Thopas is a tiny knight, probably modeled after a child's figurine, and the story is so cloying that it's cut off mid-stanza. The host also observes that the narrator can't quite seem to settle or look anyone in the eye: "Thow lookest as thou woldest fynde an hare, / For ever upon the ground I se thee stare" (L6–7).⁷ This recalls Hoccleve's description of his own shifting feet and wandering glance in the later *Compleinte*, as we discussed in the introduction. Like the Franklin's magician, the narrator is an enigmatic figure, tied to a

---

3 "[The house] did not lack for food that might please them."
4 "Our revel has ended!"
5 "I release you from your thousand pound [obligation]—you've paid well for my hospitality."
6 "He seems Elvish [sketchy; mystical] by his countenance. For he pays no attention to one single person."
7 "It looks like you're searching for a rabbit / since you're always staring at the ground."

sort of indefinable magic and a shifting physical presence. I'd argue that this description also mirror's Yergeau's idea of a neuro-queer rhetoric as one that negotiates with space in unexpected ways. This sidling, side-stepping, possibly stimming narrator opens up an affirming space for neurodivergent readers, who may also see themselves as non-traditional storytellers and neuro-queer spell-casters.

Ultimately, in a tale designed to criticize the folly of trusting false magicians, Chaucer gives us, slyly, a true one. Now we'll turn to the ways in which these academic figures, and their schools, are adapted in YA fiction.

Earthsea and the Roke School of Wizardry

Le Guin's *Earthsea* series—which she worked on from 1968 to 2001—focused primarily on a dark-skinned wizard named Ged who attended a seaside magic school. Like Samuel Delany's work, Le Guin's fantasy literature was concerned with issues of race and class, though the disappointing 2004 TV adaptation of *Earthsea* whitewashed the main character. Maria Sachiko Cecire notes that *Earthsea* "provides a counterpoint" to white fantasy narratives, "as Earthsea is a world of predominantly non-white people, in spite of the castles" (Ch 4, N76). Le Guin has also observed, in interview, that J. K. Rowling may have gained some uncredited inspiration from *Earthsea*. Rowling's Potterverse has been criticized for its overwhelming whiteness, and in *The Dark Fantastic*, Ebony Thomas mentions: "I had trouble imagining the origin stories for *Harry Potter*'s characters of color—most of whom were relegated to the background" (Introduction). In addition to her appalling transphobia, Rowling never seemed to give much thought to making the Potterverse reflect diversity in the UK. The series never improved in this manner, as she doubled down on Harry as the protagonist, while failing to create any central characters who weren't white, straight, and able-bodied.

It's difficult to ignore the similarities between Rowling's and Leguin's worlds. Both Ged and Harry Potter are young, orphaned, precociously powerful wizards who attend magic school. Both end up being pursued by a malevolent shadow, and both have upper-class rivals (Jasper/Draco) and loyal, working-class friends (Ron/Vetch). Fantasy literature is a palimpsest of ideas, always being adapted and re-fit—perhaps Rowling, like Chaucer, was merely reframing an earlier story. Like many authors, Le Guin was inspired in turn by Jungian psychology, as well as her own publisher's request to write something middle-grade: "[I] thought about kids. Boys. How does a boy learn to be an old guy with a white beard who can do magic?" ("Ursula Le Guin Q&A" n.p.). Her second novel would focus on the priestess Tenar receiving a more cloistered education, with Ged as a supporting character. Laura Comoletti describes Le Guin's wizards as "medieval Christian priests" and "celibate males, trained in textualized lore" (114). Though it's worth noting that when Ged casts a spell that goes wrong—leaving him with a vicious shadow—he does it to glimpse Elfarran, a beautiful queen. The celibacy of Le Guin's wizards appears to be relatively recent, or only lightly enforced, since Elfarran was married to a Mage-King.

In her article on queering virginity, Lisa Weston notes that "determined marriage resistance—an integral part of medieval virginity narratives—inherently disrupts the normativity of heterosexuality" (24). In addition to resonating with asexual identities, the concept of medieval virginity can be an active decision, rather than simply a renunciation of physical ties. Medieval saints' legends often feature characters whose celibacy offers a form of radical alienation from medieval marriage, as well as sociability in general. I often describe medieval saints in the classroom as the superheroes of the Middle Ages, since their bodies have unique powers which make their faith visible. In her early thirteenth-century saint's legend, Christina the Astonishing undergoes a number of physical transformations to demonstrate her connection with the divine. In addition to avoiding all physical contact, she "fle[es] the presence of human beings with wondrous horror into deserts, or to trees, or to the tops of castles" (Stouck 439). Christina skims along the branches of trees, and at one point, hangs onto a water-wheel and lets it repeatedly douse her. She seeks out these intense experiences, choosing them over the equal intensity of physical contact. In this sense, both medieval and medievalist characters who've chosen celibacy can exist in kinship with queer readers, who challenge dominant ideas on intimacy through their own forms of connection.

Ged begins life on the Island of Gont, where he's first tutored in magic—not by a wizardly professor, but by his aunt, who is a witch. Rather than a classroom, she works magic in "a low, dusky, windowless [hut], fragrant with herbs" (*Wizard of Earthsea* Ch 1). The witch "was no black sorceress, nor did she ever meddle with the high arts." Unnamed and unlamented—she flees the village when it's attacked by barbarians—the witch feels like a deeply minor character. Like Morgan, she camps out in the margins. But she also teaches Ged his first magical lessons, and when Le Guin quotes the old village saying "wicked as woman's magic," her sense of irony is sharp. From the beginning of the *Earthsea* series, we see a consciously gendered divide between wizards and witches, just as we do in the *Discworld* novels. Witches are often expected to perform care work, while wizards are free to devote themselves to research. In a later story, Le Guin has the wizard Heleth (who taught Ged's own teacher, Ogion), muse about his mistress Ard: "I wonder what difference it made to her wizardry, her being a woman . . . Or to mine, my being a man. What matters, it seems to me, is whose house we live in" (*Tales from Earthsea*, The Bones of the Earth). In this circular way, Ged's first teacher is a woman, and his second teacher—Ogion—learned his craft ultimately from Ard.

The "house" is an apt wizarding metaphor, and it recalls an even earlier adult fantasy novel: Stella Benson's 1919 *Living Alone*. Benson's writing has largely been forgotten, but she, like Le Guin, was interested in feminist recoveries of magic and fantasy. *Living Alone* focuses on a witch who runs a boarding house for solitary people, including other witches. "Magic people are always obvious," Benson observes, "they are never Modern" (Ch 2). Her novel blends medievalism with anachronism, just as T. H. White would do with *Sword in the Stone*. The witch describes her boarding house as "a monastery and a convent for monks and nuns dedicated to unknown gods," where each cell has "a little inconvenient fireplace." Solitude is the only rule in this early precursor to a magic boarding school. Benson's novel was highly influenced by the first world war, just as *Earthsea* was influenced by the social upheavals, anti-war riots, and anti-racist demonstrations of the late 1960s. As Le Guin has observed, fantasy can't escape the political. Her young wizard, Ged, soon finds himself at the Roke School of Wizardry. Like a late medieval university, the school is part of a city—it stands in "a square rimmed on three sides by the houses with sharp slate roofs and on the fourth side by the wall of a great building . . . [a] fort or a castle, it seemed" (*Wizard of Earthsea* Ch 3). His first test is to pass through the gate by offering his true name to the porter. Once inside, Jasper serves as an icy tour-guide, leading him through "the open courts and the roofed halls, the Room of Shelves were the books of lore and rune-tomes were kept . . . [and] the small cells where the students and Masters slept." There's even a noisy dining hall, which Rowling echoes to great effect in *Harry Potter*.

Ged makes friends with a kind boy named Vetch, who teaches him more spells, including levitation: "Vetch sat cross-legged, eating roast chicken up in mid-air. One of the younger boys tried to pull him down to earth, but Vetch merely drifted up a little higher (Ch 3)." Le Guin is subtle in her descriptions of Vetch as "heavyset," and darker than Ged, but a picture emerges of a powerful, fat, and soft-spoken Black wizard, never demonized for his size. Le Guin does something similar in one of her first *Earthsea* stories, "The Rule of Names" (published four years prior to the novel), where soft, middle-aged Mr. Underhill turns out to be a dragon. In *The Dark Fantastic*, Ebony Thomas recalls wondering where the Black wizards were in the fantasy novels she grew up reading: "Had witches and wizards of color been somehow subjugated—was their magic less powerful?" (Intro). Vetch was a rare instance of a Black wizard crafted by a white fantasy author, when the genre was still forming. His kindness offers Ged a model for empathy, and even after Ged has unleashed a murderous shadow through forbidden magic, he sees that "Vetch looked at him . . . [with] no less love but more wizardry, perhaps" (*Wizard of Earthsea* Ch 4). Vetch becomes a wizardly horizon for Ged's future, someone to live up to, as they struggle through the Roke school's enchanted and dangerous curriculum. Diana Wynne Jones will also adapt Le Guin's wizard school in her novel *Charmed Life* (1977), where siblings Gwendolen and Eric attend a smaller school for magic. Both authors would influence virtually every wizard school narrative to come, including *Carry On* and *The Magicians*.

The Magicians: Magic and Disappointment

Lev Grossman's *The Magicians* is focused on the story of Quentin Coldwater, a depressed, fantasy-loving teen who describes his precarious friend group as "the nerdiest of the nerds" (4). His dreams come true when he's selected to enroll in the magical Brakebills university, though this experience quickly turns into a nightmare, as school so often does. Grossman's series was adapted for television in 2015, and my discussion will focus on a mix of episodes and sections from the first novel in the series (also called *The Magicians*—I'll refer to it as the TV *Magicians*). Both the show and the print series attempt to leave school behind when the characters enter a magical secondary world (Fillory), but I want to stay with the school narrative, in part to show how they *don't* succeed in leaving it behind. What happens at wizard school doesn't stay at wizard school—instead, it shapes their lives out of the classroom, and brings them back to campus time after time. I also want to talk about the character Eliot Waugh, who forges a complex relationship with Quentin. As I'll argue, this relationship comes into focus when we read it alongside Rainbow Rowell's *Carry On*, which also features two queer wizards in love. Both Grossman and Rowell also deal with mental complexity in a variety of ways.

Kelly Kramer's article, "*The Magicians*, Narnia, and Contemporary Fantasy," analyzes Grossman's novel as "[one that] deconstructs traditional fantasy elements like quests, and reveals them for the fallible human creations they are" (159). As Quentin learns to navigate the dangerous landscape of Brakebills, it becomes clear that the school is also designed to mirror what Robbi Nester calls "the sheltering bubble of elite institutions from which most of [Grossman's] characters have emerged" ("Do You Believe in Magic?" n.p.). In this sense, *The Magicians* becomes a sort of adaptation of queer school novels like *Brideshead Revisited* and *A Separate Peace*, with the radical difference of magic. Both of these YA texts also stress a classist experience of university, where white male characters have access to particular networks that exclude everyone else. Brakebills isn't much different, since it privileges the children of wizards, just as Ivy League schools privilege legacy applicants. Quentin's first look at Brakebills is a commonplace moment in the wizard school narrative. In *Wizard of Earthsea*, Ged is enchanted by the towering spires of the Roke School of Magic, hidden like Hogwarts on its own island. Willow Rosenberg, in the fourth season of *Buffy the Vampire Slayer*, is in awe of the UC Sunnydale library when it's first revealed to her in a majestic tracking shot.

Though this library isn't magical, it still feels that way to Willow, coming from the small town of Sunnydale. I had a similar experience when I first encountered the very modest, two-floor library at my community college. And part of making these wizardly characters accessible means recognizing that some wizards go to community colleges and state schools. Quentin emerges from a dense thicket, and is greeted by the sight of an idyllic, sheltered campus:

> In the middle distance beyond the wide lawn a large house stood, all honey-colored stone and gray slate, adorned with chimneys and gables and towers and roofs and sub-roofs. In the center, over the main house, was a tall, stately clock tower that struck even Quentin as an odd addition . . . [it] was in the Venetian style . . . [over] one wing rose what looked like the green oxidized-copper dome of an observatory. (*The Magicians* 16)

Brakebills offers the type of upper-class bonding space that's common to Ivy League universities. Fountains and quads are re-christened by students, and the whole campus has a feeling of well-worn entitlement. Students even play a campus-specific game called "Welters," which allows Grossman to refashion the athleticism of Rowling's "Quidditch" into a strategic game that's closer to chess or go. The classrooms are designed to marry opulence with medievalist tradition: "The walls of [the] room were old stone. It was full of sunlight, and it stretched back and back and back. It looked like a trick with mirrors" (24). Brakebills isn't going to have its liberal arts program cut any time soon. It's a space of power and privilege, where students like Eliot are marked by certain differences in appearance and desire.

Eliot is the first classmate that Quentin meets, and there are some subtle (and big) differences in the way that both the show and the novel deal with this pivotal introduction. In many ways, Eliot *is* the wizard school. He's internalized its myriad of social rules, he moves through its fraught campus with ease, and he's even become its ambassador. In *The Magicians*, Quentin emerges, bewildered, from a magical hedge, only to find Eliot "leaning against a tree, smoking a cigarette and watching him" (16). Quentin offers a brief physical description: "[He] wore a button-down shirt with a sharp collar and very thin, very pale pink stripes . . . [the] heat didn't seem to bother him" (ibid.). Grossman waits a few more pages to acknowledge his physical difference: "There was something about Eliot's face. His posture was very straight, but his mouth was twisted to one side, in a permanent half grimace that revealed a nest of teeth sticking both in and out at improbable angles" (18). Eliot's appearance is mentioned only a few times throughout the novel. It seems both a deeply significant part of his character, and a physical trait that isn't important to the broader story.

In a particularly cryptic scene, Quentin stumbles upon Eliot engaging in role-play with a nameless student. Both are following a well-worn script, and the student makes Eliot beg for sex, then spits in his face. As Quentin watches them have sex, he's struck by the brutal intimacy of the moment, and his position as an outsider: "He was looking directly at the exposed wiring of Eliot's emotional machinery . . . [On] some level Quentin was hurt: if this was what Eliot wanted, why hadn't he come after Quentin?" (66). This is the reader's first inkling of Quentin's bisexuality, though Quentin swiftly discards this possibility—imagining how he'd ultimately disappoint Eliot, if he *did* ask. Quentin is eighteen years old at this point in the novel, and seems to be flirting with sexual fluidity, or with the complex feelings of an intense same-sex friendship. From their first meeting, Quentin admits that "Eliot had an air of effortless self-possession that made Quentin urgently want to be his friend, or maybe just be him period. He was obviously one of those people who felt at home in the world" (19). Eliot's sexuality and unconventional appearance prevent this performance from being "effortless," but they also drive him to create multiple personae for dealing with a hostile world. Ambrose, from *Chilling Adventures of Sabrina*, has a similar struggle with public personae. His breezy, sociable manner is often at odds with his own anxieties around whether he'll find a meaningful relationship—a valid concern, given that the show keeps killing his love interests.

Eliot, perhaps more than any character, is the one who pops Quentin's romantic balloon when it comes to magic. Quentin's girlfriend Alice will later remark that Quentin is one of the last people who *believes* in magic (as opposed to just practicing it), but Eliot unravels this from day one.[8] When Quentin expresses admiration that Eliot gets to live at Brakebills, he quips back: "If you can call it living" (19). Throughout the novel, Eliot's opinion of magic remains the most critical. In a nod to *Harry Potter*, he scolds Quentin early on: "You don't just wave a wand and yell some made-up Latin" (44). He also retains what Quentin describes as "an air of magnificent melancholy" (42), which draws him to Eliot as another sad person in search of strategies for dealing with his own depression. Like Jack Halberstam's notion of queer failure—which we'll discuss in the next chapter— Eliot has turned his sadness into a style or mood. When Quentin tries to talk about using magic to help people, Eliot quickly becomes the voice of realism: "What have people ever done for me? People don't want my help. People called me faggot and threw me in a Dumpster at recess when I was in fifth grade because my pants were pressed." The TV adaptation develops this in some nuanced

---

8 Alice's blunt manner and intense academic focus led to a classroom conversation about whether she might be on the spectrum, and how the novel often sees her awkwardness as antisocial, whereas Quentin's awkwardness is meant to come off as endearing. This made us think about how men on the spectrum have very different social expectations, as opposed to women and nonbinary people on the spectrum.

ways, and I'll get to that below. Eliot's anger seems one of the clearest reflections of Dean Fogg's claim that magic is about pain:

> I think you're magicians because you're unhappy. A magician is strong because he feels pain. He feels the difference between what the world is and what he would make of it . . . [You] have learned to break the world that has tried to break you. (247)

Magic always costs something, and sometimes that cost breaks you. Eliot will break the world in a number of interesting ways, and so will Quentin. Is this what magic schools teach us? How to break the world?

Magic schools, like any other schools, offer rules for us to learn and break. College is about deepening some rules, transforming others, rejecting still more. After graduation, Quentin shares a flat with Eliot and Janet (a character who, like Eliot, is a slow burn when it comes to development). They drink and they party and they fight together, like a magical version of *Who's Afraid of Virginia Woolf?* Unlike the wizards in some stories—who are too busy saving the world to interrogate the nature of magic—Grossman's characters engage in the type of metaphysical sparring matches that we'd expect to see in a grad studies classroom, or a creative writing workshop. Eliot is particularly skeptical of religion and its impact on magic: "God save us from Christian magicians" (234). He defines the problem of magical responsibility during a drunken argument: "No one gets punished for anything. We do whatever we want, and that's all we do, and nobody stops us, and nobody cares" (235). This is what separates Brakebills from Hogwarts. If nobody cares, then what *is* magic? The characters are so desperate to find this meaning that they embark on an ill-advised quest to find Fillory, which, like grad school, results in more disappointment than answers.

I remember having conversations like this as a grad student—often at the campus pub, where we could relax a bit and take off the social mask. Why, exactly, were we doing all of this? Would there be any jobs for us? And even if there were—didn't that place us all in direct competition? Fueled by exhaustion, cheap fried food, and the cosmic energies of our anxiety, we asked each other increasingly desperate questions about the state of academia, trying to figure out what was expected of us. Like apprentice wizards, we felt beholden to supervisors who would drop tantalizing bits of information about an unseen world, then suddenly clam up and refuse to tell us any more, because we weren't considered colleagues. Our teaching and marking labor was extracted for a less-than-living wage, sometimes our ideas were even stolen, but we never seemed to get any closer to understanding what it *meant* to be a teacher within this system. Those who came from academic families had a distinctive advantage, while first-generation grad students often grappled with rules and terminology—everything from how to write a conference paper, to what outfit we should wear, what food we should eat, what topics to avoid. These young witches and wizards seem to be in a very similar position to early-career academics.

But what type of magic do these students actually learn in Grossman's "darker" version of *Harry Potter*? In a memorable scene near the end of the Brakebills section of *The Magicians*, Quentin has to invoke a "cacodemon," which becomes a part of his body. The medieval meets the modern here, as Quentin accepts invasive physical pain in order to continue his studies. The earliest use of this term seems to come from Bartholomew de Glanville's fourteenth-century *De Proprietatibus Rerum*, translated by Trevisa in the fifteenth century, as a signifier for the devil. *Caco* has a tangled etymological thread, emerging from the Greek *kakós* for "bad," though also linked to the Latin *cacāre* (to shit). This references a medieval tradition of demons being connected with excrement. Ruys cites a demonic "association with refuse" in the twelfth-century stories of Peter the Venerable, in which two demonic invaders "make their escape from the monastery by diving headfirst into the latrine" (37). The students use a magic circle to summon this demon, similar to circles invoked in medieval spell-books. But rather than crafting a demon who simply does the operator's bidding—or a demon that needs to be defeated—Grossman creates a being who shares the lives of his characters. This is similar to Ged's shadow, if the shadow had actually climbed inside the young wizard. There's an intimacy to this dark magic, which is at the very heart of the school's curriculum. In his thirteenth-century work on miracles, Caesarius of Heisterbach opens the section on demons with a nod to their seductive qualities: "Demons are called tempters, because they are either the authors or provokers of all the temptations that draw men to sin" (313). It's only fitting that Quentin's internalized cacodemon represents the seduction of the magic school itself, and the permeability of his own desire for power.

Earlier I mentioned the minor character Emily Greensleeves, and we find out that she attempted a magical cosmetic spell to change her own appearance. This has disastrous results when Alice's brother tries to reverse the spell, and in the process, becomes a demonic entity called a "Niffin" that resembles a kind of energy elemental. We see a similar link between magic/experimentation in *Buffy the Vampire Slayer*, when Willow's magical lessons grow more intense, until dark magic actually possesses her in Season 6. Her girlfriend Tara criticizes her for using spells to solve problems that actually require intimacy and communication. Medieval spell-books also warn operators against biting off more than they can chew, and they stress the importance of creating an inviolable protective circle. But is there anything in these books that resembles Grossman's "Niffin," which appears as a tower of blue flame? The *Sworn Book of Honorius* contains spells for invoking spirits that are similar. The *Sworn Book* is mentioned as early as the fourteenth century, though the British Library has a fifteenth-century copy. I had the pleasure of reviewing their copy with my mother in the reading room, and we whispered about demons and spells.

My mother had introduced me to the Middle Ages—buying me a copy of *The Boy's King Arthur*, and showing me books about Vikings—so it made sense to introduce her to the British Library. During the various interactions required to get her a limited reader pass, I could see how so much medieval scholarship is inaccessible. It was only through the protective spell of my own tenured position that I could negotiate this access, and we had to state clearly that we were reading the same specific manuscript, down to the date and shelf mark. She could never have simply wandered in, with her own fierce intelligence and knowledge of medieval history, and asked to see it. In the hushed reading room, we both felt like imposters. I struggled with reading the print text, my vision swimming as I tried to make out some of the fainter impressions. I would whisper partial translations to her, while we both found ourselves sweating in the hot, dry archival room. In spite of very practical reasons why manuscripts need to be housed in a certain way, this reality also points to the inaccessibility of so much premodern literature and scholarship.

I wondered if a medieval student had also taken the book out of a library, anxious to be seen reading such a text. It's mostly taken up with long sections on the proper names of angels, but there are also discussions of how to summon "spirits of the air," warning the reader that "some are mild and others wild" (CXVIII). Some resemble "dark and obscure clouds," while others shine "like polished gold." The Spirits of the North have "bodies [that] are long and slender, full of wrath and anger . . . [their] movement is the moving of the wind" (CXXII). The warlike Spirits of the South are closest in resemblance to the Niffin: "Their nature is to cause war and plague, murders, treasons, and burnings . . . [their] movement is somewhat like the burning of part of their true appearance . . . [lightning] and thunder will be seen to fall near the circle where they are invoked" (CXXI). We can imagine a medieval clerk summoning this entity, and fearing that they might lose control of it, just as Alice's brother does.

And what of the cosmetic spell that goes awry? Like a love spell, this seems to be a forbidden part of the Brakebills curriculum—students can summon demons, but they're warned away from both metamorphic and psychological magic. Medieval spells of illusion and seduction crop up in magic manuals like the fifteenth-century Munich handbook (CML 849 in the Bavarian state library). There are spells for summoning a banquet, or invoking a phantasmatic castle with its own staff (more on that in the later chapter on *Sir Gawain and the Green Knight*). Kieckhefer argues that the manual presents magic as a spectacle: "Even when the point is for the magician to become invisible, his very state of non-visibility is a way of relating to others" (Ch 3). By this, Kieckhefer seems to be saying that even invisibility is a showy affair in the spell-book, attended by ritual, and meant to signal the privilege and power of the operator. Like Quentin, who's searching for power and a more defined sense of self through magic, the operators of this necromancy manual were pulled into spectacular rituals that couldn't help but make them feel othered, more than human. There are several love charms with fervid language: "As the raven desires the cadavers of dead men, so should you desire me." Most are focused on unsuspecting women, and involve a fair bit of light stalking and mystical imprisonment. But one spell has a fascinating queer tone:

> If you wish to do this for a man or a woman, first make it known to him where you can be found, for he [or she] will go mad with fury on not being able to find you . . . [and] by this conjuration I command you [spirits] to seduce the heart and mind of [name] to love me, immediately and swiftly . . . [and] just as this shoulderblade [bone] grows hot and burns, so may you cause him or her . . . [to] burn and grow hot with the fire of love. (Kieckhefer Ch 4).

Did Eliot think of casting such a love spell, perhaps on Quentin, or another boy? Does Brakebills forbid this kind of psychological magic because it doesn't work, or because it works too well? As I mentioned in the previous chapter, Theo from *Chilling Adventures of Sabrina* actually does attempt a spell of transformation, which fails. In the case of Emily Greensleeves, the Niffin serves as the consequence—a dark supplement that slips into her enchanted life. Grossman's text draws, in interesting ways, upon both medievalist and early modern magic traditions, while showing their danger as well.

The TV *Magicians* expands upon the queer relationship between Eliot and Quentin, though, like a spell, it remains fragile. Much of the show is focused on Quentin's sadness—both his clinical depression and his metaphysical sadness about flawed magic. In the penultimate episode of the fourth season, Quentin delivers a monologue that bitterly crystallizes the failures of magic, and his own personal failures as someone with a complex headspace:

> You know the worst part of getting exactly what you want? When it's not good enough. Then what do you do? If this can't make me happy then *what* would? Fillory was supposed to mean something. I was supposed to mean something here . . . [Honestly] fuck Fillory for being so disappointing. You know, maybe I was better off just believing that it was fiction. The *idea* of Fillory was what saved my life. This promise that people like me . . . can somehow find an escape. (S4E11)

Quentin tries to say "fuck Fillory," tries to lay aside childish things, but can't walk away. *The Magicians* offers that particular stretch of early adulthood—now called the New Adult genre—when we're still deciding what place magic will have in our lives. It leans into the disappointments rather than miracles. In many ways, this mirrors the medieval idea of the fallen world, which we must negotiate with only partial understanding.

We can draw many parallels between Fillory—any magical realm, really—and the experience of academia. In arguing against the often brutal pace of the academic world, Rick Godden asks for "a temporality marked less by solitude and more by community and collegiality" ("Getting Medieval in Real Time" 274). Fewer deadlines, more fellowship. But Godden is also writing specifically as a disabled academic, and he brings up the issue of accessibility when he can't climb the stairs to join a party: "I feel as though I am not quite living *at the same time* as everyone who can climb the steps" (270). This exposes how even the pleasurable sites of academia are often only accessible to able-bodied and able-minded people. I often had to avoid parties where I might have participated in fellowship—or simply made contacts—because I knew the loud, confusing environment would send me into a meltdown. Many grad students enter academia with a sense of hope, and a conviction that their own perspective is needed, only to discover that they've been locked out of the most vital conversations. This could be as dramatic as never seeing yourself reflected on the syllabus, or as subtle as not securing the extension needed to hand your seminar paper in a few days late, because the instructor thinks you should be "resilient." Suddenly, Fillory isn't looking so magical anymore.

Part of Quentin's disappointment lies in the fact that magic can't cure his clinical depression. He's been chasing the cure narrative that's often foisted upon disabled and neurodivergent communities, looking for a supernatural, rather than a medical, fix. But even deeper is the suspicion that his dream *itself* is fundamentally flawed—that the kind of magic he imagined never existed in the first place. This feeling may be particularly relevant to medieval studies as a discipline, which often promises a world of magic and medievalism, but fails to encourage or even welcome the work of BIPOC scholars. When I attended the 2019 International Congress on Medieval Studies in Kalamazoo, the murmured conversation everywhere was how Medievalists of Color (MOC) had had five panels on anti-racist pedagogy rejected, while white-led panels had all been approved. Many scholars boycotted the conference, and the Q&A sessions resulted in difficult, often raw conversations. BIPOC scholars who did show up to panels were often placed in impossible situations, asked to comment on the MOC boycott, while simultaneously being expected to educate white scholars on the racism within medieval studies.

In their statement entitled "The Youngest of Old Fields," the Medievalists of Color collective states clearly that "by virtue of its subject matter as constructed over its history, medieval studies has a legacy of fortifying structural racism and other engines to silence the marginalized." This silence was overwhelming at the 2019 Kalamazoo meeting, as the visible absence of BIPOC scholars combined with an often flustered silence on the part of white scholars, grappling with their own racism while also wanting to believe that there was hope for the discipline. Like Quentin, white scholars didn't want to believe that the field they'd devoted their lives to—perhaps what had even saved their lives—was based on a racist curriculum that excluded the students and teachers whose voices were most needed. We didn't want to feel guilty teaching *Beowulf*, or reading *The Lord of the Rings*, even knowing that there was a much wider world of medieval literature that we might learn about. Perhaps most keenly, we didn't want to think of the composition of our own classrooms, or wonder how we might have created an unwelcoming space for students of color. It was easier to think of the magic and ignore all the problems that magic wouldn't fix.

The work of diversifying medieval studies—and academia in general—is often carried out by non-tenured academics. They deal with daily storms of online harassment from people who see a very specific and specious view of the Middle Ages, which doesn't involve people of color. Many of these scholars are working with scant job stability or resources, while fearing that their labor may be precisely what keeps them from gaining that security. That, and an academic system based on the exploitation of contract instructors and graduate students, in much the same way that medieval feudalism created an entitled and incestuous aristocracy. Tenure also seems like a kind of magic—a spell that will make everything worth it. But as universities lay off scores of precarious instructors in the wake of COVID, while continuing to advertise for high-salaried administrative positions, it's become clearer than ever that this magic is rotten. Disabled students are being told that their accommodations can't be honored in the new digital environment. Academics who've spent decades teaching the bulk of their department's classes are being dismissed without compensation. Instructors and students are protesting institutions that continue to raise tuition and cut full-time posts while denying basic health care. Zoom meetings are electric with anger and despair. And we see that, like Fillory, the magic of academia was wildly flawed to begin with. It needs to be rebuilt with queer and radical love, just as all of creation comes to Wart's aid in *The Sword in the Stone*, "on account of love." Not Feudalism, nor Fealty, but Family.

Part of Quentin's journey lies in realizing how flawed magic really is, which allows him to appreciate and even love his own flaws. He moves from romanticizing both his powers and his desires, to connecting with something deeper and more human. In the Season 3 episode "A Life in the Day," Eliot grows old with Quentin while the two attempt to solve a magical mosaic (resembling an episode of *Star Trek: The Next Generation*, where Captain Picard experiences an alternate lifetime when he's struck by an alien probe). Up until this point, Eliot and Quentin have had a playfully affectionate friendship (including a disastrous drunken threesome). This episode forces them to solve an unsolvable riddle, and Eliot wryly observes: "Don't you love it when all the metaphors turn out to be real?" They fight and make up and comfort each other in the face of this impossible task. A year into it, they toast each other, and Eliot says: "Happy anniversary Q." Quentin's response is a kiss. His expression suggests that he's attempting to solve another puzzle—quizzical but also shyly excited. The next morning, Eliot is quick to smooth over the moment: "Let's just save our over-thinking for the puzzle." Whenever Quentin gets too close, Eliot reacts like a queer kid who wants to carefully hedge his bets. *Don't get too invested. Don't expect too much.* He dies at the end of the episode (in this timeline, anyhow), and Quentin writes: "We led full, good lives, and we took the quest as far as we could." It's the happiest we ever see two magicians in the series, bickering and all.

Wizards can experience imposter syndrome, too. In a later episode in Season 4, we're taken back to the end of "A Life in the Day": the moment after the spell wears off, when Quentin and Eliot are still in disbelief about what happened. Quentin perhaps surprisingly, perhaps not, says: "We work. And we know it cuz we've lived it. Who gets that kind of proof of concept?" As with everything, he approaches this like an academic, putting forth a shaky but personal thesis: "What if we gave it a shot?" Eliot shuts down the moment, just as he did before. But the version of Eliot *observing* the scene says: "You knew this was a moment that truly mattered and you just snuffed it out . . . [I] was afraid, and when I'm afraid I run away." He chooses to rewrite history and kisses Quentin. Earlier Eliot says to Quentin: "I know you, and you aren't—" We don't get to hear the word *bisexual*. Quentin responds: "What's the matter?" It's a delightful archaism—what *is* the matter? How does sexuality work? How does magic work, and are these answers reasonable, livable?

Eliot's powers don't necessarily give him the confidence to pursue a relationship with Quentin, or the certainty of trusting that relationship. He can summon demons, but he can't quite work up the nerve to kiss a boy in real time. And here, wizards and academics tend to share a similar mistrust of their own abilities. Both academies—the magical one, and the more terrestrial version—are invested in gatekeeping and strategies of psychological warfare. We're taught how to point out flaws in essays and presentations, and eventually, this translates into pointing out our own flaws as teachers and writers. One of my first memories of grad school was being told by a senior academic that I would never amount to anything—that I should quit in my first semester. When I talk with colleagues about their teaching and research, the mood is often self-deprecating, or outright negative. We're always comparing ourselves to more senior academics, people working at bigger schools, or simply people with more job security and manageable teaching loads.

Like magic, a full-time job is held out as a dangerous gift—something we can't refuse or question, even if it's devouring us. Peer review can also be a way of keeping new scholars in line, just as a master scolds their apprentice for trying to meddle with powers they don't fully understand. What these young wizards often demonstrate, however, is that the masters don't understand magic either. Each new class tries to unmake the system into something more accessible, and academia needs that.

Does *The Magicians* fail to deliver on the bisexual potential of its storylines? In an article for *The Series Regulars*, Tyrone Carroll notes that "the show purposely leaves the specifics of Quentin's sexuality open to interpretation, which allows many viewers to see a little bit of themselves in him." In a 2019 *Mashable* article, Alexis Nedd is cautiously optimistic, but still critical: "Sure, Quentin is bi, but the impact of the revelation felt hollow. Outside of the loop, Quentin still felt defined by his relationship with Alice." The ending of Season 4 makes it difficult for "Queliot" to exist, even if Quentin is now a confirmed "bisexual King." By the end of Season 4 of *The Magicians*, it's clear that both Eliot and Alice are the loves of Quentin's life. Even if the show refuses labels, the representation is still important, and unexpectedly moving. If we include Margot, then three of the magicians on the show are queer, which sounds about right. Magic itself is queer.

Fantasy is often accused of recycling stock characters, when in fact, authors like J. R. R. Tolkien and Ursula Le Guin drew their characters from medieval myth cycles, epic poems, and chronicles, while connecting those sources with the concerns of their current era. Grossman continues this tradition by reimagining a secondary character, like Eliot, in a more epic role. In spite of Eliot's prickliness and shades of emotional maturity, he saves Quentin at the end of *The Magicians* by rescuing him from a corporate job. He reminds Quentin that they built a queer family together, and the show takes this further by developing a queerly indefinable relationship between them. In the end, Brakebills does teach them how to break the world, but not as an act of destruction. By revisiting their own traumas and failures, they break the notion of compulsory happiness that drives so many other stories. They take the quest as far as they can. As academics, we're also scarred by a system that extracts our labor, while often ignoring the challenges it poses to our minds and bodies. As Godden argues, academic time can feel like something otherworldly, unattainable—a pace that few can follow. In response, we need to insist upon queer and crip temporalities. This can be as clear as stating, as Alison Kafer does, that: "If I go to this talk now, I'll be too tired for class later" (39). Admitting this should be opening a channel of communication, rather than feeling the deep shame of being an imposter. Because we have lessons to teach the academy, too. By imagining something different, we can secure open futures and express what

Kafer describes as "a lust to see bodies like [our] own . . . [because] we lack such futures in this present" (45).

Carrying on with Queer Wizards

Carry On was in some ways a prequel to Rainbow Rowell's book *Fan Girl*, which included a medievalist fandom: the world of Simon Snow. *Fan Girl* revolves around the main character's love of this fandom, while *Carry On* makes the fan world the *real* world, by immersing the reader in Snow's medievalist realm. There's something inescapably medievalist about this transformation from fanfic to central narrative. We're glimpsing a world at a remove, just as the Middle Ages look askance within medievalist adaptations. That queer feeling of being "askance" may also be at the heart of fanfic, which asks us to re-imagine familiar characters, just as medieval romances often play on familiar biblical narratives and historical events. Medieval mystery plays—often put on by various guilds, in partnership with local churches—are in some ways the ultimate form of medieval fanfic, since they often place central biblical characters in outlandish and entertaining situations. The fifteenth-century *Digby Mary Magdalene* play, for instance, has a character who plays the entire globe, and includes a memorable scene of temptation at a local tavern. In a conference paper on medieval fanfiction, Anna Wilson positions the fifteenth-century writer John Lydgate as a Chaucerian fanfic author. She cites "Lydgate's . . . [insistence] on inviting comparisons with Chaucer that never go in his favor" (3), which forces readers to ask whether he is a "good" poet, or simply derivative. But this also leads to productive conversations about fanfiction in general, which Wilson defines importantly as "a form of reception by desiring or loving readers who are lacking in cultural capital and/or lacking a controlling stake in the text" (2). We've already mentioned how Cassandra Clare's book series began as fanfic, and Wilson's model reminds us that all readers should have the right to re-imagine beloved texts. In fact, all writers are doing just that, as they gather threads from their favorite texts together, in order to write the very book they need.

Rowell's novel is more firmly YA than *The Magicians*, since it takes place at a medievalist boarding school, and its characters are all in their late teens. This also more closely mirrors a medieval university, where, as Ruth Karras notes, "the majority of entrants [were] between sixteen and eighteen" (70), though some schools admitted students as young as fourteen. Long-running grammar schools, like Magdalen College at Oxford, would admit even younger students—and we'll examine some compelling accounts of student life there, from Nelson's *Fifteenth Century Schoolbook* (MS Arundel 249). Simon Snow has to fight an ecological disaster while trying to survive at the Watford School of Magicks.⁹ A force known as the Insidious Humdrum is creating magical dead-zones that resemble holes in the ozone layer, with nothing left behind except "[a] mundanity that creeps into your soul" (*Carry On* 93). In the end, Watford can only be saved by its students. The university model only works if it recognizes the strengths and needs of individual students, rather than shoring up the privileges of instructors and administrators. This is all the more evident during the pandemic, as institutions rush to purchase expensive proctoring software to invasively monitor students taking exams, while ignoring the very reasonable accessibility requests that disabled students are struggling to make.

Records of medieval universities confirm that these odd spaces have always been complex and contested. In *A History of the University in Europe*, Aleksander Gieysztor notes that the medieval university was a "corporate body . . . distinguished by [its] privileges," and that *universitas* "meant any type of corporation or community" (108). The thirteenth-century University of Bologna, which we mentioned earlier, might have given Watford and Hogwarts a run for their money in terms of sheer bureaucracy. It was organized not merely into faculties, but also "nations," which changed constantly depending upon the makeup of the current student body (110). We might trace the "houses" of Hogwarts to this type of sorting, where students were grouped on the basis of cultural alliances. As early as the twelfth century, the University of Paris also formed "colleges," which were actually closer to "boarding houses for groups of students or fellows" (116). In *Carry On*, Simon's most profound wish is that he might remain at Watford over the summer, though the Mage [Simon's mentor and, spoiler alert, also his dad] insists that living with "normals" will build character: "Let hardship sharpen your blade, Simon" (*Carry On* 9). This is likely the opposite of what most medieval students wished for. In the Magdalen College schoolbook, the teacher Robert Wittinton offers up *vulgaria*: passages in English about daily life, which students must translate into Latin. Nicholas Orme states that these passages "[were] meant to criticize what the boys say as much as to sympathize with them" (306). In this way, they represent a fraught but often unvarnished look at students' speech patterns. In one passage, a student dreams of going home: "Well is my scole felows which have

---

9 Though I've never been to Watford, it's apparently quite a non-magical suburb. This reminds me of Neil Gaiman's use of "Night's Bridge" in his fantasy novel *Neverwhere*, since the actual Knightsbridge area in central London is quite posh, and also decidedly un-magical. The choice of Watford makes the "Humdrum" a British in joke, given the character of the neighborhood. However, suburbs can be magical too, and we need young readers to see magic in their own, often diverse suburbs.

leve to go se ther fathers and mothers to sport them, as for me, I cannot so moch as a moment departe from my maisters side" (Nelson, *Fifteenth-Century Schoolbook* L53).[10] As Simon grows more dependent upon his mentor, the Mage, and delves into the headmaster's past, this medieval echo feels more prescient. Simon is longing for a family—instead of complaining about school, he's begun to romanticize it. I did this too as a grad student, looking for the family structures in academia that might sustain me. But academia is the shite boyfriend who's only available when he needs something. And Simon realizes, over the course of the novel, that Watford isn't helping him. If anything, the school's structure is forcing him to internalize childhood trauma and failing to work with him on developing alternative modes of communication. Though the medieval students had family problems as well. The outside world is scary, and medieval teachers like Wittinton understood these shocks—a later passage reads "I love my father and my mother best of all the worlde, howebeit, thei be not all the kyndest to me" (Nelson, *Fifteenth-Century Schoolbook* L57).[11]

The relationship between Simon and his roommate, Baz, turns out to be the central romantic pairing within the novel, but it's not without a variety of issues. Baz is a classist vampire from an "old family," and his initial treatment of Simon is cruel. This mirrors the Harry/Draco relationship so popular in *Harry Potter* fanfic, since these opposites attract each other across an enormous class divide. Baz is allegedly mean to hide his world-sized crush on Simon, but his admission of love tends to smooth over his past transgressions, while insisting that a boy who treats you badly is simply in love with you.[12] Simon also has to deal with the megalomaniacal tendencies of his mentor, the Mage, who radicalizes the school under the cover of being a good Marxist. *Carry On* is quite openly an adaptation of *Harry Potter*, and my students have entered into spirited debates on whether it's fanfiction, homage, or a literary text that stands on its own. The main difference between the two series is that, while Harry Potter emerges as a kind, socially adept character in spite of his trauma, Simon stays brittle, awkward, and questioning He's in many ways a more realistic teen hero, whose magic sends frac-

---

10 "I envy my school fellows who have leave to visit and enjoy their parents, since I don't have so much as a moment to leave my master's side."
11 "I love my father and mother best in all the world, though they aren't always kind to me."
12 Reminiscent of the relationship between Catra and Adora in *She-Ra*—Catra is both physically and psychologically abusive to Adora, but they end up falling in love. The creator, Noelle Stevenson, has noted in interviews that they didn't know until the final season whether or not Netflix would allow the queer romance, so they had to keep drawing Catra as a villain until the very end.

tures through his world. He has trouble with words, in a way that defies the very linguistic rules of the novel's magic system:

> None of it comes naturally to me. Words. Language. Speaking. I don't remember when I learned to talk, but I know they tried to send me to specialists. Apparently, that can happen to kids in care, or kids with parents who never talk to them. (*Carry On* 108)

The magic in *Carry On* is based on idioms and popular sayings (such as yelling "Up, Up and Away" to cast a flying spell), which makes Simon's lack of articulation a problem. Rowell blames his communication difficulties on being left in care, which suggests that lack of intimate contact has rendered him speechless. Thinking of Simon as neurodivergent opens, perhaps, a more inclusive space for young readers who might also identify with Simon as a character with trouble speaking "properly." His difficulties with traditional speech might resemble the experiences of people with selective mutism (myself included), who can be "phobic of initiating speech/being overheard in the proximity of a given trigger person or group of people" (Sutton and Forrester 15). This aligns him with young readers who have also been sent to specialists, and whose own methods of communication have been criticized. In this light, Simon materializes as an important character for marginalized readers—a neuro-queer, anxious kid who has trouble expressing his thoughts and feelings.

I mentioned the ABC show *Speechless* in the introduction, which revolves around a non-verbal teen character (JJ) with cerebral palsy, played by actor Micha Fowler (who also has CP, but isn't non-verbal). JJ uses an AAC (augmentive and assistive communication) board to speak, with the help of his aid, Kenneth. I bring this up again because Simon's issues with communication are a reminder that not every wizard has facility with traditional speech. *Speechless* was canceled after three seasons, but it endures as an important show that explored ableism in every episode. Fowler has also discussed how the show made him a better actor, because he needed to communicate meaningfully through gestures and facial expressions. In S1E3 (cheekily named "Inspirations"), Kenneth actually uses JJ's disability to get them free things—until JJ puts a stop to it. He says firmly to Kenneth: "You took my voice—you don't get to do that." Later in the season, when his younger brother Ray is frantic because JJ has gone off on his own, JJ reminds him: "I'm the big brother—it's my job to take care of *you*." The show's focus on alternative communication even introduces the audience to disability technologies (like eye-tracking screens), and this makes me think about how Rowell could have pushed a bit further with Simon's non-traditional communication. Baz could also make more of an effort to read Simon's silences, rather than always worrying about them.

Simon's ellipses become as important to his own characterization as Baz's raillery. They're all modes of communication that find value in Rowell's post-Potter world. They also resemble the silences of Le Guin's wizard Ogion, who is famously laconic, but still respected.

When I recently taught *Carry On*, my students were intrigued by the ways in which Simon was *not* Harry Potter. We compared the characters at basic and nuanced levels, and they agreed that Rowell was trying to refashion Harry as a character whose trauma would become central to his story. But they also criticized the ways in which Simon had *more* trauma piled on throughout the book. One student made the point that *Carry On* ends with Simon in therapy, which is a realistic move. We talked about how teen heroes—fundamentally unready to face the horrors of their own fantasy stories—are nevertheless charged with saving worlds that are often weaponized against them. Upon learning that she must sacrifice her sister to save the world, Buffy Summers observes near the end of the fifth season of *Buffy the Vampire Slayer* (S5E21): "I don't know how to live in the world, if these are the choices." All she really wants is advice and comfort from her mother. What we demand of these heroes, the pain that we expect them to deal with, is unfair. We linked this conversation to what had been a particularly bad semester for students (and this was pre-pandemic). Counseling services on campus were overwhelmed (and underfunded), while attendance was affected by barriers to physical and mental health. It raised a compound question: what do we expect of teen heroes in these stories, and what do we expect of real-life students analyzing those stories? Our term for this shared precarity among teen wizards and students was "mental complexity," a variation on neurodiversity[13] that acknowledges the failure of terms like *diversity* to fully embody how different minds can be from each other, and how damaging it can be to work at what Peta Cox terms "passing as sane" (100).

Hogwarts and Watford are full of rituals, uniforms, and hierarchies that are fundamentally medieval in their thinking. I'm interested in what these fantasy school narratives draw from medieval structures, and how the medievalist elements of *Carry On* allow unexpected opportunities for Simon and his chosen family. Simon is essentially a medieval clerk, like Chaucer's Nicholas. He carries a sword, memorizes charms, and depends upon the shelter and protection of Watford, just as a young medieval clerk might depend upon their school. There was also medieval financial aid for students, and Toswell notes that "the sliding scale

---

13 In the edited volume *Loud Hands: Autistic People Speaking*, Nick Walker clarifies this term by stating that "there is no 'normal' style of human brain or human mind" (228).

of tuition charged according to means in the medieval period seems actually fairer and more sensible than modern funding packages" (47). Simon is just such a student, living on financial aid, surrounded by more privileged classmates like Baz. He observes that Watford is "the only place magicians live together, unless they're related" (*Carry On* 18). The school functions as a community and queer version of the biological family, and its gates proclaim a message of unity and tolerance: "MAGIC SEPARATES US FROM THE WORLD. LET NOTHING SEPARATE US FROM EACH OTHER" (25). Simon is quick to deflate this, calling it a "nice sentiment" that probably doesn't hold true. But he also sees the campus as a comforting home, rather than a place to gain a magical education.

In contrast to the esoteric subjects that students at Brakebills have to deal with, the students at Watford cleave to a fairly traditional liberal arts curriculum. This includes classes in Greek, Latin, Political Science, History, and Elocution, which turns out to be the major skill behind spell-casting. This mirrors the seven liberal arts that underpinned medieval universities, including "[the] Trivium (Grammar, Rhetoric, Logic) and Quadrivium (Arithmetic, Geometry, Music, Astronomy)" (Norton 8). As we've seen, magic was also an area of medieval academic study, though it was generally seen as a dangerous upper-class vice. Catherine Rider goes on to situate demonology and other mystical studies within the realm of scholarly adolescence: "For some students magic may have been a form of youthful experimentation, like much of the drinking and visiting prostitutes which also went on in medieval universities" (111). Both *Magicians* and *Carry On* extend a long tradition of linking magic with experimentation, and Simon is immediately in over his head with magic, because he can't control it. We often want young people to grow out of "magical thinking," which just feels like the adult way of saying "abandon hope." But these narratives challenge us to imagine wizards who integrate magic into their lives. Merlin grows into magic, not out of it. And when readers are urged to grow out of YA fantasy, their response should be to read more of it—especially if those stories are bound up in their own sense of survival. In his poem "NymphaeAceae" (like nymphs, or possibly, for [those] like nymphs), David Ly describes his own queer adolescence as "a bud / of tangled magic, / a page from a childhood grimoire," ending with a message to his younger self: "Boy, magic exists" (n.p.). Something we should all remember.

While Brakebills seems to impart knowledge that's only designed to encourage magical skills—knowledge that the characters must surpass—Watford is a functional liberal arts high school. Students are segregated by their assigned sex, and Penelope lives in "the Cloisters," described as "a long low building . . . [it] has only one door and all the windows are made up of tiny panes of glass. (The school must have been mega-paranoid when it started letting girls back in in the 1600s)" (*Carry On* 59). This mirrors Arha's living conditions in Ursula Le Guin's

Tombs of Atuan.¹⁴ It begs the question: did medieval universities expressly forbid girls to attend? In a word—not exactly—though the situation varied across Europe. Karras observes that English universities employed women as laundresses, hairdressers, and sometimes porters, but they were not admitted as students (76). She also notes that men were sometimes appointed as hairdressers, and one should dearly like to read their stories. "Aristocratic women," Karras says, could be "donors or potential donors" to the university, and of course the campus "would also have to deal with townswomen over rent" (ibid.). Fourteenth-century didactic texts, like Landry's *Book of the Knight of the Tower*—written for his daughters—assumed a community of elite and educated women readers. Abbesses like Hild of Whitby were accomplished writers and scholars, who exchanged sophisticated letters in Latin. In the fifteenth century, Margaret Paston wrote scores of letters to her husband while managing his properties, and her mother-in-law Agnes wrote to him often as well. Scholars like Héloïse d'Argenteuil received (infamous) private tutoring, though this doesn't seem to have always been the case. In his fourteenth-century romance *L'espinette amoureuse* (a "spinet" is like a harpsichord), Froissart writes of being in school at twelve years old: "There were little girls there . . . [I] gained great prowess through their grace" (Skinner Ch 25). Watford was behind the times, it seems.

Students there have realistic assignments, like inventing a new spell, and Simon casually practices medieval dueling in his tower bedroom. All of this is tongue-in-cheek, but Rowell is also deconstructing the wizard school narrative by trying to visualize how these students would actually have been educated. Simon, Penelope, and Baz study a traditional literary canon (including *Hamlet* and Victorian literature), and smart-phones are banned, while taxes are enforced by the Mage.¹⁵ In this respect Watford diverges from a medieval university, whose instructors and administrators were exempt from taxes. As Norton explains, it was not the university itself as a corporation that enjoyed this exemption, but rather "masters and scholars as individuals" (88). The Mage reverses this practice by charging the old families taxes, which is one of the acts that causes Baz's family to move against him. Watford also issues diplomas, and the students appear to learn a wide variety of topics, from "magic words" to medieval history. Simon even mentions that Penelope's mother teaches medieval history at "a Normal

---

14 Arha is a young priestess in the book who rebels against her own cloistered society. She forms a partnership with Ged, the protagonist from the previous book, who is now aging and less sure of himself.
15 Rowell doesn't expand upon the taxation system, but the "old families" seem particularly offended by this, so I assume that it's an extra (reasonable) cost for them.

university. She's published a whole shelf full of mage books, but she doesn't make any money doing it" (312). Even in this magical medievalist world, adjunct instructors are struggling to survive. Watford seems to mirror an ordinary academic institution, with a few esoteric subjects. So how does it prepare these students to be wizards in the wider world?

In short: it doesn't. But perhaps it prepares them better than Brakebills, though, like *The Magicians*, much of *Carry On* is invested in narratives of disappointment. While Brakebills seems to fail its students as an institution, Rowell is a bit more optimistic about the value of the magical school. The Mage is the one who fails Simon. He fails to be an ethical mentor, a decent father, or a credible instructor in any subject, and much of the novel explores this failure as a slow burn. In an episode of the podcast *Witch, Please* (S2E7), Hannah McGregor and Marcelle Kosman note that *Carry On* refuses any type of narrative closure. Like Morgan's multi-faceted story, this narrative plays with the reader's expectations. Baz's mother—Watford's former chancellor—tries to send him a message from beyond the grave, but it's never quite delivered. The Mage also dies before he can reveal to Simon that he is, in fact, Simon's father (a fact which might help Simon process his own trauma). Simon's mother, Lucy, never gets to meet her son. Baz's mother never gets to see that her son has survived, even thrived, after being turned into a vampire. McGregor argues that "we never get the satisfaction of seeing a character fully understand anything" in the novel, given the splintered narrative perspectives. This feels like a peculiarly medieval failure—in that context, you never "fully understand anything" in a fallen world, because humans lack a divine perspective.

Old English elegies—one of my favorite genres—are full of mourning and inarticulate sadness, because their pagan characters lack any sort of biblical instruction or reassurance. They are *anhaga*, "wretched exiles," wandering down dark paths, at the mercy of wolves in the margins. In early medieval literature, sadness and confusion are conditions of life, rather than symptoms to be treated. The seafarer has only birds as his silent companions; the wanderer mourns a world already gone, while unable to see what will come. Through this refusal of narrative closure, Rowell's novel is, perhaps, being *more medieval* in its conversation about trauma. While other YA texts might choose a course of treatment, *Carry On* avoids cure in favor of moving forward. We carry on—we are not cured. In *Brilliant Imperfection*, Eli Clare has argued against cure-based narratives within disability studies: "At the centre of cure lies eradication . . . [it] arrives in many different guises, connected to elimination and erasure in a variety of configurations" (26). This rings especially true for me as a medievalist on the spectrum, who has been treated at various stages for clinical anxiety and depression. Medication has helped at times, and it helps a lot of people—this is management, not cure. But cure itself is often a genocidal solution, proposed by organizations like Autism Speaks, or directed at trans and nonbinary people by those who want to "cure" their difference. Autism Speaks is an organization run entirely by non-autistic people, and until recently, all of their marketing focused on finding a "cure" for neurodiversity. They see us as apprentice humans in need of being corrected, rather than as the wizards we are. Harmful practices like applied behavioral analysis are still suggested as a way to treat many forms of cognitive difference that are themselves *lives* rather than problems, natural variations, sacred and necessary ways of being. The medieval mood of *Carry On* is at odds with its contemporary setting, though it leans more towards embracing difference.

It's also worth noting that in *Wayward Son*, the sequel to *Carry On*, Simon admits to having difficulty with sex—not because he isn't sure of his own attraction to Baz, but because he has undergone mental and physical trauma. Andrew Gurza notes that "we don't talk about sexuality and disability at all in queer spaces or hetero spaces. We don't really talk about disability at all" ("This Ability"). His podcast, *Disability after Dark*, is designed to correct this by exploring the varied, hot intersections between disability and sexuality. YA novels of queer empowerment don't often feature characters who are disabled or neuroatypical. I discuss most of them in this book, at least in a fantasy context. So Simon stands out here as a queer, neuro-atypical character who struggles with physical intimacy. Rowell never presents a "cure" for this, because it's just who Simon is, and Simon is still growing and changing. Like Merlin, he tries on different forms, and that process of transformation is a vital one. The book offers a somewhat rare exploration of a queer, supernatural character with cognitive complexity who doesn't achieve either a straightforward queer romance, or a tragic rejection. Instead, Rowell's point is to show Simon living within this complexity, from book to book.

Simon and Baz must live with their failures—live in a sad world—while finding ways to make that living tender, endurable. Baz sums this up in *Carry On* when he delivers a Gothic speech to his mother's bones, which lie in Watford's medieval catacombs:

> You came back, and I missed you. And then I did the thing you wanted me to do, so you probably won't ever come back again . . . [But]—I just wanted to tell you that I'm going to carry on. As I am. No matter how much I think about it, I don't think there's any scenario where you'd want me—where you'd *allow* me—to go on like this. (510)

Simon never hears this speech, which might tell him so much about Baz—instead, he gets the short version, which is Baz's gently teasing: "Carry on, Simon," at the end of the novel. The full speech, however, is vital to understanding Rowell's project. Baz and Simon cannot understand each other, yet they fall in love and form a kin group with Penelope. Baz understands that his mother—whose flame-scarred hands touched him gently as a child—would kill him if she knew he'd become a vampire. Simon claims that there are no "magickal orphans," but that's precisely what he is.[16] Baz chooses to "go on like this," in spite of having no evidence that this will be a viable, bearable life. Both characters reshape their worlds by imagining futures that should not exist. In a medieval sense, what they both envision is a kind of mercy—an access to love and survival that must exist in spite of all evidence to the contrary. A challenge to *desperatio* through survival. In this way, I'd argue, the phrase "carry on" becomes a kind of medieval riddle that haunts Rowell's novel from beginning to end.

I often teach riddles in literary survey classes, offering them as proof that the "Dark Ages" were actually fueled by intellectual and spiritual curiosity. Does the pleasure of the riddle come from solving it, or *not* solving it? Like magic, riddles are both pedagogical and fundamentally unknowable. We fail to solve them, and this queer failure is what makes them matter, because not knowing things is one of our first and most continuous lessons. "Carry on" functions much like the curious refrain in the Old English poem "Deor": *Þæs ofereode / þisses swa mæg* (L13–14). The phrase can be translated as "this, too, shall pass," or "that passed over, so this may [too]." The key word is the subjunctive phrase *swa mæg*, which locks the refrain in a sense of indeterminacy. We don't know if the dark thing is going to pass over—it *might*. Presumably, we must carry on as if it will. "Deor" is a riddle in itself, because so few Anglo-Saxon poems have refrains at all. Why this one? What is the true obstacle that we must, or might, endure? I've seen medievalists with this phrase tattooed on their bodies, in a beautiful display of solidarity in ambiguity. I have an image from *The Little Prince* tattooed on my body—an homage to a children's text that many autistic kids connected with, since the main character was an interstellar traveler. We have to carry on as medievalists in an academic system that devalues premodern knowledge, and sometimes that means turning our bodies into vital manuscripts. We carry on as teachers under changing governments which are increasingly hostile or apathetic towards universities.

Simon and Baz share an epic kiss, which is also a kind of magnificent failure. I'll discuss a similar queer kiss, in *Sir Gawain and the Green Knight*, in Chapter 5. After dealing with the pain of sharing a room with his crush for years, Baz cannot even imagine a relationship between them. Yet he also tries to come out to Simon a number of times, each one a failure. In the end, it's Simon who kisses him, and Baz fears that "Simon Snow is going to die kissing me" (342). Baz has positioned

---

16 This is an enigmatic note that the book doesn't fully explain. I see it as a cheeky nod to *Harry Potter*, while also serving as a repudiation of certain elements in Rowling's series—an insistence that Simon is a different wizard.

Simon as his rival, and assumed for years that they will murder each other, hero vs. vampire, as would happen in another story. As their rivalry dissolves, Baz must also admit that he's never kissed anyone before ("I was afraid I might bite"). Simon fails here at being the straight teen wizard we expect him to be, while Baz fails at being the more experienced queer boy that his background and reputation might suggest. As they continue to kiss, Simon questions his own sexuality ("I'm kissing a bloke. That *is* different"), while also refusing to classify his desires. Later, in Baz's room after a stilted Christmas dinner with Baz's posh family, the two of them keep failing to learn anything about one another. Simon wishes he knew what Baz was thinking, and when the narrative switches to Baz's point of view, his first thought is: "I don't know what I'm thinking" (351). When Baz asks Simon why he hasn't thought more about his sexuality, Simon replies: "I make lists of things not to think about" (354).

In class, we talked about *Carry On* in relation to bi-erasure, and why Simon couldn't simply be bisexual. Similarly, Baz describes himself as queer earlier in the novel, but then comes out to Simon as gay. We discussed this as, perhaps, an element of the novel's commitment to queer failure and a sense of indeterminacy. Neither character is allowed to understand anything fully, including their own sexualities, because they remain fluid and unknowable. Unlike the character Elliot Schafer in Sarah Brennan's *In Other Lands*, who comes out firmly as bisexual, Simon's sexuality remains as much of a riddle as that gnomic phrase, *carry on*. His excuse for not thinking more about it—"I've got a lot on my plate"—offers a strong argument. He *does* have a lot on his plate. The horrors of his world make it impossible for him to consider this part of his life in detail. But his failure to classify himself is also a resistance to being solved, in spite of Baz's teasing that he should really arrive at a firmer conclusion about himself. He chooses Morgan's complexity, over a more stereotypical idea of what a wizard should be.

This queer romance might feel far from something that could be explored at a medieval university. Karras mentions one student at the Sorbonne, in 1431, who was punished for spending time at a bathhouse (brothel) with "a foreign man" (81). Richard Edmund, a fellow at Merton College, was dismissed in 1491 for committing "the sin against nature" (ibid.). But queer romances obviously happened within these all-male spaces. Imagine being the student whose job it was to trim and wash hair—the intimacy that required—as well as sharing beds in close quarters. The Magdalen College schoolbook makes no mention specifically of same-sex attraction, but does contain a number of sweet love notes between boys engaged in passionate friendships. On the death of a friend, one of Wittinton's student narrators says, "I cannot tell in good faithe what losse may be comparede to this . . . [we] had onn mynde in every matter" (Nelson, *Fifteenth-Century*

Schoolbook L196).¹⁷ The student being addressed is often named John, and in another note, the writer says: "John, it is 7 yere agone sens I lovede the first. I dide never repent me of it for" (L197).¹⁸ Like Baz, one of the narrators is overwhelmed by his love for another student: "And thou myghtest se with thyn Eyn how moche I love the thou woldist marvell of the habundance of it . . . [I] wyll not only spende my goode for the but the best bloode in my body" (L199).¹⁹ Perhaps there was hope for medieval queer teens after all. And at the risk of committing what T. H. White jokingly calls "filthy anachronism," all these maybe-queer Johns remind me of the titular character in David Bowie's song "John, I'm Only Dancing." It seems like Bowie is dancing with someone to make John jealous, but the song hints at complex queer desires.

Carry On ends with a dance, where Simon and Baz are allowed to be public boyfriends (though Simon has a tail at this point—now a bit of a cacodemon himself). The close of the novel pivots back to desire and belonging. And as we've seen, the constant tension between desire and academia was a medieval concern as well. The thirteenth-century *Carmina Burana*—the Songs of the Benedictine Beuern monastery, in Bavaria—include a number of poems about ditching your schoolwork and heading to the tavern. One poem (CB 75) is entitled *Obmittamus studia*, or "Down with study!" David Parlett's translation captures the bouncing joy of throwing away your grammar books:

> Down with study! Books away!
> Come and learn a sweeter truth
> finding pleasure in the play
> and the greenery of youth . . .
> *Days go tumbling headlong by,*
> *gone to waste on learning:*
> *young-at-heart were made to ply*
> *trades of less discerning* (81–82).²⁰

---

[17] "I cannot tell in good faith what loss may be compared to this . . . [we] had one mind in every matter."
[18] "John, I've loved you for seven years, and never regretted it."
[19] "If you could see how much I loved you, you'd marvel at the abundance of it—I'll devote not only my goodness for you, but the best blood in my body."
[20] "Obmitammus studia,
  dulce est desipere,
  et carpamus dulcia,
  iuventutis tenere,
  res est apta senectuti
  seriis intendere.
  Velox etas preterit

The "sweeter truth" is charged with youthful desire, but the part that gets me—already what my students might call "an old"—is the line about days "gone to waste on learning." The days do tumble headlong by, and I often wonder what I missed by focusing on a decade of schooling. Even professors want to flee the classroom sometimes. The way we gather nervously in hallways, and ask each other to coffee with a pang of guilt. The fear of never being productive enough, beholden to those tumbling years, when we should just say *obmittamus studia*! Instead, we need to find our passions beyond the structures of academia, and pursue the joys that we need in order to survive—since the academy can't save us. Though we can save it by creating a space where all bodies and minds are able to thrive.

The *Carmina Burana* manuscript also includes work by the enigmatically named "Archpoet," whose twelfth-century "Confession" paints a beautiful picture of dissolute youth. He begins his confession with the words "estuans intrinsecus / ira vehementi," which Parlett translates lyrically as "boiling over in the mind / angry indignation" (151). This could very well be Simon, trying to articulate his rocky emotions. The poet makes a number of delightful negative claims, such as never being one to study while thirsty, and never passing up a game of dice at a tavern. In the poem's climax, he bursts forth with the raw material of his confession:

> Sum locutus contra me, quidquid de me novi,
> et virus evomui, quod tam diu fovi.
> Vita vetus displicet, mores placent novi;
> homo videt faciem, sed cor patet Iovi.
>
> [I confess to everything,
> everything against me:
> spit the poison out, which long
> cankered and incensed me:
> shame attends my former life,
> hope the paths that guide me:
> men see me, but only God
> can see the heart inside me.] (Parlett 157)

Here, the act of confession justifies the many desires within the poem. But it also suggests a moment of exasperated admission: *Fine, I did it! I confess to it all!* By confessing, the poet creates a new life, leaving his old one "scattered" (*displicet*) behind him. Baz has a similar experience when he confesses before

---

studio detenta,
lascivire suggerit
tenera iuventa. (Waddell 214).

his mother's tomb. He doesn't repent his life—he confesses it, and moves on. Like the Archpoet, he finds that speaking out, and owning his anxieties, creates new *mores* (paths) to follow with Simon. His heart opens (*cor patet*).

While *The Magicians* is sparse on happy endings, *Carry On* gives us the final scene of Simon and Baz moving in with each other. Simon may still have a cumbersome tail, and Baz has certainly been traumatized, but they're still able to form a relationship. Penelope remains in the picture, and everyone moves forward, in spite of the fact that Watford is collapsing after the death of its leader, the Mage. In both of these series, the characters move past what they learned in school, though the experience continues to shape them. Simon literally kills the head of Watford, and Quentin discovers multiple dimensions beyond Brakebills. Both protagonists remain tricky, sad, and complex, without ever fully dismantling their anxieties. Magic doesn't relieve them of their feelings, though it does connect them with wild and ineffable power: what Tolkien, in "On Fairy Stories," calls "Joy beyond the walls of the world, poignant as grief" (153). We can also see this as Tiffany's deep experience of matriarchal connection on the Chalk, or Morgan's insistence on remaining visible within narratives that attempt to exclude her. *Both The Magicians* and *Carry On* deconstruct the wizard school narrative by producing characters who actually, or nearly, destroy their alma mater. But this is all part of the process, as they become adult wizards who critique the rules they learned, the classes they took. If the point of magic school is to break the world, they break it again and again, finding the pain and beauty as it re-seams itself, as it heals.

I'll end with a moment of academic connection that felt like magic. While attending the International Medieval Congress in Leeds, I met up with a group of queer and nonbinary medievalists. We'd connected previously through Twitter, though I'd only met one person face-to-face, at the Kalamazoo conference earlier that year. When I was exhausted from travel, and anxious about the distance between my hotel and the university where the conference was held—could I manage this trip each day?—two of these new friends took me on a ramble through downtown Leeds. We capped off the day at a queer gathering, in a queer-inclusive cafe delightfully named Flamingos. Away from the buzzing campus grounds, we were able to connect over tea and campy rainbow cake. Our close-knit group ended up going on a day trip to York, where we, queer souls, moved through the medieval neighborhood known as The Shambles. Eating curry take-aways, chatting about our work and lives, we made our way to York Abbey. Someone suggested taking a photo, and we immortalized ourselves—real, visible, connected—queer medievalists who'd unexpectedly found each other. The experience was as significant as the conference itself. Leaning against centuries-old stone walls, looking up at the arches that still endured, we saw a place for ourselves in a field that hadn't always welcomed our perspective. Alive in those beautiful ruins.

Chapter 4
Bad Magic: Wizardry and Queer Failures of Communication

This chapter focuses on failure as a necessary and even productive element of medievalist fantasy texts. We'll look at self-conscious adaptations of the Middle Ages that pay close attention to flaws and failures, like Peter S. Beagle's *The Last Unicorn*, Sarah Rees Brennan's *In Other Lands*, and Anne Ursu's *The Real Boy*. These YA texts align with the broader failures of medievalism as an expansive genre: how critics accuse it of failing to "get the Middle Ages right," even as the Middle Ages (*whose Middle Ages?* to quote Andrew Albin's recent edited volume) evade any conservative desire to be fully knowable, white, straight, or European.

Critiques of medievalism can be straightforwardly racist, as when fans of the BBC TV show *Merlin* protested the casting of Angel Coulby, who is Black, as Guinevere. In a 2009 Livejournal[1] post, zahrawithaz cites the "'anachronism' battlecry to disparage the inclusion of a black character in a fantasy show," which emerged as a backlash to Coulby's casting. She describes how meaningful it was, as a biracial viewer, to see Gwen played by Coulby—but goes on to say that the show "undid a lot of that [good] by making her a maid . . . [it was] a little bit of we-can't-imagine-black-people-actually-in-charge, even in a fantasy world" (n.p.). Though Gwen is eventually crowned queen on the show, Ebony Thomas notes that she "remains trapped in the past, alone with a kingdom to run . . . [she] haunts the text" (Ch 3). Ultimately, the show doesn't know what to do with this version of the queen, and so her story ends unhappily ever after—she rules with little support or trust, and doesn't usher in the golden age that the show initially suggests. In this sense, medievalist adaptations can be profoundly ambivalent in their handling of diverse characters, even when they try to do good. Medievalism, in trying to undo perceived "failures" of the Middle Ages, can also fail spectacularly.

Adaptations can also be used to shore up racism and sexism that's seen to have *already existed* in the Middle Ages, as happened in *Game of Thrones*, where endless storylines involving sexual assault and torture were justified as being "medieval." With this in mind, it seems particularly important to examine medievalist adaptations that focus on their own failure as worlds, and on the failures of

---

[1] Livejournal was (and still is) an important platform in which fans can praise and critique shows, as well as whole genres. When I was working on my first novel, I often read posts in the Livejournal *Fangs, Fur & Fey*, to see what other fantasy and paranormal romance writers were saying about the genre.

https://doi.org/10.1515/9781501515330-005

their heroes. This also allows us to discuss shifting medieval viewpoints on failure, sin, and being "fallen" as a shared experience. In the Arthurian sense, we need failure—Arthur must die, and Lancelot must sin, if the audience is going to learn about negotiating a fallen world. Just as there's no single medieval treatment of gender diversity, race, or disability, there's also no universal perspective on what it means to succeed as an ideal human. These medievalist characters are important, not only in what they manage to accomplish, but also in their refusals to live up to certain social standards that remain relevant to contemporary readers.

Many of the medievalist characters I'll talk about in this chapter simply fail to engage with their medievalist worlds. Schmendrick, from *The Last Unicorn*, is a stylishly incompetent magician. Elliot Schafer, from Sarah Reese Brennan's *In Other Lands*, fails to uphold the social rules within his own portal fantasy. Oscar, from Anne Ursu's *The Real Boy*, fails at neurotypical communication (and is failed in turn by the wizards around him). I'll also look at seemingly minor characters whose failures actually drive the stories that have marginalized them, including Molly Grue from *The Last Unicorn*, and Elliot's boyfriend Luke Sunborn, who both succeeds and fails at being an ideal warrior. Thinking alongside medieval philosophers, such as St. Augustine, Thomas Aquinas, Boethius, and Peter Abelard, will give us a more nuanced view of sin as "falling short," and how this necessary failure informs much of Christian medieval life. Chaucer's work offers, as well, a valuable perspective on "lak of Stedfastnesse" (lack of stability), and the mutability that shades late medieval secular writing. In order to think about how these sometimes contradictory philosophies and theologies might have appeared in popular conversation, we'll also examine one of the York Corpus Christi plays, *The Fall*.

Failing in the Middle Ages

A medieval studies classroom will often contain failures of various kinds. Instructors might fail to convey the diversity of the period. Students might fail to read a series of difficult languages, or fail to see the relevance of the material to their contemporary lives. The class as a whole might fail to move past certain stumbling blocks, such as the casual misogyny of writers like Malory, or the glossed poetry of Chaucer that still feels alien. Though these are presented as things to work through, rather than issues to solve, many will fail to engage with the writing because it simply feels too remote. And instructors, of course, must fail to encompass *all* of the Middle Ages in their teaching—even academics who conduct truly global research can't hope to cover such a vast expanse of entangled texts and cultures. When you're studying a manuscript, a literal hole or burn in the text can also create shared failures of understanding. I've had many conversations with medievalists who felt somehow out-classed by the discipline itself, as if they were failing to live up to it; and just as many colleagues who felt that medieval studies failed to welcome and support them as diverse scholars. All this is to say that a certain "mood" of failure permeates both medieval literature itself, and the disciplines that engage with it.

While we were talking about medievalism in my Teen Fiction class, a student said: "Chaucer sucks!" This surprised me. I'd just taught a Chaucerian class, and though I wouldn't say the students *loved* the material, their essays and discussions revealed that they'd all found something engaging. I had to push through an initial urge to defend medieval literature in general, and ask why the student thought this way about Chaucer. They explained that Middle English was difficult to read, which made *The Canterbury Tales* hard to get into. And once you did manage to get into the tales, it seemed as though they were mostly about men, since the vast majority of Chaucer's pilgrims are men. This led to a broader discussion of how medieval literature can be inaccessible. Students voiced concern over being judged by how well they could read, or pronounce, Middle English. They also noted that Chaucer was almost exclusively taught in a single survey course, and the tales they encountered were canonical ones—like "The Miller's Tale"—which struck them as sexist and even violent. We talked about ways in which Chaucer's work could be made more accessible: stressing the tales by and about women; illuminating the complex gender politics, such as the Pardoner's potential trans, nonbinary, or intersex identity; presenting Middle English as a fun learning experiment, rather than as a punitive method for judging students' competency with reading.

Our conversation exposed how medieval studies can fail to be accessible, or relevant, to students who lack familiarity with the era. And even fantasy-loving students, who'd normally consume an epic medievalist novel, don't necessarily find kinship in medieval literature. As we've already discussed, the field itself can be actively hostile to BIPOC students and early-career researchers, as well as students who may struggle with the sexism and transphobia of some of these early texts. When scholars like Dorothy Kim and Mary Rambaran-Olm try to explain why a term like "Anglo-Saxon Studies" is both historically inaccurate and pointedly racist, the backlash from white scholars is constant and violent (Kim, in particular, was attacked by a senior scholar, and Rambaran-Olm is regularly harassed on Twitter). Trans and nonbinary scholars focusing on medieval studies may find that their discussions of gender—and their defense of trans rights—can disqualify them for financial support, teaching opportunities, and stable positions within the field. Their work can also be labeled as gender studies, which some medievalists see as "not really medieval," which means that the work receives far less support and attention. Finally, being trans, nonbinary, or gender non-conforming in a medieval studies classroom can open instructors and students up to harassment—

especially if someone decides simply asserting that trans people exist is a form of "indoctrination." Medieval studies has failed to create a safe space for all kinds of students and scholars, and we must do better.

But how did medieval thinkers reconcile the notion of failure? Were people allowed, even expected, to have "epic fails," as we'd call them now?

Medievalist shows like *Game of Thrones*, and even more historically precise shows like *The Last Kingdom*,[2] often present us with medieval theology that lacks any kind of nuance. The priests in *Game of Thrones* are either portrayed as cunning cultists, or hopelessly old-fashioned; theological figures in *The Last Kingdom* are often outright crooks; the priest Athelstan in *Vikings*[3] is probably the most complex portrait, though he also dies as a martyr. A survey of the actual Middle Ages, though, reveals—as it should—that philosophies of sin, transgression, and failure were complex, often contradictory. Talking about sin was like talking, today, about WiFi, climate change, or artificial intelligence—both scholars and laypeople had individual opinions that often clashed with each other. On the first day of a medieval class, someone will always mention the "corrupt church." Which is good—because it forces us to deconstruct both of those terms. There was no single church, and no easily defined religious character, just as there was no single type of medieval person. William Callin states that "the notion of a Christian Middle Ages—simple, unproblematic, uniform, communal" (35), did not exist—or existed only as a construct placed against the equally-constructed Renaissance. And there was, of course, no single punishment for failure, no single way to fail in the world.

St. Augustine gives us some of the most evocative—and queer—depictions of youthful failure in his *Confessions*. Like Boethius's *Consolation of Philosophy*—whose narrator challenged the embodied character of Fortune to explain his own political imprisonment—this late antique / early medieval text would become an enormous influence on later medieval writers. Composed at the very beginning of the fifth century, *Confessions* is both a failed biography (being incomplete), and a meditation on youthful failure resulting from Original Sin. Augustine describes

---

2 Adapted from the medievalist novels of Bernard Cornwell, this series focuses on an English character living at the height of the Viking invasion period, who's adopted by a Viking family and has to negotiate two worlds.
3 This show focuses on a Viking community, beginning with the sack of Lindisfarne (793), and going on to narrate their connections with England and the Carolingian empire that encompassed parts of what are now France and Germany. The show has some sly references to queerness: in the pilot episode, Ragnar propositions Athelstan for a threesome, and a minor character also has a brief dalliance with a eunuch. But the show has also received criticism for its treatment of a disabled character, "Ivar the Boneless," who is modeled loosely after a historical person. Ivar is portrayed as a psychotic villain whose rage stems from his disability, and unlike his able-bodied siblings, he never seems to develop past a desire for revenge.

this, in Letter 144 to Jerome, as "that which is fastened on the soul at its birth and from which it can only be freed by being born again" (*Complete Works* n.p.). But there were several exceptions to this idea. The popular fifth-century Pelagians believed that Original Sin wasn't transmitted upon birth, and that all humans could achieve perfection. Augustine himself, among others, noted that Mary was not subject to Original Sin. As a concept, it wasn't monolithic. The *Confessions*, as their name implies, deal quite exclusively with sin—and particularly with youthful sin. Augustine describes "a shadowy jungle of erotic adventures"[4] (*Confessions* Book 2), which practically sounds like a tagline for *Game of Thrones*. He states, quite poignantly, that "the single desire that dominated my search for delight was simply to love and be loved. But no restraint was imposed by the exchange of mind with mind, which marks the brightly lit pathway of friendship."[5] That pathway is, instead, filled with "clouds of muddy carnal concupiscence," as well as "the bubbling impulses of puberty."[6] Given that many of Augustine's early recollections are focused on teenage transgressions, the *Confessions* does read almost like a queer YA text, whose protagonist has developed unwelcome romantic feelings for a friend (or several friends). He clearly notes that, when he was sixteen, he gave himself "totally" to "acts allowed by shameful humanity, but under your laws illicit."[7]

In one scene that's oft-cited in discussions of medieval adolescence, Augustine mentions going to the bathhouse with his father: "[When] my father saw that I was showing signs of virility and the stirrings of adolescence, he was overjoyed to suppose that he would now be having grandchildren."[8] Whenever I read this scene, I can't help but think of Martial's bathhouse poetry in the *Epigrams*,[9]

---

4 "sed exhalabantur nebulae de limosa concupiscentia carnis" (*Augustini Confessiones* II.ii).
5 "Et quid erat, quod me delectabat, nisi amare et amari? sed non tenebatur modus ab animo usque ad animum, quatenus est luminosus limes amicitiae" (*Augustini Confessiones* II.ii).
6 "sed exhalabantur nebulae de limosa concupiscentia carnis et scatebra pubertatis, et obnubilabant atque obfuscabant cor meum, ut non discerneretur serenitas dilectionis a caligine libidinis" (*Augustini Confessiones* II.ii).
7 "vesania libidinis licentiosae per dedecus humanum, inlicitae autem per leges tuas?" (*Augustini Confessiones* II.ii).
8 "quin immo ubi me ille pater in balneis vidit pubescentem et inquieta indutum adulescentia, quasi iam ex hoc in nepotes gestiret" (*Augustini Confessiones* II.iii).
9 Martial's epigrams (first century CE) are brief, engaging poems about city life in Rome. Like his earlier contemporary, the poet Catullus (d. 54 BCE), Martial writes in an accessible, often snarky way, about morals in ancient Rome. Both poets talk about boyfriends and girlfriends—as well as intimate love for male friends—and while Roman sexuality is complex, readers might connect with these poets as bisexual men. Bisexuality is essentially the default in ancient Roman sexuality, which focuses on the tension between activity/passivity for men in particular, rather than strictly on categories of identity. Martial mentions same-sex marriage in

which talks about "draucos" (queer jocks) cruising each other in the intimate space. Is Augustine shyly, ashamedly doing the same thing, as his father comments on his own heterosexual virility? Looking over the older man's shoulder to spy one of those beefy draucos, or the slender youth that kept the fourth-century poet Ausonius awake at night?[10] So much of the *Confessions* is a continual resistance to a queer adolescence that Augustine can't condone. In his famous story about stealing from a neighbor's pear tree, he says "the fruit was beautiful, but was not that which my miserable soul coveted."[11] It's being bad that enchants him, and being bad that gives him a context for how to be good. He further describes Original Sin as "that one sin . . . [that] in one man the whole human race in its origin and, so to speak, in its very root, was condemned" (*Complete Works* Original Sin). Sin isn't simply a thing to be avoided, but the condition that makes mortal, human life possible. We live by failing, in this regard, echoing ancestral failure. Since human generation duplicates this sin, one of the problems that medieval thinkers had about homosexuality was that it didn't continue the cycle. By failing to generate children and carry on a family name, queer people not only avoided social responsibilities, but also missed out on the experience of penance occasioned by marriage and childbirth.

As medieval Europe moved into the university age of the twelfth century and beyond, scholars like Thomas Aquinas, Peter Lombard, and Peter Abelard would shape a new curriculum focused on "dialectic," or productive debate. This dialectical model still shapes contemporary classrooms, which serve as spaces that can be both safe and challenging—a place to question ideas, so long as your own existence isn't what's being questioned. In *The Nature of Things*, Aquinas says straightforwardly that "the human soul falls short of the perfection of divine life" (*Selections* n.p.). The impossibility of knowing God ensures that we're all failing, in some way, and that failure is a necessary condition of mortal existence. In *On the Teacher*, he also reminds us that "although the science we acquire through teaching is of indefectible things, none the less, knowledge itself can fail" (*Complete Writings* n.p.). The medievalist texts that we'll look at tend to approach failures of knowledge, as well. Elliott Schafer fails to

---

Rome, though he's somewhat cranky about it. The Latin term *cinaedus* also seems to have been an identity-marker for people we might now think of as queer femme males—the term originally referred to sexualized male dancers, and eventually became indicative of all cis queer men who were known for bottoming.

10 Ausonius, writing as the Roman Empire collapses, serves as a fascinating bridge between the classical world and the emerging early medieval one.

11 "dicat tibi nunc ecce cor meum, quid ibi quaerebat, ut essem gratis malus et malitiae meae causa nulla esset nisi malitia (*Augustini Confessiones*, I.iv).

understand, for instance, that the unicorns in his world are carnivorous, since he's been conditioned by medievalist fantasy to see them as beautiful and harmless. But sometimes these characters deal with failures to act, as well—failures to be heroic, or to be *anything* that matters within their own societies. In his discussion of agency in *The Human Good*, Aquinas manages to crystallize a medieval view of action mixed with good intentions: "Every agent, in acting, intends some end . . . [but] there is in any activity something beyond which the agent seeks nothing further; were this not so, actions would extend into infinity" (*Complete Writings* n.p.). A proper agent, then, is one who acts decisively, for a good purpose. Everything must have an end, just as "fire generates fire, and the olive an olive." He cites failed agents as doctors who fail to cure their patients, and artists who fail to produce true art. Total failure to act is what produces the possibility of evil, because it interrupts the circuit between action and goodness. If God is the ultimate end, but we fail to act towards that, we fail to apprehend God. Failure to call out racism and transphobia in medieval studies amounts to the same issue. It isn't enough to feel bad about it. If you're asked to appear on a "manel" (a panel of all cis men)—say no and explain why. When you see scholars being attacked for calling out racism in the academy—deal with their attackers, so the scholars can continue on with their lives. And don't leave this work to racialized academics. As we saw at Kalamazoo in 2019, this is work that desperately needs to be done by white scholars.

Medieval views on being fallen weren't negative in any simple sense. Scholars like Peter Abelard wrote that our fallen state didn't necessarily make us wrong, or lesser: in the *Ethics*, he says that "the body's very nature or structure makes many people prone to wantonness, just as it does to anger. But they don't sin by the fact that they are like this" (*Ethical Writings* 2). The real sin is in having "scorn for the creator" (3), which amounts to a kind of negative being—"as if we define shadows by saying they are the absence of light" (ibid.). Various sins take on a shadowy quality here, somewhat indefinable, while Original Sin shades us from every angle. But Abelard creates a fascinating escape from punishment: "If what were at one time illegal and prohibited deeds are later permitted and so legalized, they are committed now without any sin at all" (8). There's always a future where you might not be illegal. In this sense, a present failure might transform into a future triumph, as laws and societies change. All three of these philosophers view mortal failures—of flesh, and of understanding—as necessary elements of earthly life and learning.

Popular dramatic texts about the fall of humankind, like *The Fall* and *The Expulsion* (from the York Corpus Christi Cycle) tend to focus on shame, while also being fascinated by knowledge's temptation. In *The Fall*—which was likely first performed in the late fourteenth century—Satan the serpent describes himself as

"A worme that wotith wele how / That yhe may wirshipped be" (Davidson 2).[12] After eating the fruit, Adam laments "that bittir brayde / And drery dede that I it dyde" (4). A flaming cherubim drives them both to "middilerth," and we can see how Tolkien drew upon this existing medieval concept of the world as a "middle yard" between eternities. In *The Expulsion*, an angel tells the audience of the couple's fall: "Fro thaym is loste bothe game and glee" (1). Adam then describes a state of perpetual grief, where "mournynge makes me mased and madde" (2).[13] Yet there are ways of moving on, and unexpected acts of defiance. After listening to a tirade in which he blames her entirely for their misfortune, Eve snaps: "Be stille, Adam, and nemen it na mare. It may not mende" (4).[14] They're living in something that cannot be mended—a mortal tear in the celestial fabric. But Eve does choose to go on, and tells Adam to hush. Like the character of Miss Wardwell in *Chilling Adventures*—who turns out to be Adam's first wife, Lilith—Eve defies convention here. This sense of I can't go on, I must go on, is a mode of life that centers failure; and, like Eve, we can look failure in the eye and tell it to shut up.

This creates a sort of impossible mood: we must act, but we always act imperfectly. We must go on, but we're forever limited by our lack of essential knowledge. It sounds a lot like adolescence. And while Aquinas praises productivity as something that always has God in mind, Chaucer critiques what he calls the "wrastling world" (wrestling/bustling world) in his poem "Truth." Rather than urging us on towards perfect goals, he exhorts us to run from them: "Flee fro the prees and dwelle with sothfastnesse; / Suffyce unto thy thing, though it be smal" (L1–2, Benson 653).[15] This is an ode to anti-productivity—he tells us to focus, instead, on that kernel of interest that sustains us, "though it be smal." Several of his shorter poems focus on mutability and "lak of Stedfastnesse [stability]," a slippery condition that defines his fourteenth-century experience. Things, and people, fail to cohere. Perhaps he defines this best in the prologue to *Parliament of Fowls*, when his narrator comments upon the essential ache of life: "The lyf so short, the craft so long to lerne . . . [The] dredful joy alwey that slit so yerne" (L1–2, Benson 97).[16] He's specifically thinking of love, but this is really a meditation on all things that "slit so yerne" (slip out of our grasp). We're constantly failing, grasping, losing. Those very absences, might-have-beens, and crucial mistakes are what structure life in a fallen world. Failure isn't something to be feared—it's something that

---

12 "[I'm] a snake [worme] who knows well how you should be worshipped."
13 "Mourning makes me amazed [lost in a maze] and mad."
14 "Silence, Adam, and let it go—it can't be fixed."
15 "Flee from the crowd and dwell with patience/wisdom / be satisfied by one thing, though it be small."
16 "The life so short, the craft so long to gain / the dreadful joy that always slips away."

engenders hope. Failure is a condition of living, where we can always change and grow. And that medieval space of hope, rather than cure, is what occupies the heroes in our medievalist adaptations. *It's okay to fail—the world beat you to it. Failure has made you—failure loves you.*

The Last Unicorn

Why is medievalist YA so focused on failure? Epic fantasy for adults tends to glory in world-building, and while it can subvert generic conventions (for example, Diane Duane's funny and very queer *Middle Kingdoms* series), it often focuses on completion. Quests come to an end, characters get married, storylines move on. But middle-grade/YA fantasy goes in a sometimes very different direction. Michael Ende's *The Neverending Story*—a fantasy novel about a boy who inhabits a magic book—has a space that's literally called "The Swamp of Sadness" (RIP Artex). In Nick Sullivan's *The Seventh Princess*, the protagonist Miranda is attacked by vicious harpies while desperately trying to escape her own fantasy daydream. Mercedes Lackey's *The Last Herald Mage* trilogy was both radical in its inclusion of queer main characters, and unrelenting in its focus on alienation, suicide, and death. This fulfills Tison Pugh's "gay ghost" trope, which notes that queer characters in fantasy YA "are often metaphorically ghosts and specters" (*Innocence* 85). Rowling proved this trope by citing Dumbledore's queerness only after the character had died. Even a fantasy show that I love—*Wynonna Earp*, about a gunslinger who sends demons back to hell—manages to kill two gay characters in a single first season episode while inviting us to celebrate the memory of their love for each other. I'll discuss later how the show improves, but this is an early false start that plays into the "bury your gays" trope—that is, introducing gay characters only to write them out violently later. Yes, having two queer demons in love is an interesting move—but what use is this representation when both die in the end? We need living queer characters, not metaphorical ghosts.

Magic is a force that bends reality, a force that should be full of hope. But in many YA novels, there's a failure at the core of magic, and many of the particular novels that I've mentioned lean into this failure. Readers are supposed to see these failures, the exposed wiring of medievalist worlds that can't quite live up to our daydreams, but do often invoke nightmares. This failure disrupts what Jack Halberstam calls "the toxic positivity of contemporary life" (3). It also exposes the failure of those medievalist tropes we hold so dear—castles, princesses, wizards—and slyly suggests that we need to queer these concepts to make them our own.

Peter S. Beagle's novel, *The Last Unicorn*, was released in 1968, at the height of anti-racist protests on university campuses across the United States. Unlike the work of Le Guin, which came out in the same year, Beagle's novel doesn't approach race in a meaningful way. It's more invested in providing a melancholy satire about the fairy tale genre. *The Last Unicorn* is by no means a critical failure—it's been in print for over fifty years and was adapted as a cult-classic animated film. Twitter is full of *Last Unicorn* GIFs. But analysis of the novel remains modest, given its enduring popularity. Articles by David Stevens and R. E. Foust appeared in the 1970s and '80s, reading the novel as both a postmodern fantasy and light satire. Geoffrey Reiter's more recent (2005) article in *Mythlore* reads the unicorn as a medieval Christ figure. Indeed, Hildegard of Bingen offered the same metaphor in her twelfth-century *Book of Divine Works*. Finally, Weronika Kaszkiewicz, in her 2014 article, notes that the unicorn finds a balance in her "struggle to move from innocence to experience" (63). All of these authors find medievalist echoes in Beagle's novel, from Boethius's *Consolation of Philosophy* to the apocryphal story of the unicorn banished from Noah's ark (was she too spirited, or did she simply fail to make the cut?). I'd suggest this is because the novel fails, in many ways, to cohere as a standard fantasy text. It dramatizes radical failure in ways that don't fit neatly into Tolkien's framework of eucatastrophe/dyscatastrophe. In "On Fairy Stories," he defines *eucatastrophe* as "the consolation of fairy stories . . . [the] happy ending," while *dyscatastrophe* is "[the] sorrow and failure . . . [necessary] to the joy of deliverance" (13). You can't have one without the other, and the mourning mood of dyscatastrophe is what defines any treatment of medieval magic—it has to fail, somehow.

The Last Unicorn drags us and invites us closer to the fire, then deflates our epic fantasies with cold water. Beginning with a unicorn seems promising enough, but Beagle reminds us in the very first sentence that the unicorn is alone. She leaves her lilac wood because she can no longer bear the anxiety of living with herself. Medievalist readings of unicorns imagine them as placid creatures; medieval manuscripts more often see them as battle-hungry, their horns dipped in blood. Brennan's *In Other Lands* will imagine them the same way, as failing to live up to Elliot's expectations: a hungry (and horny) unicorn becomes one of Elliot's first red flags about the fantasy world he's been dropped into. In a fourteenth-century French decretal manuscript (Royal MS 10), a unicorn fights off two bears in the margins. Other manuscripts depict unicorns in battle. Beagle—rejecting both the purity and battle images—is perhaps the only writer to imagine a truly anxious unicorn.

Much of the novel's beginning focuses on the unicorn's failure to exist as a proper myth. The hunters who stroll through her grove are divided about whether she exists at all. Later, when a man on the road tries to capture her, the unicorn is stunned to realize that he sees her as a common horse: "Is that what you take me for? Is that what you see?" (10). The unicorn moves through a world where only precious few can see her for what she truly is—an experience that many readers might relate to. After smoothly evading the man, she meditates on the failure of his own intentions: "I never really understood . . . [what] you dream of doing with me, once you've caught me" (9). And why do we pursue unicorns? Because they resemble Christ's purity? Because they are impossible? Surely they don't grant wishes, or hoard treasure like dragons, or fly like Pegasi. There's something pointless about this unicorn in particular. The failed witch, Mommy Fortuna (ripped straight out of Boethius), has to fashion a magical horn so that the customers of her Night Carnival will actually see the unicorn. As a play on fortune, Mommy Fortuna appears as a failed witch who's just powerful enough to see the unicorn. Like the unicorn, Mommy Fortuna finds herself critically underestimated in a world that sees her—and her magic—as nothing but a parlor trick.

This is the point at which she meets Schmendrick, a failed magician who projects "an air of resolute bewilderment" (18). Schmendrick fails so hard, so spectacularly, at being a magician, that his mentor proclaims it to be something epic: "[Your] ineptitude is so vast, your incompetence so profound, that I am certain you are inhabited by a greater power than I have ever known . . . [you are] eternally inefficient" (151). The unicorn is also "eternally inefficient," a mostly forgotten myth, visible only to a mediocre witch and a crappy wizard. You can see why my students might not have taken an immediate liking to this novel, with its insistent focus on scrapping myths and destroying dreams. Schmendrick and Mommy Fortuna are both failed mages, keenly aware of their own magical mediocrity. Schmendrick notes that her power amounts to "spells of seeming . . . [she] cannot make things" (27). His spells also fail to produce concrete results. This is anti-generative magic, immaterial, without a future. It flies in the face of what we know about "real" magic, which is supposed to change the world.

Schmendrick's failure recalls the many failures that form an ableist, capitalist mode of life, where time is a commodity. He is actually quite old as a character, but hasn't learned the necessary magical skills in the time given. He's working on a different timeline from the court sorcerer in King Haggard's court, who seems to have received a more traditional education. In this sense, Schmendrick participates in the concept of crip time as someone learning at his own pace. Reacting against capitalist time in her work *Feminist, Queer, Crip*, Alison Kafer notes that the very act of being disabled or cognitively different issues "a challenge to normative and normalizing expectations of pace and scheduling" (27). Part of being human is being late, and when your body and mind have an extra layer of complexity, you're going to be late more often. This isn't a failure, but rather a call for flexibility and a desire to "imagine crip futures, because disabled people are continually being written out of the future, rendered as the sign of the future no one wants" (46). Even something that seems objective, like time, is actually wildly subjective, and narratives of pacing within disabled life are acts of resistance to the unhealthy pace of life under capitalism. By exposing the artificial nature of a certain kind of normalized productivity, we leave more room for failure, because so many people are failing humanly to live up to these expectations. We need narratives that are uneven, narratives that don't quite track, like *The Last Unicorn*, where Schmendrick can be "eternally inefficient" while still being regarded as worthy of care.

A certain queerness breathes in this bad, cobbled-together, underwhelming power. Mommy Fortuna's spells are campy in their performative nature, turning a depressed spider into Arachne, a toothless lion into a manticore, and a real unicorn into a fake one. At one point she references her own evil childhood in a way that opens up fascinating possibilities for queer, witchy kids: "Trudging through eternity, hauling my homemade horrors—do you think *that* was my dream when I was young and evil? Do you think I chose this meager magic . . . [because] I never knew the true witchery?" (37–38). What does it mean, to be young and evil? What would a young Maleficent, a young Wicked Witch of the West, dream of? Mommy Fortuna's *youthful* evil suggests a surprisingly powerful mode of being, a kind of enthusiastic chaos. Her barbed comment imagines a whole generation of young and evil witches who failed to mature into really impressive villains, an evil in-between that makes space for all levels of dark magic. We can imagine Morgan, or Madame Mim, saying something similar—that we need space for evil witches, as well as good ones.

Mommy Fortuna echoes a number of medieval and medievalist enchantresses who have failed to resonate. There's Sebile from the pre-Malory Arthurian stories, who fails to defeat the Dame d'Avalon (or to be remembered beyond a few scrappy scenes). There's Canile, the Saxon enchantress of the *Prose Lancelot*—in love with Arthur—who "knew more about enchantments than any damsel in the country" (Corley 371). She keeps her spell-books in a sealed chest, and when Kay burns it, Canile throws herself off a cliff (though she survives). Eilonwy, the brilliant and sarcastic enchantress in Lloyd Alexander's *Prydain* series, gives up her magic in order to marry dull Taran—*why?* Evil-Lyn, who openly defies Skeletor, admitting that she wants his mystical power. Like Morgan, she's able to shift shape: an old woman, a peasant girl, a ball of flame. What I loved about her was that she was angry—a proud villain. In a 2017 episode of Matt Baume's *Sewers of Paris* podcast, Anthony Oliveira talks about the villains in *He-Man*, noting that queer viewers "identify with villains because they got through something . . . [and] the queer experience is Skeletor trying to get to power" ("Failed Mystics," Episode 277). More on this queer cartoon medievalism later, but it serves as a frame for thinking about villains like Mommy Fortuna.

In *The Queer Art of Failure*, Halberstam describes a stylish mode of failing that "turns on the impossible, the improbable, the unlikely, and the unremarkable. It quietly loses, and in losing it imagines other goals for life" (88). Along with Sara Ahmed's refusal of happiness, this notion of radical failure has become a rallying cry for LGBTQ+ people who cruise through a variety of failures. This might include the failure to meet hetero milestones (getting married, buying property, having kids), as well as the failure to embody acceptable forms of masculinity and femininity in a world that pivots on the gender binary. It's enchanting to imagine, as Halberstam suggests, that "failing is something queers do and have always done exceptionally well; for queers failure can be a style" (3). I've had conversations about this with queer, trans, and nonbinary friends and colleagues, and I think it's fair to say that we're all skeptical of the liberatory properties of queer failure. Failure to pass as straight or cis at work can (does) result in termination. Failure to appear sufficiently straight in public can (does) result in violence.

My own failures to pass as neurotypical have often resulted in moments of bottomless shame, as well as warnings about how I should be more affable, sociable, clear, straightforward, pleasant, quiet, still, happy, normal. In a recent Twitter post, Cody Jackson unpacks this celebration of queer failure: "Folks want to academize failure. We need to understand that failure can be falling flat on our asses with no recourse or plan" (July 22, 2019). For many, failure can actually be the difference between life and death. But it can also be what Jackson calls "an ethical path of un/learning . . . [queer] failure is so excessive that we can't map it as failure (as such). [I]t's leaky and cannot be contained in a terrain of hetero logics" (ibid.). If we're going to frame this failure as a life mode rather than a style, we need something in-between celebration and hopelessness, a politics that acknowledges both the pleasures and the dangers of failing in a world that literally kills in the name of success.

The medievalism of *The Last Unicorn* is designed around stylistic failures. Very few characters recognize that the unicorn actually exists, including an addled butterfly whose speech is inter-mixed with poetic references. At one point, Schmendrick eats a taco in what we must presume is a medieval town. The very idea of a wizard eating a taco is queer comic perfection, but it's even more obvious as a wink to the reader because this fairy-tale world is already a pastiche of different cultures and time periods. Stevens notes that Beagle's novel "presents a serious theme . . . with a comic technique" (230). We see this most keenly when Schmendrick and the unicorn meet Captain Cully and his crew of rogues. They want to frame themselves as Robin Hood and his merry men but know that they're actually opportunistic thieves living on the margins of society. Cully initially mistakes Schmendrick for a noted fabulist, a figure like Jacob Grimm, who might record their less-than-impressive story. "One always hopes, of course,"

Cully tells him, "even now—to be collected, to be verified, annotated, to have variant versions, even to have one's authenticity doubted" (82–83). As an academic, this line strikes me to my core: the piercing desire to be cited, archived, "verified." *The Last Unicorn* actually claps back at critics in this moment, ironically anticipating how we'll continue to analyze it as a medievalist text that defies classification.

The late medieval Robin Hood ballads—which Beagle plays with here—also circulate within a space of failure. When Robin Hood first appears in Andrew of Wyntoun's fifteenth-century chronicle, he and his companion Little John are described as "waythmen," or forest outlaws (Knight, *Robin Hood*). But by the time Walter Bower mentions Robin in 1440, he's called a "famous murderer" and a cutthroat. Similarly, J. C. Holts clarifies that Maid Marian, Robin's love interest in popular culture, "only made her way into the legend via the May Games" (155) of the sixteenth century. In the earliest Middle English ballads, Robin has no love interest but Little John, with whom he shares a volatile camaraderie. The action of the mid-fifteenth-century "Robin Hood and the Monk" pivots on a disagreement between Robin and Little John. Even when Little John rescues him in the end, Robin sharply observes that "I make the maister [. . .] / Of alle me men and me" (Knight, *Robin Hood* L313–14).[17] In order to free Robin from prison, Little John casually murders both a monk and his young companion. In the slightly later "Robin Hood and the Potter," Robin is physically bested by the potter, whose "acward stroke / Smot the bokeler owt of hes hand" (Knight, *Robin Hood* L67–68).[18] Finally, the more expansive sixteenth-century "Gest of Robyn Hode" ends not in triumph, but with Robin having been *bled to death* by a prioress with shades of Evil-Lyn (Knight, *Robin Hood*). In his reimagining of Robin's "merry" men, Beagle seems to be drawing upon the Robin Hood tradition's own focus on failure and deceit.

When Molly Grue finally sees the unicorn, her response is to upbraid her for failing to appear sooner, in a moment that cries out to adult readers:

> *Where have you been?* . . . [And] what good is it to me that you're here now? Where were you twenty years ago, ten years ago? How dare you, how dare you come to me now, when I am *this* . . . [It] would be the last unicorn in the world that came to Molly Grue. (97)

The unicorn arrives at the wrong time, in the wrong place, appearing before the wrong person. As the (presumably) last unicorn in the world, she also has no future. Unicorns have become something of a gay shorthand, highly GIFable. It can be empowering to think of oneself as a unicorn. But the real thing is world-destroying. And Molly Grue's accusation might as well be the rage of queer kids

---

17 "I am the master of all men, and myself."
18 "[The potter's] backward stroke threw the shield out of [Robin's] own hand."

and queer adults alike. *Where were the unicorns when we needed them?* I thought of this recently when a student on the spectrum described how they were trying to start a campus fanclub for *Bronies*—male fans of the *My Little Pony* cartoon/toy franchise. How unlikely unicorns do exist for readers and viewers who might not have found kinship with the medieval variety. And how a 1980s franchise originally aimed at young girls can also be taken up by all kinds of fans (just as *He-Man* was aimed at boys but has a diverse fandom).

In his study of the unicorn tapestries housed at the Cloisters, Adolfo Cavallo notes that the unicorn's biblical significance "is based on what is likely to have been an error in translation from the Hebrew to the Greek" (23), when the Hebrew word for ox (*re'em*) was replaced with the Greek *monokeros*. This act of (mis)translation became an act of creation, and the unicorn "earned a permanent place in the Bible, which later served as irrefutable proof of its existence" (ibid.). This might serve as a form of queer generation, or a misreading that creates something new. The unicorn tapestries are serene from a distance, but they actually dramatize a violent hunt. Beagle's novel works in much the same fashion, beginning with an idyllic first line—"the unicorn lived in a lilac wood"—but ending with a violent confrontation between the unicorn and the Red Bull. Even Molly Grue, the unicorn's closest companion, observes that "a unicorn is an absurd animal when the shining has gone out of her" (139). Beagle's world turns around useless wizards, outdated unicorns, and broken knights "clad in homemade mail—rings, bottle caps, and links of chain sewn onto half-cured hides . . . [their] faces were invisible behind rusted visors" (155). His whole world is rusting, decaying, and this allows readers to question their own assumptions about myth and medieval fantasy. But it also has the potential for queer liberation. In his *Sewers of Paris* interview, Oliveira makes a point about "cheap" medievalism in *He-Man*. It was queer, he said,

> Precisely because [the show] had to be so cheap and rushed . . . [what's] so great about pulp, especially as a kid, is that it lets you take so many cultural points and learn them quickly, and put them into contact with each other very expediently . . . [and this] is also part of the queer experience: you learn to manipulate the things that aren't yours in an expedient and mannered way (Baume, "Failed Mystics," Episode 277).

Oliveira learned to speak English from watching *He-Man*, and I certainly learned early lessons about queerness, gender, and power as I developed attachments to characters like Evil-Lyn, Skeletor, and the Sorceress. This "cheapness" can be productive, and it mirrors the anecdote about medievalism at the beginning of Carolyne Dinshaw's *How Soon Is Now?* While at a medieval/Renaissance festival, Dinshaw sees a young man "in a terry cloth bathrobe," meant to echo a monk's habit, and she thinks: "Even in the absence of a costume he did his best" (x). His connection between past, present, and future echoes, for Dinshaw, medievalism's playful queerness, as well as its "multiple temporalities . . . [and] serious fun" (xi). Beagle is also engaged in a project of queer, serious fun.

Schmendrick, in particular, offers a forgiving queer space for "bad" magicians. He's cursed to wander the world, and he talks about magic in the same way that we sometimes talk about gender: "[It] knows what it wants to do . . . [but] I never know what it knows" (73). Upon recognizing the unicorn, Schmendrick declares his own power in singularity: "I too am *real*. I am Schmendrick the magician" (44). He calls *himself* a magician, even when others don't. In a recent Twitter conversation, medievalist Ellis Light notes: "Schmendrick gave me sooooo many trans feels" (July 16, 2019). As a queer kid growing up in the 1980s, I found Schmendrick to be one of few non-toxic male characters in fantasy media. Wizards like Gandalf and Merlin were too old to be relatable (at the time—I certainly relate to them now), but Schmendrick was a soft boy who looked young and wasn't actually *good* at magic. His failures were somehow encouraging. You could be a screw-up and still save the world. And his lack of romantic entanglements was more visible, in this case, than if he'd been a much older character. His enigmatic character opens up a whole host of opportunities for trans, nonbinary, and neurodivergent readers to see themselves in Schmendrick, and in the fantasy genre as a whole. You don't have to look, sound, or be a certain way in order to become a magician—name yourself, and the magic will move through you, knowing the way all along.

Elliot Schafer in Sarah Reese Brennan's *In Other Lands*

Elliot Schafer—the protagonist of Sarah Reese Brennan's *In Other Lands*—is another character who learns that unicorns are more than they seem. In the beginning of the novel, Elliot qualifies for a mysterious training program in a medievalist world, separated from our own by an invisible wall. This mirrors the structure of the Ivory Tower (which also happens to be a magical structure in *The Neverending Story*). The ways in which fantasy realms are often separate from our world can also serve as academic metaphors—if we want medieval studies to be accessible, we need to ensure that it isn't hidden behind a curtain of gate-keeping, classism, and spaces that remain physically inaccessible to students.

Rather than wandering accidentally into this world, Elliot is quite literally driven there in a van full of students (most of whom don't qualify). When a well-meaning teacher attempts to explain what's happening, Elliot's reply gives us an idea of his highly contemporary point of view: "I don't need you to explain to me the concept of a magical land filled with fantastic creatures that only certain special children can enter. I am acquainted with the last several centuries of popular culture" (2). In this way, Brennan skips over a whole genre of children's fantasy literature, in order to present a character who's no wide-eyed Harry Potter or academically intense Hermione. Elliot's only power within this new world is what I've come to think of as critical snark.

We'll get to the various ways in which Elliot negotiates this hostile world through irony, sarcasm, and brazen critique. For now, this early description serves to illustrate his mood throughout the novel: "Elliot refused to accept other people's version of reality" (28). Believing in magic—believing in yourself—can be a daily act of refusing other people's versions of reality for you. Growing up as a neuro-atypical kid, I would have related keenly to Elliot's philosophy of rejecting those putative realities that threatened his own. That's actually what I was doing, though I didn't have a name for it at the time. Elliot isn't simply refusing to listen to whatever people tell him. In fact, he does listen, and then argues with them about the factual accuracy of their statements. Even at the awkward age of thirteen, he's questioning the fundamentalist assumptions that produce violence, hierarchy, and social alienation. By refusing to accept these versions of reality, he fights for the world that he actually perceives.

The novel takes aim at everything from *Harry Potter* to *The Chronicles of Narnia*, while crafting one of the rare bisexual characters within the hybrid genre of YA fantasy. Elliot's sexuality is apparent from the first few chapters, when he mentions a previous crush on a male classmate, while also falling hopelessly in love with an elf named Serene-Chaos-in-the-Heart-of-Battle.[19] Brennan imagines elves as a highly structured matriarchy, where male elves have feminine stereotypes projected socially upon them. Serene blithely describes all men as innocent, soft, and helpless, with the casually sexist logic of an eighteenth-century male philosopher. This allows Brennan to puncture various sexist stereotypes within the fantasy genre,[20] and it gives Elliot the chance to consider his own complicated masculinity as an avowed pacifist who focuses on forging treaties rather than waging war. This is made all the more apparent when he becomes uneasy

---

19 Elves are seen in the novel as culturally distinct from humans, with their own inverted gender politics (men are expected to be sensitive, and women wage war), as well as complex patronymics. One of the things that makes Elliot a successful diplomat in the series is his willingness to learn about the fantasy realm's various cultures.

20 The animated program *The Dragon Prince* also features a queer romance between two elves, Runaan and his husband Ethari, as well as an interracial queer relationship between Queen Annika and Queen Neha. The show further disrupts white-centric fantasy narratives through the main character of Prince Ezra, who is mixed-race.

friends with Luke Sunborn, a warrior who just wants to fit in to the medievalist hierarchies of his world. Boy gets boy (and harpy—more on that shortly).

After two of Luke's cousins knock him out of a tree and bloody his nose, Elliot frames the event as an argument: "Kids at my old school used to hit me all the time, I have collected data on this subject, and I am in the perfect position to tell you that it has no useful results whatsoever" (56). He tries to appeal to the logic of his bullies, even when he knows that it won't work. This scene makes my heart ache because I can remember having the same conversation, to no avail. Elliot refuses to stop, and this makes him a hero, even if it results in alienating the people around him. Luke doesn't understand why he won't fight back, and Serene is scandalized that Luke's rowdy cousins would attack a defenseless boy. Like Quentin Coldwater from *The Magicians*, Elliot realizes quickly that this fantasy world is going to be just as bullshit as the world that he escaped from. This is similar to Quentin's rejection of Fillory, and we might also connect it to the experience of teaching in academia. The class-heavy "life of the mind" vs. the reality of teaching 4–5 classes per semester as an adjunct instructor, without health benefits. When I taught on contract for a major metropolitan university in the United States, I had to pick up each diminutive check in person, and made so little money that I routinely crossed the border when I needed to see a doctor. A colleague was ordering hormones on the internet, and hoping that they would be safe, due to lack of health funding. The fantasy of academia is the sweet unicorn; the reality is running for your life through the forest.

Nowhere is this more apparent than when Elliot encounters a unicorn for the first time. An awkward scene ensues when he has the idea to use virginal Luke as bait for the unicorn hunt. He thinks the unicorn will simply lay her head in Luke's lap, just like in the tapestries. But the unicorn nearly gores Luke, and as Elliot gets a good look at the creature of his dreams, he realizes how wrong the myth was: "He looked down at the unicorn. He saw, suddenly, that it wasn't as lovely as he had thought at first. Its shiny horn was too sharp, and its eyes were red with the light of murder" (204). I'd argue that Brennan's novel is adapting the work of Beagle when she reframes the unicorn as predatory, while rewriting her harpy characters as complex and socially responsible. This is driven home when we discover that Luke is actually half-harpy, and has a set of golden wings that surprise him (hello puberty!) In *The Last Unicorn*, the harpy Celano is an ancient murder-bird whose wings are razor sharp. But when Elliot touches Luke's wings (later apologizing for not asking first), he finds them to be soft and miraculous. Brennan plays a similar trick with mermaids when she re-casts them in a firmly medieval light as violent sirens who drown men to protect their underwater home.

Elliot rejects any notion of growth or redemption in this fantasy world: "Every bit of reality in the fantasy reminded him that miracles were not for him" (47).

Where other characters find their niche, Elliot just keeps researching, but never arrives at a role that fits. What he does best is argue. Sara Ahmed crystallizes this, in her book *Willful Subjects*, when she discusses the incapacity of a rule-bound world to accept children who actually know themselves: "Some wills appear as too full of will, a fullness that is also narrated as an emptying or theft of will from others" (17). This also echoes Melanie Yergeau's discussion of people on the spectrum as "non-rhetorical" and difficult. Elliot is read immediately as being "too full of will," and even his close friends react to this with confusion and hostility. Jase—a musician that Elliot dates briefly—makes an unavoidable point during their breakup: "[You'd] be difficult for anyone to put up with" (242). Elliot's willfulness puts him in danger at several points in the novel, and sometimes prevents him from connecting with people who want to help him. But it also keeps him alive, and preserves his own reality—which is a good one.

Elliot's biggest disappointment is that magic doesn't truly exist in this "magical" world: there are mythical creatures and vague enchantments, but no wizards, and no magic for *him*. Near the end of the novel, Elliot discovers that his mother also fled to this world, and has been operating stealthily as a medic the whole time. The scene in which they meet, and talk, is not one of reconciliation. His mother feels no guilt for leaving him, and sees her departure as a matter of survival. She does not miss him, or even think about him, though she does recognize him as her son. This is one of Brennan's most powerful and heart-aching subversions of epic fantasy, as Elliot realizes that he is neither a prince, nor a magician, nor a crafty orphan. Afterwards, Elliot plants himself firmly within the dyscatastrophe phase of Tolkienian fantasy. In fact, he terrorizes a group of kids that he's supposed to be teaching, by offering them a speech that is precisely the opposite of Sam's lovingly queer speech to Frodo in *Return of the King*:

> We're too young to know any better, to know we won't triumph and be heroes, that we won't be returned to the other world as if no time had passed, that the lies in the stories aren't about mermaids or harpies—the lies are about us. The lies that we might be good enough, and we might get out. We could fail at everything we try to do here, and we will never be able to get back home. (219)

This mirrors Quentin Coldwater's speech in Season 4 of *The Magicians*, in which he expresses what an "incredible disappointment" the magical world of Fillory has been. Both characters take these failures of magic personally, because both had held out so much hope that magic might improve their lives.

Elliot does still try. He keeps coming back to this world, after all. He discovers that his analytical and treaty-making abilities do, in fact, earn him a social niche. But he doesn't lose his snark, or his capacity to be overwhelmed. He says to Luke: "I'm terrible at feelings, it's like they're knives, I don't really know what to do with them and I end up throwing them with too much force" (150). At one point—when he should probably do something nice for Luke, who is hurting—Elliot observes: "He didn't feel there was much kindness left in him, and any kindness there was he fiercely wanted to save for himself" (221). The idea of a character saving kindness for himself isn't precisely heroic, but it is realistic. This also aligns with Ahmed's work on refusing happiness, and her exploration of willfulness as a politics that actually signals our varied humanity: "A willful politics might involve a refusal to cover over what is missing, a refusal to aspire to be whole" (*Willful Subjects* 184). Expanding on work by Audre Lorde, Ahmed also describes self-care as a kind of warfare. Self-care can be about "how to live for, to be for, one's body when you are under attack" ("Selfcare as Warfare"). Self-care can be an act of heroic resistance, especially for disabled people fighting to exist in a world that doesn't see our needs as cost-effective.

Elliot calls himself "vexing," but might this also be a potentially positive category, like willful? To vex is to harass, but also to agitate (from *vexare*), to question, to worry the edges of the norm. I'm also vexing. I often fail to perceive things, or perceive them too intensely. I vex with my worries and my questions ("so, you're saying there will be *five* people at the symposium? And where's the nearest bathroom?"). Many students feel vexing when they ask for accommodations—because universities are designed to make them feel as if they're requesting special support. Vexing can also be a needed thing—an act of inquiry, even love. Elliot is vexing, but he also *vexes* the foundations of an imperfect fantasy world. He says to Jase: "I always do exactly what I want, and I never care what anyone else thinks of it" (232). This isn't a typically heroic statement, but it could be a rallying cry for readers who don't fit in, readers who have themselves been called vexing. As a queer hero, Elliot gives us permission to vex our way through multiple worlds.

Oscar and Autistic Medievalism in *The Real Boy*

In Anne Ursu's medievalist middle-grade fantasy novel *The Real Boy*, Oscar is presented as an autistic boy in a medieval world that doesn't necessarily have the language to describe his point of view. In an interview with *Disability in Kidlit*, Ursu notes that she wrote *The Real Boy* after her son was diagnosed: "Both are loving, are easily overwhelmed, and they both feel things very deeply—too deeply, really, to function easily in a world that doesn't allow for such tremendous empathy" ("Interview with Corinne Duyvis," 2015). In her review of *The Real Boy*, author Corinne Duyvis states: "After reading many disappointing portrayals of autism, I truly wanted *The Real Boy* to be good . . . [it's] now my go-to recommendation" ("Review: *The Real Boy*," 2015). Duyvis's current YA novel, *On the Edge of Gone*, also features a protagonist on the spectrum, who must negotiate a hostile dystopia. Both books present thoughtful portrayals of autistic protagonists, written by authors who are connected with the community (though Ursu doesn't identify as autistic, she is careful in her representation of Oscar). As I'll go on to argue, Oscar's dystopia is one of miscommunication—he fails to pass as neurotypical, while succeeding to hold onto his own, valuable way of looking at the world, just as Elliot does in Brennan's novel.

Oscar works in the poor quarter of a thriving city, whose wealthier inhabitants depend upon magical trinkets and charms to make their lives easier (much as we depend upon technology). Though he has no innate magical ability, Oscar does have an instinct for herbs and their complexity. Because he's not a trained apprentice, he works behind the scenes of an apothecary run by Master Caleb, a chemist "so skilled he called himself a magician" (1). Oscar is tormented by an older apprentice named Wolf, and at first, his marginality is reminiscent of Harry Potter (also confined to a small room, out of sight). But differences between them are readily apparent: "[Oscar was] kept company by the quiet, the dark, the cocoon of a room, and a steady rotation of murmuring cats. It was a good fate for an orphan" (2). Both *Carry On* and *The Real Boy* are interested in deconstructing the "magic orphan" trope in the YA genre, and Ursu shifts it to a "good fate," rather than a site of trauma.

It's a particularly good fate for Oscar because he's sensitive to the complexity of the outside world, and his room in the cellar becomes a refuge instead of a prison. Oscar's outside stressors mirror Kamila and Henry Markram's "Intense World Theory" of autistic experience, which blames neuronal hyper-reactivity for the fact that "autistic children can be overtly sensitive to sensory stimulation."[21] As a person on the spectrum, I'm wary of any unifying theory or attempt to explain, and therefore "solve," my experience. But the phrase "intense world" does roughly describe Oscar's interactions with the outside. There are also hints of Oscar's traumatic past, including a remembered, hostile refrain: "*Look me in the eye, boy*" (95). But Oscar seems to have settled into a satisfying routine of preparing herbal remedies—until his bully, Wolf, is killed by a supernatural force. Master Caleb pulls Oscar from his safe space and thrusts him into the middle of the busy apothecary, where his social difficulties immediately become visible.

Oscar notes how hard it is to puzzle out the intentions of strangers: "When he went out into the marketplace and tried to apply what he'd learned to other

---

[21] Markram and Markram's research isn't necessarily helpful to autistic communities—in fact, the way they characterize autism as a developmental disorder is outright harmful. That said— their comments on the world being "intense" might actually resonate with some readers.

people, their faces all moved in different ways and their voices did all different things" (31). This is in sharp contrast to his experience with plants, which allows him to exercise his strengths: "With plants, there was a system" (82). Fantasy novels often employ a magic system, and Ursu plays with this by contrasting the order of medieval herblore with the chaos of human interaction. We see this as well in the medieval herbal tradition, including the early medieval *Lacnunga*, or "Leech-Book," manuscript of recipes and spells (MS Harley 585). This collection contains the "Nine Herbs Charm," which names "Waybroad" as "the Mother of herbs" / "wyrta modor" (Grattan 151). The herbs are given their own unique perspective: "Over thee [Waybroad] have chariots rumbled / over thee have queens ridden" (Grattan 153).[22] Part of Oscar's power is his own perception of the herbs as living things—just as they're seen in *Lacnunga*. His quest involves not only solving a supernatural mystery, but also reconciling his intuitive, silent knowledge of herbs with the challenges of loud medieval sociability. This hearkens back to Merlin's natural magic, as well as Tiffany Aching's understanding of the Chalk as something in her bones.

Ursu finds a balance between teaching Oscar these rules and having him impart his own perspective to Callie, who becomes his friend and ally. In this way, the novel avoids being a neurotypical "how-to" manual and concentrates instead on Oscar's experience of the world. At a certain point in the novel, Ursu introduces a further twist: the idea that Oscar might actually be a wooden boy, like Pinocchio, or a Pygmalion-style statue come to life. As a reader, I found this suggestion to be deeply unsettling. Autistic kids are often criticized for a perceived "lack of empathy," though Ursu herself argues that Oscar has a surplus of feeling. As a kid growing up on the spectrum, I'll admit that I identified keenly with robots, like Johnny 5 from *Short Circuit* and Data from *Star Trek: The Next Generation*. Data, in particular, was a humanoid struggling to understand humanity—always grappling with a new social rule—and I shared that struggle. The thought that Oscar might be an automaton come to life, and thereby play into theories about the (in)humanity of autistic kids, was particularly fraught. In her review, Corrine Duyvis shared this unease:

> Autism is so often associated with being not quite human, with being magical and otherworldly, that this explicit comparison to a magical, inhuman being leaves me worried that readers less knowledgeable about autism and disability representation might not grasp the way Ursu played with this trope. ("Review")

---

22 "Ond þu, wegbrade, wyrta modor,
   easten openo, innan mihtigu;
   ofer ðe crætu curran, ofer ðe cwenu reodan" (L7–9, Delanty and Matto 470).

Ursu does play with the trope—Oscar's misgivings about his own potential inhumanity are proven false—but reading him *debate* this was excruciating. At one point, he thinks: "*Yes, you are a creature that thinks and moves and walks and even talks, though you don't enjoy it very much. You may be a doll, but you can do these things*" (207). I've certainly thought of myself along these lines, as a failed boy. The very title of the novel announces that it will be about Oscar's realness, and though Ursu cleverly deflects ableist sentiment, Oscar's struggle with this will no doubt be triggering to readers on the spectrum. In her memoir, Sarah Kurchak describes this as a fear connected with autistic kids: "It was the crux of my recurring nightmares . . . [that] I was a copy that my parents had been forced to take in" (*I Overcame My Autism*, Introduction). This also taps into the medieval idea of the "conjeoun," or changeling-child, which Rose Sawyer describes in their discussion of Merlin in the Middle English *Arthour and Merlin* (94). Medieval literature discussed the changeling as a fairy child, substituted for an abducted human infant. In *Arthour and Merlin*, young Merlin is accused of being a changeling, though the Middle English romance ultimately follows the commonplace that Merlin's father was a demonic incubus.

One of the book's most interesting moves is to place Oscar, a lover of systems, into a medievalist society that's highly ordered. Ursu's city of Asteri runs on the medieval guild system, and more or less follows the structure of late medieval guilds in England, Italy, and the Netherlands. Guilds are a staple of medievalist fantasy, as evidenced by web series like *The Guild*,[23] and the plethora of role-playing games that include magical guilds. They likely had their origins in the Roman world, but emerged coherently in the twelfth-century. In his monograph *Wage and Labor Guilds in Medieval Europe*, Steven Epstein argues for the corporate significance of this flexible model: "Guilds proved to be durable institutions because they became effective ways for a group of people to promote their own interests while still competing against one another" (102). One of the earliest examples that Epstein mentions is—delightfully—a group of twelfth-century pillow makers in Cologne, who form a *fraternitas* "for their own common good" (52). The guilds in *The Real Boy* operate along the same principle of brotherhood, which is most visible after Master Caleb's shop is decimated, and the masters pitch in to repair it. However, like actual medieval guilds, they are also engaged in competition.

---

[23] Running from 2007 to 2013, this low-budget but charming web series starred Felicia Day as the long-suffering member of a computer-gaming RPG (role-playing game) guild. While the show was a comedy, it also explored realities of gaming, such as trying to afford a gaming computer and looking for community at conventions.

We learn that Caleb is profiting on tax schemes, and that he's importing magical goods in spite of the dangers involved, while denying those same goods to poor residents of the Barrow neighborhood. The gradual plot reveal—that Caleb has also been *building* children for rich families—allows Ursu to subtly question eugenicist debates around disability. Caleb profits by creating "perfect" children from magic-infused wood, and when these children unexpectedly grow sick, it's Oscar and Callie who must solve the mystery. Much of this action takes place within a medieval apothecary, loosely based on historical examples. Apothecaries seem to have been near the top of the guild structure, in terms of wealth, though not quite as affluent as those who made arms and armor. Epstein places them on the edge of the *arte maggiore* in Florence, just below luxury metalworkers (148). As late as the early modern period—as evidenced by Shakespeare's *Romeo and Juliet* and other texts—the apothecary remained a site of magic and mystery. On the counter of the apothecary, science and magic were linked in ways that would have been natural for a late medieval and early modern audience.

In her article on Venetian apothecaries, Louisa Matthews notes that official or *speziale* apothecaries were "defined by their relationship to doctors," while less-official apothecaries, or *vendecolori*, might offer a "bewildering variety of wares . . . [including] pigments . . . candles, soaps, cosmetics, ink, paper, string, dyes, sweets and spices" (680). These items might be made on-site, and turn a nice profit, which means that an assistant like Oscar could be commonplace at a busy apothecary. Matthews's article includes a reproduction of an anonymous fifteenth-century fresco (Castello di Issogne, in Valle d'Aosta), which shows an apothecary's assistant grinding materials. The master behind the counter is well-dressed, while the assistant—like Oscar—wears more humble clothing, and sits away from the transactional space of the counter. Late medieval Spanish texts, like *La Celestina* by Fernando de Rojas (both the date and the author are contested), dramatized the apothecary as an illicit site. Celestina is both a bawd and a chemist, and we get a glimpse of her cobbled-together apothecary:

> Y en su casa hazía perfumes, falsava estoraques, menjuí, ánimes, ámbar, algalia, polvillos, almizcles, mosquetes. Tenía una camara llena de alambiques, de redomillas, de barrilejos de barro, de vidrio, de arambre, de estaño, hechos de mil facciones. (115)

> [In her home she made perfumes, false sycorax [for making amber], *benjamin, gum-anime*, amber, civet, powders, mixtures, musk, *mosqueta*. She had a room full of alembics [for distilling], little vials, pots of clay, of glass, of brass, of tin, made in a thousand ways.]

Celestina's apothecary offers everything from mistletoe to glass beads to abortifacients to cosmetics. In this way, it resembles a *vendicolori* with its capacious inventory, similar to the space of endless invention where Oscar works. Like medievalism itself, the apothecary fuses materials and minds in order to craft an experience.

When he's forced to deal with customers for the first time, Oscar doesn't know how to anticipate their questions. With Callie's help, he creates a "map of the essential phrases in his mind . . . *How may I help you? . . . Why don't we try some ____? . . . Perhaps you might try this instead*" (145). As if creating a recipe, he has to draw this map of questions and responses. This could mirror the act of consuming a medieval conduct manual, except, rather than trying to become a knight, Oscar is trying to pass for neurotypical. And these small-talk phrases are themselves charms, which create safe, efficient interactions. I had a similar experience to Oscar growing up—it was extraordinarily difficult to understand the rules of conversation, or anticipate how one exchange might differ from another. A variety of people on the spectrum discuss having to design this type of social map, including Rudy Simone (*Aspergirls*) and Cynthia Kim (*Nerdy, Shy, and Socially Inappropriate*). Oscar's experiences tend to be grounded in both autism culture and medieval culture.

While the magic in *Carry On* is based on words—particularly on idioms and popular phrases—the magic in *The Real Boy* is a mixture of herblore and ecopower. Much of it remains mysterious, as Oscar reads a manuscript by ancient wizards, only to be puzzled by their process: "[If] there was a system to the magic in this book, it relied on rules in languages Oscar didn't even know" (82). This magic remains fragmentary in significant ways, and this allows Ursu to dig into the essential mystery of apothecaries. Master Caleb's customers don't understand how their charms work, and Oscar's talents at herblore are first discovered when he substitutes one recipe for another of his own design. To borrow the title of an equally subversive film, it's *practical magic*, more attuned to herblore passed down by women in early medieval texts like the *Trotula*. The above-mentioned film focused more on kinship between women in a magical family than it did on the spectacle of magic, and the *Trotula* was a series of remedies for women, authored by a woman. Here we see the difference between magic as male spectacle (summoning a dragon) vs. magic as responsible practice (as when Simon communicates with the dragon in *Carry On*). When Oscar has to brew a remedy for one of the sick kids, he thinks about the process, halfway between science and magic: "At each step [of mixing] there is a small amount of transformation that cannot be overlooked or rushed. And these moments should not be, because they are beautiful" (283). These little miracles come in steps, which are part of an order that he has learned through study, but also through his senses, just as Tiffany and Sabrina learn to follow their instincts as witches. Given the environmental sensitivity of many people on the spectrum, it's a brilliant move for Ursu to make this anxiety a strength in Oscar. His attention to detail, his bottom-up processing, turn this magical recipe into a loving system where each step is beautiful.

Master Caleb is killed by a monster made of earth and scraps, a kind of medieval Golem.[24] This is the same material Oscar feared *he* might be made from. But as the novel progresses, we learn that this monster is a response from the earth itself. The ancient wizards died "to try to kill [a] plague from the soil up" (183), pouring all of their magic into the soil, which resulted in the enchanted trees that Caleb uses to manufacture children. When Oscar faces off against the earth-monster, he realizes that it's simply an ecological response to excess magic. The Humdrum, in *Carry On*, is a similar, ecological response to Simon's excess magic. These novels feature wizard characters who have upset the natural order, and it's up to their teen protagonists to restore that balance. Oscar devises a way to preserve the system of the old wizards, and he does it through his unique way of understanding details. At first he sees this as a problem: "He couldn't look at anything but the different pieces" (169). But in the end, he's able to weave those details into a plan, just as he combines the correct herbs to address plague-like symptoms in the kids. The novel is ultimately more about Oscar's way of seeing the world, than it is about fighting any kind of supernatural evil. What makes this all the more interesting is how the precisely medieval structures of Oscar's world—the apothecary and the guild system—become sites of unexpected power for him. These old systems, rather than being challenged or overturned in a contemporary move, become sites of knowledge and growth for Oscar, who uses them to translate the mysteries of social interaction. The medieval is instructive, not curative.

If not for the familiarity of the apothecary, Oscar would have no sense of home, no safe space. I'll return to this point in the epilogue, where I mention David Rose's apothecary in the Canadian show *Schitt's Creek*. At the same time, the human organizers of these systems tend to fail, even if the systems endure. Master Caleb turns into a bloodthirsty capitalist, and his death leaves Oscar alone and bewildered, suddenly responsible for the survival of the apothecary. Callie is also abandoned by her mentor, Madame Mariel, and must learn a kind of "leechcraft" on her own. As a team, Oscar and Callie are both attendant to details: Oscar knows exactly what ingredients to combine, and Callie knows exactly how to talk to her patients. But Oscar still fails to connect with people in a consistent way, and though Callie helps him to draw social maps, there are still problem areas. He doesn't quite understand how she "covered her meaning in cushions and invited people to settle back into them" (105). His questions, often abrupt, lead to confusing exchanges and hurt feelings. At one point, Callie tells him to "pretend" that

---

[24] A golem is a creature from Jewish folklore, animated by a sacred word.

he's more socially adept. Oscar replies: "I don't know how to pretend." Callie's response: "[Well], pretend you do" (159). Callie exposes the performance aspect of social interaction, the "imposter syndrome" that suggests we're all just pretending, somehow. It reminds me, as well, of an anecdote from Jenny Lawson, who has written elegantly about her own anxiety in *Furiously Happy*. When faced with the challenge of recording an audiobook, she laments to Neil Gaiman that she doesn't know how. Gaiman responds: "Well, pretend that you do."

Oscar's unwillingness to pretend is a hallmark of literary autistic characters (think the protagonist of *The Curious Incident of the Dog in the Night-Time*), who cleave to particularly rigid ways of thinking. This brought me up short, because I didn't know exactly what Oscar was saying. Did he not know how to pretend in this particular scenario, or *at all*? The latter would suggest a more stereotypical view of young autistic protagonists, and Duyvis mentions this in her review: "There's a difference between naiveté and simplifying a character's emotional landscape. The latter bothers me immensely given how often disabled people are infantilized" ("Review"). As with the twist about Oscar's realness, Ursu also plays with this idea of literalness in Oscar's thinking. When he carves some of the magic wood into a cat figurine, he names it "Cat"—not because he can't think of a more imaginative name, but because that's the name that fits. This also reminds me of a moment in John Elder Robison's autistic memoir *Look Me in the Eye*, where he talks about naming his cat "Small Animal." To me, this is hilarious, and suggests irony rather than any kind of imaginative failure.

Oscar is amazed to have created the figurine at all, since it's the first time he's made something from a mental image, rather than simply following recipes. It's both orderly and artistic, which is the point I believe Ursu intends to make about mapping vs. pretending. Callie's suggestion—"pretend that you [can pretend]"—exposes the artificiality of social interactions in a playful way. Oscar's resistance is earnest, rather than stubborn or unknowing: he *wants* social interactions to have meaning, and doesn't see how he can manufacture an illusion. The novel is ultimately concerned with the tension between binaries like real/fake, charm/spell, truth/fiction. The magic that seems artificial, a bit like Schmendrick's magic, parceled out in charms, turns out to be very real. Oscar fears that he might be fake, but comes to a gradual understanding of his own realness. That knowledge, however, does not erase his trauma at having to live in a world that fails to understand him.

And it recalls Sarah Kurchak's discussion of being seen as a "real" autistic writer: "There is something about the word 'real,' though, that hits me particularly hard as an autistic human . . . [and] what people are really doing when they're trying to determine if I'm really autistic is figuring out if I make them uncomfortable or sad enough to count" (*I Overcame My Autism*, Introduction) This roughly describes many interactions I've had with well-meaning people who wanted to assure me that I was either "very high functioning" or "not really autistic" because I could make eye contact or go out on a date. Neurotypical society creates definitions of "realness" that we don't fit into, then decides whether we count as "really" different or not. As someone with an ambiguous diagnosis—wavering between "high-functioning" and what my neuropsychologist evocatively termed "residual autism"—I get the double-edged experience of that elusive realness. Not just the fear that you might not be "really" one person or another, but that the category itself is forever out of your grasp. This can refer to the difficulty in securing a diagnosis—especially as an adult—as well as how neurotypical people will deny your existence even with a diagnosis.

People of color on the spectrum are even more vulnerable to this shifting category of "real autism," which refuses to recognize them while mobilizing racist violence against them on a daily basis. Autistic writer ChrisTiana ObeySumner criticizes the lack of autistic narratives for Black and femme people: "I feel left out, alone, erased from the sociopolitical discourses of what it means to be autistic/disabled . . . [Autism] doesn't occur in a vacuum and neither do any aspects of our intersectionality" (n.p.). Autistic people of color are far more likely to be on the receiving end of police violence, as well as the daily effects of racialized ableism. Women and nonbinary people on the spectrum also present differently from cis men, though biased testing still focuses on a particular kind of straight autistic male (completely ignoring how many people on the spectrum identify as queer, trans, and nonbinary).

Shows like *Atypical* and *Young Sheldon* focus on charming white protagonists with ample support systems, rather than individuals dealing with intersections of racism and ableism. An important counterpoint to this is Josh Thomas's recent show, *Everything's Gonna Be Okay*, which focuses on a young autistic woman trying to negotiate high school. In this show, the character Matilda challenges a number of stereotypes leveled at autistic people—she's queer, has a girlfriend, and is interested in music rather than science. Kayla Cromer, who plays Matilda, is autistic herself, and notes in an interview that "so many actors out there that have a disability or have autism are desperately trying to even get in the audition . . . [and] I could really break through the stigma attached to disability in entertainment" (Lindsay, "For Rising Stars" n.p.). Matilda struggles with sociability, but she also manages to maintain an equal relationship with another woman on the spectrum, and eventually she's accepted to the exclusive Julliard Academy. By contrast, Oscar's own "realness" in the medievalist novel is one that takes place largely outside of these concerns, and as much as we celebrate positive autistic narratives, they also need to be far more diverse.

The Real Boy dwells within a particularly medieval feeling of sadness and failure, which we began this chapter with. A sadness that is world-making, that resists curative strategies because it's our neighbor, a part of our *fraternitas*. Sadness is also a craft, and for Oscar, it remains a common perspective. He has "the sense that his whole body was charged with something, something unnatural, like his heart and brain were always spinning—and that nothing could take it away" (95). No matter how precisely he maps the social world, that "spinning" will always be there. When Oscar presents an unfinished magic doll to Callie, he calls it "a real boy . . . [Almost]. You would have barely been able to tell the difference" (250). He's speaking of himself as well—a boy rendered unreal by sadness, spinning, that sense of never quite fitting in. Oscar only relaxes in the warm, dark heart of the cellar, surrounded by cats, where he can read peacefully. As he grapples with realness, he keeps coming back to the feeling of being marginalized: "The feeling, always, of living in a different pocket of air from everyone else, not knowing how to break through it. And this, the aloneness, pressing down on his chest, the most constant company of his life" (203). Reading this hurls me back into childhood. And even though Ursu's novel ends with a moment of shy connection between Oscar and one of the children that he's rescued, that sadness remains "constant company" for him. Kinship with Callie and support from the guild members helps ease his progress through the world, but it doesn't make the world any less hostile or confusing.

We are left with his failure, not as a heartbreaking moment, but as a companion. Buffy Summers is another teen hero in a show full of medievalist imagery—from swords to spells.[25] In the finale of Season 5, she observes: "The hardest thing in this world is to live in it" (*Buffy the Vampire Slayer*, S5E22). Oscar feels the depth of this hardness, but it isn't something that he can cure with magic or herblore. When sadness is your companion, rather than your nemesis, it can lead you down unexpected paths. It can, like the cat figurine, be a comfort, even a surprise, though you intimately recognize its contours, the hard warmth of it in your hand. Oscar lacks the magical power of Caleb—he can't make life out of wood—but he can, and does, heal people. And he's able, in the end, to preserve the work of the ancient wizards by redistributing magic within the earth. Both characters are real wizards, borrowing from a number of medievalist traditions, while evolving queerly within them. Like Elliot and Schmendrick, Oscar thinks differently from those around him, and that radical difference is what allows

---

25 My own anecdotal research suggests that medievalists love *Buffy*, or at least have strong feelings about the show. I've written about how I identify strongly with the character Anya, an ex-demon who has to learn how to be human by studying the behavior of the other characters.

these mages to work. Their struggles with anxiety allow them to approach problems from surprising angles, while they re-work systems to hold their different ways of knowing. By applying their divergent minds to medievalist structures, they create firmly medieval endings—miraculous, sly, sad. Apothecaries full of mercury, fire, and hope.

In the next chapter, we'll move from failed medievalist heroes, to a medieval hero that seems to balance upon a web of failures: Sir Gawain. I'll discuss how Gawain's status as a young, untried knight makes him particularly relevant to teen readers, who may find it relatable to view medieval worlds through his perspective. At the same time, the medieval text that he's most known for—*Sir Gawain and the Green Knight*—concentrates on his many failures as a knight trying to live up to the structures of chivalry. I'll suggest that Gawain's queer adventures can make this vibrant fourteenth-century poem a kind of anti-conduct manual, or guide for growing sideways into the role of a young queer knight. This chapter will also return us to Morgan le Fay, as both a disruptive and wise presence in the poem. She challenges chivalry as something impossible to uphold, even as she offers Gawain, her nephew, the tantalizing possibility of an unwritten life outside of Arthurian convention. Along the way, we'll explore what makes the Gawain character so enduring, and what contemporary readers might be able to take from a mysterious poem about a young knight, an enchantress, and a green giant.

Chapter 5
Do You Really Want to Snyrt Me? Queer Adolescence in *Sir Gawain and the Green Knight*

A "snyrt" is a glancing blow in Middle English, and that's what it can feel like to read *Sir Gawain and the Green Knight*. Many medievalists in North America and the UK have a complicated relationship with *Sir Gawain and the Green Knight*. People specializing in the Old French tradition may be more focused on the work of Marie de France, while Iberian specialists probably have nightmares about the twelfth-century *Cantar de mio Cid* (Song of the Cid).[1] But I was trained to worry about *Sir Gawain and the Green Knight*, and it looms over me. Like *Beowulf*, it serves as a representative text within the field, a requirement for survey courses, and a text written in a tricky (West Midlands) vernacular. When I was confronted with the task of writing an M.A. thesis on *SGGK*, I felt myself drowning beneath the weight of scholarly articles that went back to the nineteenth century. How was I supposed to reckon with this imposing critical tradition? Anyone who's ever presented on the poem at a medieval conference has found that opinions remain charged. It also serves as a gate-keeping text for medievalists who feel that interpretations should line up and echo past scholarship. Don't rock the girdle. I once talked about the green knight as a queer, nonhuman figure—more of a plant than a human—and a senior medievalist was having none of this. "Where's your *proof* that Bertilak isn't human?"

It was a funny question. In a text whose entire core is a magic spell, where's the proof that Bertilak *is* human? Are any of the supporting characters in *SGGK* identifiable as medieval humans, or are they extensions of Morgan le Fay's enchantment? The story of *SGGK* is both deceptively simple and devilishly knotted. A monstrous character—the Green Knight—appears at King Arthur's court and challenges him to combat. Gawain takes Arthur's place—but after beheading the unwelcome visitor, he watches in astonishment as the Green Knight calmly picks up his head, demanding to return the favor a year later. Gawain searches far and wide for the mysterious knight, and eventually finds himself in the castle of Lord Bertilak, who is actually the Green Knight in disguise. They strike a bargain to

---
[1] This text—incorporating far older material than its twelfth-century copy—has much of the same fraught national resonance for Spain as the *Morte Darthur* has for Britain. It focuses on the titular character's resistance to Muslim rule in medieval Iberia, and gives shape to a vernacular romance tradition, which begins to develop separately from the extant Arabic and Hebraic literary traditions centered around Córdoba.

offer each other the "winnings" they receive each day, so Bertilak offers Gawain the animals he's hunted, while Gawain offers Bertilak the kisses he "wins" from the lord's wife. She also lends him a green girdle that will protect him from harm, and—crucially—Gawain *doesn't* offer this up to Bertilak, thereby breaking the rules and disrupting his own knightly virtue of honesty. When the Green Knight finally faces Gawain, he gives the knight a wee "snyrt" to the back of the neck, as a reminder of this small betrayal. The entire game, or "gomen" as it's called in Middle English, turns out to be a trick engineered by Morgan le Fay—all in the name of frightening Queen Guinevere, or so she claims at the end of the poem. This leaves us wondering what's real, what's fantasy, and what's a metaphor designed to challenge the structure of chivalry itself.

How do we separate fantasy from reality in the poem? It may be more useful to read this text through the concept of "entwinement," which Seeta Chaganti applies to an inscribed early medieval stone cross from the village of Ruthwell in her article on "The Dream of the Rood."[2] She notes that, like the entwined carvings on the cross, the inscribed runes "are woven into a complicated program of representational carving instead of existing as exterior to it" (56). Similarly, the characters in SGGK are entwined within Morgan's magic, and at the heart of this spell lies Gawain's coming-of-age story. In a poem concerned with young Arthur and untested Camelot, the central images pertain to adolescence. Cindy Vitto notes that "the number of available children's versions [of SGGK] should cause us to ponder just why this story remains so popular" (118). In this chapter, I'll link SGGK explicitly to YA literature, as a text whose focus on "a young knight's testing" (119) continues to resonate as a story about magic, deception, and queer adolescence.

One of the arguments of this book has been that criticism of the YA genre tends to focus on dystopian novels,[3] while medievalism is more clearly connected with children's literature and its celebration of fantasy. But the raw material of adolescence is often present in medieval poems like SGGK, which focuses clearly on Gawain's coming of age. And the figure of the wizard, in particular, is a staple of YA texts which draw their material from a long process of medievalist adaptation. Recent scholarship by Clare Bradford, Seth Lerer, and J. Allan Mitchell has

---

2 This early medieval poem (difficult to date, but definitely one of the earliest literary works in Old English), imagines the cross of the crucifixion as a living being that also mourns for the death of Christ, while blending early medieval Christian imagery with symbolism that might be drawn from Old Norse spirituality (Odin sacrificing himself on the World Tree), and possibly Romano-British spiritual elements, as well.

3 The dystopian fantasy cartoon, *Kipo and the Age of the Wonderbeasts*, features a romance between two queer teen POC characters (Benson and Troy). It also winks at romance tropes by having a cloud of sparkling light appear—with soft music—whenever the two exchange a knowing look.

opened up significant conversations around medieval childhood and how contemporary children's texts have adapted medieval material. With this conversation, I want to stress the pliable links between children's and YA genres that both take up the medieval world in unique ways, depending upon their young protagonists.

Gawain is somewhere between adolescence and adulthood, while having to deal with his "somewhat childish" uncle, the hot-headed King Arthur. He has a reputation for "love-talking" that belies his actual awkwardness as a potential lover, and nowhere is this more apparent than when he hides from Lady Bertilak under the covers, like a terrified frat boy. To borrow Geraldine Heng's terminology in her oft-cited article on women's relations in *SGGK*, we can think of this text as a knot that links both adolescent and childhood perspectives in medieval literature. We've previously discussed Heng's imagery of the knot in this poem, and Morgan appears at several points as a kind of "punctum" or gathered point, drawing our attention to one transition or another. Gawain is thrust into what we'd now describe as "adult situations," but retains a fluid and uncertain perspective as he deals with two worlds: one real, the other magic. The laughter throughout this text, and at its end, suggests that these worlds are slyly knotted together, and that learning this is part of Gawain's journey into adulthood. A little "snyrt" to the neck can feel like the end of the world, even if it's really the beginning. I'll argue that the poem's gentle celebration of Gawain's failings can represent a model of medieval adolescence that's surprisingly supple. For this reason, teens can draw lessons from the poem's depiction of a young knight who *must* fail in order to grow.

The Rise of Gawain

One of the common elements across the Gawain romances is the knight's youth and beauty. He's graceful but untested. Several romances focus on the infancy and illegitimacy of Gawain, whose parentage must often be kept a secret. The thirteenth-century Latin *Rise of Gawain* goes one step further in attempting to describe his adolescence. The unknown author also wrote *The Story of Meriadoc*, where Arthur appears in an equally unflattering light, and both texts seem interested in the formation of England alongside other cultures (Roman or Celtic). Mildred Day notes the unusually realist character of *Rise*, in its attempt to link Gawain's upbringing with Roman history (he even encounters Greek fire while fighting a battle—according to the text, this requires a lot of toads and the blood of a dragon).

This teen version of Gawain is both thoughtful and hot-headed. He spends a great deal of time assessing situations and trying to construct battle strategies, though sometimes he rushes into the fray, literally screaming at his enemies. Day describes how young Gawain "must learn to balance his strength with sound planning, pain with renewed effort, and pride with patience" (xxiv). Since his adventures are "missions for the emperor of Rome" (xxvii), this romance adds a layer of realism that presents his adolescence as a bit magical, but still plausible. He's known as "the knight of the surcoat," because he's apparently the first knight to think of wearing a red surcoat over his armor. Day links this detail to *Sir Gawain and the Green Knight* as a fashionable signifier for Gawain, since *SGGK* also describes Gawain's brand new surcoat. Because Gawain in *Rise* can't be told of his secret parentage, young Gawain is known simply as *puer sine nomina*, the Boy with No Name. This nameless boy takes on the courtly characteristics that are expected of him, while remaining anxious about his own secrets.

Gawain's secret—not knowing his true parentage—is something that he carries into battle. It becomes part of a romance tradition, "the knight with the secret," which we see as well in Gawain's decision to keep the green girdle a secret in *SGGK*. These open secrets depend upon dramatic irony (the audience knows), as well as public knowledge within the text (everyone *but* Gawain seems to know what he's up to). I don't think it's a stretch to link this with Eve Sedgwick's axiomatic definition of the closet, which she describes as both "*the* open secret" and "a silence that accrues particularity by fits and starts, in relation to the discourse that surrounds and differentially constitutes it" (*Epistemology of the Closet* 3). Gawain's secret, like his reputation, always precedes him. As a character, he's known for his prowess and sociability, but also for being young, which sets up an odd paradox. Gawain can't quite live up to his reputation—he can neither voice that secret nor fill his own impossible sabatons as the world's (supposedly) most courteous knight. Secrecy forms all kinds of interesting veins within the prose of *Rise*, which this section focuses on. He gives the knight Nabor "a ring and a crimson chlamys" (Day 39) as a token of remembrance, to celebrate the relationship they've formed as prisoners of Milocrates. The chlamys could be a utilitarian cloak, but we're meant to read this as a fine gift, with the color linking Nabor to Gawain's own surcoat. Both the ring and the cloak function as open secrets: revealing Gawain's relationship with Nabor while functioning within the Roman context of the story.[4] As a knight, Gawain's potential queerness would need to be quite literally cloaked—but as a Roman boy with no name, he's free to give a love-token to Nabor,

This scene is curious for its play on secrecy and truth. Gawain (still unnamed) watches Nabor from the shadows, remembering the ring and the chlamys. The narrator delivers a curious fact about shadows: "Mos quippe est quod

---

[4] In this romance, Gawain is raised in Rome, and ends up serving in the crusades. He eventually makes his way back to Britain, where he reunites with his uncle, King Arthur.

in umbra constituiti, luci presentes clare aspiciant; ipsique ab illis incircumspecti maneant." Day translates this using parentheses: "(Those standing in the shadows see clearly those in the light while they themselves remain unseen by others)" (39). Gawain is invested in remaining shadowed, a position that is itself halfway between light and darkness. As he remembers Nabor from the shadows, Gawain decides to "[gamble] on this friendship" (41), and ask for help. He's often caught between thought and action. Verbs like "pondering" and "gambling" and "considering" appear throughout *The Rise of Gawain*, as it attempts to dramatize an adolescent hero still coming into his own identity. This shadowy scene with Nabor, though not explicitly important to the plot, still suggests a wide range of queer possibilities for the unnamed knight.

The game or *gomen*, so important to *SGGK*, also circulates within *The Rise of Gawain* as a medieval YA text. When Gawain (still a stranger) faces his uncle, King Arthur, he utters a gnomic statement that might have been pulled from an Old English maxim: "I wander because I do not know the roads. No flight of an exile drives me" (105). Arthur responds by trying to cut him down a notch: "You rely on your quick tongue. I see your game" (ibid.). The Latin phrase, translated as "your game," is *versuciam tuam*: this comes from the adjective *versutus*, which means "quick" or "cunning." In many ways, the Gawain of this romance must learn to be cunning, to play the game. Various characters educate him on how to balance war with wit, and he doesn't always succeed. In a dazzling moment of mirror images, Gawain must fight the nephew of Milocrates, called simply "the nephew of the king"—which, of course, also describes Gawain himself. The two nephews clash, and when Gawain gets blood in his eyes, he grows "frantic with fear that his vision would be dimmed" (57). This is a Gawain who screams, who panics, who watches from the shadows.

When everyone calls him "the new knight," we're reminded not just of his fashionable armor, but also his essential newness as someone young and untested. In his chapter on the Gawain romances, Thomas Hahn identifies Gawain as "the Young Man, available for both adventure and love" ("Gawain and Popular Chivalric Romance in Britain" 220). Often introduced as a child, forever branded as Arthur's nephew, he "pursues, from one romance to the next, the attractions of open-ended, opportunistic errancy" (219). Hahn notes the inter-generational relationship between Gawain and Arthur, which often defines the former as "the good 'son'" (223), the pliable knight, always up for anything. *The Rise of Gawain* adds a matrix of cleverness to this growing shoot of a knight, who tries to absorb military strategy like a seasoned commander, but can't resist the adolescent temptation of throwing his own uncle into a pond. He constantly shifts from courteous knight to boy in armor, still half-baked, and that greenness of body and mind open him up to various queer temptations in the poem. But this youth also lets him appear as a fallible teen, undecided in matters of gender and sexuality, still trying to tell which parts of the game will mean the most to him.

Gawain's Offshoots

I'll argue in this section that Gawain's youth is one of the most significant elements of his character—that he's always been a YA figure, so to speak. A potential version of Gawain appears as early as the eleventh century, in the Welsh tale *Culhwch and Olwen* (existing today only in a fourteenth-century copy). The story focuses on Culhwch's romantic pursuit of Olwen, which necessitates a number of increasingly complex quests only loosely associated with Arthur's court. He has to chase down a boar, slice a witch in two, and battle a vicious one-eyed giant. The tale begins with Culhwch arriving at Arthur's court, where he must participate in obscure pre-chivalric rituals, like having his hair cut by the king. Sir Kay also appears as Cai, retaining his temper. When I teach this text, it's always met with a bit of confusion, since it doesn't resemble any of the later, more familiar Arthurian stories. But there's also something discreetly magical about this story, with its wild deeds and majestic catalogs of names (including Fflewdwr Fflam and Duach from the Uplands of Hell). Rachel Bromwich links Gwalchmai to an early Latin figure—Walwen in William of Malmesbury's twelfth-century *De rebus gestis Anglorum*—described as King Arthur's "not degenerate nephew" who "reigned in Walwethia" ("Gwalchmei m. Gwyar" n.p.). *Culhwch and Olwen* describes him as Arthur's nephew "[who] had never come home without [succeeding] in the mission in which he had gone out to seek" ("Culhwch and Olwen," trans Bromwich). He's also an expert rider, which may have led to him adopting a named horse (Gringolet) in later stories.

As early as the Welsh story *Peredur* (part of the *Mabinogion*)[5] Gwalchmai is noted for his civility. Arthur states that "he does more with his words than we do with our fair arms" (Bromwich, "Gwalchmei m. Gwyar" n.p.). This sets the scene for Gawain's reputation as a "love-talker," which various stories will take up or challenge. By the time we reach the thirteenth-century Old French "Gauvain" romance *Le Chevalier à l'épée*, Gauvain is a cultured and courtly knight, exemplary both on and off the battlefield. The romance opens by citing Gauvain's "loiauté,

---

[5] *The Mabinogion* is a cycle of Welsh myths whose content likely dates back to the tenth century and earlier. Both *Culhwch and Olwen* and *Peredur* focus on early Arthurian stories with a Welsh context, and are often included in Arthurian volumes, though their oral tone (including invocation and repetition) makes them very different in character from Monmouth's more efficient narrative.

proëce et anor" (loyalty, prowess, and honor) (L5, Armstrong 7), establishing both his military prowess and his honor. This story mirrors *SGGK* in several ways: Gauvain loses himself in a forest, encounters a mysterious stranger, rests at his home, and eventually marries his daughter. The marriage dissolves when she meets a more handsome knight, and immediately leaves Gauvain. They both argue for possession of her greyhounds, leading to Gauvain's misogynistic conclusion that dogs are more loyal than women. What links Gauvain with the later Gawain is his enjoyment of gaming and pleasures off the battlefield ("prist tot jorz talent / D'aler desduire et deporter" [he was known for / sporting and enjoying himself]). The anonymous author of the Old French romance also complains that Chrétien de Troyes has "forgotten" Gawain, suggesting that he was a popular knight with a less-established tradition than Lancelot or Percival.

Le Chevalier á l'épée also begins with an incident that stresses Gauvain's youthfulness and inexperience, despite his stated prowess. He enters the forest deep in thought, so that "il perdi son chemin" (he loses his path). The Old French grammar (*his path*) speaks to a deeper loss than just the forest path. Like the protagonist of Dante's *Comedia*, Gauvain seems to lose his coordinates entirely. I bring this up as a youthful transgression because it mirrors a scene from Ramon Llull's *Order of Chivalry* (adapted in the fifteenth century by Caxton), where a young squire "becomes so exhausted that he falls asleep on his horse" (Caughey 10). Since both horsemanship and proper focus are attributes of knighthood, the squire's immaturity sets him up for a long lecture on these very subjects. Gauvain seems to fail in a similar way, not just by losing his way, but by brooding instead of taking decisive action. He shares several qualities with this squire, who is also singled out to participate in a didactic test of chivalry. While the squire receives this information explicitly as a student, Gauvain is launched on an adventure that will reframe his own understanding of loyalty. This paves the way for romances like *SGGK*, which are visibly concerned with tests that challenge both the structures of late medieval chivalry and the genre of romance itself.

My last youthful Gawain example comes from the thirteenth-century Middle Dutch *Walewein* (surviving in a fourteenth-century copy). This is an expansive poem (over ten thousand lines), and it features a number of marvels, like *SGGK*. It begins not with a giant intruder, but with a magical flying chess set, whose rude and mysterious entrance disrupts Arthur's feast. Walewein is sent after the chess set, which seems like a very odd quest, considering that he is "at the fore in knightly deeds of virtue" (in dogheden es ghetrect voort [L105, Johnson and Claassens 35]). At the same time, the poem describes him at several points as "mild," and later Middle English romances will use this designation as well to note Gawain's mannered behavior. The fact that *Walewein* includes somewhat endearing magical monsters—a baby dragon, a were-fox, and the flying chess set itself—suggests that young readers may have been particularly engaged by the more whimsical scenes. When Walewein disturbs a dragon's nest, he has to face a baby dragon who "was fierce, even if it was small" (het was ghewect met onghemake [L345, Johnson and Claassens 42]). When he slays the elder dragon, its boiling blood eats through his armor, leaving him further exposed. We might imagine a young knight returning with damaged armor, saying, preposterously, *a dragon did it*! Only it's true, in Walewein's case.

The destructive armor motif continues when Walewein falls asleep in a grove that happens to belong to Roges, who Mitzi Meyers, at the Arizona Center for Medieval and Renaissance Studies Conference, once described as "an adorable werefox." Roges was cursed by his enchantress stepmother, and now he haunts this grove, harassing any knights who happen to come by. After Walewein breaks the first rule by falling asleep, the fox steals his sword. Curiously, the poet tells us not to blame the knight: "This is what happened / it is lost / it is gone" (L5171–72, Johnson and Claassens 242).[6] Sometimes a fox steals your sword and there's nothing you can do about it. But Roges doesn't stop there. The "vos [fox] sinen halsberch trecken ende scoren / Ende maecte veinstren ende doren" (he began to pull and tear at his hauberk / opening up doors and windows in it [L5181–2, Johnson and Claassens 243]). Anyone who's ever lived with a cat, and watched them shred a book in plain sight, is familiar with this scene.

Roges gleefully claws twenty holes in Walewein's already-damaged armor, exposing his body in the most comical way possible, while also objectifying him. Now the tale is even wilder: *first a dragon bled on me, then a fox chewed on me*. A bit like Chaucer's toy knight Sir Thopas, Walewein faces childlike adversaries that would have appealed to a younger audience. Walewein also questions Roges a bit like a child would, asking not *which devil sent you*, but rather, *do you live under this linden tree? How can you talk?* He enters into the marvel without questioning it. He learns that the fox speaks six languages, and decides to adopt him as a companion—the sort of human/animal blending we'd see in the Disney *Robin Hood*, where the titular character is a talking fox. Roges returns his sword, and though Walewein observes somewhat acidly that "he is a fool who trusts a fox" (L5898, Johnson and Claassens 274),[7] he does in fact place his trust in a helpful fox. In this way, *Walewein* presents a number of moral lessons that it simultaneously tweaks and challenges, and the young knight is just receptive enough to learn alongside a menagerie of magical creatures. We can then recognize, in the fourteenth-century Middle English Gawain, a character based on a prototype that

---

6 "Maer nu eist also vergaen: / Het es verloren, het es ghedaen."
7 "Maer hi es dul die vos betrouwet."

includes civility, cleverness, and a certain openness to being tested. His youth is bound up in this sense of flux and transformation—Gawain is still becoming himself, and that makes him flexible in a variety of ways. Like a character in a YA text, he's discovering what he wants, what he values, and how to find living space between the rules of his society and his own desire for independence.

Queer Youth in *Sir Gawain and the Green Knight*

SGGK is full of youthful images, as well as a kind of essential "newness" that casts its young hero as a half-forged, untested weapon. Aside from Arthur's childish demeanor, we have the power of the New Year, which looms over the text as a combination of suspense and rebirth. The freshly painted pentangle on Gawain's shield is an old symbol made new, stamped onto gleaming armor that hasn't yet been broken in. In class, I often compare the arming scene in *SGGK* to a hockey player putting on brand new gear (I am Canadian, after all), and we can't deny that Gawain's knightly image is a bit too fresh and ill-fitting. The courtiers murmur that he's too young to take on such a task, that his flower will be crushed. He simply doesn't cohere as a ready knight, but rather, a pretty young actor who's taken on the role with gusto, like someone from *High School Musical*. Even Gawain himself acknowledges his own youth, when he accepts the Green Knight's initial challenge. He begs, as Arthur's nephew, to strike the blow that will hopefully eliminate this gruesome marvel that has disrupted the court. His justification is not only that Arthur's life can't be spared, but that "this note is so nys that noght it yow falles" (L358). The task is so little, or "nice," that it would be undignified for a king, but perfectly reasonable as a young person's trial. Gawain doesn't exactly trumpet his own prowess when he reminds the court that "I am the wakkest, I wot, and of wyt feblest" (L354).[8] Later, at steamy Castle Hautdesert, Lady Bertilak will disagree with this underestimation by citing Gawain's sparkling reputation for wit and love-talking (a skill he's actually terrible at—though maybe it's unreasonable to expect that he could outwit Morgan le Fay). How Gawain sees himself is different from the way the court sees him. He's an awkward teen who feels imposter syndrome underneath his fashionable armor. He may also be participating here in a politics of humility more commonly applied to women in medieval romances— saying little, watching more, and searching for a place in the narrative.

In his early dialogue with the Green Knight, we also see a line of questioning that would fit with the curious but cautious hero from *The Rise of Gawain*.

---

8 "I am the weakest, and feeblest of wit."

He knows that he has to seek out the mysterious Green Chapel, but how is this possible when he doesn't know anything about the Green Knight's own lands or lineage? While Arthur's immediate response is to issue a challenge, Gawain enters into a tentative series of questions that we might expect from a first-year undergrad who's trying to puzzle out an Arthurian syllabus:

> "Where schulde I wale the?" quoth Gawan, "Where is thy place?
> I wot never where thou wonyes, bi hym that me wroght,
> Ne I know not the, knyght, thy cort ne thi name.
> Bot teche me truly thereto . . . ."
>
> (L399–402)

He practically asks: "What even *is* a Green Knight?" It almost feels like a personal ad or missed connections post—*did I see you? Did you see me?* Gawain's questions take on an air of urgency, even anxiety. *Where should I look? What's your address? You never told me any of this—not even your name!* He reveals here a fundamental ignorance of courtly traditions, a lack of experience which provokes him into further anxious questioning. His pedagogical language here, "teach me truly," suggests a squire needing to draw information from an older knight. And since this information will either save or kill him, the stakes are high. I can't help but observe how Gawain's rapid-fire questions resemble my own, when I'm confronted with a new social event. *Where will it be? How many people will be there? What do I know about them, and what do I need to know?* I've asked these exact questions to exasperated friends, who've inevitably replied, *it's just a party*. Might as well say: *it's just the Green Chapel.*

When he sets out on this uncertain adventure, the court is "in yonge yer" (still in its infancy) (L490). Lady Olenna, from *Game of Thrones*, would call these courtiers "summer children." Gawain's battles with monsters are practically disregarded by the poem, the way we'd nod sagely at someone's discussion of trapping rare Pokémon. It's not the point of the romance, really. But what *is* the point? Cindy Vitto describes *SGGK* as representing both "a coming of age ritual" and "a poem about the importance of reading signs along the way, signs that Gawain excusably misses" (108). The monsters are signs that don't quite signify. Or perhaps they form a continuum of monsters, including Bertilak/the Green Knight, whose monstrosity and humanity are edges of the same queer leaf. We excuse Gawain for misreading these signs because of his youth. But as Vitto also points out, there are also "the sexual implications of the plot," which various children's adaptations "tackle to some extent" (112). Part of what makes *SGGK* a teen text, I'd argue, is that device of erotic temptation—the "adult content" that would be softened in a text for younger readers. Not exclusively—authors like Tamora Pierce deal frankly with sex in books for a middle-grade audience—but in general, this sexual content, and particularly queer content, allows the poem to fit more visibly within a YA canon.

It's not the monsters that really get to Gawain—it's the weather. The rain dousing him, the cold wind, the fear of being lost. When he calls to the heavens, it isn't God that he addresses, but "Mary, that is myldest moder so dere" (Mary, the mildest mother, so dear) (L754). He might have cited Mary's other protective qualities, but he dwells instead on her motherhood. It's like he's calling out to his own mother, Anna, in the way that we often—though not always—remember a mother's care when we're sick or scared. Gawain calls out to Mary, and Castle Hautdesert appears on the horizon: an impossible confection of spires and half-castles and bits of gemstone, like a wild art project, thrown together in the moment by Morgan. When Gawain enters the castle, he also enters Morgan's spell, becoming part of the story that she's weaving alongside the action of the poem. As the eternal nephew, he moves from the romanticized court of his uncle, to the romantic fairy court of his (half) aunt, in whose company he'll share much joy (even if he doesn't recognize her). Gawain's secret inadequacies collide with Morgan's secret presence, made tangible by the games. One more game whose rules elude Gawain, because he's still figuring out how to strategize. Vitto calls *SGGK* "at heart a family romance, a retelling of every child's need to break away from home and ultimately return again" (118–19). But what home does Gawain discover, both within and between these two unstable courts? What does he eventually accept as "home," and what does he pass over, in order to finally be seen as adult?

Just a Kiss?

YA texts often culminate in a triumphant kiss—or begin with a problematic one—and this moment becomes even more significant in LGBTQ+ stories. In *Simon vs. the Homo Sapiens Agenda*, the titular character gets a swoony kiss with Bram, inches away from the space where the two sent anonymous emails to each other for months:[9]

> I kiss him for real, and he kisses me back, and his hands fist my hair. And we're kissing like it's breathing. My stomach flutters wildly. And somehow we end up horizontal, his hands curved up around my back. "I like this . . . [We] should do this every day." (Albertalli 301)

---

[9] The conceit of the novel is that Simon and Bram exchange anonymous emails, and Simon tries to guess Bram's identity. When they finally kiss in Simon's bedroom, they're ironically next to the computer where Simon was anonymous for so many months.

When Amanda kisses her cis boyfriend Grant in Meredith Russo's *If I Was Your Girl*, both Amanda and the audience hold their breath: "I wanted [past Amanda] to see this, to feel this, so she could understand that one day she might not just be okay with her body, but that she would be able to feel things, beautiful things, inside of it" (207). The kiss becomes a form of time travel for Amanda, signaling to her past self that she has a future, in spite of the transmisogyny she's already experienced. In a more medievalist text, like *Carry On*, the kiss between Baz and Simon Snow is a kind of war. Baz thinks: "Simon Snow is going to die kissing me" (Rowell 342). Rowell stages this as both an amplification of the epic kiss trope, and a serious examination of what might happen when two opposed forces, mage and vampire, fall in love. Merlin, in McCarthy's *Once and Future*, experiences his kiss with Val as peace rather than war: "[Val's] touch had a confidence that pinned Merlin into place after so much wandering through places and times that didn't belong to him" (330). In queer YA texts, the kiss is more than just a kiss—it signals a future. It can be a utopia, a home, or an epic match.

But what about the "kissing game" in *SGGK*? Critics tend to consider this part of the "gomen," the lighter side, really, of the darker beheading exchange. In fact, the queerness of the kiss exchange hasn't produced as much sustained scholarship as you'd expect, given its centrality within the poem. Editors tend to focus on the lady's temptation while glossing over the resulting kisses between Gawain and Bertilak. James Winny notes, with a sense of brevity, that "[Gawain gives] Bertilak the kisses he has secretly received from his hostess" (xiv), then moves on from the subject. He does concede that Gawain's meeting with Bertilak is more of a "tryst" than a duel, but leaves it at that. J. R. R. Tolkien's edition of *SGGK* is still a benchmark, and in his critical essay on the poem (originally a keynote presentation), he describes the kiss exchange as a "seemingly absurd compact" (81). He notes the grave danger of desire in Gawain's scenes with Lady Bertilak, but passes over the male-male kisses entirely, except to note that Bertilak's challenge is a specifically masculine one: "It is as man to man, as opponents in a game, that he is challenging Gawain" (93). In the end, for Tolkien, even Gawain's false confession becomes "a mere game" (96), which means that Bertilak's kisses must be a "sporting" matter as well, and nothing more.

We see this queer trope—"it didn't really happen"—in a variety of YA programs where queerness becomes a plot point. In *Buffy*, for instance (S2E15), there's an awkward moment where the school bully, Larry, thinks Xander is gay. The show moves in an unexpected direction as Larry corners Xander in the locker room, only to end up coming out to him. But it also plays up Xander's discomfort that someone thinks he might be gay.[10] The show seems to open up the tantalizing possibility of Xander being queer, but only for the second of dissonance that it creates. The fantasy program *Wynonna Earp* does something similar when it introduces the character of Jeremy—a scientist with a vocal crush on Doc Holiday. As a character who's both queer and a person of color, Jeremy's inclusion in the show is quite significant, and it's frustrating to see him reduced to pining after a straight character for laughs. But *Wynonna Earp* is a show that evolves. When Jeremy comes to Doc for love advice, the conversation could be played for laughs; instead, Doc puts an arm around Jeremy and says: "You be direct. You ask for what you want" (S3E6).

Later in the same episode, Jeremy and his love interest, Robin, share a kiss. They banter for a bit at first, and then Robin grins and says: "I'm going to try something." It's almost as if they know how rare it is to see two men kissing in a fantasy show like this, and Robin wants to see if they can get away with it. In this moment, *Wynonna Earp* grows up as a show by weaving all of that prior queer comedy into an actual, intimate relationship. And given the enduring queer romance between two other characters—Wynonna's sister, Waverly, and the police chief Nicole Haught—the show's queer storylines actually outnumber its straight storylines at this point. Like *SGGK*, *Wynonna Earp* is a campy, subversive text about monsters and heroes—a low-budget Canadian production that rewrites the cowboy ethos by giving Wynonna her ancestor's gun—and it shouldn't quite work, but works spectacularly because of its self-awareness. It's an example of how a text can push past queer-baiting[11] and create meaningful romance and representation.

---

10 There's a persistent rumor in the Buffyverse that Xander was supposed to be gay, but creator Joss Whedon didn't think the WB network would allow it. So he waited until the show had switched to UPN, and eventually decided to make Willow gay (but was simultaneously worried that her bisexuality might be interpreted negatively by the audience at the time, so wrote over her past relationship with Oz). Instead, Xander became a stand-in for straight male viewers, and his incessant focus on heterosexuality served to make him creepy—even predatorial at times.

11 This term refers to a strategy whereby shows continually hint at a queer romance to gain viewers, but never actually deliver the relationship in question. A prime example is the flirtation between characters Stiles and Derek on *Teen Wolf*, but shows can approach this issue differently. *Chilling Adventures of Sabrina*, for instance, has a pansexual character (Ambrose) who only ever has relationships with men in the first season. A show like *Killing Eve* focuses on an intense psychological relationship between an agent and a killer, which involves an element of attraction on both their parts, but always seems to exist in a gray area designed to keep people watching. Queer-baiting can also involve introducing a queer character and then killing them for the sake of the plot, as happens with Willow's girlfriend Tara on *Buffy*. The queer character becomes a metaphor, while the straight characters survive.

Tolkien's dismissal of the Gawain/Bertilak kissing scenes actually points to homophobia within medieval studies as a whole. Straight scholars often dismiss same-sex desire in medieval literature as problematic, or comedic, or designed to drive home a lesson, or some reverse strategy of the author to actually condemn the act by focusing intensely on it. And this may be the case with some depictions—we have no way of knowing authorial intentions, especially in an anonymous text like *SGGK*—but it doesn't make the *visibility* of that desire any less meaningful. If the kiss is merely a game, then we move past it. But if love is the game—if Gawain's whole life is embroiled in playing this game of sociability—then the queer romance of the poem becomes every bit as significant as the straight temptation scenes. As the poem blurs lines between fantasy and identity, Tolkien does point us to Gawain's coming of age through his own sense of imperfection: "His 'perfection' is made more human and more credible . . . [by] the small flaw" (97). Gawain is ultimately too hard on himself, as any anxious young person would be, and this is what Tolkien sees as the art of the poem: not simply its stylish focus on conduct, but how it dramatizes "that twofold scale with which all charitable people measure: the stricter for oneself, the more lenient for others" (ibid.). The Gawain that emerges, for Tolkien, is a young, self-critical knight, who tends towards guilt and shame rather than deeper reflection.

Tolkien routinely describes the exchange game as a "trap," which suggests that the kissing is merely a part of this. David Boyd's essay in *Arthuriana*—one of the only sustained critical analyses of queerness in the poem—argues that the kissing game is "whimsically intended (though homophobically grounded)" (78). In their work *Cleanness* (see Andrew, *Poems of the Pearl Manuscript*), the *Gawain* poet is clear about their appreciation of sodomy as a grave sin, for which God was justified in wiping Sodom and its surrounding cities from the face of the earth. In a conference paper at the medieval congress in Leeds, Matthew McCall described this act as "God [tearing] a page out of the book of creation" ("Underneath It All"). *SGGK* can't possibly valorize an erotic relationship between Gawain and Bertilak. Nevertheless . . . I'd argue that this remains one of the most strangely positive depictions of queer intimacy in late medieval literature. Part of this interpretation hinges upon how we interpret the kisses as a performance, and various YA adaptations of *SGGK* have done this in different ways. Is Gawain kissing Bertilak simply as payback? Are his kisses chaste? Or are they something else? Boyd reminds us that, in spite of the humor, "the threatening implications of the exchange game for Arthur's knight (who traditionally represents the height of chivalry, masculinity, and heteronormative sexuality) are formidable" (82). Sex with Bertilak, as a logical extension of the game, would bring social ruin. But is Gawain really "the height of chivalry" in this poem? Much of this dissonance stems from a reputation that Gawain can't possibly fill. The poem finds its sense of play in that space between Gawain as he *should* be, and not-yet-Gawain, like the Nameless Boy of *The Rise*, whose options are open.

The conduct that the poem teaches is fraught, because Gawain is supposed to fail. As a conduct text, it sees failure not only as a part of adolescence, but a broader part of humanity. To grow up, we first need to feel that *snyrt* on the back of our necks—the scar tissue of failure that will make us who we're meant to become. But objectively, Gawain should remain chaste. In the *Confessio Amantis*, John Gower includes multiple sections on avoiding temptation. Isabel Davis notes how Gower chooses "the bizarre illustrative example" (161) of David as a paragon of chastity, in spite of his polygamy: "King David hadde many a love, / but natheles alwey above / Knyhthode he kepte in such a wise" (L4345–48).[12] King David's most well-known queer relationship was with Jonathan, whom Gower neglects to mention (though this would paradoxically be a plus, since David still avoids "lust to ligge in ladi armes"[13] by staying with Jonathan). As a call to chastity for young princes, it's about as mixed a message as anything we see in *SGGK*. In the previous book of *Confessio*, Gower also calls out the sensuality of Nero:

> Of Nero whilom mai be told,
> Which agein kinde manyfold
> Hise lustes tok, til ate laste
> That God him wolde al overcaste.
> (L1155–59)

> [Much may be said of Nero,
> Whose lusts were so varied
> Until God at last
> Cast him asunder.]

Like Sodom, Nero is "overcaste" by God for his literally manifold lusts. The word that Gower keeps returning to is "delicacy." Lust is to be avoided as a matter of course, but "delicacy," as a cipher for both sodomy and effeminacy, ties into the necessary "hardening" of knights that chivalry manuals outlined. Gawain is green, soft, and vulnerable, which means that he needs to fear delicacy and its many soft pleasures. Brewer notes that green has a panoply of meanings in the poem, as it

---

12 "King David had many loves, but always valued [chaste] knighthood above them."
13 "Lust to lie in the arms of women."

did in the Middle Ages more generally, including "green sickness [a nutritional deficit]", or "a fairy color," or perhaps even an indicator of decay (181–82). The Green Knight is allowed to be green because he's an actual fairy, but Gawain's greenness is a point of vulnerability, the spot where he feels the *snyrt*. We have to assume that the poet is also invested in hardening Gawain, and what better temptation to provide than the very delicacy that Gower warns boys about? The kisses, then, are more than kisses. They represent a fundamentally bisexual temptation, where two potential lovers—Lord and Lady Bertilak—are both separate beings and two queer shadows of Morgan le Fay. Both are violations of chivalry, but Bertilak's kiss, in spite of his beard, is the softer and more delicate one.

I want to trace an evolution of queer desire in Gawain's kisses with Bertilak. Whenever I teach *SGGK*, my students are always curious about how serious the kisses might be. Are they simply a performance—tit for tat, as it were—or are they "real?" I point to the West Midlands original text and ask students to consider the poet's original adjectives for each kiss. The first kiss is *comlyly*, the second *hendely*, and the third both *saverly* and *sadly*. All of these words have a constellation of meanings, and those meanings shift over the progression of time within the text, as Gawain becomes a better kisser. *Sadly* is one of the most curious adjectives, which I'll discuss in a moment, because it connects explicitly to the training of knights. But let's start with the common translations for these kissing descriptors.

The first kiss is generally read as the most innocent. James Winny translates *comlyly* as "pleasantly" (79), while Casey Finch supplies the translation "kindly and courteously" (271). Both interpret the original "as he couthe awyse" (as he could devise) in the sense of an effortful performance—Gawain is reciprocating as politely and firmly as he can manage. There's absolutely no sense that he *dislikes* the kiss, though Morpurgo's YA adaptation will be explicit about this as a homophobic warning to young readers (more on that shortly). The sense that we get from this first kiss, across multiple translations, is that it's very public. Winny's translation renders this as: "[Gawain] kisses him as pleasantly as he could devise" (L1388, 79), which suggests that he's "devising" a strategy. There's an uncertainty to it, as well. Gawain is doing what he thinks is required, but he's still stepped off the *mappa mundi* and into the true *wirral*: the space where anything might happen. Bertilak's court responds with mirth, rather than anything close to censure. It's like that moment when you kiss a first date tentatively outside the movie theater, then look around quickly to see if anyone noticed. The court responds to this same-sex kiss with the same winking charm that of Arthur's court responding to Gawain's mark of the garter. They laugh and then resume their own varied performances. And perhaps their laughter authorizes the desire itself, since it's rendered unreal—just as we laugh at two straight male characters whose hands touch by accident in a romantic comedy.

There's clearly an upping-the-ante within the wording of the second kiss. I see this as an evolution of desire, as Gawain moves from doing what he thinks is required, to doing what he *maybe wants to?* His desire for Lady Bertilak is socially dangerous in a clear way, and he feels bad about it, as he's been trained to. But his potential desire for Lord Bertilak is part of the poem's texture of secrecy, and he doesn't quite have a language to respond to it. In a kind of dizzying scene of meta-text, I imagine young Gawain discovering a copy of *Cleanness* in Lord Bertilak's spacious library. He reads about the destruction of the cities on the plain, and wonders if Hautdesert might be the inheritor of that ruin. Is he in the same mortal danger? He knows that he must be hard, not soft. But he's still green—and what does that mean?

Gawain delivers the second kiss *hendely*, or "handily." Chaucer famously applies the adjective *hendy* to his clerk Nicholas, who's both confident and too free with his hands. Nicholas assaults Alison by reaching under her dress—a move that Chaucer views with sporting indulgence, made all the more unnerving by the charge of assault leveled against the author by Cecily Chaumpaigne.[14] The adjective *hendely*, then, has a number of sexual connotations, both playful and violent. When Gawain kisses Bertilak *hendely*, he makes a new and perhaps unexpected move in this game. He kisses with purpose. With the first kiss, Gawain clasps his arms politely around Bertilak. The second kiss is more dynamic: "He hent the hathel aboute the hales" (he grabbed the man by the waist) (L1639). The Middle English verb *henten* means "to seize," as well as—even more romantically—"to catch [something] as it falls" (*Middle English Dictionary*, University of Michigan). Bertilak quite literally swoons in Gawain's arms here, and suddenly the lord of Hautdesert seems in danger of falling himself. Gawain's gambit pushes them both off the board, somewhat. Did Morgan expect Gawain to reciprocate with such gusto? Is he still playing her game, or a game of his own?

The third and final kiss is checkmate. After once again grabbing Bertilak, Gawain kisses him "saverly and sadly" (L1936). Our modern adjective "savory" derives from *saverly*, which gives us an idea of how this kiss must feel. In his glossary, Tolkien notes that *saverly* can refer to the spicing of a dish, meaning both "with relish" and "to [one's] liking" (209). Various translators use "relish" to

---

14 The charge of "raptus" against Chaucer was ambiguous, since that term can mean kidnapping as well. Though Chaumpaigne did withdraw the claim, that doesn't mean the claim itself wasn't entirely valid. On an episode of the BBC *Arts and Ideas* podcast, Elizabeth Robertson (in conversation with Hetta Howes and Alicia Spencer-Hall), notes that "the original charge *clearly* was a charge of sexual assault . . . [however], all we know is that [Chaucer] was *released* from the charge . . . [and] generations of critics have tried to brush this event under the rug" ("A Feminist Take on Medieval History").

represent the general feel of the kiss, and Finch uses "heartily," making us think of the strong, "locked" letters of the poem itself. Now we would probably describe the kiss as *spicy*. The character Seth Cohen in the teen drama *The O.C.* described such a kiss as "minty," which queerly fits with the Green Knight's distinctive color. Cordelia Chase on *Buffy* might call it "salty goodness" (S1E5). Bottom line: it's impossible to read this as anything other than a firm, passionate kiss, and even if this is part of the game, it's still clear that Gawain is enjoying himself.

The second adjective, *sadly*, may seem odd—what's *sad* about the kiss? This wording hinges upon a knowledge of chivalry manuals, where knights were hardened, or "saddened," into warriors. The task of knighthood is to make the soft body hard, to knead dough into steel. Male bodies are never supposed to be soft, and the Latin adjective for soft—*mollis*—was applied to eunuchs and queer men. Even now, we judge pornographic representation by whether it reveals an erect penis (with ridiculous controversy around what "erect" means). This focus on hardness also fails to consider the bodies of trans men, since only one particular type of cis penis is considered the standard. Knightly conduct manuals were also deeply concerned with toughening up soft bodies. In her article on medieval battlefield emotions, Katie Walter identifies this process as being literally sad: "The natural heat and softness of a boy's body needs to be tempered by the cold, or be *saddened* . . . [in] order to become a knight" (Walter 26, emphasis added). The Middle English verb means to harden, which is also precisely what sadness can feel like.

In his translation of a conduct manual—Aegidius Romanus's *Governance of Kings and Princes*—Trevisa describes a baking process that ends in cooling: "Colde fastneth the lymes and membres and maken hem sad, so that thei ben the more able to do dedes of armes" (Trevisa 238).[15] All knights endure a saddening process—they sadden to iron. We might argue that wizards undergo a similar process, learning proper magic, while letting go of childish charms. Is this the moment when Gawain becomes a knight? Does this final kiss with Bertilak mark his entry into adulthood? The kiss ranges across textures, from soft to sad to hard. Finch curiously translates *sadly* as "handily," returning to the *hendy* adjective of the second kiss to form a fascinating continuity. Here we may even see an echo of Nabor's advice, in *The Rise of Gawain*, to embrace cleverness alongside strength. You can be handily sad, or sadly clever, or feel queer in "lymes and members" (limbs and members). This third kiss adds to Gawain's own library of desire.

---

[15] "Cold fastens the limbs and members, saddens [hardens] them, so [boys] are more able to do deeds of arms."

Green, G, or PG-13?

In her thorough review essay on Arthurian adaptations, Roberta Davidson asks a deceptively simple question: what happens "when King Arthur is PG-13" (5)? She surveys a number of texts, some YA, some adult, while coming to the conclusion that more explicitly feminist adaptations "have the power tell the old stories in a new way ... [and are] our latest contribution to the Matter of Arthur" (15). While the Arthur/Guinevere plot has been adapted in a number of YA stories, the Matter of Gawain is less commonly adapted. Part of this may stem from Thomas Hahn's description of Gawain as more of a "narrative function" ("Gawain and Popular Chivalric Romance in Britain" 223) than a knightly character with his own layers. But Hahn also concludes that many of Gawain's adventures focus on "a trial of social ties" (224), which suggests that he may actually be the *sine qua non* version of the adolescent knight, forced to negotiate a bewildering series of social and familial connections. *SGGK* is a difficult poem to adapt under any circumstances, due to what Geraldine Heng has called its "knotted" narratives, as well as its overflowing material details in the hunting/arming scenes. And then there's the "PG-13" content. As mentioned earlier, Cynthia Vitto sees this as difficult material that all children's and YA adaptations must take on, in one form or another. I'll focus on two versions in the remaining section: Michael Morpurgo's popular 2004 *Sir Gawain and the Green Knight* (illustrated by Michael Foreman), and the less popular (but highly acclaimed) 2002 animated film by Tim Fernee. The former makes a point of disowning the poem's queer content, while the latter sees it as an essential part of *SGGK* and assumes that a young audience can handle it.

Morpurgo's edition with Candlewick Press is beautifully illustrated, but one of the scenes that's obviously missing is the Gawain/Bertilak kiss. Foreman depicts Gawain stripped to the waist (when Lady Bertilak first creeps up on him), and then later, as possibly naked (though the framing retains his modesty). The second image is undeniably sexual, which suggests that the publisher imagined this content was suitable for a middle-grade audience. Lady Bertilak clearly has all the power in these scenes, and Gawain is a pale lad with little to no control over the weirdness present at Castle Hautdesert. He's so gently clueless that he asks himself: "She cannot have come here simply to talk about the weather, can she?" (60). There's also a particularly striking image of the Green Knight's head sailing through the air, streaming blood like a sprinkler, with the green/red making it a kind of Christmas horror. In short, the YA text doesn't shy away from sex or violence. But the kisses with Bertilak seem to have posed a thorny problem for Morpurgo, who is careful to reiterate that Gawain and Bertilak are *just friends*. He presents the first kiss as a slurping performance: "Gawain stepped forward, put his arms around the lord of the castle, and kissed him once on the cheek, very noisily so that everyone could hear it" (65). In the original, this kiss is not on the cheek, though the aspect of public performance is still important. Morpurgo amplifies this by making the kiss a clear strategy on Gawain's part. When I initially read this scene, I was more than a little shocked when Morpurgo added: "The lord wiped his cheek" (ibid.). The way you might wipe your cheek if your grandmother, or even your dog, had just kissed you. It reminds us that the pain of straight, cis manhood involves vocally rejecting same-sex intimacy at an early age. You can't "be" a man until you've loudly and repeatedly claimed to not be queer in any way. A shitty spell that fails every time.

This strategy of dismissal continues throughout Morpurgo's adaptation. The second time, we're told that "[Gawain] kissed the lord twice, once on each cheek . . . [I'm] glad it wasn't more, because as much as I like you, I really don't like kissing men with great bristly beards!" (75). The hetero avoidance is palpable. But more than avoidance, this is an explicit revision of the original text to spare young readers from its queer ambivalence. Not only does Gawain continue to kiss Bertilak on the cheek, he specifically states that *he doesn't like kissing men*. And in particular, men with "great bristly beards." The effect is to imagine Gawain kissing Santa Claus—which kids would find hilarious—rather than the truth of Gawain kissing his host with both purpose and relish. The third time, Gawain kisses Bertilak "affectionately and noisily three times, each time trying to avoid his bristling beard" (88). Foreman's illustrations also render Bertilak as a desexualized jolly old lord, rather than a bearish threat to Gawain's chastity. Both the author and the illustrator assume that a sincere same-sex kiss would be going too far in an illustrated book for younger audiences. Consider, though, that Linda de Haan's picture book for even younger audiences—*King and King*—pulls off a same-sex kiss two years earlier (and a queer marriage!) Both kings are wearing green, to boot. So this *Gawain* adaptation doesn't hit a wall in publishing, so much as create a wall as it dismisses the importance of the kissing game to the poem's narrative of secrecy/disclosure.

I'd argue that the most transgressive image in Morpurgo's version isn't the explicitly sexual moments with Lady Bertilak, but rather, a smaller image near the end whose size and placement resembles a manuscript miniature. This is immediately after Gawain receives the *snyrt*. In the miniature image, the Green Knight—now of indeterminate age—helps Gawain to rise from the earth. He places his own scarf on Gawain's neck, to staunch the blood, while holding him up. They almost appear to be dancing. Gawain looks remarkably uncertain, while the Green Knight's attention is fixed on the wound. He's a benevolent presence here, but still, there's something wildly ambivalent in their positioning. The performance has shattered. When Gawain asks what's going on, the Green Knight laughs: "All in good time, Sir Gawain" (106). Like a nurse answering a patter of irrelevant questions from their patient. The *Sir Gawain* feels ironic here, since Gawain still appears so young, especially in this illustration. Both characters are vulnerable, and nobody's puckering or trying to avoid bristly beards. We realize that we don't know, truly, who or what the Green Knight is, and that remains a dangerous knot within even the most conservative adaptations.

Fernee's 2002 animated film takes a different approach. This film won a BAFTA award, though it remains mournfully difficult to find in high-quality format. The comments section on the YouTube version is dominated by high school students and early undergrads, who have turned to the film as a substitute for the longer (and less accessible) poem. My favorite comment: "Looks like nobody reads, and we all have exams tomorrow." So the film's YA audience is fairly clear. The animation style has the quality of stained glass, and I teach this in conjunction with James Winny's *SGGK* facing translation,[16] whose cover features a fourteenth-century knight in stained glass (from Tewkesbury Abbey). The film includes all three kisses, but decides to present them more dramatically, alongside visual cues that play brilliantly into the poem's color imagery. With the first kiss, Gawain approaches Bertilak from the right, placing his right hand on the lord's cheek as he kisses him. Gawain blazes golden, while Bertilak's entire body—and the space around him—is cast in ruby-red light. Horns play dramatically in the background as they lock lips. With the third kiss, the framing is curiously reversed. Gawain's left hand caresses Bertilak's face, as if now approaching from a queer direction.[17] The middle kiss is performed in silhouette, as both characters lean towards each other. But the book-ending kiss scenes are close-ups, and in both, Gawain's eyes are closed. "Relish" is really the only adjective we can attach to these kisses, both deliberate and sensual. The hall around them vanishes in a wash of red light, matching Gawain's red surcoat. This isn't a warning, but rather,

---

16 The facing translation (Middle English on one side, contemporary English on the other), allows students to play with the sound and feel of the original language, while still offering the "decoded" version for ease of access. We talk about how the two versions are clearly different, though we can see many similarities in how words have evolved over time. As an undergrad, I was forced to puzzle through only the Middle English originals of medieval texts, and while this happened to work for me—since I enjoyed Middle English—I could see how other classmates felt like the process was too exhausting. I now recognize this as gate-keeping: the "good medievalist" students learned to read Middle English, while everyone else was weeded out of the conversation.

17 Once, when I was screening this cartoon in a survey class, a student yelled "get it boy!" It was a remarkable shift from watching queer movies in the 1990s in a small town, where the audience might actually boo a same-sex kiss, or even walk out. It reminded me how important hope is within our discipline—and that generations truly change in their perceptions of queer content.

a continuity, a link to the medieval world of the poem. Gawain is doing exactly what he should.

I'm not arguing that this animated film defines Gawain as queer, since it pays far more attention to his bedroom games with Lady Bertilak. But it does preserve the queer knotted space within the poem itself. Boyd describes this as a "crisis of masculinity" (94), produced by Morgan and her manipulation of Gawain. Whether we call it a crisis or an opportunity, the poem allows it to exist, and the cartoon does as well. I'm reminded of a moment in my class on eighteenth-century genders and sexualities, when a student delivered a compelling presentation on Milton's fallen angels as nonbinary beings. They asked, as part of the Q&A portion, whether the class thought Milton's text allowed for nonbinary identities (given its conservative seventeenth-century context). Another student answered: "I believe that, yes, it has to. It has to, because it's present in the text." Even if the *Gawain* poet is explicitly opposed to sodomy and all of its implications, *SGGK* still presents us with a moment of profound queer intimacy. Some YA adaptations shy away from this content, while others embrace it.

Kat Howard's recent Arthurian adaptation, "Once, Future," reimagines Gawain as a dancer named Nirali who takes on the Green Knight *within* a medieval studies classroom. In Howard's adaptation, Viviane (the enchantress who captured Merlin) is an English professor who continually stages the same Arthurian drama over the centuries in the hopes that she'll find a different ending. The players in this version are grad students who agree to participate in a game: they'll take on the names of Arthurian characters, and see if the myth works its will upon them. Arthur is played by Sabra, a queer woman, and Nirali plays Gawain with a kind of indifference. We sense she has better things to worry about. When the Green Knight comes knocking on their classroom door, Howard uses the same stylistic technique as the *Gawain* poet: "*Wham. Wham. WHAM*" (*A Cathedral of Myth and Bone* 124). The knight storms in, and Nirali beats him at his own game by recognizing him, by radically knowing him:

> Think of what you have seen and not seen on your journey here. There are no more great forests, no standing stones to serve as clocks. We do not ride in pursuit of wishes granted by the white hart. You are a thing unique, sole and unexpected . . . [Truly], a wonder, and so you have fulfilled your quest. (*A Cathedral of Myth and Bone* 125)

In naming the Green Knight the wonder that he truly is, Nirali/Gawain confirms the marvel of Morgan's magic, which animates the entire poem. Rather than engaging in witty rejoinders, or even kisses, she glides like a dancer to the heart of the Gawain Matter: the Green Knight is exactly the kind of immeasurable wonder that "childish" Arthur demanded. More than a Christmas game or a New Year's entertainment, he is "sole and unexpected," a true queer miracle trailing holly and sparks and, yes, a bristly beard. And when you kiss a wonder, all bets are off, because that game has no rules.

Scholars tend to approach *SGGK* with an overwhelming straightness. Aside from David Boyd's essay on sodomy in the poem, there are very few academic analyses of queerness applied to Gawain and Bertilak. I'm reminded of the first time I visited the British Library, and innocently asked to view the manuscript. I was told, gently but firmly, that this was a heritage document—a national treasure—and only scholars performing forensic analysis on the parchment would actually be allowed to view it. In spite of its digital accessibility, *SGGK* remains a part of England's own nation-building experience, and perhaps this is why we hesitate to queer the poem. I first read it in high school (thanks to my English teacher, Muriel Morris), and I think of how significant it would have been to imagine Gawain as even playfully queer. The very thought that a knight could desire a lord. At no point during my graduate experience did I ever hear queerness referenced in the poem by an instructor. The kisses were always just part of the poet's clever game. As this chapter argues, however, a kiss can matter. We need to make *SGGK* accessible to a wide readership, and reveal the essential queerness of the text as its green heart, rather than just a clever strategy by the poet. Nothing for Gawain is particularly stable, and this mirrors the chaos of adolescence, where we linger in softness and becoming.

SGGK ends with the gentle laughter of Camelot as the court reacts to Gawain's funny story, as they peer at his little wound. But immediately before this conclusion, there's a final temptation scene that few discuss as an actual temptation. Having sat patiently through Gawain's blustering misogynist tirade, this reminds us, perhaps, of the blustering instructor who refuses to teach queer medieval texts. Or the conservative student who refuses to acknowledge queer readings within historical texts (less common than the former). In a locker room, a kiss can also be a threat: a way of denying queerness by performing it. Gawain's misogyny here seems to perform a similar function—rejecting all women, but at the same time rejecting Bertilak's desire. In spite of this, the Green Knight holds out an invitation. He offers Gawain the option to stay in Castle Hautdesert, which is, after all, the self-fashioned home of his queer aunt, Morgan:

> Therfore I ethe the, hathel, to com to thyn aunt,
> Make myry in my hous; my meny the lovies,
> And I wol the as wel, wyghe, bi my faythe,
> As any gome under God for thy grete trauthe.
> (L2467–70)

[Therefore I urge you, warrior, to come to your aunt,
Make merry in my house—my servants [already] love you,

And I will love you as well, sir,[18] by my faith,
As any man [or game] under God, for your honesty.]

Let us remember how Gawain's desire, upon first meeting the Green Knight, was focused on knowledge. *Who are you? Where do you come from? Where can I find you?* In Morpurgo's adaptation, Bertilak responds to Gawain's final questions with "all in good time." In the original, Bertilak makes Gawain a tempting offer: to "make myry" (make merry) in his house, which is also the house of Morgan le Fay. It's curious that he says *my servants love you, and I will as well*, given that we aren't sure if these servants are actually magical creations of Morgan (like the castle itself, which is both beautiful and impossible). Bertilak calls himself a "gome" here: both a man and a game, while pledging "grete trauthe" (great truth/service) to Gawain. And isn't that what he's been looking for all along? An answer to his burning questions?

Morgan has the only answers to these questions—but the answers might be dangerous, as well. And the poem casts a spell over us, encouraging us to ignore Morgan's marginal presence. She's at the heart of the poem, though hidden in plain sight. At several points—before learning the true identity of his aunt—Gawain simply sees her as an ugly old woman to be dismissed. Yet, he can't quite do it. She keeps appearing alongside her lovely young counterpart, and we're told that they spend unrecounted hours together, to Gawain's great joy:

> Watz never freke fayrer fonge
> Bitwene two so dynge dame,
> The alder and the yonge;
> Much solace set thay same.
> (L1315–18)

> [Never was a man so taken up [or whirled about]
> Between two so dignified dames,
> The older and the young;
> Much solace did they find [together].]

Gawain's previous focus on her wrinkles and dark eyebrows recalls the description of Dame Ragnelle in the thirteenth-century romance "The Wedding of Sir Gawain," as well as the loathly lady in Chaucer's "Wife of Bath's Tale." Both of these Middle English romances feature a hag-like woman who transforms into a beautiful damsel. Like Bertilak, Ragnelle has a prodigious appetite, and her hag's body is what offends prudish Gawain the most—the way she takes up space. Ragnelle is transformed through the same type of "nygramancy" that

---

[18] Since "wight" can mean man, human, or lord, this line could literally be "I love you, man."

Morgan wields on a grander scale. Though "necromancy" initially referred to having power over the dead, the word gradually broadened to include most ambivalent forms of magic. We also see this larger-than-life character echoed in T. H. White's Madame Mim, who earned her magical degree at "Dom-Daniel," the mythical undersea magic school. Mim, an unapologetic cannibal, uses chivalry as an excuse to invite Wart and Kay into her dangerous house. She reminds the boys that, as knights in training, they can't turn down a lady's invitation. Her spell over a boiling pot continues to blur categories: "*Mingle, mingle, mingle, you that mingle may*" (90). As an irredeemable and unrepentant version of Ragnelle, Mim represents a chaotic model of magic that Wart must overthrow, in order to side with Merlyn.

Disney's 1963 film, *The Sword in the Stone*, pushes her anti-sociability even further (though with a lighter touch on the cannibalism). While White's version is a beautiful, raven-haired woman who crackles with electricity, the cinematic Mim is a gray-haired woman of indeterminate age, first seen playing a game of solitaire. She lives happily on her own, and dislikes people. When she hears Wart cough, she says "sounds like someone's sick—how lovely." Rather than deferring to Merlyn, she calls back: "I've got more magic in one little finger." Which may be true, given that she later transforms herself into a dragon. Her withering magic "[finds] delight in the gruesome and grim," which in some ways makes her even more chaotic than Morgan. The Arthurian enchantress lives to challenge the structures of chivalry, but she still acknowledges those structures, and even sometimes helps. Like Roges when he first shreds Walewain's armor, Mim is gleefully destructive. She's "mad" but also "marvelous," and can flicker from a giant to a mouse in a moment. Not only does she demonstrate an evil alternative to Merlyn's model of magic—she also demonstrates a model for living as a woman, unattached, unbothered by social rules, with a raven as company. You can sleep late, curse the sun, and still be a feared sorceress. Merlyn only bests her through anachronism, by becoming a germ that infects her body.

In Chapter 2, we discussed Morgan as part of a sisterhood of enchantresses, rather than a lone witch prowling the margins of the *Morte*. She appears among a dynamic group of empowered women, and while the medieval romance tradition doesn't always know what to do with them, the genre's ambivalence can't erase their community. *SGGK* allows us to imagine Bertilak joining the sisterhood. We know very little about how his powers work. Did Morgan curse him into transformation, like some kind of were-tree? Is his actual form green, and lordly Bertilak is only the disguise? He appears to us as a queer, not-entirely-human character whose life is an untold romance of its own. I was always taught to read Bertilak as Morgan's henchman, but the poem clearly states that they live together, perhaps as equals. Both characters are forever transing—they change shape, from flesh to stone, skin to moss, mundane to magic. I return to my point at the beginning of this chapter, which is that the Green Knight resembles a kind of queer plant, more than a cis man. If we see them as fluid, always grafting and editing their bodies within the text, we can open up space for trans and nonbinary readers to join this community as well. As someone who's always on the verge of getting a Baobab tree tattooed on my back—in further homage to *The Little Prince*—I vibe deeply with the queerness of plants and all their genders. The act of seeing both Morgan and Bertilak as queerly embodied, never confined to one form, can be an act of welcome to trans and nonbinary medievalists.

Thinking outside the lines can also look like collective thinking and community formation. In the fantasy/science-fiction show *Sense8*, we're presented with a group of characters who can read each other's thoughts, and even control each other's bodies. All of the sense8 characters are positioned as outsiders, but they need to cooperate and empathize with each other, in order to fight against a corporation that wants to control their abilities. Two of the show's creators (Lana and Lilly Wachowski) and one of its central characters, Nomi, are trans women, with Nomi played by trans actress Jamie Clayton. Nomi has Entrapta's programming and tech skills, as well as Morgan's defiance against the narratives imposed upon her. In S1E9, Nomi has a psychic conversation with Lito, a gay Latinx man who's struggling with his sexuality. They "meet" in a museum, surrounded by structures proclaiming what art should be, who should own it, how we should receive it. But the museum is also where Lito met his partner, Hernando—making an erotic connection that the space neither expected, nor sanctioned. Nomi recalls a traumatic moment as a child, when a group of boys tortured her in the shower. Lito calls the boys "monsters." But Nomi offers a different reading of the moment:

> That locker room . . . [made] me the woman that I am . . . [I] quit trying to fit in, trying to be one of them. I knew I never would be. But more importantly, I didn't want to be. Their violence was petty and ignorant, but ultimately it was true to who they were. The real violence—the violence that I realized was unforgivable—is the violence that we do to ourselves, when we're too afraid to be who we really are.

With all of Morgan's tenacity and self-knowledge, Nomi becomes the person she's been all along. *Sense8* isn't specifically for teens, but scenes like this invite trans children to see themselves through Nomi's experiences. She is a character valued for her mind, and her ability to craft and break codes at the same time. Though *Sense8* doesn't shy away from Nomi's transness, it also doesn't focus exclusively on her body, as so many narratives do when they decide to include trans characters. Though she's framed by a giant painting at the museum, Nomi eludes any type of narrative frame, just as Morgan so often does. She speaks of the locker room's transformative capacity, but also of her own, an enchantress in her own right.

Trish Salah's poetic work also engages with Morgan as a transformative figure. In her first collection of poems, *Wanting in Arabic*, she describes Morgan le Fay as a trans woman searching for narrative space:

> She was aware of the necessity of certain fictions, more certainly of their failing . . . / [Never] the less she prized her freedom. Stole / yours. Love demands that, and one needs to be able to work. A certain / and *then*, or *until*, the backward swoop. Fiction will do that for / you. More, if you are a beautiful girl, as she was, and determined to be.
>
> ("Fata Morgana," *Wanting in Arabic* 62).

Salah envisions Morgan as a working enchantress ("one needs to be able to work"), and one who's keenly aware of her own fictional representation. The "backward swoop" could be the *snyrt* of the Green Knight's axe, but also Morgan herself, looking back queerly and *swooping* into the text on currents of dark air. She's both a beautiful girl, and someone "determined to be" how she's just described herself. An enchantress becoming. Salah's Morgan knows how fiction can squeeze her character into a single meaning, but rebels against this. The poem's title—"Fata Morgana"—also refers to a kind of mirage. A play on the simultaneous visibility and invisibility of trans women in medieval literature, just as Bychowski describes the trans women in the *Prose Merlin* as "invisibly present" ("Quantum Objects" 12). This Morgan invites readers to discard the fictions trying to define them, and instead, to swoop into the pages they deserve. Imagining both Morgan and Bertilak as members of this transformative, supernatural community extends the Middle Ages to trans and nonbinary readers, who may not have imagined themselves there at all. But you were there. Always, you were there, in every century.

What Bertilak is offering Gawain, then, amounts to more than simply the "merry" house of Aunt Morgan. What he holds out to Gawain is "solace." The chance to learn from his magical aunt, to laugh with her and discover all the secrets of her fairy castle. And to be loved—by Bertilak, his people, and Aunt Morgan herself, forming a queer family that runs parallel to Camelot. We imagine them partying in the Green Chapel, swapping jokes and (likely) kisses. At the base of this scene, Bertilak is promising Gawain to love him better than any other man on earth. As queer romances go, it's certainly as dramatic as Simon kissing Bram on the Ferris Wheel in *Homosapiens Agenda*. But Gawain says no. Morpurgo interprets this moment as Gawain saying: "Not on your life." And perhaps this emphatic register does match with the Gawain of the poem. He rejects Bertilak's offer because it would lead to a very different poem, a Fifth Fitt,[19]

---

[19] The poem is divided into four Fitts—a Middle English word meaning both "round of singing" and "short measure of time."

where the game was even less certain. He has to return to Camelot so that his failure can be made public. Living in Morgan's house would, by contrast, be a more embodied acceptance of queer failure. A joyful knowledge that queer failure, to quote Jack Halberstam, "is something queers do and have always done exceptionally well; for queers failure can be a style" (3). Gawain's failure is definitely stylized in the poem, and made material by the garter that symbolizes his transgression (and the court's gentle pardon). But failing with Morgan and Bertilak would be deeper than this, and the game doesn't stretch that far, at least not for Gawain. He rejects the Green Chapel in much the same way that Charles ultimately rejects Sebastian in *Brideshead Revisited*, while still acknowledging the temptation of the queer alternate life that Sebastian offers him.

The young knight's endearing failures also remind me of a more contemporary character who cannot live up to his own reputation—Otis from the UK teen show *Sex Education*. Otis knows a great deal about sexual health because his mother is a sex therapist, but he's also virginal and extremely uncertain about his own investment in sexuality. With a bit of Gawain's cleverness, he starts a kind of "tutoring" service at school, where classmates pay for sex advice. As with Gawain, his reputation for "love-talking" serves to shield his own personal clumsiness when it comes to sex (the first season lingers over his failure to masturbate). Joseph Gamble has linked the program to early modern narratives of sexual instruction ("How to Do It"), and I'll link it further back, to *SGGK*, since both texts are so concerned with intimate failures of reputation. In one particularly medieval episode, Otis and his friend Eric get lost in the woods (filmed on location in Wales, so comparable to the *Wirral* that Gawain must navigate). His father, who's supposed to be a guide, turns into a blustering Arthur figure who can't read a map, until they're forced to take shelter in a nearby hotel. Straight Otis and his gay best friend, Eric, share a bed without fuss—they have a physical intimacy in the show that's uncommon between male friends in most YA programming. Eric takes this moment to tell Otis that a boy named Adam—who viciously bullied Eric for years—may now have feelings for him.[20] The register is doubly knotted here, since Eric is looking for love advice, but he's also confiding in Otis as a friend, blurring the boundary:

Otis: "He bullied you—for years! Eric, he's a horrible person!"

Eric: "People can change."

---

[20] In an episode of the *Hazel & Katniss & Harry & Starr* (*HKHS*) podcast (S2E25), Brenna Clarke Gray discusses how Otis becomes the audience's point of view here—telling Eric what we already know—but the show also crucially "gives Eric the agency" to reject Adam's internalized homophobia on his own.

Otis: "If he's changed, then why is he making you sneak around at night?"

Eric: "It's romantic—something that you wouldn't understand because you're too busy pretending to have feelings for your girlfriend." (S2E5)

Eric enacts a dangerous queer fantasy here—sleeping with your bully—even though he knows it will end in disaster. So many queer people find their desires frozen into loving the bodies that were fatal to us—the straight people who made us unsafe. Harry/Malfoy fanfic plays on this desire, but ignores the very real harm that a character like Malfoy does to Harry. Villains-becoming-lovers is an entire genre within queer romance (particular MLM, or Men Loving Men stories), and it often takes advantage of that adolescent fantasy where the bully kisses us, instead of beating us down. *Sex Education* explores this trope without flinching, and Eric has to reckon with the way in which he's romanticized his abuser.[21] Adam does eventually come out as bisexual, though Eric can't deal with his shame—much as Bertilak will advise Gawain against shame.

In this moment, Eric punctures Otis's bubble of expertise by exposing his hypocrisy as a "sexpert": he can't actually practice the level of honesty that he recommends to others. Throughout the series we see Otis dispensing sensible advice which he fails to heed, or advising people beyond his experience while failing to diversify how he thinks about his own sex life. During a party—which Katy DeCoste noted on Twitter mirrors Camelot's New Year's celebration (May 10, 2020)—Otis fails to advise Anwar on how to prepare for anal sex with his boyfriend. He's too drunk to remember his own advice, so Rahim (Eric's boyfriend) has to step in as advisor. The result is a character who, much like Gawain, fails to achieve his own potential while also learning about the impossibility of living up to social expectations. At the end of the medievalist episode, he puts his head on Eric's shoulder, and a long shot frames them in the doorway of the hotel as if it were a looming castle—small and open to dangers, but also queerly kin to one another.

The way that *SGGK* enshrines failure gives it, perhaps, a special resonance with academic readers—students and instructors alike—who are trying to survive difficult academic conditions. I write this while under lockdown for COVID-19, and my university's optimistically named "pivot to digital" plan was actually a flaming ball of chaos that exposed wild inequalities within our grading system.

---

21 In the above-mentioned *HKHS* podcast episode, Clarke Gray and Joe Lipsett also discuss Adam's whiteness, and how he breaks up a developing relationship between Eric and Rahim. Given the paucity of queer people of color in relationships on television, Adam's meddling here also takes on a racist tone, as Rahim is edged out to make space for the much more problematic white love interest.

Many students were expected to hand in assignments as normal, with the same amount of "rigor" (a word we can throw out), while dealing with acute mental and physical trauma. A vast gendered divide between academics was made even more visible, as women and nonbinary mothers found themselves shouldering the bulk of childcare duties, while cis male academics seemed relatively unphased by the shift to working from home. This point has been raised numerous times at town-hall-style meetings, with little to no response from the university administration. I have seen colleagues break down while discussing their mental health at these meetings, while administrators looked on in uncomfortable silence, or offered slim platitudes about wellness. Please fuck off with wellness. We don't need yoga—we need accessible counseling and a reasonable workload.

As Jay Dolmage writes in *Academic Ableism*, "academia powerfully mandates able-bodiedness and able-mindedness, as well as other forms of social and communicative hyperability, and this demand can best be defined as ableism" (7). His description of "communicative hyperability" is particularly resonant with me, since, in spite of my vocabulary and training as an educator, I often struggle to communicate verbally—especially under pressure. I thought of this while hosting an online thesis defense, where a student shyly admitted that they had trouble with words. "Me too," I chirped. At that very moment, I was having trouble keeping my body still and organizing my mind. There's no one way to be a reader, a writer, or a student in general. There's no one way to signal that you're listening, or that you're taking up space "appropriately." Students reading *SGGK* may be curiously empowered by its mercy, its celebration of *snyrts* and screw-ups. As an academic, I find it soothing to know that even Arthur's nephew can ruin his quest, and still be fine.

We've talked already about crip time as a necessary antidote to academic over-scheduling and the ruthless expectation of able-bodied competency. How academia discriminates against disabled students and faculty by enshrining ableist practices, harming us physically and mentally, and preserving inaccessible spaces. In her article, entitled "The Future We—and the Middle Ages—Want," Usha Vishnuvajjala describes a sense of hope within medieval literature: "Writers of medieval romance imagined an alternative past—and therefore an alternative present, and perhaps a possible future—in which people who were held apart by patriarchal structures and discourses could be allies to each other" (3). This sense of a liberating temporality is something we can apply to medieval studies as well, just as Dinshaw argues that medievalist atemporality produces a sense of queer kinship. We have to unseat academic time, in favor of something softer, more attenuated, more human. Bertilak seems to offer Gawain something similar—an escape from the rat race of medieval romance, with its expectations of hard masculinity and complex chivalry. A ticket to Morgan's fairy castle instead, where time flows like sap, and you don't need to die to be successful. A better Fitt. A queer and demi-present life, locked in Sappho's eternal tense of always-now, always greening. Gawain's refusal crystalizes the limits of the author, but not the poem itself—this safe choice isn't necessarily a comment on the young knight's true desires.

Gawain as a character is both much-adapted and, perhaps, ill-adapted at times, due to his ambivalent status as a knight frozen in adolescence. Malory makes his youthful stubbornness one of the great downfalls of Camelot, since he's incapable of forgiving Lancelot. Various YA adaptations read him as either an innocent ingenue (more Percival than Gawain), or a sly character whose coming of age involves a mixture of strength and craft. As a witty character, Gawain fits in well with the YA canon, where sarcasm and anxiety vibrate along the same frequency. *SGGK* may not explicitly be a conduct manual for young knights, but it does pivot on matters of secrecy, sociability, and sexuality, which are also elements of the LGBTQ+ YA genre.

Morgan appears as a significant part of Gawain's journey, even if she's forever in the background. Morgan and Bertilak extend an invitation, beyond the edge of the poem, where anything is possible. Gawain has to think queerly in order to see the potential in Morgan's offer, and we might read his negative response as one of fear, rather than repudiation. It takes courage to read your own story backwards, to read against the grain of every medieval romance, and envision something different. I don't think it's a leap to claim Gawain as a queer teen character within the medieval canon, whose future adaptations must reckon with his sexuality. Even when YA adaptations don't officially depict queer intimacy, it remains knotted in space and time. The kiss is more than just a kiss, and Gawain's greenness, his delicacy, his canonical bisexuality, make him a medieval model for LGBTQ+ readers—as well as queer medieval readers who saw in him, perhaps, a green core of transformative living, never satisfied by one form.

Epilogue: Gandalf's Charm

This final section is about charms—not just spells, or songs, or even quarks, but also how wizards themselves might be charming. If you've ever played an RPG (role-playing game), the value of "charisma" is one that's often neglected in favor of vitality or intelligence. Certainly, magic-users aren't supposed to be charming. But Gandalf, Tolkien's famous wizard, *is* inescapably charming. Gandalf deals in charms that might appear less impressive when we think about the magic of *The Lord of the Rings*, but which fit the particular mood of *The Hobbit* as a middle-grade text leading into the YA genre. Tolkien wrote *The Hobbit* in multiple versions, based on stories he'd told to his children. It was published in 1937, and he immediately set out working on *The Lord of the Rings* as a more expansive sequel, written between 1937 and 1949. *The Hobbit* focuses on Bilbo Baggins, who is lured out of his comfortable hobbit hole by the wizard Gandalf, and forced into an adventure that changes how he sees the world of Middle-Earth. *The Lord of the Rings*, by contrast, focuses on Frodo Baggins, Bilbo's cousin, who is thrown into an even more epic adventure by Gandalf. While Bilbo's journey ends after rescuing an ancient treasure from the hoard of the dragon Smaug, Frodo must trek across Middle-Earth with a fellowship of companions, in order to destroy the evil ring of Sauron. *The Lord of the Rings* became the blueprint for the fantasy genre that followed, along with the role-playing tie-ins that would emerge in the 1970s and '80s. *The Hobbit* is still regarded as more of a children's story, and perhaps a young adult story—as I'll argue—though it crosses multiple types and genres of literature.

I was certainly charmed by Gandalf, and still find their brand of magic to be a fascinating one. A *charm* can be many things: a middling spell, a din of music, a human outcry, or a type of particle that gives form to the universe. A charm is more accessible—something even an apprentice can manage. It's often seen as a lesser form of magic, but as the love charms that we dealt with earlier prove, it can be powerful. *The Hobbit* exerts a particularly charming force as a text that's sometimes difficult to classify. Arriving as it does at the edge of modernist fantasy in 1937, it's both an outlier and a fairly conservative medievalist text whose structure has made an indelible mark on the genre. Bilbo is the protagonist, but Gandalf is the lightning that moves through it—the queer instigator, the unreliable storyteller, the presence that can't quite be contained. Like both Merlin and Morgan le Fay, Gandalf is a kind of unstable particle, sometimes disrupting the very narrative. Gandalf also thinks differently from the hobbits, by virtue of understanding how magic works. I'll attend to some of this wizardly thinking, and how this reinforces ways of being different, charmed.

One of the earliest appearances of the word "charm" is in the Middle English *Cursor Mundi*, a sprawling historical-religious text composed anonymously around 1300. Here, charm appears in connection with unlawful desire: "Lucheri has me reft resun / With charm and conurisun" (Lust has ravished my reason / With charm and conjuration [L28520–21]). *Cursor* means "runner," and the poem itself runs (or drags us) across a world of stories, trying to construct what is essentially a vast history of biblical and secular moments. Given that focus on building history, it's perhaps surprising that "charm" and "conjuration" appear so loosely, as causes or effects of desire. A charm is something like a spell, it seems, but ill-defined, and not recognized by popular medieval terms such as *nigromancy*. Chaucer uses it, in "The Knight's Tale," to describe more specific medical magic: "To oothere woundes and to broken armes / Some hadden salues and some hadden charmes" (L1852).[1] Translations of earlier texts, like "Against a Sudden Stitch," are often grouped together as "charms"—though the flexible OE word "spell" would be more appropriate. There's a sense that a "charm" is what you call something that has no other classification. Between-the-lines magic.

The Hobbit is often described as children's literature—perhaps even as a more simplified version of *The Lord of the Rings*. In many ways, it belongs to the category of middle-grade literature, which stretches just to the edge of readers beginning high school. Maria Sachiko Cecire places it within a canon of both "children's and YA fantasy literature" (Ch 2). To think of it as a middle-grade or early YA text, I'll also return to Brenna Clarke Gray's definition of YA as something "focalized through a teen" that's "immediate and vivid" (*Hazel & Katniss & Harry & Starr*, S1E22.5).[2] Gray mentions *The Hobbit* as a text falling under this designation, since it's really about Bilbo growing up. At the end of the book, Gandalf even observes: "My dear Bilbo . . . [you] are not the hobbit that you were" (Ch 19). We know that Tolkien began *The Hobbit* as a series of stories for his children, and the text often serves as a bridge to more "adult" fantasy. Given Bilbo's "adolescent" journey, from sheltered, middle-aged hobbit, to seasoned adventurer, the novel is closer to a teen text like Lloyd Alexander's *Taran Wanderer* than it is to Rowling's *Philosopher's Stone*. While Alexander's novel focuses on adolescence and becoming—Taran is literally wandering through life—*The Philosopher's Stone* is more firmly interested in childhood. When I re-read *The Hobbit* as a teen, I found it to be darker than I'd remembered—full of gallows humor, near-death experiences, and foreboding. It's also a fundamentally anxious text, since it's filtered through Bilbo's nervous perspective.

---

1 "For other wounds, and for broken arms / some used salves, and others used charms."
2 Clarke and Lipsett also mention in this episode that Bilbo is "young for a hobbit."

In *A Modernist Fantasy*, James Gifford describes *The Hobbit* as a product of Tolkien's "disappointment with the world as it is," but also as a conservative example of "sentimental nostalgia" (Intro). Compared with T. S. Eliot, Hope Mirlees, or Stella Benson, Tolkien does feel conservative in his politics and world-building practices. At the same time, I'd argue, a character like Gandalf might represent the "core of anti-authoritarian radicals" that Gifford associates with other modernist writing and philosophy. *The Hobbit* may have emerged from a medieval studies curriculum with which Tolkien and C. S. Lewis were intimately familiar, but it's still radical in its desire to pair an acerbic wizard with an awkward, unheroic protagonist. Gawain is really the closest thing we have to a fumbling knight in the romance tradition, but even he doesn't curl up on the floor screaming *struck by lightning* at the very mention of an adventure, like Bilbo. As many critics have noted, *The Hobbit* also concerns itself with highly nuanced discussions of good and evil—particularly the evil we do while trying to be good. In a cast of unlikely characters with less-than-perfect motivations, Gandalf is perhaps the most ambiguous. Their true identity as an angelic spirit, or Maiar, won't be revealed until well into *The Lord of the Rings*. For now, Gandalf is mysterious, contrary, and often at a loss, just like Bilbo. In *The Last Unicorn*, the wizard Schmendrick observes with self-loathing: "Wizards don't matter." They do, of course. But they matter differently, strangely, charmingly.

In *The History of The Hobbit*, John Rateliff notes that the story "is so familiar, it has taken on an air of inevitability" (Introduction). That's why it's so surprising to read Tolkien's earlier drafts, where Gandalf is named *Bladorthin* and the subterranean villain Gollum helps Bilbo, rather than trying to eat him. Smaug is Pryftan[3] the Dragon, and Thorin's royal grandfather—King of the Dwarves—is named Fimbulfambi. We can see the story's genesis as something for young children, and also how, through various revisions, Tolkien refined it into something for older readers as well. Gandalf may have even originated in Tolkien's *Letters from Father Christmas*—a magic-wielding Santa Claus (Rateliff n.p.). Nobody can quite agree on when he began the story, but the Tolkien children have suggested that it would have been as early as 1931–1932. "The Pryftan Fragment"—so named for Smaug's original name—seems to be the earliest incarnation. In this version, Bladorthin is even more cranky than Gandalf, telling everyone to hush when Thorin (confusingly named Gandalf) tries to speak. When the dwarves argue about Bilbo's suitability for the mission, Bladorthin reminds them that they chose the hobbit by scratching a personal mark on the door:

---

[3] From the Old Welsh "pryf," meaning "worm."

"I put it there," said Bladorthin from the darkest corner. "With my little stick I put it there. For very good reasons. I chose Mr. Baggins for the fourteenth man and let anyone say He is the wrong man or his house the wrong house who dares. Then I will have no more to do with your adventure, and you can all go and dig turnips or coal." (Pryftan Fragment)

The published version includes the dig about coal, but omits the turnips (which feels like the better insult), as well as Gandalf's position, glowering from the darkness.[4] There's no mention of a staff in this scene in the 1937 edition, but in his draft, Tolkien calls it, charmingly, "my little stick." This perhaps recalls Gandalf's Old Norse origins as an Odin figure (that and the broad-brimmed hat). The Old English "Nine Herbs Charm," with which Tolkien was certainly familiar, describes a remedy against a "wyrm" strike:

ða genam Woden VIIII wuldortanas
sloh ða þa næddran þat heo on VIIII tofleah. (Delanty and Matto 475)
Then Woden seized 9 wondrous twigs / and broke the worm to pieces.

Gandalf's "little stick," rather than a proper staff, resembles the *wundortanas* that Odin mysteriously uses against the dragon. Their magic, I'd argue, also resembles what Old Norse literature describes as *seiðr*: a middling power that queers genders and power structures. We see this in the Old Norse *Poetic Edda*, which collects a number of mythological poems. The existing copy is from the thirteenth century, though the stories are far older. In an insult-poem known as "Lokasenna" (Loki's Verbal Duel), the gods Odin and Loki both accuse each other of using "women's magic" (Loki uses it to become a mare and a milkmaid at various times). Gandalf's charms are linked to the unstable magic of Odin and Loki, while their sharp but kind demeanor also has something in common with Monmouth's wounded Merlin in the *Vita*. This earliest version of Gandalf shows us how Tolkien was working through what Gwendolyn Morgan calls "the undeniably medieval world" of *The Hobbit*, which is steeped in "mythologies of early England" (28), while also playing with Gandalf's register as a sarcastic magus.

---

4 The bitterly sarcastic wizard Raistlin Majere, in the *Dragonlance* series (highly popular serial books by Margaret Weis and Tracy Hickman, which thrived during the 1980s and '90s), is likely an echo of Gandalf's acerbic wit. In *Dragons of Autumn Twilight*, the first *Dragonlance* novel, Raistlin also glowers at his company from the shadows, unwilling to join in drinking or dancing at the Inn of the Last Home. Raistlin paid a physical cost for gaining magical power, and now lives with chronic pain and cough similar to pneumonia or tuberculosis. He can certainly be read as a disabled wizard, though the metaphor implied—power in exchange for disability—remains troubling.

I'm using they/them pronouns for Gandalf throughout this discussion. Tolkien's wizards are essentially angelic beings, which makes them nonbinary, and all the more important for young readers. In his "Essay on the Istari," Tolkien notes that these beings are "clad in bodies as of Men, real and not feigned" (*Unfinished Tales* 389). This makes them subject to a variety of pains, temptations, and desires. At the same time, the Istari are "forbidden to reveal themselves in forms of majesty" (ibid.), which reminds us that they are, in fact, nonbinary by nature. Perhaps, when reading Tolkien's phrase "bodies . . . [as] of Men," we might think instead of the OE noun "mann," which is gender-neutral. The Istari become *people*, not simply men, even if the few active wizards in Middle-Earth do resemble cis men. Tolkien's wizards might serve as unique role models—particularly for nonbinary and neurodivergent readers who connect with the wizard as a shifting figure. Why do these medievalist demi-gods still resonate for LGBTQ+ readers? What can old wizards teach us about how to survive our current world?

There is no single definition of what being nonbinary means. In their recent edited volume, Rajunov and Duane speak to the issue of community, rather than definition: "Communities are blossoming around the experience of being something other than a man or a woman," thereby affirming "not only the complexity of gender, but . . . [the] complexity of the individual" (Introduction). I use he/they pronouns in a (relatively safe) academic setting, though I'm less likely to use them in mixed spaces. And I'm hesitant to identify as nonbinary, because I don't want to draw attention away from individuals who experience daily harm by being mis-gendered. The idea of fluid gender was not a new concept to medieval audiences. In his work on Christ's body and its depiction on the cross, Robert Mills notes that the wounded Christ demonstrates "an ambiguous and indeterminately gendered performance that renders attempts to conceive it in terms of binaries and 'role-reversals' highly problematic" (161). This expands Carolyn Bynum's work on Christ's feminized body, suggesting that Christ's body is actually visualized in nonbinary terms. Jonah Coman also writes on the transness of Christ's body, noting Christ as a figure "whose humanity is figured as his cloak . . . [What] body does Christ reveal if he were to take this cloak off?" (3–4). Sacred understandings of Christ's body hinged upon its openness and flexibility.

Nonbinary angels (and demons) weren't a new concept, either. Caesarius of Heisterbach wrote about demons who were made of smoke and shadows, who had no fixed, corporeal form. They're closer to beings like Odo, the changeling from *Star Trek: Deep Space Nine*, who can only hold onto a physical form for so long. Ruys notes that medieval questions about angelic corporeality and movement can feel a bit "nonsensical . . . [until] we substitute the word 'atom' for 'angel'" (66).

Medieval philosophers were actually asking complex questions about the nature of materiality itself when they thought about (and with) angelic bodies. Medievalist texts like Neil Gaiman's *Good Omens* declare explicitly that their angels are nonbinary, and what made the angels who visited Sodom deeply compelling was, we assume, their beautiful difference. Perhaps Tolkien's Maiar only took on male form because, in a medieval society, maleness was equated with power. But Gandalf also wears high-femme robes, amazing boots, and a silver scarf: *be a wizard, but make it fashion*. It's important to acknowledge the character's core, nonbinary identity, because this welcomes young trans and nonbinary readers.

There are also limits to the relatability of Gandalf for readers—particularly when we consider the wizard's whiteness. Regardless of Tolkien's own ambiguous personal politics as someone who saw himself as an outsider, the racial politics within Middle-Earth are damaging to BIPOC readers. We've already discussed in the introduction how Tolkien's narrow view of medieval literature shaped medieval studies in ways that made it inaccessible to a variety of students and scholars. The impact of this in his *Lord of the Rings* series is even more dramatic, since the work has been so widely read and absorbed. In his essay on racism and colonialism in fantasy literature, Daniel Heath Justice (member of the Cherokee nation) argues that "Tolkien's epic story of English pastoral goodness besieged by swarthy techno-fascist hordes added a moral certitude, literary cachet, and coherent secondary-world mythology to heroic fantasy" (n.p.). This is a world were good people are literally white, and anyone with dark skin is either a goblin, an orc, or a monstrous spider. Heath Justice offers the term "wonder" as a corrective to "fantasy"—which, as a genre, is particularly harmful to Indigenous readers "because it's so deeply entangled in settler-colonial logics of dead matter, monolithic reality, and rationalist supremacy."

When I teach the fantasy/horror novels of Haisla/Heiltsuk writer Eden Robinson, we discuss how her fantasy is rooted in the protocols and stories of her own connected communities, as well as in an understanding of British Columbia as unceded Musqueam territory. Her YA book *Son of a Trickster* focuses on a teen whose father is the mythical trickster figure Wee'git (local to Haisla and Heiltsuk traditions). Jared's love interest, Sarah, is also a witch who identifies as Two-Spirit[5] and nonbinary. Work like this challenges the racist structure of Tolkienian

---

[5] In an interview about his book of poems, *Full Metal Indigiqueer*, Oji-Cree writer Joshua Whitehead (from Peguis First Nation in Manitoba) describes his queerness and cultural identity as "a braiding of two worlds . . . [I] go by both two-spirit and Indigiqueer. One to pay homage to where I come from, from Winnipeg, being kind of the birthplace of two-spirit in 1990. But I also think of Indigiqueer as the forward moving momentum for two-spiritness" (n.p.).

fantasy by rooting stories in an experience of colonial genocide, rather than a good/evil binary focused on whiteness as brilliance. The upper-level classes where I teach *The Hobbit* are often overwhelmingly white, but this doesn't prove that only white people read Tolkien—rather, it confirms that the *study* of Tolkien seems to be welcoming only for white students, as does most of the curriculum in English studies. This is why it's important to include fantasy literature in general-education and introductory courses, where the classroom is more diverse. As instructors, we can grapple with Tolkien's racist narratives, while holding space for BIPOC students who may fear that they aren't reflected in the fantasy genre.

I think what first drew me to Gandalf was how they were always changing. Even their name changed: Olórin, Mithrandir, Gandalf, Grey, White. The idea of having a secret name—one you fear to reveal, or one you can't reveal—might connect with all kinds of transitions, processes of self-naming, and experiences of passing in a world that doesn't quite see you. Tolkien's wizards aren't particularly masculine (beards aren't necessarily male), and instead appear at a remove from social interaction, wearing robes that make them appear soft and indistinct. Throughout *The Hobbit* and *The Lord of the Rings*, Gandalf also has a slyness, a wit, that separates them from more binary characters: a neuro-queer way of thinking. In their first interaction with Bilbo in *The Hobbit*, Gandalf's response to Bilbo's "good morning" is a master-class in both verbal and tonal analysis:

> What do you mean? . . . [Do] you wish me good morning, or mean that it is a good morning whether I want it or not; or that you feel good this morning; or that it is a morning to be good on? . . . [What] a lot of things you do use *Good Morning* for! (Ch 1)

This almost perfectly mirrors my own chain of thought when someone asks: *how are you?* My instinct is to answer in a way that's both logical and impossibly granular ("well, after waking up—"), but I know that this is socially unacceptable. Often I say "fine" while grimacing, because it's hard to lie both verbally and facially at the same time.

I don't mean to play into stereotypes about autistic literalness here. Sarcasm was an uphill battle for me, but I figured it out (mostly) after a lot of trial and error. Unlike the character Sam on *Atypical*, as discussed in Chapter 1, I don't take everything literally. But I am, often, the person in the room to most likely inquire about word choice. This also takes us back to our discussion of witches, in the *Tiffany Aching* books, as people who analyze the world and themselves. Gandalf wants to know precisely what Bilbo is saying, just as Tiffany wants to know the measurements of a monster's glaring eyeballs: because details matter. The wizard later announces both their singularity and circularity by saying: "I am Gandalf, and Gandalf means me!" Aside from Tiffany's rallying cry about thinking differently, I can't imagine a better charm for declaring your own neuro-queerness: *I am Gandalf, and Gandalf means me. I mean myself. I can't be anyone other than who I am.* Bilbo associates Gandalf with the wizard who makes excellent fireworks and magical cufflinks, but Gandalf is just Gandalf. This declaration of identity is similar to a person coming out as trans and nonbinary. *I'm me. These are my pronouns.* There's no justification or explanation required. Declare yourself a wizard.

I was drawn to wizards as a neuro-queer kid because they held out the possibility of neurological and narratological difference. Their minds were magic, and made me believe that my queer mind could be magic too. Their asynchronous relationship with the world seemed like a mirror to my own experiences, as I tried to reason with social conventions that, quite often, were designed to make me feel like an alien. In *Autistic Disturbances*, Julia Miele Rodas describes neurodivergent language as "language hacking, the joyful breaking down and retooling of conventional language in ways that defamiliarize and implicitly critique seemingly seamless and intuitive communicative practice" (8). I'd argue that the charms (songs, from *carmen*) in *The Hobbit*, along with Gandalf's sarcastic asides, and even the weaving together of ancient languages represent a kind of neuro-queer rhetoric. Gandalf sees Bilbo as most changed after the hobbit spontaneously composes a poem: *Roads go ever ever on / Under cloud and under star / Yet feet that wandering have gone / Turn at last to home afar.* A poem he creates in that moment, as an archive of everything he's experienced. These interruptions are little flashes of grace that are actually radical in their potential to disrupt what could be a wholly traditional epic story.

Like Merlin, Gandalf also has an expansive view of the past and future. Peter Goodrich notes of the Arthurian Merlin figure: "It is as if he can step outside the conventional reality of the narrative world and reenter it anywhere he desires" (12). Gandalf was the same. They have a kind of magical queer-view mirror, like T. H. White's Merlyn from *The Sword in the Stone*, who saw everything back to front and was only ever confused by the present. Gandalf always seemed to be watching the action unfold, never hurried, never startled. Except by the one ring itself, and its capacity to stir unspoken desires. But Gandalf is also unique: Frank Riga notes that the wizard is "by no means a carbon copy of previous exemplars" (22). Drawing upon Arthurian tradition, while forging a distinct path, Gandalf presents a model of transformation for readers. I've maintained in a number of academic texts that this epic foresight confers a particular kind of sadness. A wizardly sense of non-belonging. To many, the wizard's loneliness feels like "home afar."

There's a popular Twitter meme with Gandalf wearing sunglasses (which magically slide over their face), with the text: *deal with it*. This is my Gandalf. A bit camp, a bit tired, a bit over it. When you live your life in an epic register, it's all the more annoying to deal with hobbit micro-aggressions, tedious questions, and the little insecurities and selfish acts that accumulate to form Tolkien's metaphor of draconic greed. The wizard snaps at Bilbo and Thorin. They go missing for long periods of time, "just when a wizard would have been most useful, too." Like Monmouth's Merlin, Gandalf insists upon autonomy from the quest. While Gawain is presented with one dangerous choice after another—rarely in control— Gandalf seems to skim directly above or below the narrative in a unique pocket of space. When Thorin asks why the wizard has ridden apart from them, Gandalf answers laconically: "To look ahead." When Thorin asks him to be more plain, Gandalf launches into a story, then snaps "don't interrupt!" when Thorin interjects for clarification. It doesn't matter if Gandalf is talking to royalty, or a hobbit, or an elf, or, presumably, another wizard—Gandalf is Gandalf. When Elrond discovers the secret of entering Smaug's lair, Gandalf is even "a little vexed" that the elf has decoded this first. There is about the wizard, at times, a sense of delightful irritation—a Dorothy Zbornak sense of comedic timing and critical snark. On *Golden Girls*—a 1980s comedy (with a queer following) that centered on the lives of older women living in community with each other—Dorothy's character was a teacher and often delivered the most critical raillery.

Gandalf's sexuality is hard to define. As an immortal demi-god, they have no real need for a traditional romantic relationship. We can read them along the LGBTQ+ spectrum, and their fraught relationship with Saruman could easily be the echo of a past romance (made more plausible by Gandalf's own interest in the mortal pleasures of Middle-Earth). In his article on medieval sexualities in *The Lord of the Rings*, Christopher Vaccaro notes that "Gandalf signifies hope and encouragement" (98) as they try to change Saruman's path. In spite of exiling Saruman, Gandalf "continues to hope" for their "friend's reform" (99). It's difficult to know how Istari love one another. For ace/aromantic readers, Gandalf's asexuality can also be empowering. Queer readers can spin stories of a past romance between both wizards. Magic destabilizes romance in all kinds of interesting ways.

In a 2002 interview with *The Guardian*, Sir Ian McKellen makes Gandalf's queerness canonical: "I was suggesting to Peter [Jackson] yesterday that he should insert some love interest for Gandalf in a later [movie]. He suggested Galadriel . . . [I] said, no, I was thinking more of someone like Legolas" (n.p.). Many fans would probably argue that Legolas is already in a committed relationship with Gimli, which I also stan. But would an overt queer relationship make Gandalf a more empowering figure for LGBTQ+ readers? Only if we define queerness within the space of an erotic relationship, which is, frankly, limiting and incorrect. Readers don't need to be told that they aren't queer until they've had sex; instead, they need to be shown queerness as a delicate texture of possibilities and feelings that don't necessarily conform to one act or one desire.

Gandalf is also willful. The wizard leaves at unexpected moments, and fights in unpredictable ways (such as throwing their voice to distract trolls in *The Hobbit*). In her book *Willful Subjects*, Sara Ahmed talks about the figure of the willful girl in children's literature. She describes this girl as "one who insists on getting her own way, who comes to you with her own explanations of what it is that she is doing" (21). We might read Morgan le Fay along these lines, as well—Geraldine Heng describes her in *SGGK* as embodying "an imperfect knot . . . [that] situates identity as more tenuous and incomplete—a fragile, uncertain prospect that is always on the verge of unraveling" ("Feminine Knots" 504). Ahmed notes that willfulness also "might be what we do when we are judged as being *not*, as not meeting the criteria for being human, for instance" (*Willful Subjects* 15). This links back to Yergeau's previous discussion of what counts as rhetorical among neurotypical writers and speakers. Gandalf shows us that a wizard zags, a wizard talks back, a wizard has thorns. This willful wizard can serve as a model of neuro-atypicality for readers who also don't conform to binary ways of thinking. It's okay to be a knot, rather than someone who fits into a heroic template.

Wizards, in spite of their slanted perspective, can also belong to a community. In his essay on Radagast the Brown, Nicholas Birns notes that wizards do technically form a kind of pack: "One assumes that there are a reasonable number of wizards wandering around Middle-Earth. In fact, this sense of wizards as a class suggests that Tolkien at first expected to have more wizards in *The Lord of the Rings*" (115). After misdirecting Gandalf, Radagast disappears. Very little is ever known about the character, and it seems like they just wanted to live peacefully with animals, rather than helping the Fellowship. While Tolkien casts Saruman as a victim of dragon fever,[6] Birns suggests that Tolkien "almost seems embarrassed by Radagast" (ibid.). They don't really fit into the narrative, but at the same time, their disappearance signals "an elegy . . . [for] a kind of storytelling that is now gone from a re-conceived Middle Earth" (125). Radagast's very failure to make an impact is, in some ways, a defining element of their character. We might argue that their non-compliance demonstrates Jack Halberstam's "queer art of failure," which "turns on the impossible, the improbable, the unlikely, and the unremarkable. It quietly loses, and in losing it imagines other goals for life" (88). Radagast's failure to matter within the series is, paradoxically, an act of defiant selfhood.

---

6 This is Tolkien's term for greed (capitalism, really) in *The Hobbit*—since dragons famously don't know the precise value of their hoards, but they still count every coin. Saruman falls under the same spell of greed, only his greed is for power.

And their willful footsteps away from the path of good—towards a more vegetal neutrality—suggests that there may be whole communities of quietly unknowable wizards carving different paths throughout Middle-Earth.

Gandalf, like all wizards, contains queer multitudes. As I've tried to show in this book, the medievalist tradition of the wizard—going back to Merlin and Morgan—has always been a story of radical difference. Wizards are uncourtly, uncontainable. They are not all white, cisgender, or able-bodied. A medieval fantasy studies that refuses to acknowledge the actual racial and gender diversity of the Middle Ages is precisely what white supremacists have tried to weaponize, and Middle-Earth is one of the most popular medievalist fantasy texts. In her piece on medievalism and white supremacy in *Time* magazine, Dorothy Kim urges medievalists to "resist the medieval narratives that activate violent hate" and "create counter-narratives" (n.p.). We need a medievalism that reflects the diverse Middle Ages—wizards and all—more than ever. There are stakes involved when we imagine Gandalf, and other wizards, as neurodivergent and nonbinary. We need to ensure that readers see themselves reflected in fantasy worlds, because world-building can also be world-healing, and wizards can be a tool against ableism, homophobia, and transphobia.

If this book has a core argument, it's the necessity of diverse wizardry for audiences who are consuming both medieval and medievalists texts. I wanted to show not simply that certain medieval structures survive in YA literature, but that we can actually learn about both traditions by placing them alongside one another. In medieval literature, we find flawed, anxious knights, neurodivergent wizards, and enchantresses who refuse the status quo. In medievalist YA, we find teen characters who share all these qualities, even as they try to challenge and reinvent the tropes of fantasy. *Sir Gawain and the Green Knight* was also invested in challenging tropes, so this transgression is adapted, rather than entirely novel—but each iteration is still new. Like medievalism itself as a crafty assemblage, teen readers can take what they need from diverse medieval cultures, and forge new links of memory, belonging, and desire. Reading *The Hobbit* can be deepened by reading the work of Chaucer, or Marie de France. But Tolkien's work can also influence how we approach these medieval texts as part of a long story about growing up. Those of us who work in this seemingly very old field must be attuned to what's new, what's changing; those who read medieval texts can also take new lessons from them.

My argument, really, is that medieval wizards saved my life. As a queer autistic person, I squinted at Gandalf across fire and smoke, and saw myself. In their subtlety and riddlic ways, I saw Galadriel's power. In their wit, I saw Merlin chuckling at future selves. In willfulness, I saw Morgan le Fay as both a marginal figure, and a member of mystical community. And I realized that I didn't have to choose between being simply Aragorn or Galadriel. The title of this section also refers coyly to a moment when I was talking to my partner. "You're charming," they said, "at first." We both laughed, and *charming at first* became a common descriptor. Gandalf is also charming at first, until he starts disappointing people. Being charming—that is, appearing as "quirky" rather than "weird"—can be exhausting. It's truth, not charm, that forges relations and makes a living space. But, as these wizards demonstrate, a good charm can also get you through a difficult situation. Charms exist everywhere—more accessible than academic magic.

Perhaps the most powerful magic that wizards possess is time. Merlin and Gandalf are both long-lived, watching regimes rise and fall. Morgan's age is often indeterminate, but we get the sense that she can be anyone or anything. We see her as a young scholar in the *Vita Merlini*, an older politician in *Sir Gawain and the Green Knight*, and a royal presence at the prime of her life in the *Vulgate*. T. H. White's Merlyn teaches Wart about the precious queerness of time, and disability scholars say the same thing about crip time as something essential. For anyone who isn't neurotypical or able-bodied, it can be nearly impossible to thrive in a world that extracts your labor and denies you the right of being lost in thought—what Tolkien calls fantasy as a human right. If we're going to teach medieval and medievalist literature, then we need to make our classrooms a place where students can revise and reflect their ideas, without fear of censure. In his work on disability and academic productivity, Travis Chi Wing Lau argues that "a 'crip slow' approach pushes us to be more critical of larger structures of productivity that are tied to academic progression . . . [rather] than having scholars work at the mercy of strict academic clocks, we can bend those clocks to meet disabled bodies where they are" (19). Like Morgan bending space and time to forge Castle Hautdesert, we can create more wizardly classrooms, where students aren't forced to write ableist comprehensive exams or simply replicate the language of popular critics. Instead, they can learn their own spells of community and survival.

Now that we're under lockdown, I've returned to my old stims. Squeezing a foam ball. Snapping my fingers. Pacing. Lining things up. Staring at the bright spines of books. The cat curls up with me and we watch the Canadian show *Schitt's Creek*. In an episode about wine-tasting, Moira Rose tells her son, David: "You and I — we're two potent grapes" (S6E7). Good, but potent. Two people who can never quite fit into this small town, while at the same time, people keep inviting them back. As someone who crashes scenes, speaks in riddles, and wears a feathered cape with gauntlets, Moira Rose has more than a little of Morgan le Fay in her character. David wears gender-fluid cloaks and gowns that make him stand out in a small town. But Schitt's Creek is also a magical space, free of homophobia, where David can be openly pansexual without fear. David, often acerbic and unapologetically queer, is shocked when his boyfriend Patrick proposes to him, because he never imagined something like that happening to such a grape. Wine flows throughout the show, a medieval metaphor of blending and expansive taste. In the very first season, when declaring his pansexuality, David says: "I like the wine—not the label" (S1E4). He also wears gowns and robes, bringing a queer wizardly aesthetic to a small, utopian town where his visibility is celebrated. The show makes me think about queerness, wine, and mind labels: the pleasures and shocks of being a potent grape.

One of David's path-breaking decisions is to transform the vacant general store into Rose Apothecary, a shop that will also serve as a community space in the town. This is what puts him in Patrick's orbit for the first time, since Patrick has to help him fill out the necessary paperwork. Standing in the empty space, gently stoned, David calls Patrick and awkwardly but delightfully describes what he wants to create: "It's basically a general store, um, that will support local artists, under the brand of the store. Which—which would also be my brand—oh—sorry I just got a text—Oh God! Yeah, the text cut us off—" (S3E8). His business plan plays with space and time, mirroring the ways in which we often have conversations about important things—including the pauses and hesitations. Patrick is able to visualize David's plan of supporting the local community, and stitches his many calls together like a palimpsest, saying: "The good thing about the messages was that I was able to get enough information to fill out your forms." This is precisely what students should hear when they're seeking an accommodation: *You are understood*. We can't keep forcing students to write essays that replicate a particular form, either. Instructors can listen to oral essays, full of the same pauses and hesitations, where students can show what they've learned without having to hammer it into shape. Though Patrick and David are radically different, they comprehend each other in a way that signals kindness and curiosity. The show gives David time to grow and make mistakes—queer and precious time that we can bring to our classrooms as well. We can make spaces of learning more like a medieval apothecary, full of possibilities.

This book emerged because I kept seeing wizards relegated to particular genres—either children's literature, or adult fantasy literature—when in fact, they seemed to be everywhere. And in particular, they resonated in literature aimed at adolescent readers, on the edge of post-secondary education, who were being told they'd need to take a break from magic and learn "resilience." But wizards, if anything, are survivors, just like our students. And addressing wizardry in medieval literature, and medievalist YA, reveals that these magic-users have particular lessons to teach a diverse spectrum of teen readers. They aren't restricted to children's stories, nor are they defined by post-Tolkienian adult fantasy. Wizards move through their own supernatural adolescence, which readers can identify with.

They can be queer, trans, and nonbinary (often, challenging the gender binary is their default). They can have disabled bodies, inseparable from their magic. They can be neurodivergent, and their ways of thinking serve to strengthen them, rather than making them outcasts. They are imperfect. Merlyn cries when Wart fails to recognize him; Madame Mim delights in being anti-social; Simon pushes Baz away, struggling to process his own trauma. Wizards and enchantresses are us, and we can bring their magic into the classroom in order to replace academic rigor with practical magic. Wizards belong to everyone. They show readers who don't fit in that fitting in doesn't have to be the only choice. You can be a queer ranger, like Radagast. You can be lost like the original Istari who vanished off the map. You can smoke weed, raise a fire, and dance with a Balrog, like Gandalf. And you don't have to answer to the name you were given. You can name yourself, slip into your own wyrd robes, and be angelic. My green leather-bound copy of *The Hobbit*, with its gold runes along the edge, contained all of these possibilities. Runes are never binary—neither are we. A seemingly "young" genre like YA draws upon old roots, and what feels remote—worlds away—can actually be a toolkit for you, now. Gandalf is what you are. Wizards matter—then, now, always.

Appendix: Texts and Media

This appendix offers brief summaries of the central medieval, YA, and fantasy-themed texts discussed in the book, in order to make them as accessible as possible. These are concise descriptions, at times accompanied by suggestions for pursuing further research. Think of this as a series of open lecture notes.

Medieval Texts

Anglicus, Bartholomaeus. *On the Properties of Things*
This thirteenth-century Latin text offers detailed descriptions of childhood and adolescence, expanding upon work by Aristotle and Isidore of Seville. It was translated into Middle English by John of Trevisa in the fourteenth century. An e-book is available in modern English, edited by Robert Steele (*Medieval Lore from Bartholomaeus Anglicus*).

Anon. *The Black Book of Carmarthen*
This thirteenth-century Welsh text includes a number of early stories about Merlin—particularly his experiences on the battlefield. It also includes several prophecies that Merlin relates about the conflict between Wales and Saxon invaders. Meirion Penner has an affordable paperback edition (with the Welsh original in facing translation).

Anon. *Mabinogion*
These ancient Welsh stories, compiled in the thirteenth century, were drawn from far older traditions of oral storytelling. They contain a slightly different look at Arthurian mythology, including more imaginative monsters and supernatural quests. Sioned Davies has an edited version with a scholarly supplement.

Anon. *Poetic Edda*
This thirteenth-century collection of Old Norse poetry is drawn from older stories. Fascinating parallels between Norse and Arthurian stories (dragons, magic, and even Odin as a potential Christ figure) can be identified. Carolyne Larrington has an excellent translated edition, and translated versions are available on the *Sacred Texts* website: https://www.sacred-texts.com/neu/poe/index.htm.

Anon. *Les Prophésies de Merlin*
This early fourteenth-century manuscript includes a magic duel between Morgan le Fay and an enchantress called the Dame of Avalon. It stresses a sense of community between Morgan and other enchantresses. The manuscript pages

can be viewed at E-Codices: https://www.e-codices.unifr.ch/fr/searchresult/list/one/fmb/cb-0116.

Anon. *Prose Merlin*
This fifteenth-century Middle English text is essentially a translation of all the Merlin material in the earlier *Vulgate*. However, the *Prose Merlin* also contains some original elements (Merlin has a baby dragon!) and paints the character as a bit less isolated. The University of Rochester has an annotated version: https://d.lib.rochester.edu/teams/publication/conlee-prose-merlin.

Anon. *The Rise of Gawain*
This thirteenth-century Latin text details the youth of Gawain, while taking several liberties (it is the only text to imagine Gawain living in Rome and joining the crusades). It is primarily of interest because it imagines Gawain on his own adolescent journey, beyond Camelot (Queen Guinevere also appears as a witty, self-assured character). Mildred Day has a translated edition, which should be available by order from college or university libraries.

Anon. *Sir Gawain and the Green Knight*
This fourteenth-century manuscript, written in a dialect of Middle English (what we might think of as a regional accent), focuses on a young Sir Gawain and his struggle to face off against the supernatural Green Knight. Along the way, he fails to uphold his knightly training, but the poem gently insists that failure is human. Derek Brewer's *Companion to the Gawain Poet* explores the poem and its context in detail, while Geraldine Heng's essay, "Feminine Knots" (*PMLA* 1991) explores Morgan le Fay's central role in the poem. James Winnny has an accessible facing translation of the poem (English on one side, Middle English opposite). The manuscript images can be viewed at the University of Calgary's *Gawain Project* (http://contentdm.ucalgary.ca/digital/collection/gawain/search) and a translated edition is available through the University of Rochester: https://d.lib.rochester.edu/camelot/text/weston-sir-gawain-and-the-green-knight.

Anon. *The Sworn Book of Honorius*
This fifteenth-century spell-book was one of the most frequently banned texts in late medieval history and contains a number of spells for summoning elemental-like spirits. The physical copy is in the British Library, but a version in modern English can be read here: https://fliphtml5.com/kymf/wtsy/basic.

Anon. *Vulgate* (or *The Lancelot-Grail Cycle*)
These multi-authored thirteenth-century French stories—spanning ten volumes—gather together a diverse range of tales about King Arthur's knights. Though the focus is on Lancelot as a fallible knight, they also explore characters like Merlin,

Morgan le Fay, and Guinevere, as well as the queer romance between Lancelot and Galehaut (edited out in later texts). The most accessible version of selected tales is Norris Lacy's *The Lancelot-Grail Reader*. Searchable editions of the Old French original can be found on Archive.org.

Barney, Stephen. *The Etymologies of Isidore of Seville*
This edition collects what we would now call an encyclopedia by the seventh-century writer Isidore of Seville, including detailed descriptions of how early medieval thinkers conceptualized childhood and adolescence.

Chaucer, Geoffrey. *The Canterbury Tales*
In this unfinished fourteenth-century masterwork, Chaucer's pilgrims engage in a storytelling contest during their pilgrimage to Canterbury. The text is known for its detailed use of characterization, ironic sense of humor, and memorable personalities like the Wife of Bath and the possibly queer, nonbinary, or intersex Pardoner. An online facing translation is available here: http://sites.fas.harvard.edu/~chaucer/teachslf/tr-index.htm. More information can be found at the Open Access Companion to the Canterbury Tales: https://opencanterburytales.dsl.lsu.edu/.

de Boron, Robert. *Merlin and the Grail*
This thirteenth-century French cycle of stories expands upon Merlin's origins, describing how his father was a demonic figure. Robert de Boron places the wizard squarely in the middle of good and evil forces, while also humanizing him by describing his unusual childhood. Nigel Bryant's translated edition presents the story in an affordable paperback.

de France, Marie. *Lais*
These twelfth-century French stories contain several Arthurian tales, including "Lanval" (about a knight forgotten by Arthur's court, who seeks the help of a fairy enchantress). Marie de France has adapted earlier stories told in "Breton"—before the Norman conquest—some of whose structure survives in living languages like Cornish. Claire Waters has an excellent scholarly edition, and the *lais* can also be read in translation online, compiled by Judith Shoaf: https://people.clas.ufl.edu/jshoaf/marie_lais/.

Delanty, Greg and Michael Matto. *The Word Exchange*
This volume of early medieval poetry includes some of the riddles and elegies mentioned in the book, like "The Wanderer" and "The Wife's Lament," with facing translations. It also includes spells and charms, which were a part of early medieval medicine. The complete corpus of Old English poetry can be read at the Old English Poetry Project, hosted by the University of Rutgers: https://oldenglishpoetry.camden.rutgers.edu/.

Monmouth, Geoffrey of. *The History of the Kings of Britain*
This enormously popular twelfth-century Latin text was one of the first to offer a detailed look at the origins of King Arthur. It presents the story of Merlin using magic to facilitate Arthur's birth, as well as a young Arthur pulling the sword from the stone. Monmouth places Arthur within the context of a long line of English kings, and his text is involved in English nation-building in some complex ways (particularly because he was living under Norman occupation). Michael Faletra has a very accessible edition with a scholarly supplement.

Monmouth, Geoffrey of. *The Life of Merlin*
This twelfth-century Latin text expands upon the character of Merlin, who is only briefly mentioned in Monmouth's more popular *History of the Kings of Britain*. As a poetic text, it is far more creative in how it approaches the wizard figure, and depicts him as an anxious survivor of battlefield PTSD. It also provides one of the earliest descriptions of Morgan le Fay as a scholar and healer who lives on an island with her sisters. The *Vita Merlini* is included in Faletra's edition of *History of the Kings of Britain*.

Gower, John. *Confessio amantis* (The Lover's Confession)
This fourteenth-century epic poem also serves as medieval conduct literature, since several of its sections are designed to separate good behavior from bad. It includes a number of stories adapted from both medieval and classical folklore. An online version compiled by the University of Rochester is available here: https://d.lib.rochester.edu/teams/publication/peck-confessio-amantis-volume-1.

Hoccleve, Thomas. *My Compleinte*
In this fourteenth-century poem, Thomas Hoccleve includes episodes of depression, social anxiety, and cognitive difference that we might now describe as neurodiversity. Though Hoccleve focuses on how he managed to outgrow this social anxiety, the poem provides a window into the life of a young, anxious medieval person. Roger Ellis has published a scholarly edition of *My Compleinte* and other works by Hoccleve. Much of Hoccleve's poetry is also available on Archive.org.

Kieckhefer, Richard. *Forbidden Rights: A Necromancer's Manual of the Fifteenth Century*
This translated version presents a medieval Latin spell-book, currently housed in Munich. It contains a number of spells that medieval university students may have actually studied, including what I've described as a bisexual love spell. Kieckhefer's edition is available as an affordable e-book.

Knight, Stephen. *Robin Hood and Other Outlaw Tales*
Knight collects a variety of tales about the late medieval figure Robin Hood, from the fourteenth century all the way through to the seventeenth-century versions that would influence popular cinema. An online version is available through the University of Rochester: https://d.lib.rochester.edu/teams/publication/knight-and-ohlgren-robin-hood-and-other-outlaw-tales.

Malory, Thomas. *Le Morte Darthur*
This fifteenth-century version of Arthurian stories, printed by William Caxton, has become the standard. Many readers are familiar with tropes about Camelot and King Arthur without even having read Malory's work, since its influence is so far-reaching. Malory edited the *Vulgate* quite heavily, and the version he presents is the most coherent, though not necessarily complete. An online version is available on the *Sacred Texts* website: https://sacred-texts.com/neu/mart/. Leitch and Rushton's *A New Companion to Malory* provides detailed analyses of the text, and the University of Rochester's online *Camelot Project* is also an excellent resource: https://d.lib.rochester.edu/camelot-project.

Nelson, William. *A Fifteenth-Century Schoolbook from a Manuscript in the British Museum (MS. Arundel 249)*
This facsimile edition reprints lessons from a fifteenth-century schoolbook, and offers a fascinating look at how medieval students might have viewed their university experience. It is available in an affordable e-book edition.

Stehling, Thomas. *Medieval Latin Poems of Love and Friendship*
This collection includes queer Latin poetry by Marbod of Rennes, Baudri of Bourgueil, and other early medieval poets who deal in themes of gender and sexuality. Stehling provides Latin originals and English translations, and this volume is one of the only places to find translated work by these lesser-known medieval poets (including poems between women). It can be ordered through a college or university interlibrary loan system.

Vostaert, Pieter and Peninc. *The Romance of Walewein*
This epic poem, written in Middle Dutch somewhere between the thirteenth and fourteenth centuries, tells a story about Sir Gawain that is not seen in other Arthurian texts. Walewein (Gawain) leaves Camelot in search of a magic chessboard and encounters a talking fox who becomes his companion. It is a hard romance to track down, but David Johnson has a facing translation through D. S. Brewer's Arthurian Archives series.

Young Adult Novels

Albertalli, Becky. *Simon vs. the Homo Sapiens Agenda*
Not a medievalist novel, but it does focus on an epistolary exchange (through email) between Simon and a secret love interest. The novel was adapted into a successful 2018 film, which was one of the first mainstream movies to focus on a gay teen romance.

Alexander, Lloyd. *Taran Wanderer*
Alexander's children's fantasy series—set in the world of Prydain—is a loose retelling of the Welsh *Mabinogion* stories. In this book, he explores the adolescence of his hero, Taran, who is explicitly searching for his identity while also struggling to complete a series of quests. It is the most YA-feeling of Alexander's medievalist books, and also features a witch named Eilonwy whose sarcasm tempers Taran's earnestness.

Beagle, Peter S. *The Last Unicorn*
This gently satirical—and melancholy—novel focuses on the world's last known unicorn and her desire to find others like her. Along the way, she meets a failed magician named Schmendrick and a scullery maid named Molly Grue—two of the only people who recognize her for what she truly is. Every hero is ambiguous, and like a true fairy tale, the ending also leaves us wondering. In 1987 the novel was adapted into a popular animated film, directed by Arthur Rankin (who also directed the 1977 animated *Hobbit* film).

Brennan, Sarah R. *In Other Lands*
This YA fantasy focuses on Eliot, a snarky bisexual teen who finds himself transported to a medievalist realm where heroism is enforced. Brennan dissects a number of fantasy tropes in this book (e.g., her Elvish women are all warriors, while the men are pacifists). Eliot's eventual role as a diplomat and treaty expert subverts what we have come to expect from a fantasy hero, and he has an adorable romance with a harpy.

Capetta, Amy Rose and Cori McCarthy. *Once and Future*
This book reimagines T. H. White's *Once and Future King* series: Arthur becomes Ari (a queer Arab woman), Merlin falls in love with Percival, and Guinevere has her own spaceship. It is an exciting mash-up of medieval fantasy and space opera, whose characters live on a broad spectrum of gender and sexuality.

Clare, Cassandra. *The Red Scrolls of Magic*
This novel focuses on the romance of Magnus Bane (a centuries-old mage) and Alec Lightwood (a shadow hunter—technically the enemy of someone like Magnus). It is

both a complex romantic story and a fantasy-mystery hybrid, and the queerness of the relationship is announced on the very cover with Magnus and Alec holding hands. Magnus is also a person of color, and his adventures can be followed in the TV series *Shadowhunters*.

De Haan, Linda. *King and King*
This illustrated children's book was one of the first to depict a fairy-tale romance between two boys. It tells the story of a prince who is supposed to find a princess to marry, but instead falls in love with—and marries—another prince. The book was critiqued and banned when it came out in 2003, but has endured as a queer children's classic.

Duane, Diane. *A Wizard Alone* [Millennium E-Book Edition]
The sixth book in Duane's series focusing on teen wizards, *A Wizard Alone* has an autistic main character who is also a wizard. Duane heavily revised the 2003 edition to craft a more sensitive portrayal of an autistic character, and the updated edition received positive reviews from sites like *Disability in Kidlit*. The book is not strictly medievalist, but Duane's language-based magic system shares much in common with Ursula Le Guin's medievalist *Earthsea* novels.

Duane, Diane. *A Door into Fire*
This was one of Duane's first novels (previously she had been known for her work on *Star Trek* series books), and it features a queer wizard in a medievalist world. The book was well ahead of its time in 1979, depicting a complex society where pansexuality was the norm, and the main characters—Herewiss and Freelorn—are in a committed relationship. Their queer adolescence is depicted as being largely without incident, and this series lacks the tragedy that would have normally been inflicted on queer characters in the genre.

Grossman, Lev. *The Magicians*
This New Adult story focuses on Quentin Coldwater, a wizard-in-training who attends the magical Brakebills Academy (these characters are slightly older, so Brakebills is more like a magical university). It also includes a portal fantasy involving a magical realm, Fillory, which is a dark adaptation of C. S. Lewis's *Narnia* series. Quentin deals frankly with depression and social anxiety throughout Grossman's trilogy of books.

Lackey, Mercedes. *Magic's Pawn*
Though not marketed as YA, this fantasy novel explores the queer adolescence of the mage Vanyel, including his journey towards self-acceptance. This is not a happy book—every tragedy you can imagine does occur—but it is also an early

positive portrayal of a queer character in the fantasy genre. Certainly, it's one of the earliest depictions of a queer teen in medievalist fantasy fiction.

Le Guin, Ursula. *A Wizard of Earthsea*
The first book in Le Guin's *Earthsea* series focuses on Ged, a young wizard (also a person of color) who attends the Roke Island School of Wizardry. This is one of the first depictions of a magic school within the fantasy genre, and Le Guin subverts many of Tolkien's tropes (e.g., the majority of her wizards are people of color, while the "barbarians" are light-skinned). A morally complex story of a wizard's adolescence, which does not go smoothly.

Morpugo, Michael. *Sir Gawain and the Green Knight*
This illustrated children's book adapts the fourteenth-century poem *Sir Gawain and the Green Knight*. The illustrations are striking, but the narrative is surprisingly homophobic, as it tries to render the queer kisses between Gawain and Bertilak as a pointed joke. Still, the book cannot quite suppress the delightful otherness or monstrosity of the Green Knight.

Pratchett, Terry. *The Wee Free Men*
This is the first book in the Tiffany Aching series and focuses on Tiffany's childhood. Growing up on the remote Chalk, she is far removed from any knowledge of magic. But when her little brother is kidnapped by a monster, Tiffany begins a journey that will transform her into the witch she has always been. Tiffany's thoughtfulness, social anxiety, and love of logic make her a non-traditional heroine and someone who might resonate with neurodivergent audiences.

Rees, David. *In the Tent*
This early gay YA novel focuses on Tim, a Catholic teen from Exeter who grapples with his sexuality while camping in the medievalist countryside. It is one of the first examples of gay YA literature that includes an open romance, sex, and a relatively happy ending.

Robinson, Eden (Haisla/Heiltsuk). *Son of a Trickster*
This YA fantasy/horror novel focuses on teen Jared and his struggle to reconcile the fact that his father is Wee'git, a legendary trickster local to Haisla/Heiltsuk culture. Jared's mother is a witch, and his girlfriend, Sarah, identifies as Two-Spirit. The first book has been adapted to a TV series with the CBC network.

Rowell, Rainbow. *Carry On*
This novel tells the story of Simon Snow and his experiences at the magical Watford Academy, including his romance with Baz the vampire. Rowell subtly critiques many elements from J. K. Rowling's *Harry Potter* series within the book,

dealing with trauma and its relationship to magic. Since Simon's world is actually part of a fanfiction series in her earlier book, *Fangirl*, Rowell is also commenting on fandom in *Carry On*.

Russo, Meredith. *If I Was Your Girl*
Not a medievalist novel, but Russo's debut book focuses on Amanda, a trans girl negotiating a new high school, and a potentially fraught relationship with a cis boy (Grant). Russo adapts a number of YA conventions—a prom, a secondary mystery, divorced parents—in ways that feel fresh and relevant.

Tolkien, J. R. R. *The Hobbit*
In many ways, this children's/YA book launched the modern fantasy genre. It focuses on Bilbo Baggins, a hobbit who is torn from his comfortable hobbit hole when he joins a mission organized by the wizard Gandalf. Not only does *The Hobbit* re-weave medieval stories in fascinating ways, it also delivers the emotional intensity and growth of character that we tend to associate with the YA genre. The lack of women in this book is frustrating, but Tolkien's later series—*The Lord of the Rings*—does deliver more complex characters who are women.

Ursu, Anne. *The Real Boy*
This middle-grade fantasy novel focuses on Oscar, an autistic boy living in a late medieval world structured around the guild system (what we might think of as early trade unions). Oscar is a gifted herbalist who is forced to take over the apothecary, after his master is killed by a monster. The novel explores his journey to solve a magical mystery, as well as his anxiety and struggles with sociability (Ursu consulted with her autistic son while creating the character).

White, T. H. *The Sword in the Stone*
The first novel in White's *Once and Future King* series focuses on a young Arthur (nicknamed Wart) and his magical education under the wizard Merlyn. White plays with many of the ideas found in Malory's *Morte Darthur*, but under the gentle comedy of this book lies an exquisitely melancholy look back at the Middle Ages. White also adapts Morgan le Fay into the evil enchantress Madame Mim—a villain so powerful she could only be allowed to exist in one book (and his editors even urged him to remove the now-classic character).

Wynne Jones, Diana. *Hexwood*
This fantasy/science-fiction hybrid offers a re-reading of Merlin's story, told from the perspective of Ann Stavley, a child recovering from illness who discovers Merlin in the forest near her house. The book reimagines Camelot as a totalitarian regime in space, and borrows from Welsh legends about the bard Taliesin. It is a strange and haunting novel that remains a critically under-valued Arthurian

adaptation. (Thank you to my former student, Apolline Lucyk, for introducing me to the book!)

Media

Aguirre-Sacasa, Roberto, Creator. *Chilling Adventures of Sabrina*
This adaptation of the *Sabrina* comics focuses on Sabrina Spellman, a teen witch who tries to balance her magical upbringing with her desire to be a normal high school student. The show is filled with medievalist images, from the devil as a physical being, to witch covens and animal familiars. It presents queerness as fairly unremarkable within the witch community, though YMMV (your mileage may vary) in terms of queer characters being relegated to hetero-centered storylines over the course of each season. Like the Tiffany Aching novels, *Chilling Adventures* does center the stories of supernatural women in a significant way.

Andras, Emily, Creator. *Wynonna Earp*
This show—based on the comic series by Beau Smith—tells the story of Wyatt Earp's distant descendent, Wynonna, who sends demons back to hell using Earp's antique gun (Peacemaker). The show is filmed in Canada and has a mostly Canadian cast. It is notable for its queer content, including two central queer relationships, as well as the ways in which it subverts masculine cowboy narratives.

Benioff, David and D. B. Weiss, Creators. *Game of Thrones*
Not strictly a teen series, though it has been widely consumed by younger viewers. This adaptation of George R. R. Martin's *Game of Thrones* series focuses on the medievalist world of Westeros, and its geographic neighbor, Essos. The show concentrates on the Stark children, who must negotiate an almost relentlessly hostile medieval society. Martin was highly influenced by actual medieval conflicts like the Wars of the Roses and the Hundred Years War.

Butchard, Stephen, Executive Producer. *The Last Kingdom*
Adapted from the medievalist novels by Bernard Cornwell, this series focuses on Uhtred, who is abducted by Vikings at an early age. His character is split between two cultures as he tries to negotiate the chaotic early medieval kingdoms of the ninth century. Several historical figures appear, including King Alfred the Great.

Gadsby, Hannah. *Douglas*
This comedy special is the sequel to Gadsby's show *Nanette*, which explored her relationship with trauma as a queer autistic woman. *Douglas* delves more into Gadsby's autistic identity, and she also spends some time cutting down male fantasies within art history. The special is notable in how it addresses queerness,

gender, and neurodiversity, while also presenting the autistic community as far-reaching and positive.

Halperin, Michael, Creator. *He-Man and the Masters of the Universe*
This 1980s cartoon/toy franchise focused on the realm of Eternia, which combined medievalist castles with futuristic technology. Many queer viewers have found a kindred spirit in Skeletor, the show's campy villain, whose wit is often thwarted by He-Man's brawn.

Harmon, Dan, Creator. *Community*
Though not specifically medievalist or teen-centered, *Community* is notable for its focus on fantasy—including an episode devoted to D&D (Dungeons and Dragons)—as well as its commentary on fandom. One of the characters, Abed Nadir, is described in the first episode as having ASD, though the show coyly avoids labeling him after that. Abed's love affair with fantasy culture is connected with his own difficulties negotiating social rules; however, the show is very clear that this is not because Abed confuses fantasy with reality, but rather because he prefers the structure of fantasy to the randomness of reality.

Henson, Jim, Director. *Labyrinth*
This 1986 film—with a screenplay by *Monty Python* alum and medieval historian Terry Jones—tells the story of a teen girl (Sarah) who must rescue her baby brother from the Goblin King's magical labyrinth. The film included several nods to late medieval culture, from a Quixotic[1] knight in the form of a raccoon, to combat with swords and cannon balls. The Goblin King is an androgynous wizard figure, played by David Bowie, who wears feather cloaks and dances joyfully at the thought of wreaking havoc on the mortal world.

Hirst, Michael, Creator. *Vikings*
This medievalist show focuses on a group of Vikings living in the eighth and ninth centuries. The show's initial protagonist, Ragnar Lothbrok (Ragnarr Loðbrók), is a historical figure described in various medieval texts. Viewers also watch the character Björn, Ragnar's son, as he grows up, which offers an interesting glimpse of Viking childhood and adolescence. As I discuss, the show has been criticized for its depiction of a disabled villain—Ivar the Boneless (Ívarr hinn Beinlausi)—whose thirst for power seems problematically linked with his own disability. The show also tends to depict a great deal of warfare, in spite

---

[1] This term refers to Miguel de Cervantes's character Don Quixote, an older gentleman who takes medieval romances too seriously. *Don Quixote* critiques both medieval and early modern culture in Spain, and is considered a classic of satirical literature, as well as a nation-defining novel.

of the fact that medieval Norse communities were principally invested in farming, trade, and textiles (Viking raids were a part of this culture, but not *all* of it).

Howard, Ron, Director. *Willow*
This 1988 fantasy film focused on Willow Ufgood, a little person, who was portrayed by actor Warwick Davis. Willow's quest focuses on protecting the infant Elora Danan, and the movie weaves in medieval material on fairies and magic. It includes a duel between two enchantresses in the film that has much in common with Morgue's magic duel in the *Prophésies de Merlin*. Much of the film's cast were also little people, in comparison with the dwarves in the *Lord of the Rings* film franchise, who were created using CGI (computer generated imagery).

Jones, Julian, Creator. *Merlin*
This YA show—airing on the BBC—focused on teen Merlin and his rocky friendship (and sometimes passionate relationship) with a young, inexperienced King Arthur. Guinevere was played by Black actress Angel Coulby—a decision challenged by critics who refused to accept that Black people existed during the Middle Ages.

Levy, Daniel and Eugene, Creators. *Schitt's Creek*
This Canadian show focuses on a small town (Schitt's Creek) which seems disagreeable at first, but turns out to be a kind of utopia, where the misfit Rose family is able to evolve and pursue their own passions. Creator Dan Levy has mentioned in interviews how he wanted the town to be entirely free of homophobia, and the show tackles a number of stereotypes about small towns, while also refusing to romanticize the setting. Both David and his mother, Moira, have a queer self-presentation that I've come to think of as medievalist nonbinary fashion.

Lorre, Chuck, Creator. *The Big Bang Theory*
This show focuses on four nerdy friends, including Sheldon Cooper, a physicist who has always seemed to be coded autistic (the showrunners deny this). Cooper has many phobias, and often misinterprets social cues, but the show also crafts him as an ultimately sympathetic character. Its focus on fantasy and nerd culture makes *The Big Bang Theory* of interest to a variety of viewers, though there has also been significant criticism that the show tends to trade in stereotypes.

Lorre, Chuck, Creator. *Young Sheldon*
This show focuses on the childhood of Sheldon Cooper, the acerbic physicist and star of Lorre's *The Big Bang Theory*. *Young Sheldon*'s exploration of the titular character's childhood delivers a potentially relatable experience for neurodivergent viewers—though Sheldon's behavior is sometimes wholly designed to cause drama and get laughs, his very real anxiety and issues with sociability might ring true with many people.

Marx, Christy, Creator. *Jem and the Holograms*
A 1980s cartoon and toy franchise that focused on the rock star Jem—who was the secret alter ego of the businesswoman, Jerrica Benton. Though not medievalist, the show was fantastic in the sense that Jerrica used a pair of cyber-magic earrings to transform into Jem, and was also guided by a Morgan-like mentor (the hologram, Synergy).

Mulcahy, Russell, Director. *Highlander*
This 1980s film franchise focuses on an immortal warrior, Connor MacLeod, who battles other immortals for a mysterious power known simply as "the prize." The initial film, starring Christopher Lambert, was particularly medievalist—Connor lived as a mortal in late medieval Scotland, and was tutored by a foppish (but dashing) immortal named Ramírez. The films also saw a TV spinoff in the 1990s, combining medieval combat with magic in an urban setting.

Nunn, Laurie, Creator. *Sex Education*
This teen comedy addresses sexuality through its main character, Otis, who becomes an unofficial sex therapist by borrowing knowledge gained from his mother (who actually is a sex therapist). I reference the show in relation to *Sir Gawain and the Green Knight* in part due to its setting (pastoral England), and also the way in which it un-works highly knotted stereotypes within the YA genre in an effort to portray teens as flawed and human.

Petersen, Wolfgang, Director. *The NeverEnding Story*
Based on the German novel by Michael Ende, this 1984 adaptation tells the story of Bastian Balthazar Bux, a boy who discovers a magic book while running into a shop to escape his bullies. Both the book and the film are considered classics of the fantasy genre—particularly in their use of meta-analysis (e.g., Bastian communicates with Atreyu, the hero of *The NeverEnding Story*, then finds himself within the book, telling his own story). In both the film and the book, Atreyu is portrayed as pan-Indigenous, though the actor who played Atreyu was not Indigenous or a person of color. Bastian is described as fat in the book, but the movie does not take this up.

Rashid, Robia, Creator. *Atypical*
This show focuses on an autistic teen, Sam, who has trouble dealing with the stresses of high school. Sam is portrayed by a non-autistic actor, and the show has received criticism for lack of community consultation. Rashid involved autistic actors in the second and third seasons, though their presence was still fairly marginal. Some viewers have found a sense of kinship with Sam, while others see his character as a constellation of stereotypes. *Atypical* is significant for being one of the first TV programs to center a young autistic character.

Reitherman, Wolfgang, Director. *The Sword in the Stone*
This Disney film adapts T. H. White's *Sword in the Stone*, while lessening some of the darker elements (i.e., Madame Mim is less threatening than the cannibal enchantress in White's novel). Though the film is familiar to many—especially the duel between Merlin and Mim—it was not a particular critical success. Merlin is almost wholly a comedic figure, rather than the ambivalent enchanter who appears in the novel.

Sechrist, Radford, Creator. *Kipo and the Age of the Wonderbeasts*
This Pixar animated show focuses on a fantastic and post-apocalyptic world, full of giant talking animals and rebellious humans who have survived an ecological catastrophe. The cast is notably diverse, and includes a queer romance between two POC (person of color) characters (Benson and Troy). The show touches upon mutation as a metaphor for difference (or queerness) in much the same way as the *X-Men* comics and films.

Silveri, Scott, Creator. *Speechless*
This show focuses on J. J. DiMeo, a teen with cerebral palsy who is non-verbal (portrayed by Micha Fowler, an actor with cerebral palsy). The show skewers all kinds of tropes around disability representation, including an episode in which J. J.'s classmates "ship" him with another student who happens to be a wheelchair-user. It manages to be a palatable comedy while still delving into some challenging material about ableism. Silveri based the character of J. J. on his brother, Gregory, who also had cerebral palsy.

Stevenson, Noelle, Creator. *She-Ra and the Princesses of Power*
This Netflix reboot of the 1980s original focuses on the friendship between She-Ra/Adora, Princess Glimmer, and their friend Bow, as they battle a fascist empire. Like its predecessor, *He-Man*, *She-Ra* blends medieval elements with technology. Stevenson's version is highly queer-inclusive, featuring a nonbinary character, multiple queer romances, and an anti-oppressive message. The show also features an autistic character (Entrapta) who was designed with some community consultation.

Thomas, Josh, Creator. *Everything's Gonna Be Okay*
This show explores a group of orphaned siblings, and plays on tropes in earlier orphan narratives, like *Party of Five*. One of the central characters, Matilda, is autistic (the actress who plays her, Kayla Cromer, is also autistic). The show presents a meaningful look at how a young queer woman with autism negotiates high school and, later, post-secondary education.

Wachowski, Lana, Lilly Wachowski, and J. Michael Straczynski, Creators. *Sense8*
This fantasy/science-fiction show focuses on a group of characters—sense8s—who can read each other's thoughts and control each other's bodies. They exist as a collective, and most of their decisions require consultation and radical forms of empathy. The show is notable for its inclusion of multiple queer and trans characters, along with a diverse cast and global shooting locations that challenge shows merely focusing on a single North American town.

Whedon, Joss, Creator. *Buffy the Vampire Slayer*
This cult-classic show focuses on teen vampire slayer Buffy Summers, along with her friends Willow (a queer witch) and Xander (a non-supernatural teen boy). The show adapts a number of medievalist elements, from sword-fighting to biblical demons, and it was well ahead of its time for depicting a queer romance. By the second season, Marti Noxon was also heavily involved in shaping the program.

Bibliography

@bitterbleue. "Autism is incredibly diverse and varied spectrum wise." Twitter, August 23, 2020, 8:52 p.m. https://twitter.com/bitterbleue/status/1297728554738778112.
@cjacksonAR. "Folks want to academize failure." Twitter, July 22, 2019. [Account deleted.]
@DubiousCA. "I have very complex feelings around Entrapta." Twitter, August 24, 2020, 11:04 a.m. https://twitter.com/DubiousCA/status/1297942851062398978.
@elissawashuta. "Outside the video game." Twitter, January 2, 2019, 2:12 p.m. https://twitter.com/elissawashuta/status/1080587587536994310.
@hamlethologram. "If everyone in the world transitioned it would still be fine." Twitter, July 12, 2020 2:15 p.m. https://twitter.com/HamletHologram/status/1282408341541654534.
Abelard, Peter. *Ethical Writings*. Translated by Paul Spade. Indianapolis, IN: Hackett Publishing, 1995. Kindle edition.
Adair, Torsten. "C2E2 Is Bigger Than New York Comic Con." *The Beat*, April 5, 2014. http://www.comicsbeat.com/c2e2-is-bigger-than-new-york-comic-con-and-can-grow-even-bigger-than-san-diego/.
Ahmed, Sara. *Living a Feminist Life*. Durham, NC: Duke University Press, 2017.
Ahmed, Sara. *The Promise of Happiness*. Durham, NC: Duke University Press, 2010.
Ahmed, Sara. "Selfcare as Warfare." *feministkilljoys* (blog), August 25, 2014. https://feministkilljoys.com/2014/08/25/selfcare-as-warfare/.
Ahmed, Sara. *Willful Subjects*. Durham, NC: Duke University Press, 2014.
Albertalli, Becky. *Simon vs. the Homo Sapiens Agenda*. New York: Balzer + Bray, 2016.
Albin, Andrew, Mary C. Erler, Thomas O'Donnell, Nicholas L. Paul, and Nina Rowe, eds. *Whose Middle Ages?* New York: Fordham University Press, 2019.
Alexander, Lloyd. *The Chronicles of Prydain*. New York: Henry Holt and Co., 2013. Kindle edition.
Al-Udhari, Abdullah, ed. *Classical Poems by Arab Women*. London: Saqi Books, 2001.
Andrew, Malcolm. *The Complete Works of the Pearl Poet*. Berkeley: University of California Press, 1993.
Andrew, Malcolm, ed. *The Poems of the Pearl Manuscript*. Exeter: University of Exeter Press, 1996.
Angel Daniel Matos. "'Without a Word or a Sign': Enmeshing Deaf and Gay Identity in Young-Adult Literature." In *Lessons in Disability*, edited by Jacob Stratman, 221–41. Jefferson, NC: McFarland and Company, 2016.
Aquinas, Thomas, *The Complete Works of Thomas Aquinas*. Edited and translated by John Henry Parker. N.p.: Catholic Publishing, 2018. Kindle edition.
Aquinas, Thomas. *Selected Writings*. Edited and translated by Ralph McInerny. London: Penguin, 1998. Kindle edition.
Armstrong, Edward, ed. *Le Chevalier à l'épée*. Baltimore, MD: John Murphy, 1897.
Atypical. Created by Robia Rashid. Sony Pictures and Exhibit A, 2017–.
Augustine. *Augustini Confessiones*. Edited by O'Donnell, James. https://faculty.georgetown.edu/jod/latinconf/latinconf.html.
Augustine. *The Complete Works of Saint Augustine*. Edited by Philip Schaff et al. N.p: n.p. 2011. Kindle edition.
Augustine. *The Confessions*. Translated by Henry Chadwick. Oxford: Oxford University Press, 2009. Kindle edition.
Barnhouse, Rebecca. *The Middle Ages in Literature for Youth*. Lanham, MD: Scarecrow Press, 2004.

Barnhouse, Rebecca. *Recasting the Past: The Middle Ages in Young Adult Literature*. Portsmouth, NH: Heinemann, 2000.

Bartelink, Gerard. "Denominations of Demons and the Devil in the *Missale Gothicum*." In *Demons and the Devil in Ancient and Medieval Christianity*, edited by Nienke Vos and Willemien Otten, 193–209. Leiden: Brill, 2011.

Bartlett, Claire. *We Rule the Night*. Boston: Little Brown and Company, 2020.

Batman, Stephen. *Batman vppon Bartholome his booke De proprietatibus rerum, newly corrected, enlarged and amended: with such additions as are requisite, vnto euery seuerall booke: taken foorth of the most approued authors, the like heretofore not translated in English. Profitable for all estates, as well for the benefite of the mind as the bodie*. 1582.

Battis, Jes, ed. *Supernatural Youth: The Rise of the Teen Hero in Literature and Popular Culture*. Lanham, MD: Lexington Books, 2013.

Battis, Jes, and Susan Johnston, eds. *Mastering the Game of Thrones: Essays on George R. R. Martin's A Song of Ice and Fire*. Jefferson, NC: McFarland & Company, 2015.

Baume, Matt. "Behind the Queens." *Queens of Adventure* (podcast), Episode 9, May 30, 2018. https://queensofadventure.com/episodes.

Baume, Matt. "Failed Mystics." *The Sewers of Paris* (podcast), Episode 277, March 12, 2020. http://www.mattbaume.com/sewers-shownotes/2020/3/12/failed-mystics-ep-277-buffy-x-men-he-man-and-lwaxana-troi.

Beagle, Peter S. *The Last Unicorn*. New York: Ace Books, 1991.

Bec, Pierre. *Chants d'amour des femmes-troubadours*. Paris: Stock, 1995.

Benoît de Saint-Maure. *Le Roman de Troie*. Edited by Léopold Constant. Paris: Librairie de Fermin Didot, 1904.

Benson, Stella. *Living Alone*. Scotts Valley, CA: CreateSpace, 2016. Kindle edition.

Biblia Vulgata. Edited and translated by Alberto Colunga and Laurentio Turrado. Madrid: Biblioteca de Autores Cristianos, 1995.

The Big Bang Theory. Created by Chuck Lorre. Warner Brothers, 2007–2019.

Birns, Nicholas. "The Enigma of Radagast." *Mythlore* 26, no. 1 (Fall 2007): 113–26.

Blud, Victoria. *The Unspeakable: Gender and Sexuality in Medieval Literature*. Cambridge: D. S. Brewer, 2017.

de Boron, Robert. *Le Livre de Merlin*. MS Additional 38177. British Library Catalogue of Illuminated Manuscripts. https://www.bl.uk/catalogues/illuminatedmanuscripts/record.asp?MSID=6730&CollID=27&NStart=38117.

de Boron, Robert. *Merlin and the Grail*. Edited by Nigel Bryant. Cambridge: D. S. Brewer, 2008.

Boureau, Alain. *Satan the Heretic*. Translated by Teresa Fagan. Chicago, IL: University of Chicago Press, 2006.

Boyd, David. "Sodomy, Misogyny, and Displacement: Occluding Queer Desire in 'Sir Gawain and the Green Knight.'" *Arthuriana* 8, no. 2 (Summer 1998): 77–113.

Bradford, Clare. *The Middle Ages in Children's Literature*. Basingstoke, Hampshire: Palgrave, 2016.

Brennan, Sarah. *In Other Lands*. Easthampton, MA: Big Mouth House, 2017.

Brewer, Derek. "The Colour Green." In *A Companion to the Gawain Poet*, edited by Derek Brewer, 181–90. Cambridge: Boydell & Brewer, 1997.

Bromwich, Rachel. "Gwalchmei m. Gwyar." In *Gawain: A Casebook*, edited by Raymond Thompson and Keith Busby, 95–102. New York: Routledge, 2014.

Bryant, Nigel, ed. *Merlin and the Grail*. Cambridge: D. S. Brewer, 2008.

Buffy the Vampire Slayer. Created by Joss Whedon. Mutant Enemy Productions and WB/UPN, 1996–2003.

Bychowski, M. W. Gabrielle. "Quantum Objects: Transvestism in *Estoire de Merlin*." *Transliterature: Things Transform*, April 5, 2014. http://www.thingstransform.com/2014/04/.

Bychowski, M. W. Gabrielle. "Were There Transgender People in the Middle Ages?" *The Public Medievalist*, November 1, 2018. https://www.publicmedievalist.com/transgender-middle-ages/.

Bynum, Carolyn. *Fragmentation and Redemption: Essays on Gender and the Human Body in Medieval Religion*. New York: Zone Books, 1992.

Caesarius of Heisterbach. *The Dialogue on Miracles*. Translated by Henry von Essen Scott. 2 vols. New York: Harcourt, Brace and Co., 1929.

Callin, William. "Christianity." In *Medievalism: Key Critical Terms*, edited by Elizabeth Emery and Richard Utz, 35–42. Cambridge: D. S. Brewer, 2014.

Camelot. Created by Chris Chibnall. Starz Entertainment, 2011.

Campbell, Lori, ed. *A Quest of Her Own: Essays on the Female Hero in Modern Fantasy*. Jefferson, NC: McFarland and Company, 2014.

Capdevila, Isabel. "Age and Rage in Terry Pratchett's 'Witches' Novels." *European Journal of English Studies* 22, no. 1 (2018): 59–75.

Capetta, Amy Rose, and Cori McCarthy. *Once and Future*. New York: Jimmy Patterson Books, 2019.

Carroll, Tyrone. "*The Magicians* Bewitches Us with Its Portrayal of Bisexuality." *The Series Regulars*, February 17, 2019, https://theseriesregulars.com/the-magicians-bewitches-us-with-their-portrayal-of-bisexuality/.

Carruthers, Mary. *The Book of Memory*. Cambridge: Cambridge University Press, 2008.

Cart, Michael. *Young-Adult Literature: From Romance to Realism*. Chicago: American Library Association, 2017.

Cart, Michael, and Christine Jenkins. *Representing the Rainbow*. Lanham, MD: Rowman & Littlefield, 2018.

Carter, Julian B. "Sex Time Machine for Touching the Trancestors." *TSQ: Transgender Studies Quarterly* 5, no. 4 (2018): 691–706.

Castillo, David. *Baroque Horrors: Roots of the Fantastic in the Age of Curiosity*. Ann Arbor: University of Michigan Press, 2010.

Castle, Terry. *The Apparitional Lesbian*. New York: Columbia University Press, 1995.

Caughey, Anna. "Adult Ideologies in Late-Medieval Advisory Writing." In *Literary Cultures and Medieval and Early Modern Childhoods*, edited by Naomi J. Miller and Dianne Purkiss, 3–20. Cham, Switzerland: Palgrave Macmillan, 2019.

Cavallo, Adolpho. *The Unicorn Tapestries of the Metropolitan Museum of Art*. New York: The Metropolitan Museum of Art, 2005.

Cecire, Maria Sachiko. *Re-Enchanted: The Rise of Children's Fantasy Literature in the Twentieth Century*. Minneapolis: University of Minnesota Press, 2019. Kindle edition.

Chaganti, Seeta. "Vestigial Signs: Inscription, Performance and 'The Dream of the Rood.'" *PMLA* 125, no. 1 (2010): 48–72.

Chappell, Cailtin. "Why *She-Ra's* Entrapta Means So Much for Autistic Representation." *CBR. com*, May 31, 2020. https://www.cbr.com/she-ra-entrapta-autistic-representation-matters/.

Charmed. Created by Jessica O'Toole. CW and Poppy Productions, 2018–.

de Charney, Geoffroi. *The Book of Chivalry*. Edited by Richard Kaeuper and Elspeth Kennedy. Philadelphia: University of Pennsylvania Press, 1996.

Chaucer, Geoffrey. *The Riverside Chaucer*. Edited by Larry Benson, Robert Pratt, et al. Oxford: Oxford University Press, 2008.

Chen, Lysa and Shauna Nakasone. "Women of Actual Play." *Behold Her* (podcast), Episode 3, May 13, 2018. https://dontsplitthepodcastnetwork.com/behold-her-podcast/.

Cheng, Patrick. *Radical Love: Introduction to Queer Theology*. New York: Seabury Books, 2011.

Chilling Adventures of Sabrina. Created by Roberto Aguirre-Sacasa. Warner Brothers and Netflix, 2018–.

Cixous, Hélène. "The Laugh of the Medusa." Translated by Keith and Paula Cohen. *Signs* 1, no. 4 (Summer 1976): 875–93.

Clare, Cassandra and Wesley Chu. *The Red Scrolls of Magic*. New York: Margaret K. McElderry Books, 2019.

Clare, Eli. *Brilliant Imperfection: Grappling with Cure*. Durham, NC: Duke University, 2017.

Clare, Eli, and Kelly Fritsch. "Resisting Easy Answers: An Interview with Eli Clare." *Upping the Anti*, no. 9, November 23, 2009. https://uppingtheanti.org/journal/article/09-resisting-easy-answers/.

Clarke, Basil. *Life of Merlin*. Cardiff: University of Wales Press, 1973.

Clarkson, Tim. *Scotland's Merlin*. Edinburgh: John Donald, 2016.

Clay, Beatrice. *King Arthur and His Round Table*. Illustrated by Dora Curtis. London: J. M. Dent, 1949.

Cohen, Jeffrey J. *In the Medieval Middle* (blog). http://www.inthemedievalmiddle.com/.

Cohen, Jeffrey J. *Stone: An Ecology of the Inhuman*. Minneapolis: University of Minnesota Press, 2015.

Collodi, Carlo. *The Adventures of Pinocchio/Le avventure di Pinocchio*. Edited by Nicholas Perella. Berkeley: University of California Press, 2005.

Coman, Jonah. "Trans-Historical Touches: A Musing on Handling Books, Textiles, and Queer Community." Roundtable discussion for "Queer Textures of the Past," International Medieval Conference, Leeds, July 1–4, 2009.

Community. Created by Dan Harmon. NBC and Krasnoff Productions, 2009–2015.

Comoletti, Laura. "How They Do Things with Words." *Children's Literature* 29 (2001): 113–41.

Conlee, John, ed. *Prose Merlin*. TEAMS Middle English Text Series. Kalamazoo, MI: Medieval Institute Publications, 1998.

Corley, Colin, ed. *Lancelot of the Lake*. Oxford Classics. Oxford: Oxford University Press, 2008.

de Corral, Pedro. *Cronica del rey don Rodrigo con la destruycion de España: y como los moros la ganaron*. 1587. https://archive.org/details/cronicadelreydon00corr/page/n5/mode/2up.

Cover, Jennifer. *The Creation of Narrative in Tabletop Role-Playing Games*. Jefferson, NC: McFarland & Company, 2010. E-book.

Cox, Carolyn. "The Mary Sue Interview: The Ladies of Geek & Sundry's *Critical Role* Explain How D&D Changed Their Lives." *The Mary Sue*, March 31, 2016. https://www.themarysue.com/the-mary-sue-critical-role-interview/.

Cox, Peta. "Passing as Sane, or How to Get People to Sit Next to You on the Bus." In *Disability and Passing: Blurring the Lines of Identity*, edited by Jeffrey A. Brune and Daniel J. Wilson, 99–110. Philadelphia, PA: Temple University Press, 2013.

Croft, Janet B. "The Education of a Witch: Tiffany Aching, Hermione Granger, and Gendered Magic in Discworld and Potterworld." *Mythlore* 27, no. 3/4 (2009): 129–42.

"Culhwch and Olwen." Translated by Rachel Bromwich. 2017. http://www.culhwch.info/.

Davidson, Clifford. *The York Corpus Christi Plays*. TEAMS Middle English Text Series. Kalamazoo, MI: Medieval Institute Publications, 2011.

Davidson, Roberta. "When King Arthur is PG-13." *Arthuriana* 22, no. 3 (2011): 5–20.
Davies, Sioned, ed. *The Mabinogion*. Oxford Classics. Oxford: Oxford University Press, 2008.
Davis, Isabel. *Writing Masculinity in the Later Middle Ages*. Cambridge: Cambridge University Press, 2007.
Davis, James. *Medieval Market Morality*. Cambridge: Cambridge University Press, 2012.
Day, Mildred. *Rise of Gawain*. New York: Garland Publishing, 1984.
DeCoste, Katy. "The episode where he throws the party." Twitter, May 10, 2020, 11:08 a.m. https://twitter.com/katydecoste/status/1259712031055200257.
De Fougères, Étienne. *Le Livre de manières*. Edited by J. T. E. Thomas. Paris: Peeters, 2013.
Delanty, Greg and Michael Matto, eds. *The Word Exchange*. New York: W. W. Norton & Company, 2011.
Dinshaw, Carolyn. *How Soon Is Now?* Durham, NC: Duke University Press, 2012.
Dolmage, Jay. *Academic Ableism*. Ann Arbor: University of Michigan Press, 2017.
Drake, Graham, ed. *Four Romances of England: King Horn, Havelok the Dane, Bevis of Hampton, Athelston*. TEAMS Middle English Text Series. Kalamazoo, MI: Medieval Institute Publications, 1997.
Duane, Diane. *A Door into Fire*. Scotts Valley, CA: CreateSpace, 2019. E-book edition.
Duane, Diane. *So You Want to Be a Wizard*. 1983. Reprint, San Diego, CA: Harcourt, 2003.
Duane, Diane. *A Wizard Alone*. Dunlavin, Ireland: Ebooks Direct, 2014. E-book edition.
Duyvis, Corinne. *On the Edge of Gone*. New York: Harry N. Abrams, 2016.
Duyvis, Corinne. *Otherbound*. New York: Amulet Books, 2016.
Duyvis, Corinne. "Review: *The Real Boy* by Anne Ursu." *Disability in Kidlit*, April 13, 2015. http://disabilityinkidlit.com/2015/04/13/review-the-real-boy-by-anne-ursu/.
Eddy, Nicole. "Merlin: International Man of Mystery." *British Library Medieval Manuscripts Blog* (blog), February 20, 2013. https://blogs.bl.uk/digitisedmanuscripts/2013/02/merlin-international-man-of-mystery.html.
Emery, Elizabeth, and Richard Utz, eds. *Medievalism: Key Critical Terms*. Cambridge: D. S. Brewer, 2014.
Epstein, Steven. *Wage Labor and Guilds in Medieval Europe*. Chapel Hill: University of North Carolina Press, 1995.
Eribon, Didier. *Insult and the Making of the Gay Self*. Durham, NC: Duke University Press, 2004.
von Eschenbach, Wolfram. *Parzival*. Edited by A. T. Hatto. London: Penguin, 1980.
Everything's Gonna Be Okay. Created by Josh Thomas. Freeform, 2020–.
Ewalt, David. *Of Dice and Men*. New York: Scribner, 2013.
Excalibur. Directed by John Boorman. Orion Pictures, 1981.
Eyler, Joshua, ed. *Disability in the Middle Ages: Reconsiderations and Reverberations*. London: Routledge, 2010.
Finch, Casey, trans. *The Complete Works of the Pearl Poet*. Berkeley: University of California Press, 1993.
Finn, Kavita Mudan, and Jessica McCall. "Exit, Pursued by a Fan: Shakespeare, Fandom, and the Lure of the Alternate Universe." *Critical Survey* 28, no. 2 (2016): 27–38.
Finn, Kavita Mudan, and Jessica McCall. "High and Mighty Queens of Westeros." In *Game of Thrones versus History: Written in Blood*, edited by Brian A. Pavlac, 19–31, Malden, MA: Wiley Blackwell, 2017.
Firefly. Created by Joss Whedon. Mutant Enemy Productions and 20th Century Fox, 2002–2003.

de France, Marie. *Lais: French Texts*. Translated by Glyn Burgess. London: Bristol Classical Press, 1998.
Friedman, Albert. "Morgan le Fay in *Sir Gawain and the Green Knight*." Reprinted in *Sir Gawain and Pearl: Critical Essays*, edited by Robert J. Blanch, 135–58. Bloomington: Indiana University Press, 1966.
Fries, Maureen. "From the Lady to the Tramp: The Decline of Morgan le Fay in Medieval Romance." *Arthuriana* 4, no. 1 (1994): 1–18.
Gadsby, Hannah. *Hannah Gadsby: Douglas*. Directed by Madeleine Perry. Netflix, 2020.
Gamble, Joseph. "How to Do It: Sex Education and the 'Sex Life.'" *Nursing Clio*, March 19, 2019. https://nursingclio.org/2019/03/19/how-to-do-it-sex-education-and-the-sex-life/.
Game of Thrones. Created by David Benioff and D. B. Weiss. HBO and Television 360, 2011–2019.
Ganze, Ronald. "The Neurological and Physiological Effects of Emotional Duress on Memory in Two Old English Elegies." In *Anglo-Saxon Emotions*, edited by Alice Jorgensen, Frances McCormack, and Jonathan Wilcox, 211–26. Farnham, Surrey: Ashgate Publishing, 2015.
Garland, Rosemary Thomson. "Integrating Disability, Transforming Feminist Theory." *NWSA Journal* 14, no. 3 (Fall 2002): 1–32.
Garmonsway, G. N. *Aelfric's Colloquy*. London: Methuen, 1967.
Geoffrey of Monmouth. *The History of the Kings of Britain*. Edited by Michael Faletra. Peterborough, ON: Broadview Press, 2008.
Geoffrey of Monmouth. *Life of Merlin*. Edited by Basil Clarke. Cardiff: University of Wales Press, 1973.
Geraghty, Lincoln. "Heroes of Hall H." In *Superheroes on World Screens*, edited by Rayna Denison and Rachel Mizsei-Ward, 75–93. Jackson: University Press of Mississippi, 2015.
Gieysztor, Aleksander. "Management and Resources." In *A History of the University in Europe: Universities in the Middle Ages*, edited by Walter Rüegg, 108–42. Cambridge: Cambridge University Press, 2003.
Gifford, James. *A Modernist Fantasy*. Victoria, BC: ELS Editions, 2018. Kindle edition.
Gladir, George. *Archie's Madhouse #22*. Pelham, NY: Archie Comic Publications, 1962.
Godden, M. R. "Anglo-Saxons on the Mind." In *Learning and Literature in Anglo-Saxon England*, edited by Michael Lapidge, 271–98. Cambridge: Cambridge University Press, 1985.
Godden, Rick. "Getting Medieval in Real Time." *postmedieval* 2, no. 3 (2011): 267–77.
Goodrich, Peter, and Raymond H. Thompson, eds. *Merlin: A Casebook*. New York: Routledge, 2004.
Gower, John. *Confessio Amantis*, Vols. 1–3. Edited by Russell Peck. TEAMS Middle English Text Series. Kalamazoo, MI: Medieval Institute Publications, 2006. Rochester University, Robbins Library Digital Projects. https://d.lib.rochester.edu/teams/publication/peck-confessio-amantis-volume-1.
Grattan, Charles. *Anglo-Saxon Magic and Medicine Illustrated Specially From the Semi-Pagan Text "Lacnunga."* London: Oxford University Press, 1952.
Gray, Brenna Clarke, and Joe Lipsett. *Hazel & Katniss & Harry & Starr* (podcast). 2018–. https://hazelkatnissharrystarr.simplecast.com/.
Grossman, Lev. *The Magicians*. New York: Penguin, 2010.
Gurza, Andrew. *Disability after Dark* (podcast). 2016–. http://www.andrewgurza.com/podcast.
Gurza, Andrew. "This Ability: Andrew Gurza on Queer Disability and Sex." *Xtra Video* (video), March 10, 2020. https://www.dailyxtra.com/andrew-gurza-on-queer-disability-and-sex-168258.

Gutt, Blake. "Transgender Genealogy in *Tristan de Nanteuil*." *Exemplaria* 30, no. 2 (2018): 129–46.
Gwenogvryn, J. Evans. *Poems from the Book of Taliesin*. London: Forgotten Books, 2015.
Gygax, Gary. *Dungeons & Dragons Player's Handbook*. Lake Geneva, WI: TSR, 1980.
de Haan, Linda, and Stern Nijland. *King & King*. Berkeley: Tricycle Press, 2003.
Hahn, Thomas. "Gawain and Popular Chivalric Romance in Britain." In *The Cambridge Companion to Medieval Romance*, edited by Roberta Krueger, 218–35. Cambridge: Cambridge University Press, 2000.
Hahn, Thomas, ed. *Sir Gawain: Eleven Romances and Tales*. TEAMS Middle English Text Series. Kalamazoo, MI: Medieval Institute Publications, 1995.
Halberstam, J. *The Queer Art of Failure*. Durham, NC: Duke University Press, 2011.
Hatto, A. T., ed. and trans. *Parzival*. London: Penguin Classics, 1980.
Heaney, Seamus, ed. *Beowulf*. New York: W. W. Norton & Company, 2001.
Heath Justice, Daniel. "Indigenous Wonderworks and the Settler-Colonial Imaginary." *Apex*, August 10, 2017. https://apex-magazine.com/indigenous-wonderworks-and-the-settler-colonial-imaginary/.
Hebert, Jill M. *Morgan le Fay: Shape-Shifter*. New York: Palgrave Macmillan, 2013.
He-Man and the Masters of the Universe. Created by Michael Halperin. Filmation, 1983–1985.
Heng, Geraldine. *Empire of Magic: Medieval Romance and the Politics of Cultural Fantasy*. New York: Columbia University Press, 2003.
Heng, Geraldine. "Feminine Knots and the Other *Sir Gawain and the Green Knight*." *PMLA* 106, no. 3 (1991): 500–514.
Heng, Geraldine. "Race in the European Middle Ages." *Humanities and Social Sciences Online*. February 27, 2018. https://networks.h-net.org/node/113394/discussions/1454005/teaching-essay-race-european-middle-ages.
Hildegard of Bingen. *Scivias*. Translated by Mother Columba Hart and Jane Bishop. New York: Paulist Press, 1990.
Hillman, Richard. "Chaucer's Franklin's Magician and *The Tempest*." *Shakespeare Quarterly* 34, no. 4 (1983): 426–32.
Hobgood, Alison, and David Houston Wood, eds. *Recovering Disability in Early Modern England*. Columbus: Ohio State University Press, 2013.
Hoccleve, Thomas. *My Compleinte*. Edited by Roger Ellis. Exeter: University of Exeter Press, 2001.
Hollander, Lee, trans. *The Poetic Edda*. Austin: University of Texas Press, 2010.
Holt, J. C. *Robin Hood*. London: Thames & Hudson, 1983.
Hostetter, Aaron. *Medieval Appetites: Food in Medieval English Romance*. Columbus: Ohio State University Press, 2017.
Hostetter, Aaron, trans. "The Wanderer." *Anglo-Saxon Narrative Poetry Project*. https://anglosaxonpoetry.camden.rutgers.edu/the-wanderer/.
How to Train Your Dragon. Directed by Dean DeBlois and Chris Sanders. DreamWorks Animation and Mad Hatter, 2010.
Howard, Kat. *A Cathedral of Myth and Bone*. New York: Saga Press, 2019.
Hsy, Jonathan. *Trading Tongues: Merchants, Multilingualism, and Medieval Literature*. Columbus: Ohio State University Press, 2013.
Hutton, Ronald. *The Witch: A History of Fear*. New Haven, CT: Yale University Press, 2017.
Isidore of Seville. *The Etymologies of Isidore of Seville*. Translated by Stephen A. Barney, W. J. Lewis, J. A. Beach, and Oliver Berghof. Cambridge: Cambridge University Press, 2006.

Jackson, Cody. "How Disability Labor Justice Can Help Reimagine a Discipline." *Medium*. May 26, 2019. https://medium.com/@cody72471/rhet-comp-disabilitylabor-justice-43dacf642553.

Jackson, Cody. "Loving Jim: Jim Wheeler and the Matter of Queer Archives." *Medium*. August 1, 2019. https://medium.com/@cody72471/loving-jim-jim-wheeler-and-the-matter-of-queer-archives-21557b4e991a.

Jackson, Steve, and Ian Livingston. *The Citadel of Chaos*. London: Puffin, 1983.

Jackson, Steve, and Ian Livingston. *The Crown of Kings*. London: Penguin, 1985.

Jackson, Steve, and Ian Livingston. *The Warlock of Firetop Mountain*. London: Wizard Books, 2007.

Jem and the Holograms. Created by Christy Marx. Sunbow, 1985–1988.

Jenkins, Christine. *Representing the Rainbow in Young-Adult Literature*. Lanham, MD: Rowman & Littlefield, 2018.

Jenkins, Henry. "Super-Powered Fans: The Many Worlds of San Diego's Comic-Con." *Boom* 2, no. 2 (2012): 22–36.

Johnson, David, and Geert Claassens, eds. and trans. *Roman van Walewein*. Cambridge: D. S. Brewer, 2012.

Joy, Eileen. "Blue." In *Prismatic Ecology: Ecotheory beyond Green*, edited by Jeffrey Jerome Cohen, 213–32. Minneapolis: University of Minnesota Press, 2013.

Kafer, Alison. *Feminist, Queer, Crip*. Bloomington: Indiana University Press, 2013.

Kane, Vivian. "How Women Are Driving the Dungeons & Dragons Renaissance." *The Mary Sue*, May 10, 2018. https://www.themarysue.com/women-in-dungeons-and-dragons/.

Kann, Claire. *Let's Talk About Love*. New York: Swoon Reads, 2018.

Karras, Ruth Mazo. *From Boys to Men*. Philadelphia: University of Pennsylvania Press, 2002.

Kaszkiewicz, Weronika. "Peter S. Beagle's Transformations of the Mythic Unicorn." *Mythlore* 33, no. 1 (Fall 2014): 53–65.

Kaufman, Amy S. "Malory and Gender." In *A New Companion to Malory*, edited by Megan Leitch and Cory James Rushton, 164–76. Cambridge: D. S. Brewer, 2019.

Kemp, Simon. *Medieval Psychology*. New York: Praeger, 1990.

Kieckhefer, Richard. *Forbidden Rights: A Necromancer's Manual of the Fifteenth Century*. University Park: Pennsylvania State University Press, 1998. Kindle edition.

Kim, Cynthia. *Nerdy, Shy, and Socially Inappropriate: A User Guide to an Asperger Life*. London: Jessica Kingsley, 2014.

Kim, Dorothy. "The Question of Race in *Beowulf*." *JSTOR Daily*, September 25, 2019. https://daily.jstor.org/the-question-of-race-in-beowulf/.

Kim, Dorothy. "White Supremacists Have Weaponized an Imaginary Viking Past." *TIME*, April 15, 2019. https://time.com/5569399/viking-history-white-nationalists/.

Kipo and the Age of the Wonderbeasts. Created by Radford Sechrist. Pixar. 2019–.

Klein, Thomas. "The Old English Translation of Aldhem's Riddle *Lorica*." *Review of English Studies* 48, no. 191 (1997): 345–49.

Klinck, Anne, ed. *The Old English Elegies*. Montreal: McGill-Queen's University Press, 2001.

Kline, Daniel, ed. *Medieval Literature for Children*. New York: Routledge, 2003.

Kline, Daniel. "Participatory Medievalism, Role-Playing, and Digital Gaming." In *The Cambridge Companion to Medievalism*, edited by Louise D'Arcens, 75–88. Cambridge: Cambridge University Press, 2016.

Knight, Stephen. *Merlin: Knowledge and Power through the Ages*. Baltimore, MD: Johns Hopkins University Press, 2009.

Knight, Stephen. *Robin Hood and Other Outlaw Tales*. TEAMS Middle English Text Series. Kalamazoo, MI: Medieval Institute Publications, 1997.
Knowles, James. *King Arthur and His Knights*. New York: Children's Classics, 1998.
Kramer, Kelly. "Common Language of Desire: *The Magicians*, Narnia, and Contemporary Fantasy." *Mythlore* 35, no. 2 (2017): 153–69.
Krueger, Roberta, ed. *Cambridge Companion to Medieval Romance*. Cambridge: Cambridge University Press, 2000.
Kurchak, Sarah. *I Overcame My Autism and All I Got Was This Lousy Anxiety Disorder*. Madeira Park, BC: Douglas & McIntyre, 2020. Kindle edition.
Kurchak, Sarah. "The Promise—and Pitfalls—of Netflix's New Reality Dating Show for Autistic People." *TIME*, July 24, 2020. https://time.com/5870971/love-on-the-spectrum-netflix/.
Labyrinth. Directed by Jim Henson. Lucasfilm, 1986.
Lackey, Mercedes. *Magic's Price*. New York: DAW, 1990.
Lacy, Norris. *The Lancelot-Grail Reader*. New York: Garland Publishing, 2000.
Lancelot-Grail. Vol. 8, *The Post-Vulgate Cycle*. Translated by Martha Asher. Cambridge: D. S. Brewer, 1996.
Larrick, Nancy. "The All-White World of Children's Books." *The Saturday Review*, September 11, 1965, 63–65.
Larrington, Carolyne. *King Arthur's Enchantresses: Morgan and Her Sisters in Arthurian Tradition*. London: I. B. Tauris, 2014.
The Last Kingdom. Executive Produced by Stephen Burchard. Carnival Film and Television, 2015–.
Lau, Travis Chi Wing. "Slowness, Disability, and Academic Productivity." In *Disability and the University: A Disabled Students' Manifesto*, edited by Christopher McMaster and Benjamin Whitburn, 11–19. Bern: Peter Lang, 2019.
Lawson, Jenny. *Furiously Happy: A Funny Book about Horrible Things*. London: Macmillan, 2015. Kindle edition.
Lee, Mackenzi. *The Gentleman's Guide to Vice and Virtue*. New York: Katherine Tegen Books, 2018.
Le Guin, Ursula K. *Tales from Earthsea*. New York: HMH Books, 2012. Kindle edition.
Le Guin, Ursula K. *Tombs of Atuan*. New York: Atheneum, 2012.
Le Guin, Ursula K. "Ursula Le Guin Q&A." *The Guardian*, February 9, 2004. https://www.theguardian.com/books/2004/feb/09/sciencefictionfantasyandhorror.ursulakleguin.
Le Guin, Ursula K. *The Wind's Twelve Quarters: Stories*. New York: HarperPerennial, 2004. Kindle edition.
Le Guin, Ursula K. *A Wizard of Earthsea*. New York: Harcourt Reprint, 2012.
Lerer, Seth. *Children's Literature: A Reader's History*. Chicago: University of Chicago Press, 2008.
Light, Ellis Amity. "Schmendrick." Twitter, July 16, 2019, 7:47 p.m. https://twitter.com/ellisamitylight/status/1151201598842032129.
Lindsay, Kathryn. "For Rising Stars Maeve Press & Kayla Cromer, Everything Is Gonna Be Better Than Okay." *Refinery29*, January 17, 2020.
Lockett, Leslie. *Anglo-Saxon Psychologies in the Vernacular and Latin Traditions*. Toronto: University of Toronto Press, 2011.
Loeppky, John. "Disabilities Are Not Curses," *The Carillon*, November 30, 2014, https://www.carillonregina.com/disabilities-are-not-curses/.
Loftis, Sonya Freeman. *Imagining Autism: Fictions and Stereotypes on the Spectrum*. Bloomington: Indiana University Press, 2015.
Lundin, Britta. *Ship It*. New York: Freeform Books, 2018.

Lupack, Barbara Tepa, ed. *Adapting the Arthurian Legends for Children*. New York: Palgrave Macmillan, 2004.
Ly, David. *Mythical Man*. Windsor, ON: Palimpsest Press, 2020. Kindle edition.
Machemer, Theresa. "New *Harry Potter* Character Uses a Wheelchair." *Changing America*, November 4, 2019. https://thehill.com/changing-america/respect/accessibility/468426-new-harry-potter-character-uses-a-wheelchair.
Macrae-Gibson, O. D. *Of Arthour and of Merlin*. London: Early English Text Society, 1979.
Malory, Thomas. *Malory: Works*. Edited by Eugene Vinaver. Oxford: Oxford University Press, 1971.
Malory, Thomas. *Le Morte Darthur*. Edited by Helen Cooper [Winchester Manuscript]. Oxford World's Classics. Oxford: Oxford University Press, 2008.
Mardoll, Ann. "The Problem with Entrapta." *Ann Mardoll's Ramblings* (blog), December 2, 2018. http://www.anamardoll.com/2018/12/the-problem-with-entrapta.html.
Markram, Kamila and Henry. "The Intense World Theory: A Unifying Theory of the Neurobiology of Autism." *Frontiers in Human Neuroscience* 21 (December 2010): 1–29.
Marshall, David W., ed. *Mass Market Medieval: Essays on the Middle Ages in Popular Culture*. Jefferson, NC: McFarland and Company, 2007.
Masschaele, James. *Peasants, Merchants, and Markets*. New York: St. Martin's Press, 1997.
Masters, Jeffrey. "Jacob Tobia." *LGBTQ&A* (podcast), February 15, 2019. https://luminarypodcasts.com/listen/jeffrey-masters-the-advocate/lgbtqanda-814/jacob-tobia-will-change-how-you-think-about-gender-330/651b9ac0-9134-489f-9e45-e06b2ce439ea.
Matthews, Louisa. "Vendecolori a Venezia: The Reconstruction of a Profession." *The Burlington Magazine* 144, no. 1196 (2002): 680–86.
Maxwell-Stuart, P. G. *Wizards: A History*. Stroud, Gloucestershire: Tempus Publishing, 2004.
McAllister, Rosemary. "I love the idea of medieval girls." Twitter, April 14 2020, 11:18 p.m. https://twitter.com/DubiousCA/status/1250292274602246147.
McCain, Kevin. "Who Is Raistlin Majere?" In *Dungeons & Dragons and Philosophy*, edited by Christopher Robichaud, 132–44. Chichester, West Sussex: Wiley Blackwell, 2014.
McCall, Matthew. "Underneath It All: Cutaneous (Mis)Identity in *Sir Gawain and the Green Knight*." Paper presented at IMC What is the place of publication?2019, Leeds, July 4, 2019.
McDonald, Robin, ed. *Re/Visioning Depression*. London: Palgrave, forthcoming 2021.
McGregor, Hannah and Marcelle Kosman. "Witch, Please and Some Other Novel." *Witch, Please* (podcast), S2E7, September 11, 2017. http://ohwitchplease.ca/2017/09/s2e7-witch-please-and-some-other-novel/.
McKellen, Ian. "A World under His Spell." Interview, Euan Ferguson. *The Guardian*, February 17, 2002. http://film.guardian.co.Uk/lordoftherings/news/0,11016,652303,00.html.
McNabb, Cameron Hunt, ed. *The Medieval Disability Sourcebook*. Goleta, CA: Punctum Books, 2020.
McRuer, Robert. "Compulsory Able-Bodiedness and Queer/Disabled Existence." In *Disability Studies: Enabling the Humanities*, edited by Sharon Snyder, Brenda Jo Brueggemann, and Rosemarie Garland-Thomson, 88–99. New York: MLA Press, 2002.
Medievalists of Color. "The Youngest of Old Fields." 2019. https://medievalistsofcolor.com/statements/the-youngest-of-old-fields/.
Mendlesohn, Farah. *Rhetorics of Fantasy*. Middletown, CT: Wesleyan University Press, 2008.
Merlin. Created by Johnny Capps et al. Shine Productions and BBC, 2008–2012.
Metzler, Irina. *A Social History of Disability in the Middle Ages*. New York: Routledge, 2013.
Micha, Alexandre. "Robert de Boron's Merlin." In *Merlin: A Casebook*, edited by Peter Goodrich and Norris Lacy, 289–300. New York: Routledge, 2003.

Mills, Robert. "Ecce Homo." In *Gender and Holiness: Men, Women and Saints in Late Medieval Europe*, edited by Sarah Salih and Sam Riches, 152–73. London: Routledge, 2011.

Mitchell, David T., and Sharon L. Snyder. *Cultural Locations of Disability*. Chicago: University of Chicago Press, 2006.

Mitchell, J. Allan. *Becoming Human: The Matter of the Medieval Child*. Minneapolis: University of Minnesota Press, 2014.

Moberly, Kevin, and Brent Moberly. "Play." In *Medievalism: Key Critical Terms*, edited by Elizabeth Emery and Richard Utz, 173–80. Cambridge: D. S. Brewer, 2014.

Moran, Mary Jeanette. "'Balance Is the Trick': Feminist Relationality in *The Amazing Maurice* and the *Tiffany Aching* series." *The Lion and the Unicorn* 42, no. 3 (September 2008): 259–80.

Morgan, Gwendolyn. "Authority." In *Medievalism: Key Critical Terms*, edited by Elizabeth Emery and Richard Utz, 27–34. Cambridge: D. S. Brewer, 2014.

Morpurgo, Michael. *Sir Gawain and the Green Knight*. Somerville, MA: Candlewick Press, 2004.

Muir, Bernard, ed. *The Exeter Anthology of Old English Poetry*, Vol. 1. Exeter: University of Exeter Press, 1994.

Muñoz, José Esteban. *Cruising Utopia: The Then and There of Queer Futurity*. New York: New York University Press, 2009.

Murray, Alexander. *Suicide in the Middle Ages*. Vol. 2, *The Curse on Self-Murder*. Oxford: Oxford University Press, 2000.

Mussett, Shannon. "Berserker in a Skirt." In *Dungeons & Dragons and Philosophy*, edited by Christopher Robichaud, 189–201. Chichester, West Sussex: Wiley Blackwell, 2014.

My So-Called Life. Created by Winnie Holzman. ABC Productions, 1994–1995.

Nedd, Alexis. "*The Magicians* Confirmed the Show's Best Ship." *Mashable*, February 21, 2019. https://mashable.com/article/the-magicians-quentin-eliot-romance/.

Nelson, William. *A Fifteenth-Century Schoolbook from a Manuscript in the British Museum (MS. Arundel 249)*. Miami, FL: Franklin Classics, 2018. Kindle edition.

Nester, Robbi. "Do You Believe in Magic?" *Hollins Critic* 49, no. 1 (2012): np.

Newman, Coree, "The Good, the Bad, and the Unholy." In *Fairies, Demons and Nature Spirits*, edited by Michael Ostling, 103–22. London: Palgrave Macmillan, 2018.

Noone, Kristin, and Emily Lavin Leverett, eds. *Terry Pratchett's Ethical Worlds: Essays on Identity and Narrative in Discworld and Beyond*. Jefferson, NC: McFarland and Company, 2020.

Norton, Arthur. *Readings in the History of Education: Mediaeval Universities*. Cambridge, MA: Harvard University Press, 1909.

ObeySumner, ChrisTiana. "Being Autistic, Black and Femme Highlights the Experience of Living Intersectionally." *The Seattle Globalist*, December 7, 2018. https://www.seattleglobalist.com/2018/12/07/black-autistics-exist-an-argument-for intersectional-disability-justice/79083.

Okun, Maureen, ed. *Le Morte Darthur: Selections*. Peterborough, ON: Broadview Press, 2015.

Orme, Nicholas. *Medieval Children*. New Haven, CT: Yale University Press, 2003.

Outhwaite, Ida, illus. *Little Book of Elves and Fairies*. London: Michael O'Mara, 2001.

Parlett, David. *Selections from the Carmina Burana*. London: Penguin, 1986.

Paul, K., trans. "Cursor Mundi." *Corpus of Middle English Prose and Verse*. https://quod.lib.umich.edu/c/cme/AJT8128.0001.001.

Pearman, Tory. *Women and Disability in Medieval Literature*. New York: Palgrave Macmillan, 2010.

Pennar, Meirion. *The Black Book of Carmarthen*. Burnham-on-Sea, Somerset: Llanerch Press, 1989.

Pérez, Christina. *The Myth of Morgan la Fey*. New York: Palgrave Macmillan, 2014.

Peterson, Joseph H., ed. and trans. *The Sworne Booke of Honorius*. 2009. Esoteric Archives, http://www.esotericarchives.com/juratus/juratus.htm.
Piepzna-Samarasinha, Leah Lakshmi. *Care Work: Dreaming Disability Justice*. Vancouver, BC: Arsenal Pulp Press, 2018. Kindle edition.
Pinsent, Pat. "The Education of a Wizard: Harry Potter and His Predecessors." *The Ivory Tower and Harry Potter: Perspectives on a Literary Phenomenon*. Edited by Lana A. Whited, 27–52. Columbia, MI: University of Missouri Press, 2002.
de Pizan, Christine. *Selected Works*. Edited by Renate Blumenfeld-Koskinski. New York: W. W. Norton & Company, 1997.
Plato. *Symposium*. Translated by Robin Waterfield. Oxford World Classics. Oxford: Oxford University Press, 2009.
The Power of Grayskull. Directed by Randall Lobb. Definitive Film, 2017.
Pratchett, Terry. *A Hat Full of Sky*. New York: HarperCollins, 2015.
Pratchett, Terry. *I Shall Wear Midnight*. New York: HarperCollins, 2011.
Pratchett, Terry. *The Shepherd's Crown*. New York: HarperCollins, 2016.
Pratchett, Terry. *The Wee Free Men*. New York: HarperCollins, 2015.
Pratchett, Terry. *Wintersmith*. New York: HarperCollins, 2007.
Pratchett, Terry and Neil Gaiman. *Good Omens*. New York: William Morrow, 2019.
Price, Margaret. *Mad at School: Rhetorics of Mental Disability and Academic Life*. Ann Arbor: University of Michigan Press, 2011.
Prophésies de Merlin en prose. Codex Bodmer 116. Fondation Martin Bodmer. https://www.e-codices.unifr.ch/fr/fmb/cb-0116/bindingA/0/Sequence-861.
Pugh, Tison. *Chaucer's (Anti)-Eroticisms and the Queer Middle Ages*. Columbus: Ohio State University Press, 2016.
Pugh, Tison. *Chaucer's Losers, Nintendo's Children, and Other Forays into Queer Ludonarratology*. Lincoln, NE: University of Nebraska Press, 2019.
Pugh, Tison. *Innocence, Heterosexuality, and the Queerness of Children's Literature*. New York: Routledge, 2014.
Rajunov, Micah and Scott Duane, eds. *Nonbinary: Memoirs of Gender and Identity*. New York: Columbia University Press, 2019. Kindle edition.
Rateliff, John. *The History of the Hobbit*. New York: HarperCollins, 2011. Kindle edition.
Rees, David. *In the Tent*. Boston: Alyson Publications, 1986.
Reiter, Geoffrey. "Two Sides of the Same Magic." *Mythlore* 27, no. 3 (Summer 2009): 102–16.
Rider, Catherine. *Magic and Religion in Medieval England*. London: Reaktion Books, 2012.
Riga, Frank. "Gandalf and Merlin: J.R.R. Tolkien's Adoption and Transformation of a Literary Tradition." *Mythlore* 27, no. 1/2 (Winter 2008): 21–44.
Riverdale. Created by Roberto Aguirre-Sacasa. CW and Berlanti Productions, 2016–.
Robertson, Benjamin. "From Fantasy to Franchise: Dragonlance and the Privatization of Genre." *Extrapolation: A Journal of Science Fiction and Fantasy* 58, no. 2-3 (Summer-Fall 2017): 129–52.
Robertson, Elizabeth, Hetta Howe, and Alicia Spencer-Hall. "A Feminist Take on Medieval History." *BBC Arts and Ideas* (podcast), October 9, 2018. http://www.medievalshewrote.com/blog/2018/10/9/bbc-arts-and-ideas-podcast-a-feminist-take-on-medieval-history.
Robinson, Eden. *Son of a Trickster*. New York: Vintage, 2018.
Robison, John Elder. *Look Me in the Eye*. New York: Three Rivers Press, 2008.
Roche-Madhi, Sarah, trans. *Silence*. East Lansing: Michigan State University Press, 1999.
Rodas, Julia Miele. *Autistic Disturbances*. Ann Arbor: University of Michigan Press, 2019.

Rogers, Will. "Complaint: Thomas Hoccleve." In *Medieval Disability Sourcebook*, edited by Cameron Hunt-McNabb, 313–23. Goleta, CA: Punctum, 2020.
de Rojas, Fernando. *La Celestina*. Edited by Dorothy Severin. Madrid: Ediciones Cátedra, 2006.
Romano, Aja. "Harry Potter and the Author Who Failed Us." *Vox*, June 11, 2020. https://www.vox.com/culture/21285396/jk-rowling-transphobic-backlash-harry-potter.
Romano, Dennis. *Markets and Marketplaces in Medieval Italy*. New Haven, CT: Yale University Press, 2015.
Rowell, Rainbow. *Carry On*. New York: St. Martin's Reprint, 2017.
Rowell, Rainbow. *Wayward Son*. New York: Wednesday Books, 2019.
Rowling, J. K. *Harry Potter and the Philosopher's Stone*. London: Bloomsbury, 2014.
Russo, Meredith. *If I Was Your Girl*. New York: Flatiron, 2018.
Ruys, Juanita. *Demons in the Middle Ages*. Kalamazoo, MI: ARC Humanities Press, 2017.
Salah, Trish. *Wanting in Arabic*. Toronto: TSAR Publications, 2002.
Salisbury, Eve. *Chaucer and the Child*. New York: Palgrave Macmillan, 2017.
Sawyer, Rose A. "Changeling Stories: The Child Substitution Motif in the Chester Mystery Cycle." In *Literary Cultures and Medieval and Early Modern Childhoods*, edited by Naomi Miller and Diane Purkiss, 87–101. Cham, Switzerland: Palgrave Macmillan, 2019.
Schitt's Creek. Created by Dan Levy. CBC, 2015–2020.
Scoville, Chester, ed. *The Digby Play of Mary Magdalene*. Peterborough, ON: Broadview Press, 2017.
Sedgwick, Eve Kosofsky. *Epistemology of the Closet*. Berkeley: University of California Press, 1990.
Sedgwick, Eve Kosofsky. "How to Bring Your Kids up Gay." *Social Text* 29 (1991): 19–27.
Sense8. Created by Lana Wachowski, Lilly Wachowski, and J. Michael Straczynski. Anarchos Productions et al., 2015–2018.
Sex Education. Created by Laurie Nunn. Netflix, 2019–.
Shadowhunters. Created by Ed Dector. Constantin Film, 2016–2019.
Shakespeare, Tom. *Disability Rights and Wrongs, Revisited*. London: Routledge, 2014.
She-Ra and the Princesses of Power. Created by Noelle Stevenson. DreamWorks Animation and Netflix, 2018–.
Shuffleton, George. *Codex Ashmole 61*. TEAMS Middle English Text Series. Kalamazoo, MI: Medieval Institute Publications, 2008.
Simone, Rudy. *Aspergirls: Empowering Females with Asperger Syndrome*. London: Jessica Kingsley, 2010.
Sir Gawain and the Green Knight. Directed by Tim Fernee. Vinegar Hill, 2002.
Sir Gawain and the Green Knight. Edited by Paul Battles. Peterborough, ON: Broadview Press, 2012.
Skinner, Patricia, ed. *Medieval Writings on Secular Women*. London: Penguin, 2011.
Snyder, Christopher. *The World of King Arthur*. London: Thames and Hudson, 2011.
Sommer, Oskar. *The Recuyell of the Historyes of Troye*. 2 vols. London: David Nutt, 1894.
Sommer, Oskar, ed. *The Vulgate Version of the Arthurian Romances*, Vol. 5. Washington, DC: Carnegie Institution of Washington, 1912.
Speechless. Created by Scott Silveri. ABC, 2016–2019.
Star Trek: Deep Space Nine. Created by Rick Berman. Paramount, 1993–1999.
Star Trek: The Next Generation. Created by Gene Roddenberry. Paramount Television, 1987–1994.
Steele, Robert, ed. *Medieval Lore from Bartholomew Anglicus*. N.p.: Good Press, 2019. E-Book edition.

Stehling, Thomas, ed. *Medieval Latin Poems of Male Love and Friendship*. New York: Garland Publishing, 1984.
Stevens, David. "Incongruity in a World of Illusion: Patterns of Humour in Peter Beagle's 'The Last Unicorn.'" *Extrapolation* 20, no. 3 (Fall 1979): 230–37.
Stockton, Katherine Bond. *The Queer Child*. Durham, NC: Duke University Press, 2009.
Stoker, Bram. *Dracula*. Edited by Glennis Byron. Peterborough, ON: Broadview Press, 1997.
Stouck, Mary-Ann. *Medieval Saints: A Reader*. Toronto: University of Toronto Press, 1998.
Stranger Things. Created by Matt Duffer and Ross Duffer. 21 Laps and Netflix, 2016–.
Stratman, Jacob, ed. *Lessons in Disability: Essays on Teaching with Young-Adult Literature*. Jefferson, NC: McFarland and Company, 2019.
Sullivan, Lou. *We Both Laughed in Pleasure: The Selected Diaries of Lou Sullivan*. Brooklyn, NY: Nightboat Books, 2019. Kindle edition.
Supernatural. Created by Eric Kripke. Kripke Enterprises and Warner Brothers Television, 2005–.
Sutton, Carl and Cheryl Forrester. *Selective Mutism in Our Own Words*. London: Jessica Kingsley, 2016.
The Sword in the Stone. Directed by Wolfgang Reitherman. Walt Disney, 1963.
Thiébaux, Marcelle, ed. *The Writings of Medieval Women*. New York: Garland Publishing, 1994.
Thomas, Ebony Elizabeth. *The Dark Fantastic: Race and the Imagination from Harry Potter to the Hunger Games*. New York: New York University Press, 2019. Kindle edition.
Tolkien, J. R. R. *The Hobbit*. New York: HarperCollins, 2009. E-Book edition.
Tolkien, J. R. R. *The Hobbit*. London: Houghton Mifflin, 2012.
Tolkien, J. R. R. *The Lord of the Rings*. 2nd ed. 3 vols. Illustrated by Alan Lee. Boston: Houghton, 2002.
Tolkien, J. R. R. *The Monsters and the Critics*. New York: HarperCollins, 2007.
Tolkien, J. R. R. "On Fairy Stories." *The Monsters and the Critics, and Other Essays*. Edited by Christopher Tolkien, 109–61. New York: HarperCollins, 2007.
Tolkien, J. R. R. *The Silmarillion*. New York: HarperCollins, 2013. Kindle edition.
Tolkien, J. R. R. *Sir Gawain and the Green Knight*. Oxford: Oxford University Press, 1968.
Tolkien, J. R. R. *Unfinished Tales*. Edited by Christopher Tolkien. Boston, MA: Mariner, 2014. Kindle edition.
Toswell, M. J. *Today's Medieval University*. Kalamazoo, MI: ARC Humanities Press, 2017.
Tracy, Kisha and John Sexton, eds. *The Lone Medievalist: Out of the Cloister*. Goleta, CA: Punctum Books, forthcoming 2021.
Trevisa, John, trans. *The Governance of Kings and Princes*. Edited by David C. Fowler, Charles F. Briggs, and Paul, G. Remley. New York: Garland Publishing, 1997.
Tsiolis, Vasilis. "La cueva de Hércules en la construcción ideológica de Toledo." In *Debita Verba: Estudios en homenaje de Profesor Julio Mangas Manjarrés*, edited by Rosa María Cid López and Estela Beatriz García Fernández. Oviedo, Spain: Ediciones de la Universidad de Oviedo, 2003, pp. 735–48.
Ursu, Anne. "Interview with Corinne Duyvis." *Disability in Kidlit*, April 13, 2015. http://disabilityinkidlit.com/2015/04/13/interview-with-anne-ursu-about-the-real-boy/.
Ursu, Anne. *The Real Boy*. Oakland, CA: Walden Pond Reprint, 2013.
Vaccaro, Christopher. "'Morning Stars of a Setting World': Alain de Lille's *De Planctu Naturæ* and Tolkien's Legendarium as Neo-Platonic Mythopoeia." *Mythlore* 36, no. 1 (Fall 2017): 81–102.
Vela i Auelsa, Carles. *L'Obrador d'un apotecari medieval segons el llibre de comptes de Francesc Ses Canes (Barcelona 1378–1381)*. Barcelona: Consell Superior d'Investigacions Científiques, 2003.

Vishnuvajjala, Usha. "The Future We—and the Middle Ages—Want." *The Year's Work in Medievalism* 32 (2017): 1–4.
Vist, Elise. "Dungeons and Queers: Reparative Play in Dungeons and Dragons." *First Person Scholar*, May 30, 2018. http://www.firstpersonscholar.com/dungeons-and-queers/.
Vitto, Cindy. "Deceptive Simplicity: Children's Versions of *Sir Gawain and the Green Knight*." In *Adapting the Arthurian Legends for Children*, edited by Barbara Tepa Lupack, 107–22. New York: Palgrave Macmillan, 2004.
Wace. *Roman de Brut*. MS. Egerton 3028. British Library Catalogue of Illuminated Manuscripts, https://www.bl.uk/catalogues/illuminatedmanuscripts/record.asp?MSID=9419&CollID=27&NStart=32125.
Waddell, Helen, ed. *Medieval Latin Lyrics*. London: Penguin Classics, 1964.
Walker, Nick. "Throw Away the Master's Tools: Liberating Ourselves from the Pathology Paradigm." In *Loud Hands: Autistic People Speaking*, edited by J. Bascom, 228–40. Washington, DC: The Autistic Press, 2012.
Walker, Nick. "Neuroqueer: An Introduction." *Neurocosmopolitanism*, May 2, 2015. https://neurocosmopolitanism.com/neuroqueer-an-introduction/.
Walter, Katie. "Peril, Flight and the Sad Man: Medieval Theories of the Body in Battle." *Essays and Studies* 67 (2014): 21–40.
Waters, Claire, ed. and trans. *The Lais of Marie de France*. Peterborough, ON: Broadview Press, 2018.
Weis, Margaret and Tracy Hickman. *Dragons of Autumn Twilight*. Lake Geneva, WI: TSR, 1984.
Weston, Lisa. "Queering Virginity." *Medieval Feminist Forum* 36, no. 1 (2003): 22–24.
Wheatley, Edward. *Stumbling Blocks before the Blind: Medieval Constructions of a Disability*. Ann Arbor: University of Michigan Press, 2010.
White, T. H. *The Once and Future King*. New York: Ace Books, 1987.
Whitehead, Joshua. "Poet Joshua Whitehead Redefines Two-Spirit Identity in *Full-Metal Indigiqueer*." *CBC Radio*, December 15, 2017. https://www.cbc.ca/radio/unreserved/from-dystopian-futures-to-secret-pasts-check-out-these-indigenous-storytellers-over-the-holidays-1.4443312/poet-joshua-whitehead-redefines-two-spirit-identity-in-full-metal-indigiqueer-1.4447321.
Wilde, Jen. *Queens of Geek*. New York: Swoon Reads, 2017.
Willow. Directed by Ron Howard. Lucasfilm, 1988.
Wilson, Anna. "Digital Reading Practices and Lydgate's Chaucerian Fanfiction." Roundtable presentation at the International Congress on Medieval Studies, Kalamazoo, MI, May 11–14, 2017.
Winny, James. *Sir Gawain and the Green Knight*. Peterborough, ON: Broadview Press, 1992.
Witwer, Michael. *Empire of Imagination*. London: Bloomsbury, 2015.
Wynne Jones, Diana. *Hexwood*. New York: HarperCollins, 2009.
Wynne Jones, Diana. *The Merlin Conspiracy*. New York: Greenwillow Books, 2003.
Wynne Jones, Diana. *Reflections: On the Magic of Writing*. New York: Greenwillow Books, 2012.
Yergeau, Melanie. *Authoring Autism*. Durham, NC: Duke University Press, 2018.
Young Sheldon. Created by Chuck Lorre and Steven Molaro. Warner Brothers, 2017–.
zahrawithaz. "What It Means to Me to Have a Black Guinevere." *Livejournal*, October 13, 2009. https://zahrawithaz.livejournal.com/3365.html.
Zarins, Kim. *Sometimes We Tell the Truth*. New York: Simon Pulse, 2017.

Index

Abelard, Peter 95, 128, 132, 133
Aelfric of Eynsham 5
Ahmed, Sara 24, 139, 145, 146, 198
Aldhelm 94
Alexander, Lloyd 21, 28, 138, 190, 208
Ancrene Wisse (Guide for Anchoresses) 7
Anglicus, Bartholomaeus 6, 203
Andrew of Wyntoun 140
Aquinas, Thomas 16, 19, 128, 132–133, 134
Aristotle 5–6, 203
Arthour and Merlin 44, 149
King Arthur 6, 10, 27, 28, 32, 33–34, 38, 43, 48, 50, 51, 52, 53, 59, 62, 66, 67, 74, 77, 80, 128, 138, 157, 158, 159, 160, 161, 162, 163, 165, 166, 170, 175, 178, 184, 186, 206, 207, 208, 211, 214
A Separate Peace 102
asexuality 51, 100, 197
Atypical 65, 154, 195, 215
Augustine 128, 130–132
Ausonius 6, 132
Autism Speaks 85, 121

Bailly, Harry 97, 98
Barney, Stephen 205
Bartlett, Claire 12
Baudri of Bourgeoil 7, 31, 207
Baume, Matt 138
Bennett, Jane 51
Benson, Stella 101, 191
Beowulf 2, 54, 110, 157
Berthelot, Anne 68
The Big Bang Theory 36–38, 85, 214
bin Ziyad, Hamda 8
Birns, Nicholas 198
bisexuality 25, 111, 112, 123, 131–132fn, 143, 172, 185, 187, 206, 208
The Black Book of Carmarthen 27, 28, 203
Blud, Victoria 7
Boethius 128, 130, 136, 137
Book of the Knight of the Tower 16–17, 119
The Book of Taliesin 29
Bower, Walter 140
Bowie, David 56–57, 124, 213

Boyd, David 170, 178, 179
The Boy's King Arthur 3, 107
Bradford, Clare 24, 158–159
Brenchley, Chaz 3
Brewer, Derek (D. S.) 171–172, 204, 207
Brideshead Revisited 102, 184
Bromwich, Rachel 162
Bryant, Nigel 34, 205
Buffy the Vampire Slayer 1, 14, 56, 70, 74, 76, 77, 80, 95, 102–103, 106, 117, 155, 168–169, (fn), 174, 217
Burt, Kathleen 82
Butler, Judith 47
Bychowski, M. W. Gabrielle 8–9, 24, 41, 45, 46–47, 75, 183
Bynum, Carolyn 193

cacodemon 106, 124
Caesarius of Heisterbach 106, 193
Callin, William 130
Cantar de mio Cid (Song of the Cid) 157
Carmina Burana 25, 124–125
Carroll, Tyrone 112
Carruthers, Mary 19
Cart, Michael 20, 22, 23
Carter, Julian B. 50
The Castle of Sorcery 55
Castle, Terry 7
Caxton, William 23, 43, 65, 96, 163, 207
Cavallo, Adolfo 141
Cecire, Maria Sachiko 2, 21, 99, 190
Chaganti, Seeta 158
Chaucer, Geoffrey 1, 5, 54, 128, 199
– and influence on Lydgate 113
– and influence on Shakespeare 98
– *The Canterbury Tales* 25, 30, 56, 93, 97–99, 117, 129, 164, 173, 180, 190, 205
– *The Parliament of Fowls* 17, 53, 134
– "Truth" 134
Chaumpaigne, Cecily 173(fn)
Cheng, Patrick 76
Chilling Adventures of Sabrina 2, 14, 23, 24, 31, 32, 54, 59, 60, 70, 74–82, 84, 88, 89, 90, 91, 104, 108, 134, 151, 169fn, 212

Cixous, Hélène 67
Clare, Cassandra 113
– *Mortal Instruments* 53, 56
– *The Red Scrolls of Magic* (with Wesley Chu) 27, 33, 53–58, 208–209
Clare, Eli 11–12, 19–20, 34, 120
Clark, Beverly Lyon 20
Clarke, Basil 39, 40fn
Clarke Gray, Brenna 21, 184fn, 185fn, 190
Clarkson, Tim 33
Cleanness 170, 173
Cohen, Jeffrey J. 2, 81
Coman, Jonah 193
Community 213
Conlee, John 43, 44, 45
Coulby, Angel 21, 127, 214
Crónica del rey don Rodrigo 96
Crónica General 95–96
Culhwch and Olwen 162(fn)
The Curious Incident of the Dog in the Night-Time 153
Cursor Mundi 190

Dame d'Avalon 67–70, 71, 138, 203
Dante 78, 163
d'Argenteuil, Hélöise 119
Davidson, Roberta 175
Davis, Isabel 171
Day, Mildred 159–160, 204
de Boron, Robert 9, 10, 24, 27, 32, 33–39, 43, 205
de Charny, Geoffroi 5
De Fougères, Étienne 7–8
de France, Marie 33, 48, 157, 199, 205
de Glanville, Bartholomew 106
De Haan, Linda 209
Delanty, Greg 205
de la Puerta, Ruiz 96
"Deor" 122
de Rojas, Fernando 150–151
de Romans, Bieris 8
de Saint-Maure, Benoit 62, 69
de Troyes, Chrétien 33, 34, 62, 163
Digby Mary Magdalene 113
Dillon, Athena 37
Dinshaw, Carolyn 1, 17, 22, 23, 41, 61, 75, 76, 83fn, 141–142, 186

Dolmage, Jay 19, 186
Dom-Daniel academy 93, 181
Donovan, John 22
Dracula 93
The Dragon Prince 143fn
drag performance 3
"The Dream of the Rood" 158
Duane, Diane 29–31, 135, 209
Duane, Scott 193
Duyvis, Corinne 12, 146–147, 148, 153

Eliot, T. S. 191
The Epic of Gilgamesh 94
Epstein, Steven 149, 150
Eribon, Didier 36
Evans, J. Gwenogvrn 28–29
Everything's Gonna Be Okay 154, 216
Excalibur 59
Eyler, Joshua 16, 17, 24

Faletra, Michael 39, 206
fanfiction 13, 54, 113, 115, 185, 210–211
Feist, Raymond E. 55
A Fifteenth Century Schoolbook (Nelson) 113, 114–115, 123–124, 207
Firefly 51
Finch, Casey 172, 174
Finn, Kavita Mudan 54, 69
Foreman, Michael 175–177
Foust, R. E. 136
Fowler, Micha 116, 216
Friedman, Albert 71–72
Fries, Maureen 62, 68, 71
Froissart, Jean 119

Gadsby, Hannah 89, 212–213
Gaiman, Neil 153, 114fn, 194
Gamble, Joseph 184
Game of Thrones 69–70, 127, 130, 131, 166, 212
Ganymede 7
Geoffrey of Monmouth
– *History of the Kings of Britain* 39, 40fn, 61, 206
– *Vita Merlini* 9, 24, 26, 28, 32, 33, 34, 37, 39–43, 57, 59, 61–62, 192, 197, 200, 206
"Gest of Robyn Hode" 140

Gieysztor, Aleksander 114
Gifford, James 191
Gildas 94
Godden, Rick 17, 34, 109, 112
Gododdin 28
Golden Girls 197
Goodrich, Peter 24, 32, 33, 35, 196
Gower, John 17–18, 171–172, 206
Grisandolus 9, 41, 45–47, 80
The Guild 149
Guinevere 10, 21, 38, 60, 70, 72, 127, 158, 175, 204, 205, 208, 214
Gurza, Andrew 12–13, 121
Gutt, Blake 9, 24, 47, 50, 57, 80

Haberkorn, Gideon 83, 91
Hahn, Thomas 161, 175
Halberstam, Jack 24, 104, 135, 139, 184, 198
Hazel & Katniss & Harry & Starr 21, 184fn, 185fn, 190
Heath Justice, Daniel 194
Hebert, Jill 60, 62
He-Man and the Masters of the Universe 63, 138, 140, 141, 213, 216
Heng, Geraldine 8, 23–24, 32, 53, 60, 70, 71, 72, 73, 92, 159, 175, 198, 204
Hercules 93
– as potential model for Godric Gryffindor 96
– Cave of Hercules myth (*la cueva de Ércoles* or *el edificio de los Cerrojos*) 95–96
Highlander 55, 215
Hild of Whitby 119
Hildegard of Bingen 15, 136
Hillman, Richard 98
Hinton, S. E. 20
Hoccleve, Thomas 15–16, 98, 206
Holts, J. C. 140
Hostetter, Aaron 1, 2
How The Good Wife Taught Her Daughter 5
Howes, Hetta 173fn
Hsy, Jonathan 23
Hutton, Ronald 75

If I Was Your Girl (Russo) 168, 211
In Other Lands (Brennan) 1, 2, 25, 123, 127, 128, 132–133, 136, 142–146, 155–156, 208
– as response to *Harry Potter* 143
Isidore of Seville 6, 51, 203, 205

Jackson, Cody 87–88, 139
Jem and the Holograms 59, 215
Johnson, David 207
Joy, Eileen 2

Kafer, Alison 17, 19, 34, 112–113, 137
Karras, Ruth Mazo 5, 24, 25, 113, 119, 123
Kaszkiewicz, Weronika 136
Kaufman, Amy S. 24, 59–60
Kempe, Margery 49
Kieckhefer, Richard 93, 107–108, 206
Killing Eve 159fn
Kim, Cynthia 151
Kim, Dorothy 2, 23–24, 54, 129, 199
King Arthur And His Knights 27
King Horn 4
Kipo and the Age of the Wonderbeasts 158fn, *216*
Knight, Steven 24, 32–33, 45, 207
Kramer, Kelly 102
Krueger, Roberta 33
Kurchak, Sarah 83–84, 89, 149, 153

Labyrinth 56–57, 213
Lackey, Mercedes
– *The Last Herald Mage* 135
– *Magic's Pawn* 55, 209–210
Lacnunga (or "Leech-Book") 94, 148
Lady of the Lake 10, 66
Lancelot 9–10, 59, 66, 67, 73, 77, 128, 163, 187, 204–5
Landry, Geoffroy IV de la Tour 119
Larrick, Nancy 20
Larrington, Carolyne 24, 59–60, 61, 62, 63, 67, 68, 69, 70, 71, 72, 78, 203
The Last Kingdom 130, 212
The Last Unicorn (Beagle) 25, 127, 128, 135–142, 144, 153, 155–156, 191, 208
Lau, Travis Chi Wing 200
Lawson, Jenny 153
Le Chevalier à l'épée 162–163
Lee, Mackenzi 12
Le Guin, Ursula 21, 112, 135–136

– and influence on *Harry Potter* 99, 101
– *Tombs of Atuan* 118–119
– *A Wizard of Earthsea (Tales from Earthsea)* 25, 45, 93, 99–102, 106, 117, 209, 210
Lerer, Seth 98, 158–159
Lewis, C. S. 191
– *The Chronicles of Narnia* 143, 209
Light, Ellis Amity 24, 142
Llull, Ramon 163
Lockett, Leslie 16
Loeppky, John 11
"Lokasenna" (Loki's Verbal Duel) 192
Lombard, Peter 132
Lorde, Audre 146
loricae 94
Lucian 94
Lupack, Barbara 24
Ly, David 118
Lydgate, John 113

The Mabinogion 162(fn), 203, 208
The Magicians (Grossman) 23, 25, 92, 93, 94, 102–113, 120, 126, 144, 209
– TV adaptation 108–113, 145
Magus, Simon 31
maleficia 27
Manlove, Colin 20
Marbod of Rennes 6–7, 22, 31, 207
Mardoll, Ana 64–65
Markram, Kamila and Henry 147(fn)
Martial 131–132(fn)
Mason, Derritt 22
Matthews, Louisa 150
Matto, Michael 205
Matos, Angel Daniel 15
Maxwell-Stuart, P. G. 31
McAllister, Rosemary 7
McCall, Jessica 69
McCall, Matthew 170
McKellen, Sir Ian 197
McNabb, Cameron Hunt 17, 24
McRuer, Robert 73
Mendelsohn, Farah 75–76
Medievalists of Color (MOC) 109–110
Meyers, Mitzi 164

Merlin 2, 3, 8–9, 10, 13, 14, 21, 23, 24–25, 26, 27–58, 59, 60, 61, 67, 68, 69, 72, 74, 80, 86, 88, 91, 92, 118, 121, 127, 142, 148, 149, 168, 178, 189, 192, 196, 197, 199, 200, 203, 204, 205, 206, 208, 214, 216
– Lailoken 27, 28, 37
– Myrddin 27, 28
Merlin (BBC) 21, 127, 214
Micha, Alexandre 35, 37, 42
Middle English Dictionary 4, 173
Mills, Robert 193
Mirrlees, Hope 191
Mitchell, J. Allan 24, 98, 158–159
Moran, Mary Jeanette 82, 83
Morgan, Gwendolyn 192
Morgan le Fay 2, 23, 24–25, 27, 28, 31, 39, 53, 57–58, 59–92, 96–97, 100, 120, 123, 126, 138, 156, 157, 158, 159, 165, 167, 172, 173, 178, 179–184, 186–187, 189, 198, 199–201, 203, 204, 205, 206, 211, 215
– Medea 57, 62, 69
Morte Darthur 9, 10, 23, 24–25, 27, 28, 32–33, 43–44, 48, 51, 52, 57, 60, 62–63, 65, 66, 73, 77, 78, 79, 82, 90, 96, 128, 157fn, 181, 187, 207, 211
– Winchester manuscript 44, 52
Munich spell-book 93, 107, 206
Muñoz, José Esteban 53, 76
My Little Pony 141
My So-Called Life 27

necromancy 62, 90, 93, 96–97, 108, 180–181
Nedd, Alexis 112
neuro-queer 10–11, 14, 26, 36, 37, 49–50, 60, 72, 87, 88–89, 91, 99, 116, 195–196
The Neverending Story (Ende) 135, 142
– 1985 adaptation 215
Nguyen, Hanh 81
"Nine Herbs Charm" 148, 192
Nodelman, Perry 20

ObeySumner, ChrisTiana 154
The O.C. 174
Oliveira, Anthony 138, 141

Once and Future (Carpetta and McCarthy) 10, 21, 23, 24, 27, 32, 33, 47, 48, 51–53, 57, 168, 208
"Once, Future" (Howard) 178–179
Orfeo 4
Orme, Nicholas 24, 114

Paston, Margaret 119
Pearman, Tory 16–17, 24
Pennar, Meirion 28
Peredur 162(fn)
Pérez, Kristina 74
Peter the Venerable 106
Piepzna-Samarasinha, Leah Lakshmi 91–92
Pierce, Tamora 166
Pinsent, Pat 93
Poetic Edda 192, 203
Pokémon 19, 166
Power of Grayskull 63
Pratchett, Terry 14, 48
– *A Hat Full of Sky* 87, 89
– *The Shepherd's Crown* 82, 83, 86, 90
– Tiffany Aching 24, 32, 59, 60, 67, 70, 81, 82–92, 148, 151, 195–196
– *The Wee Free Men* 82, 83, 84–85, 86, 87, 210
– *Wintersmith* 83, 87, 88
Price, Margaret 11, 19, 73
"The Prophecies of Merlin" 67
– *Les Prophésies de Merlin* 24, 67–70, 71, 96, 203–204, 214
Prose Lancelot 138
Prose Merlin 9, 24, 28, 32, 33, 38, 41, 43–48, 79, 183, 204
Pugh, Tison 23, 135

Rajunov, Micah 193
Rambaran-Olm, Mary 23–24, 129
The Real Boy (Ursu) 25, 127, 128, 146–156, 211
– and influence of *Harry Potter* 147
Rees, David 22, 210
Reimer, Mavis 20
Reinhardt, Verena 83, 91
Reiter, Geoffrey 136
Rider, Catherine 77, 118

Riga, Frank 196
The Rise of Gawain 25, 159–162, 165–166, 171, 174, 204
Robertson, Elizabeth 173fn
Robin Hood 139, 140, 207
– Disney adaptation 164
Robinson, Eden 14, 194–195, 210
Robison, John Elder 153
Rodas, Julia Miele 10–11, 25, 35, 85, 196
Rogers, Will 15–16
Roman de silence 8–9
Romano, Aja 13
Romanus, Aegidius 174
Rowell, Rainbow
– *Carry On* 1, 14, 23, 25, 55, 92, 93, 102, 113–126, 147, 151, 152, 168, 210–211
– *Fan Girl* 113
– *Wayward Son* 121
Rowling, J. K.
– and anti-Semitism 13
– and influence of Le Guin 99, 101
– and influence on *The Magicians* 103, 104, 106
– and influence on *The Real Boy* 147
– and *In Other Lands* as response 143
– and racism 13, 99
– and transphobia 13, 99
– as adapted in *Carry On* 1, 115, 117, 112fn, 210–211
– *Harry Potter* 1, 12, 14, 54, 93, 143, 185, 190
– *Harry Potter: Hogwarts Mystery* 12
Ruys, Juanita 25, 32, 94, 95, 106, 193
Rykener, Eleanor 47

Salah, Trish 183
Salisbury, Eve 24, 97
Sappho 8, 187
Sawyer, Rose 149
Schitt's Creek 152, 200–201, 214
Sebile 62, 63, 66, 67, 68–69, 90, 138
Sedgwick, Eve Kosofsky 4–5, 160
Sense8 182, 217
The Seventh Princess (Sullivan) 135
Sex Education 184–185, (fn), 215
Shadowhunters 53, 55, 209
Shakespeare, Tom 20

Shakespeare, William 43, 80, 98, 150
She-Ra and the Princesses of Power 63(fn)–65, 115fn, 216
Short Circuit 148
Silence 45, 46
Simon vs. the Homo Sapiens Agenda (Albertalli) 22, 167, 183, 208
Simone, Rudy 151
Sir Gawain and the Green Knight 4, 6, 8, 22, 24, 25, 32, 57–58, 52, 59, 60, 66–67, 70–71, 72, 74, 88, 95, 107, 122, 156, 157–187, 191, 197, 198, 199, 200, 204
Sir Gawain and the Green Knight (Fernee) 25, 175, 177–178
Sir Gawain and the Green Knight (Morpurgo) 25, 172, 175–177, 210
Snyder, Christopher 39
Speechless 116, 216
Spencer-Hall, Alicia 173fn
St. Patrick 94
Star Trek: Deep Space Nine 193
Star Trek: The Next Generation 110, 148
Steele, Robert 203
Stehling, Thomas 207
Stevens, David 136, 139
Stratman, Jacob 15
Stockton, Katherine Bond 4, 50
The Story of Meriadoc 159
Sullivan, Lou 80, 81
Supernatural 54fn, 76
Sword in the Stone (Disney) 56, 181, 216
Sword in the Stone (White) 24, 27, 33, 34, 48–51, 56, 68, 93, 101, 110, 181, 196, 200, 202, 211
The *Sworn Book of Honorius* 106–107, 204

Taliesin 28, 29, 41, 44, 45, 47, 61, 211
Teen Wolf 159fn
Thomas, Ebony Elizabeth 2, 20, 99, 101, 127
Thomson, Rosemary Garland 16
Tolkien, J. R. R. 112
– and eucatastrophe/dyscatastrophe 136
– and influence on white medieval culture 2–3, 54, 65, 194, 195
– and York Corpus Christi Cycle 134
– edition of *Sir Gawain and the Green Knight* 168, 170, 173

– "Essay on the Istari" 193
– Gandalf 3, 26, 33, 34, 37, 48, 142, 189, 191–202, 211
– *The Hobbit* 3, 21, 23, 26, 34, 48, 55, 189, 190, 191–192, 194–196, 198(fn), 199, 202, 211
– *Letters from Father Christmas* 191
– *The Lord of the Rings* 3, 110, 145, 189, 190, 191, 194, 195, 197, 198, 21
– "On Fairy Stories" 126
– Radagast the Brown 198–199
Trevisa, John 106, 174
The *Trotula* 151
Tsiolis, Vasilis 95
Tueller, Carson 12

University of Bologna 95
– and possible influence on *Harry Potter* and *Carry On* 114

Vaccaro, Christopher 197
Vikings 130, 213–214
Vishnuvajjala, Usha 186
Vitto, Cindy 158, 166, 167
von Aue, Hartmann 62, 79
von Eschenbach, Wolfram 32
Vostaert, Pieter and Peninc 207
The Vulgate 9, 10, 24, 33, 44, 58, 59, 62, 65, 66, 67, 70, 73–74, 77, 80, 82, 200, 204–205, 207

Wace 33, 38
Walewein 25, 163–165, 181, 206
Walker, Nick 10–11, 37
Walter, Katie 174
"The Wedding of Sir Gawain" 180–181
Weston, Lisa 100
Wheatley, Edward 17
Whitehead, Joshua 194fn
William of Malmesbury 162
Willow 68, 70, 214
Wilson, Anna 113
Winny, James 168, 172, 177, 204
witch (etymology) 14
The Witch of Endor 31, 57, 81, 97
Witch Please 21, 120
wizard (etymology and definition) 2–3, 14

The Word Exchange 205
– "The Wanderer" 205
– "The Wife's Lament" 45, 205
Wynne Jones, Diana 81, 101–102, 211–212
Wynonna Earp 135, 169, 212
wyrd 26, 73, 92, 202

Yergeau, Melanie 10–11, 15, 37, 49–50, 64, 72, 99, 145, 198
York Corpus Christi Cycle
– *The Expulsion* 133–134,
– *The Fall* 128, 133–134,
Young Sheldon 36–37, 154, 214

www.ingramcontent.com/pod-product-compliance
Lightning Source LLC
Chambersburg PA
CBHW020228170426
43201CB00007B/350